Angels and Earthly Creatures

THE MIDDLE AGES SERIES

Ruth Mazo Karras, Series Editor

Edward Peters, Founding Editor

A complete list of books in the series
is available from the publisher.

Angels and Earthly Creatures

Preaching, Performance, and Gender in the Later Middle Ages

Claire M. Waters

PENN

UNIVERSITY OF PENNSYLVANIA PRESS

Philadelphia

10   9   8   7   6   5   4   3   2   1

Published by
University of Pennsylvania Press
Philadelphia, Pennsylvania 19104–4011

Library of Congress Cataloging-in-Publication Data

Waters, Claire M.
  Angels and earthly creatures : preaching, performance, and gender in the later Middle
Ages / Claire M. Waters.
      p. cm. — (Middle Ages series)
  Includes bibliographical references and index.
  ISBN 0-8122-3753-6 (cloth : alk. paper)
      1. Preaching—History—Middle Ages, 600–1500. 2. Rhetoric—Religious aspects—
Christianity—History. 3. Rhetoric, Medieval. 4. Pastoral theology—Catholic Church—
History of doctrines—Middle Ages, 600–1500. I. Title. II. Series.

BV4207.W38 2003
251'.0094'0902—dc22

                                                                              2003065756

For my parents

Contents

Preface

"Jacob saw a ladder reaching from earth to heaven, on which angels were ascending and descending," writes Alan of Lille at the beginning of his *Summa de arte praedicatoria*. Later he interprets this image as one of preaching: "for preaching instructs now in divine matters, now in morals, which is signified by the angels ascending and descending. For the angels are preachers, who ascend when they preach heavenly things; descend, when through moral sayings they adapt themselves to those below them." Alan's image nicely captures the dual nature of the preacher's task, reflected also in the title of this book. As God's messengers, preachers did indeed take the role of angels, and their awareness of the exaltation of that position is evident in Alan's lofty image. As angels whose task was to speak with earthly creatures, they had a duty to their audiences that required them at times to descend from the heights, to make their doctrine accessible to those "below them." But the idea that, in descending, preachers must conform themselves to those they address is a reminder that, for all their angelic office, these speakers of heavenly things were themselves as earthbound as their audiences were.

This book considers the ways in which preachers dealt with their situation as angels and earthly creatures, as the human embodiments of doctrine. Although the pedagogical elements of the preacher's task were not the first object of my study when I began this project, it has been a pleasure to trace the elements and expectations of the medieval consideration of teaching as an embodied task, and the meditations of the theorists discussed below on the fallibility of authoritative bodies often took on an unexpectedly topical cast. This continuing relevance should not have surprised me; we may sometimes think of preaching as an abstract or detached activity, but these texts are a reminder of how immediate and personal a task teaching is. They offer a salutary demonstration of the commitment these medieval authors had to making their instruction come alive, in and through their words and actions, for their audiences. The preaching literature of the Middle Ages has come to seem to me less a series of precepts laid down from on high than a continuing conversa-

tion—between medieval theorists and their classical and patristic predecessors, between preaching texts and the genres that overlapped with
them, and between preachers and their audiences—about how the Word
of God might be disseminated on earth.

In this context, it is a pleasure to acknowledge the many people
whose teaching and conversation have enriched this project throughout
its development. Barbara Newman, herself no mean preacher, has shown
unfailing generosity and encouragement all along the way; my debts to
her are beyond expression here. Beverly Kienzle and Becky Krug, with exceptional kindness, each read the entire manuscript at very different mo-
ments in its evolution and offered invaluable commentary. Others who
provided welcome feedback on various chapters include Dorothy Chan-
sky, Jennifer Kolpacoff, Larry Scanlon, Fiona Somerset, and Nicholas
Watson. They and audiences who heard and responded to papers based on
this work helped to spur my thinking and shape the final manuscript. To
them, Alastair Minnis, and an anonymous press reader I owe many im-
provements, as well as the admission that sometimes I have declined to
take their excellent advice, no doubt to my cost.

I feel very fortunate to have had, throughout the creation of this
book, wonderful colleagues; chief among those who read, discussed, encouraged, and challenged are Cynthia Baule, Seeta Chaganti, and Sally
Poor. The last in particular I thank not only for more readings of various
pieces than either of us can remember but also for innumerable discussions of topics all along the range of Jacob's ladder.

I am grateful for an extremely productive and enjoyable month at
the Rockefeller Foundation's Bellagio Center, which was instrumental in
the final shaping of this project, and also for the financial assistance offered by research grants from Northwestern University and the University of New Mexico. The offices of Vice Chancellor for Research Barry
Klein and Dean Elizabeth Langland at the University of California,
Davis, have generously supported the publication of this book, and I am
happy to be able to acknowledge their help here. Parts of Chapters 4 and
5 appeared in much-abridged form in *Essays in Medieval Studies* 14
(http://www.luc.edu/publications/medieval/vol14/waters.html).
Chapter 2, in slightly different form, was included in *Studies in the Age of
Chaucer* 24 (2002). The editors of these journals have kindly given per-
mission to reproduce this work, as has Pennsylvania State University
Press, which recently published *The Vulgar Tongue: Medieval and Post-*

Medieval Vernacularity, edited by Fiona Somerset and Nicholas Watson, containing a shorter version of Chapter 3.

My final thanks go to my husband, Alan; and to my parents, to whom this book is dedicated with love.

Introduction

Et Verbum caro factum est, et habitavit in nobis.
[And the Word became flesh, and dwelt among us.]
                                              John 1:14

Who has access to the divine? How is that access achieved, and how transmitted? And what responsibilities does it carry with it? The medieval preacher, whose office required him to struggle with these questions, was a bridge between divine and human, between an eternal truth and a particular audience. He was also the representative of a clerical culture whose control over textuality, authority, and religious knowledge was increasingly centralized and codified but also in many ways increasingly precarious in the later Middle Ages. Caught between these various roles, mediating between disparate groups and milieus, the preacher found himself in a hybrid position. In this he resembled, not accidentally, his ultimate model, the Word made Flesh, who first presented the essential fusion of human body and divine truth and then passed on to his successors the responsibility to imitate him and perpetuate his message. But unlike Jesus, for whom the combination of Word and Flesh was perfect and effortless, the preachers who followed him had to struggle with their role. They worked within the limits of their human embodiment, an embodiment that even after the coming of Jesus bore the mark of Adam and thus was prone to war against their best intentions and the divine message they carried.

The appropriate interaction of life and teaching, of preaching and practice, and the significance of that interaction, is one of the main topics of the *artes praedicandi,* Latin handbooks for preachers that were produced and copied in considerable numbers all over Europe from the late twelfth through the fifteenth centuries.[1] While many of the *artes* are primarily rhetorical manuals on the construction of a sermon, most contain some attention to other matters—from the preacher's morality to his gestures, his subject matter, his deportment, even his clothing. In both immediate practical terms and a larger spiritual sense they are concerned with how a preacher should perform his role and fulfill the duties of his office. Their discussions focus around two related concepts: the preacher's personal authority—his ability to manage his own sinful nature, make use of his physical body, and present himself in a way that made him a credible and appropriate speaker of divine truth; and the preacher's institutional authorization—his status within a hierarchy and his representation of a divinely instituted lineage and its official doctrine. Authority and authorization were recognized as necessary components of effective preaching and imagined as, ideally, mutually reinforcing qualities. At the same time, though, because of the contested nature of preaching in the later Middle Ages these categories were often set against one another, and the preacher who possessed only one of them could pose a spiritual danger to himself and others.

The central contention of this book is twofold. First, I argue that the conflicted cooperation between authority and authorization is a manifestation of the fundamentally hybrid nature of the preacher's calling, one recognized everywhere in the handbooks. Standing between earth and heaven, between the institutional church and the faithful laity, the preacher saw his own liminality expressed most markedly in his own body, the physical vessel of a divine calling. That body's susceptibility to the snares of the world and the flesh presented constant anxieties for theorists of preaching, but at the same time these theorists grudgingly acknowledged the essential and, indeed, potentially enriching influence of the preacher's embodiment on his work. Exploring these contradictions as they appear in literature written by, for, and about preachers in this period provides a new way to approach questions about the relationship between body and spirit in the Middle Ages: by studying those whose professional duty was to convey the latter by means of the former. A second, and related, argument is that in pursuing the cultural implications of the *officium praedicatoris*, we must look at women's preaching in the context of and as a formative influence on ideas about men's preaching.[2] Women were energetically and vociferously excluded from a public teaching role, ostensibly because of the limitations of their gender.[3] But as the writers of the preaching manuals were all too aware, the frailty of the body—its capacity for sin, deception, and worldliness—that medieval culture often associated particularly with the feminine was equally a threat to every preacher.[4] Discussions of women preachers thus allowed theorists to raise and examine questions about personal authority and the body's role in that authority without having to address those questions directly toward male preachers. Putting women's preaching back into its full context illuminates not only the boundaries of authorized activity but also the nature of licensed preachers' connection to the hierarchy that sent them and to the divine body they represented.

The *artes praedicandi* and other works of preaching literature that explore the tensions outlined above are the foundation of this book. The aim is to offer a reading of these texts of spiritual and professional formation that is attentive to what they can tell us about the pitfalls and rewards of the activity of preaching and the demands it made upon the human beings who held this "angelic" office. The late medieval revival of interest in preaching took place, of course, in a broader landscape of religious renewal and competition, and before beginning the literary discussion that forms the majority of this argument it will be useful to sketch some of that background. Although this book by no means claims to offer a comprehensive account of the history of late medieval preaching, I have tried to situate my argument with regard to the historical specificities of the mid twelfth to late fourteenth centuries; the brief account that follows is intended to provide the reader with a context for the works and themes treated here.

Beginning in the eleventh century the reforms fostered by Pope Gregory VII emphasized the need for the clergy to be a group set apart from the world, both independent of temporal control and contemptuous of earthly goods and desires.[5] This focus both raised clerical status and laid the clergy open to critiques of their moral stature, critiques that others were not slow to make. Heterodox religious groups and freelance evangelists began to challenge the clerical monopoly on preaching, often using personal morality as a basis for criticism of the clergy.[6] Brian Stock offers a highly illuminating account of one such group, the Patarenes of eleventh-century Milan, which demonstrates that the questions addressed in the preaching manuals in the late twelfth century onward were ones that had been exercising reformers for some time already; his discussion, which sees preaching as a central facet of the Patarene movement, touches on such issues as clerical status and bodiliness (particularly the debate over clerical marriage), the effect of charismatic preaching, the relationship between preacher and audience, and questions of jurisdiction and right to preach, particularly laymen's "usurpation" of preaching—all matters that recur throughout this book.[7] The desire of individuals and groups to speak out and instruct others reflected a new conception of a central ideal of Christian life, the *vita apostolica,* which had traditionally been identified with the monastic *vita communis*.[8] In the later eleventh and twelfth centuries the apostolic life was reimagined as centering on poverty and preaching, on action in the world rather than a removed life of contemplation. This development reflects the tension between the institutional and the charismatic that plagued the late medieval church as the hierarchy tried to maintain its established power while remaining true to its radical roots. This tension lies at the heart of many of the debates about preaching.

Fundamentally important among these debates was the question of authorization and jurisdiction. Those who embraced the new understanding of the *vita apostolica* were by no means always heretical in their beliefs, but their desire to exercise the apostolic office of preaching led inevitably to clashes with orthodoxy. The monastic withdrawal from the world and laxity among the secular clergy had left a vacuum of religious instruction and exhortation, which devout laypeople were only too glad to fill—a task they often, it seems, performed with great skill and effectiveness, but one which made them a potential threat.[9] Herbert Grundmann describes an edict issued by Lucius III in 1184 that named heretical groups to be suppressed (including Cathars, Waldenses, and Patarenes) and then provided a list of heretical characteristics: "First on the list was unlicensed preaching."[10] The performance of religious instruction was thus at the heart of the battle for religious control, whether as a heretical activity, a focus of lay spirituality, an official response to challenges against orthodoxy, or a pastoral attempt to rescue straying sheep. In many ways the development of preaching theory was a defensive reaction: claims on public speech by excluded groups such as heretics, laypeople, and women influenced the formation of official conceptions of preaching.[11]

The clerical hierarchy, not surprisingly, fought to maintain its prerogatives against the incursions of nonclerics. While some of its efforts were punitive, others attempted to harness the fervor and effectiveness of marginal groups and use them to benefit the church as a whole. Some itinerant preachers were granted license to preach and encouraged to found settled orders.[12] For most of the twelfth century, however, the church's efforts to reconcile splinter groups to itself were half-hearted and ineffective. It was not until the accession in 1198 of Innocent III, the great proponent of inclusion, that the movement to bring heterodox groups back into the fold began to build steam. Innocent's willingness to reabsorb suitably chastened lay groups led him to issue a limited preaching license to the Italian Humiliati at the beginning of the thirteenth century and to attempt similar reconciliations with others.[13] As with the wandering preachers, stability seems to have been of great importance: provided such associations were willing to recognize the validity of the ecclesiastical hierarchy and organize themselves into some kind of settled structure, they could be assimilated into orthodoxy.[14]

As the twelfth century drew to a close, then, the clerical hierarchy finally began to respond to the need for improved interaction between itself and the laity.[15] In the early thirteenth century two events took place that were to have an enormous impact on the development of that interaction and particularly on the practice of preaching. The first was the Fourth Lateran Council of 1215, which codified the demand for pastoral care. The requirement that every individual make a yearly confession of sins to a priest, perhaps the most famous of the council's statutes, meant that the laity needed increased instruction in the tenets of the Christian faith so that they could make a full and valid confession, and thus that the clergy needed to be prepared to provide that instruction. The council, recognizing that bishops were no longer able to do all the preaching required and anxious to combat the spread of unlicensed preachers, also ordered that bishops appoint "appropriate" substitutes to preach in their dioceses.[16]

The second event of the early thirteenth century with special relevance for preaching was the formation of the mendicant orders. The Dominicans originated as an antiheretical movement; the Franciscans' particular focus was on perfect poverty. Both groups practiced itinerant preaching and thus looked similar, at first glance, to various heterodox associations, for whom they were sometimes mistaken.[17] They demonstrated from the beginning, however, a willingness to be part of the hierarchical church; in return, the church (in the person of Innocent III) permitted them to continue the practices of poverty and preaching central to their spiritual vocation.[18] As the Dominican and Franciscan orders developed they maintained their preaching activities, becoming important parts of the church's defense against both heresy and internal decay. But as wandering evangelists they still threatened the jurisdiction of the secular clergy, leading to ongoing battles over their right to preach.[19]

Over the course of the thirteenth century the mendicant orders solidified into enormous and enormously influential networks. Their development and the concomitant growth of the universities gave rise to the more rigorous scholastic explication of many of the ideas that originated in the apostolic reform movements. Explorations of sacramental theology and the nature of the church continued the attempt to define and control the exercise of religious authority, upholding the rights of the centralized church of which the mendicants were now a part. The scholastic interest in classification led to an outpouring of technical works such as the *artes praedicandi* (a significant number of which were written by friars) and disputation literature that often tried to define and delimit preaching in order to exclude unwanted or unauthorized groups.

Alongside this centralization of authority lay movements continued to develop. The growth of extra-liturgical forms of devotion, and of attention to the human Christ, offered possibilities for lay piety that ultimately built on the reforming zeal of earlier centuries.[20] For women especially, the new modes of piety could provide opportunities for religious expression since they tended to emphasize personal authority and morality, rather than orthodox institutional authorization, as the bases for public speech. The developments in women's religious experience have been extensively studied; they affected women of all social and religious classes, from beguines and nuns, to anchoresses, to devout laywomen of all ranks.[21]

Women's participation in the religious trends of the later Middle Ages both reflected and shaped those trends. The reforming temper that characterized much of the period, for example, can be seen in the activities and writings of extraordinary women as far apart in time and earthly status as the twelfth-century Benedictine abbess Hildegard of Bingen and the fourteenth-century Dominican tertiary Catherine of Siena. Catherine and her older contemporary Birgitta of Sweden, on the other hand, both benefited from the new emphasis on Christ's human accessibility by using their personal connections to God as an authorization of their speech. But it was not only such famous figures whose lives and activities were affected by the upheavals and controversies of the late Middle Ages; other lessknown and surely many unknown women were part of the expanding idea of what it meant to lead a religious life. The frequent complaints that heretics, particularly Waldensians, permitted women to preach are only one marker of this increase in the scope of women's activities.[22] The intense reactions, both positive and negative, to women's role in heterodox, lay, and visionary spirituality suggest that to their contemporaries these women could function as a sign of all that was both vital and threatening in these new expressions of piety.[23]

This brief historical account suggests, I hope, how many cultural concerns swirled around preaching in the later Middle Ages and why a consideration of the literature of preaching is fruitful for an understanding of the period as a whole. Faced with the threats of heresy and lay disaffection, and thus with a demand for both more and better preaching, late medieval clerics responded with innumerable aids for preachers, including collections of hagiography, collections of exempla, florilegia, model sermons, and above all *artes praedicandi*. Such texts can provide an appreciation of how medieval clerics viewed this crucially important task and how they tried to reconcile the unworldly truth of preaching with the earthly body through which the preacher expressed it. As M.-D. Chenu observes of the transformations of the twelfth century, "The dialectic between the gospel and the world . . . evoked a dual response from the individual Christian as he both returned to the gospel and remained in the world. A dual response and not two responses, for history shows it was the Christian's return to the gospel which guaranteed his presence in the world and that it was this presence in the world which secured the efficacy of the gospel."[24] The preaching that participated in this "dual response" both benefited from and struggled with the interaction of its elements in ways that reflect the efforts of the church as a whole to come to terms with the competing demands of charisma and hierarchy, spiritual authority and earthly power. Preaching offers a way to see the medieval church in the process of understanding and constructing itself, through the bodies of the men who represented it and the women who tested its boundaries.

While there is, not surprisingly, no single work offering a complete history of medieval preaching, there are many places to begin the study of sacred eloquence in the Middle Ages.[25] Most, however, tend to treat the issue of women's preaching separately from men's preaching. Drawing on the medieval handbooks written by and for preachers, this book aims to reintegrate these two traditions, which illuminate each other and clarify our understanding of what it meant to medieval preachers to be the mouth of God, to hold an angelic office in human form.[26] In so doing, it builds on and helps to connect recent areas of lively inquiry in medieval studies. While the place of the female body in religious practice, for instance, in both its negative and positive valences, has been subtly and intensively investigated in recent scholarship, the male body is only beginning to receive such attention. Several recent essay collections on medieval masculinity and book-length studies such as Dyan Elliott's work on clerical bodies and their potential for sin show the growing interest in this area; the preaching manuals can complement such work by considering the pitfalls of masculine self-presentation, the dangers offered by the male flesh in performance, and the implications of masculine embodiment for the institutional hierarchy of the church.[27]

From another angle, Christ's body, especially in its relationship to the Eucharist and to affective devotion, has been the topic of much excellent and influential work in the last few years.[28] A study of preachers, who were encouraged to model themselves explicitly on the physical presence and activity of Christ, enhances our sense of how the Middle Ages understood the ultimately important body and how that understanding reflected on the bodies of those who represented him. The study of works by preachers thus offers a "historically contingent version of Christ's humanity" that can supplement what David Aers, following Sarah Beckwith, calls the "commonplace" of "*the* humanity of Christ" as the suffering, bleeding body of Passion meditations and other late medieval devotional works. The version of Christ's humanity imagined in the preaching manuals tends to be closer to the one that Aers calls "the Gospels' Jesus . . . [m]obile, articulate, teaching, healing."[29]

Finally, the hybridity inherent in preaching can help us to understand certain competing trends of the later Middle Ages, for which the body of the preacher was in some sense a staging ground. These trends are represented by two important strands in recent medieval scholarship: the study of women's religious experience and devotion, exemplified by the work of Caroline Walker Bynum; and the literary examination of scholastic and canon-law texts, such as the work of Alastair Minnis. These fields, while not in competition, have remained more separate in modern scholarship than their subjects would have been in their original medieval context. But they have much to say to one another, and this book benefits from and will, I hope, contribute to their productive cross-fertilization. Stephen Jaeger has recently explored the relationship between bodily and textual authority in the school culture of the high Middle Ages, arguing that the eleventh and twelfth centuries saw a shift from charismatic body to charismatic text.[30] In the twelfth and thirteenth centuries a similar intensification of focus on the dignity of the office of preaching and its textual mandate, rather than on the person of the preacher, warred with the ongoing awareness of the physical side of the preacher's activity. Discussions of the office of preacher enable an examination of widespread late medieval concerns with embodiment and authority in a particular context and can offer a new window onto the medieval perception, and (attempted) resolution, of such competing ideas.

The effort to manage the physical aspect of preaching in relation to its textual foundations is a crucial undertaking of the preaching manuals. For this reason the *artes praedicandi* most closely examined here are the ones that give extensive attention to matters, such as the preacher's relationship to his office or his self-presentation, beyond the purely technical aspects of sermon construction.[31] Since appropriate transmission of the Word of God was essential to the spiritual health of the faithful laity and the institutional health of the orthodox church, the preacher's body had an importance far beyond its own boundaries—boundaries that could be unstable, as recent work suggests.[32] A study of the preacher's vulnerable humanity and his hybrid status can help us to understand the "necessary interrelationship and ultimate interdependence" of the varied and sometimes competing discourses (those of heterodoxy, canon law, pastoral care, and affective spirituality, among others) that made up the world of medieval Christianity.[33] The negotiations between textuality and embodiment, between authorization and authority, that underlie many of these conflicts are a fundamental concern of the preaching theorists and the subject of this book.

The chapters that follow explore in more detail the need both to establish and to cross boundaries that characterized medieval preaching. The first four chapters address the building blocks of the preacher's role: his authorization, his persona, and his language. "The Golden Chains of Citation" looks at the concern with definitions and boundaries that characterized late medieval discussions of the preacher's institutional authorization and draws on modern performance theory to examine the implications of their attempt to create an unbreakable and impermeable lineage of preachers. In "Holy Duplicity: The Preacher's Two Faces" I turn to the problem of the preacher's "person," both as a physical body and as a persona presented to the world; this chapter also introduces Geoffrey Chaucer's *Canterbury Tales* into the discussion, focusing particularly on the Parson and the Pardoner. Chaucer's role here and later is not merely decorative. It is clear from the *Tales* that Chaucer, as G. G. Sedgewick long ago noted, "got himself steeped in all the dyes of traditional preaching before he set about creating the Canterbury Tales and several of the pilgrims in it," an apt metaphor given how naturally preaching concerns seem woven into the fabric of various tales.[34] While many medieval literary texts respond to and are shaped by preaching traditions, it is my contention that Chaucer's poem, with its intense emphasis on speech, embodiment, and authority, illuminates some central issues in preaching theory by presenting them in concentrated (and personified) form.[35] The third chapter, "A Manner of Speaking: Access and the Vernacular," considers the preacher not only as a translator in a linguistic sense, but also as a mediator between cultures who needed both to form a connection with and to maintain his distinctness from his audience. " 'Mere Words': Gendered Eloquence and Christian Preaching" explores the long-standing association between rhetoric and femininity and the implications of using a worldly, morally neutral form to convey a spiritual message.

The final three chapters turn from the first section's primary focus on male preachers—in which women, nonetheless, often play an important part—to look at women preachers, fictional and real, more directly. "Transparent Bodies and the Redemption of Rhetoric" examines how the legendary preaching of certain women saints helped to address the anxieties raised by the allure of rhetoric and by the preacher's physicality. "The *Alibi* of Female Authority" considers the efforts of three historical women, Hildegard of Bingen, Birgitta of Sweden, and Catherine of Siena, to rework the clerical conceptions of preacherly speech and authorization that excluded them and to provide themselves with a place from which they could proclaim their message to the church. Finally, "*Sermones ad Status* and Old Wives' Tales; or, The Audience Talks Back" looks at the preoccupation of the *Canterbury Tales* with competing voices and speaking bodies in light of the work's origins in the preaching form known as *sermones ad status,* sermons to various types or classes of people. I argue that the figure of the Wife of Bath represents, in a sense, the logical outcome of trends already present in preaching and that her peculiar combination of feminine and clerical modes of speech allows Chaucer to appropriate the necessary hybridity of preachers' discourse in creating his own poetic voice.

In all of these chapters, I have tried to let the preoccupations of the medieval texts examined here—debate literature, hagiography, canon law, poetry, and above all the *artes praedicandi* themselves—direct my own interests. The extraordinary care, attention, and energy devoted to preaching by the authors of these various texts suggest the importance of their subject: a mode of speech and performance that offered, in their view, not an imitation of life, but access to the life eternal. Respect for the high aims and seriousness of preaching at its best, however, should not prevent us from exploring its human—and thus at times less than ideal—qualities and characteristics. "Official" and orthodox discussions of preaching show where the theorists' concerns lie, but if we accept these straightforwardly on their own terms, we see only half the picture. By considering theory in the light of practice, the acceptable in juxtaposition with the excluded, and above all, the productive and destructive interactions of the preacher's human body with the authoritative message he worked to convey, this book aims to provide a fuller representation and a better understanding of the activity of preaching in the later Middle Ages.

I

The Golden Chains of Citation

Quomodo vero praedicabunt nisi mittantur?
[And how shall they preach unless they are sent?]

Rom. 10:15

IN HIS *DIALOGUES*, GREGORY THE GREAT recounts at one point the story of a holy abbot, Equitius, and his preaching career. Like some later preachers, Equitius ran into difficulties over his right to proclaim the Word of God. Gregory tells Peter,

A certain man called Felix . . . since he observed that this venerable man Equitius was not in holy orders, and that he went around to various places preaching zealously, addressed him one day with the daring of familiarity, saying, "How do you, who are not in holy orders, and have not received license to preach from the bishop of Rome under whom you live, presume to preach?" Compelled by this inquiry of his, the holy man revealed how he received the license to preach, saying, "I have myself considered these same things that you say to me. But one night a beautiful youth appeared to me in a vision, and placed on my tongue a physician's tool, a lancet, saying, 'Behold, I have put my words in your mouth; go forth and preach.' And from that day, even if I wished to, I have not been able to keep silent about God."[1]

The holy man was fortunate to live in a time when, although his license to preach might be questioned, his unsupported assertion of immediate authorization from God was still likely to be accepted. Writing some eight centuries later, around 1320, Robert of Basevorn expressed what was by then a well-established distrust of such visionary justifications. His *Forma praedicandi* holds, "It is not sufficient for someone to say that he is sent by God, unless he manifestly demonstrates it, for heretics often make this claim."[2] By Robert's time it was not just the occasional holy freelancer who was in question, but whole crowds of new claimants to a preaching mission, and an individual's assertion of his or her right to preach had become not just the subject of occasional (and, Gregory implies, impudent) inquiry but the catalyst for intensive scrutiny of preaching itself.

As the example of Equitius suggests, one difficulty for late medieval theorists was the acknowledged existence of sacred precedents for inspired preaching. The need to manage the conflicting authorities that gave rise to such precedents instigated a large-scale effort to codify and clarify church law in the twelfth century and "free the church from *its* chains to the undifferentiated holy past."[3] The desire to "differentiate," to create human jurisdictions that would check the proliferation of unlicensed speakers, is part of what motivates the discussions of the nature and ownership of preaching in the later Middle Ages.[4] In freeing the church from its chains, the theorists in effect created a new, singular chain of authorities that excluded certain older models in order to solidify the contemporary assignment of ecclesiastical power.[5]

This chapter explores how changes in the conception of preachers' authority clustered around the problem of citation, of both authoritative words and authoritative individuals, as theorists wrestled with a central question: "How shall they preach unless they are sent?" The variety of answers over time points to important developments in the understanding of the office of preacher in the later Middle Ages. The preacher established his claims by re-presenting earlier models and above all the absent exemplar, Christ. This representation was simultaneously the heart of his office and its point of greatest vulnerability because the same absence that required the preacher's activity meant that it was exceptionally difficult to guarantee that activity or to exclude unlicensed practitioners from it. The potential for women and laymen to claim immediate authorization or sacred precedent increased the need for a scaffolding of theory and citation to support the claims of licensed, male preachers, a need that fueled the work of definition and distinction described above. If we look at the claims made for preachers who were "sent" in juxtaposition with the claims of those who were not, particularly women, the fragility of the licensed preachers' exclusive ownership of public religious speech becomes increasingly apparent.

Medieval theorists' troubled attempts to regulate preachers' representations can be illuminated not only by what they say about unlicensed speakers, but also by recourse to theories of performative speech and in particular by the modern chain of citation that links Judith Butler, Jacques Derrida, and J. L. Austin. The points of contact between these modern *auctoritates*—the points where Butler draws on Derrida, which in turn mark Derrida's productive disagreements with Austin—are, strikingly, also matters crucial to the medieval debate: the "iterability" or "citationality" of speech, the concept of ordinary versus extraordinary speech-acts, and the problem posed, for both Austin and the preaching theorists, by the "peculiarly hollow and void" speech of acting. All three issues ultimately lead to concerns over the ownership and origination of speech that plagued medieval theorists as they tried to work through the simultaneous presence and absence of Christ that made preachers' authority so complicated.

Defining Citations

The idea that preaching is "citational" is hardly shocking; in itself it posed no threat to the preacher's authority to acknowledge that his speech borrowed explicitly from an authoritative text, and that his activity was always a half-explicit citation of the activity and authority of the preachers who went before him. Silvana Vecchio has observed that for medieval Dominicans, "an ideal thread links the holy founder [Dominic] to the very figure of Christ" and that indeed "the chain of authorities can be even longer and run through the stages of a possible history of edification: Moses, the prophets, Christ, Gregory, Bede, Augustine, Jacques de Vitry, St. Dominic"; the Dominicans saw themselves as "the inheritors and continuers of this long tradition."[6] Her point is echoed repeatedly in medieval discussions; one of the three things Humbert of Romans, master-general of the Dominicans from 1254 to 1263, regarded as "especially powerful" in preaching was "the consideration of the methods of other preachers."[7] Robert of Basevorn takes up this suggestion, describing the methods of the persons he considers the five greatest preachers of Christian tradition: Christ, Paul, Augustine, Gregory, and Bernard. He notes, however, that Christ "included all praiseworthy methods of preaching in his own method"; as the "fount and origin of good," Christ is the source and context of all good preaching.[8]

At the same time the potential for citation by unlicensed speakers created considerable anxiety about maintaining the purity of this chain of authorities. Canon law decretals and scholastic disputations drew on and reinforced a textual and institutional tradition that was consistently opposed to unauthorized preaching, and they brought together potentially conflicting authorities to give that tradition a single voice.[9] The repeated attempts to define preaching in the twelfth century and onward were part of a "general movement to codify knowledge"; texts such as the great summas of the thirteenth century built on Peter Lombard's *Sentences* and its commentaries to create definitive solutions to all kinds of theological problems.[10] While scholastic disputation, by its very nature, required the admission of varying points of view, and while the answer provided might be quite nuanced and was even capable of leaving some room for doubt, the goal of the exercise was to resolve issues, and this was how its solutions tended to be used in later borrowings.[11] In preaching manuals, for instance, pronouncements against women preachers that derived from quodlibets and the decretals took on an absolute quality: contexts and caveats were stripped away, leaving a new and incontrovertible declaration that subsumed all earlier authoritative discourse on the subject. Throughout the period the chain of citations that excluded unlicensed preachers was imaginatively reinforced and legalistically solidified, strengthening the official position of authorized preachers and making it ever more inaccessible to outsiders.

If we examine the process by which preaching worked out its own boundaries, however, the definitional solidity claimed for the activity comes to seem somewhat illusory. Definition always involves interpretation; it can be as much a polemical tool as an objective description, as Beverly Kienzle and Pamela Walker observe with regard to women's preaching: "The name preaching has been withheld to deny legitimacy or pronounced to issue condemnation."[12] And as Simon Forde points out, modern scholars have been perhaps too ready to accept a "narrow, orthodox definition" of preaching that reflects clerical biases rather than the "range of acts that form part of the transmission of the faith and the living of the gospel" in medieval religious life.[13] His argument is supported by the fact that medieval texts may refer to such activities as disputation, prophecy, exhortation, and teaching, whether performed by men or women, as preaching, and definitions of preaching often seem to describe activities that in other contexts are permitted to women and laymen.[14]

When explicitly faced with the possibility of unlicensed preaching, however, theorists took care to regulate and define the activity so as to exclude those who were not part of the church hierarchy. The Benedictine Ranulph Higden's fourteenth-century manual asserts that "preaching is the public persuasion of many people, for the promoting of salvation, at an appropriate time and place."[15] Although he does not belabor the point, this definition implicitly excludes those who were not permitted to speak publicly and retains control over the definition of preaching by its mention of "appropriate time and place." It is clear, of course, that preaching could occur in many forms, places, and times; but there were also times, places, subjects, and certainly persons that were considered to disqualify an act from the characterization "preaching." Perhaps the best way to formulate this problem would be to say that there is a strict set of criteria that define what might be called, by analogy to J. L. Austin's concept of "explicit performatives," "explicit preaching." Though preaching almost never verbally declares itself as such ("I preach to you"), a properly authorized man standing in a pulpit, at the appropriate point in a Mass, dressed in clerical garb and speaking on the right sort of topic in the right manner could hardly be regarded as doing anything other than preaching.[16] It might be fair to say that preaching theorists would have wished to exclude from consideration as preaching any speech-act that *could not* properly have taken place in those circumstances (at Mass, from the pulpit)—a criterion that would obviously, and from their point of view desirably, exclude female and lay preaching altogether.[17] This is indeed the view promulgated by the popular fourteenth-century work *Speculum Christiani:* "A grete differens es be-twene prechynge and techynge. Prechynge es in a place where es clepynge to-gedyr or foluynge of pepyl in holy dayes in chyrches or other certeyn places and tymes ordeyned therto. And it longeth to hem that been ordeynede ther-to, the whych haue iurediccion and auctorite, and to noon othyr. Techynge es that eche body may enforme and teche hys brothyr in euery place and in conable tyme, os he seeth that it be spedful."[18] Here the notion of "iurediccion and auctorite" is specifically linked to the issues of time and place, and each is used to reinforce the other in a definition of preaching that strictly limits what kind of speech may bear that label.

Despite these attempts at definition, however, it is clear that there must have been innumerable instances when any one or a number of the ideal characteristics of licensed preaching—the appropriate time, place, type of sermon, even an officially authorized person—were lacking without that speech-act ceasing to count as preaching, and this fluidity at the definitional boundaries of preaching opened the door for persons other than priests and bishops to preach.[19] We can gain a more specific sense of how and why preaching needed to be regulated by looking at three categories frequently seen together in such texts as the *artes praedicandi*, disputations, and canon law: prophecy, preaching, and priesthood. The juxtaposition of these categories, particularly as they relate to women, helps to suggest what qualities and problems were felt to be essential to the activity of preaching, by contrast with its near neighbors.[20]

Crucial to the link between preaching and priesthood was the sense of lineage and mission referred to in Rom. 10:15. Because Christ had chosen only male disciples, only men were "sent"; they derived authorization from that original mission, rooted in the will of Christ and preserved in the ultimate textual authority of the Bible. The mission Christ gave his Apostles came to be seen as an office and one that could only be conferred by a person who already held that office.[21] This created a lineage of male priests and preachers whose words derived from the words of Christ, who were supposed to follow and imitate him, and who were authorized both by that point of origin and by the ongoing tradition of priestly office in which they stood. Compounding the importance of priestly lineage in the later Middle Ages was the reformist concept of the priesthood as "a human condition quite distinct from laity," which made it even more difficult for laymen and persistently impossible for women to take on priestly functions.[22]

Since prophets, on the other hand, were sent directly by God without human mediation, they could to some degree avoid the issue of lineage, and the role of prophet was thus open to women, as biblical example confirmed.[23] At the same time there was a consistent effort to emphasize the charismatic, noninstitutional nature of prophecy and thus to prevent women prophets from becoming models for a tradition of female public speech.[24] There was also an insistence that such charismatic authority be regulated, either by direct miracle or, more likely, by clerical approval.

If priesthood and prophecy seem fairly clear in their willingness or lack thereof to accommodate unofficial speakers, particularly women, preaching is a gray area lying between the institutional and the charismatic and thus more difficult to assess. Insofar as it partakes of the qualities of priesthood, there is a tendency to emphasize institutional authorization and thus to exclude women, among others.[25] But insofar as preaching is assimilated to prophecy, it claims a charismatic, personal authority for the speaker that is much more difficult to regulate. The negotiation between these two aspects, both of which were essential to the preacher's role, takes place largely in terms of the preacher's relationships to clerical lineage and to language, particularly the scriptural text.

The medieval concern with these matters can be illuminated by reference to similar problems in the works of Judith Butler and Jacques Derrida, focusing on the ownership of speech and on citation as a source of meaning. In her discussion of the performance of (gender) identity Butler raises the important question of who is to be imagined as the "author" of that performance.[26] She argues that a performed identity has a history that exceeds any individual performer: "The act that one performs . . . is, in a sense, an act that has been going on before one arrived on the scene . . . much as a script survives the particular actors who make use of it, but . . . requires individual actors in order to be actualized and reproduced as reality once again."[27] While the performance of preaching, like the performance of gender, has no explicit script, it draws on both Scripture and an authoritative lineage of performance, and those origins structured late medieval theorists' attempts to create and defend the boundaries of preaching.

Butler's concept of performance as repeated acts derives from the Derridean notion of "iterability," which "implies that every act is itself a recitation, the citing of a prior chain of acts which are implied in a present act."[28] For Derrida, it is precisely repetition, or rather the possibility of repetition, that makes meaning possible.[29] His concept of iterability also implies that all language is citational, that "every sign, linguistic or nonlinguistic, spoken or written . . . can be *cited,* put between quotation marks; in so doing it can break with every given context, engendering an infinity of new contexts in a manner which is absolutely illimitable. This does not imply that the mark is valid outside of a context, but on the contrary that there are only contexts without any center or absolute anchoring (*ancrage*)."[30] The notion of a sign system "without any center or absolute anchoring" would have been anathema to medieval preaching theorists; in fact, it seems to have been precisely a fear of unanchored contexts that led them to regulate preaching so energetically.[31] The attempts to prevent unauthorized speakers from entering into the chain of citations described at the beginning of this section helped to give preaching its authoritative form in the later Middle Ages. Ultimately both Butler's and Derrida's theoretical approaches raise the question of authorship or ownership of language, which proves to be central to how preaching's purity of lineage was controlled. An examination of texts that address women's relationships to the offices of priest, preacher, and prophet leads to an understanding of the importance of ownership and lineage as foundational categories for male preachers.

Lineage and Ownership

In 1210 Pope Innocent III issued a bull, *Nova quaedam nuper*, in which he expressed his surprise and disapproval at the news that certain abbesses had recently been known to "bless their nuns, hear their confessions of sins, and, reading the gospel, presume to preach publicly"; he ordered the relevant bishops to put a stop to this nonsense, noting that "although the blessed virgin Mary was worthier and more excellent than all the apostles, still the Lord commended the keys of the kingdom of heaven not to her, but to them."[32] The association of the abbesses' activities, including preaching, with the "power of the keys" conferred by ordination, the power to hear confessions and give absolution, indicates that for Innocent these two roles were closely related.[33] His reference to Mary underlines his explicit denial to women of any historical claim to priestly power and concomitantly forbids them the right to preach. Pope Gregory IX reaffirmed Innocent's ruling and reasserted women's exclusion from the ability to cite Scripture publicly in 1234 when he "took from abbesses their right of public preaching and reading of the Gospel."[34]

A text written shortly after Innocent's bull similarly addresses the relationship between reading in the church and women's proper role in ecclesiastical matters.[35] Thomas of Chobham, an early thirteenth-century pastoral theologian with a strongly pragmatic bent, permits public reading of religious texts by women, apparently on the grounds that the speaker makes no intelligent contribution of her own to what is said. Abbesses may instruct and reprehend their nuns, he says, but they may not "expound sacred Scripture by preaching"; and they may read publicly from the Epistles of Saint Paul, the legends of the saints, and the gospel at matins—this is the office of deaconesses, Thomas says—but may not put on priestly vestments or read from the Epistles or the gospel at mass.[36] Thomas's approach is more tolerant than that of Innocent III, but it still denies women access to the most characteristic marks of the clerical hierarchy (priestly vestments, participation in the Mass) and particularly, it may be noted, prohibits women from originating speech: only the "greater ones" (*maiores*) in the church may expound Scripture to the people, may offer their interpretations and make use of their own intelligence.[37] Women, and laymen, may *re*-cite Scripture or preaching from a text or from memory but may not, so to speak, cite it in their own right, as the production of their own independent knowledge.

As Franco Morenzoni notes, in drawing the line against unlicensed speech at public exposition of Scripture, Thomas is reflecting "a distinction apparently already well established at the beginning of the thirteenth century . . . that preaching is not permitted to the laity unless the word *praedicare* is used as a synonym for exhortation to good, while it is formally forbidden them when it is taken *in its proper sense,* that is, the public explication of the sacred text."[38] Similarly, Innocent III permitted the laymen of the Humiliati to offer moral exhortation in their gatherings but forbade them to discuss "the articles of the faith and the sacraments of the church"—that is, doctrinal and hierarchical matters.[39] It is important to recognize, however, that preaching "proper" is not as stable in medieval preaching texts as Morenzoni, among others, seems to suggest. The issue of whether textual exposition is the ultimate definition of preaching is called into question, for instance, by Thomas's remark, "Although many simple priests may not know the profound mysteries of sacred Scripture, but only know how to rebuke vices and build up faith and good morals, at least in simple words, we do not believe that they are to be condemned. For thus did John the Baptist preach . . . thus the apostles preached."[40] In other words, such activity—which, as Thomas notes immediately afterward, may be practiced by laypersons in private (and he later gives examples of women saints and male hermits "preaching" this way in public)—functions as preaching in a pastoral context, suggesting that here as elsewhere the more limited definition was used not so much to characterize "true" preaching as to exclude unauthorized preachers.[41]

Reading aloud and expounding Scripture thus formed one aspect of what it meant to be a priest and accordingly one axis of the argument regarding unlicensed preachers. Considerations of the nature and scope of women's charismatic authority offer another angle on the problem. Discussions of women preachers frequently take women's ability to prophesy as a counterargument to their fundamental position that women may not preach. Henry of Ghent's thirteenth-century disputation on female preachers, for instance, says, "To prophesy is no less [an act] of grace than to teach; rather it is the work of prophets to teach publicly those things that are revealed to them," and he concedes that women have been prophets.[42] However, since his final decision, like that of all his colleagues, is that women may not preach after all, this argument must be opposed. Henry does this by saying that "prophecy is given to women not for public instruction, but for private, and if they teach men by it, this is on account of special grace, which does not respect sexual difference."[43] The argument from "special grace" was a favorite since it removed prophecy, and thus women's speech, from the realm of official, replicable authority. Thomas Aquinas, on whom Henry of Ghent drew for his own argument, declared that "prophecy is not a sacrament, but a gift of God" and placed it outside the human hierarchy of the church, saying that "the prophet is a medium between God and the priest, as the priest is between God and the people."[44] The "office" of prophet that could not be denied to women, then, is defined in such a way as to make it irrelevant to issues of women's preaching or ordination.

In another instance of the desire to prevent women from citing an authoritative lineage, the preaching of certain women saints such as Mary Magdalene and Katherine of Alexandria may be acknowledged, but care is taken that they remain very much *non imitanda sed veneranda* (to be venerated rather than imitated).[45] Eustache of Arras does eventually decide that these two women are worthy of the preacher's aureole, but the contention of, for example, Robert of Basevorn that a preacher must preach repeatedly and with authorization to merit the aureole would certainly exclude most women from the strict title of preacher, even if they managed once or on occasion to perform some version of that role.[46] Thus, although preaching manuals occasionally admit that women have been known to preach, they prefer to regard this as a product of extraordinary circumstances that does not authorize imitation.[47]

The dichotomy between the ordinary and the extraordinary used to short-circuit the development of a female lineage of preachers appears, not surprisingly, to be related to the issue of ordination. A disputation by Jean de Pouilly, for instance, discusses battles over jurisdiction between mendicants who have the office of preacher "only by commission or privilege (*ex commissione seu privilegio*), that is to say, by virtue of an extraordinary right (*jure extraordinario*)"; parish curates, by contrast, are authorized to preach by "ordinary right."[48] Jean notes that parish priests have this authority because it was conferred on them (in the person of the seventy-two disciples) "immediately" by Christ.[49] "Ordinary" authority to preach thus derives from a direct mandate from Christ, a mandate not given to laymen nor, especially, to women. And since the "immediate" conferral of ordination by Christ effectively took place through a human intermediary, it turned out that the mediation of a human lineage of priests and the institutional tradition conferred a more stable authority than the truly immediate inspiration of the prophet. Anyone, that is, including a woman, could attain an authorization from God that was equally or more immediate and direct than that of a priestly preacher, but she could attain it only in an extraordinary and thus noncitable sense.[50]

Limiting women to the noncitable role of prophet or—what amounts to the same thing—to "extraordinary" and nonlineal acts of preaching was thus one way of defining women's preaching out of existence. As Alcuin Blamires points out, quoting Hugh of St. Cher, "While prophetesses might give precedent for foretelling the future or uttering praise, they do not give precedent for 'expounding Scripture in preaching' (a distinction, in fact, between *praedicere* and *praedicare*)."[51] Problems arise, however, if we look at the meaning of prophecy in other contexts, since it seems that neither prophecy as such nor its exercise by women was as clear-cut as Hugh's pronouncement or Aquinas's appeal to the "gift of grace" might suggest.[52] Thomas of Chobham says that "preaching is also sometimes called prophecy. . . . To prophesy is to explain to the people those things which are said."[53] Most of the female prophets of the Bible, like their male counterparts, prophesied in this sense and thus functioned as preachers in Thomas's definition. Similarly a commentary wrongly attributed to Thomas Aquinas treats the biblical prophets as preachers who "employed a 'mode of preaching' appropriate to the people's capacities" in its simplicity and use of parables.[54] And William of St.-Amour, arguing a point of preaching jurisdiction that has nothing to do with women, says in the beginning of his antifraternal tirade, "Prophets in holy scripture are called seers. . . . Thus in making the scriptures available by expounding them they can justly be called seers, since in those same writings they are called prophets. Eph. 4: 'And he gave to some of them apostles, to others prophets;' the Gloss [adds], 'Prophets, that is, interpreters of scripture.' "[55] Here the distinction between apostles and prophets, which could certainly have been used in other contexts as a justification for excluding prophetic speech from the realm of preaching, is set aside in favor of an interpretation that defines prophecy explicitly as textual interpretation, "making the scriptures available by expounding them."

To go back to a foundational example, it may be noted that Moses, God's prophet, conveyed the messages he received to his brother Aaron, who had the gift of eloquence; it would thus seem that Aaron is the preacher to Moses' prophet, acting as the mediator Aquinas envisioned between prophet and people.[56] At another point, however, God says to Moses, "I have made you a God to Pharaoh; your brother Aaron will be your prophet," which suggests that the distinction between prophet and preacher was not a particularly solid one and moreover that a "prophet" could directly address an audience.[57] In his early thirteenth-century preaching manual Alexander of Ashby further demonstrates the fluidity of roles when he refers to Moses as interchangeably preacher and prophet, and to Aaron simply as priest.[58] When unlicensed preachers were not directly in question, in other words, the boundaries of prophecy and preaching could be somewhat fluid. When the object was to control access to ecclesiastical power, however, prophecy consistently took on its limited meaning of direct revelation or future-telling, a meaning that had the effect of excluding female and lay male prophets from a clerical lineage of preachers.[59]

The definition of the woman prophet's role as extralineal, then, was designed to cope with one of the difficulties raised by women who addressed the church: that of what precedent they might set. There remained, however, the question of the origin of the prophet's speech, a concern akin to the question of "expounding" in preaching. When God instructed the fourteenth-century prophet Birgitta of Sweden to go and rebuke the king of Sweden, Birgitta pleaded ignorance of what to say and was told, "When you arrive, open your mouth; and I will fill it"; when she arrived, "divine words were at once poured into her."[60] This formulation accords with Birgitta's image of herself as a "channel" for God's Word, a pure conduit for the message she carried. Two centuries earlier Bernard of Clairvaux had rejected this image of a male preacher, saying that he should be a vessel, not a channel, taking in the message and incorporating it before pouring it out by teaching. To attempt to teach others without being filled oneself constituted a spiritual danger.[61] For a woman preacher, however, any activity or image that emphasized the role of her own mind or body in the transmission of her message could be risky and distracting.

A male preacher's ownership of his words seems at first glance to be more clear-cut than is that of the woman prophet. Preaching, unlike scripted, sacramental speech, always has an individual, personal component; as one thirteenth-century author notes, "no one speaks of 'my baptizing' as he does of 'my evangelizing' or 'my preaching.' "[62] This is one of the things that differentiate preaching from a sacrament, which, if performed with technical correctness, always has the same effect, regardless of the quality of the individual priest who performs it.[63] The preacher is thus involved in the work of preaching and cannot expect "his" preaching to be handed to him on a silver platter; as the preaching manuals make clear, the Lord helps those who help themselves, and eloquence in preaching is an acquired habit as well as a gift of grace.[64] Yet Birgitta's delicate balance between God's words and her own, though more fraught, is in some ways not so different from that of a male preacher. A thirteenth-century treatise on preaching says that "the preacher should not say his own words, but the words of the Lord and those things the Lord supplies to him."[65] And the reassurance given to Birgitta that her speech comes from God echoes numerous biblical verses that apply to male prophets and preachers, most notably, perhaps, Matt. 10:18–20, from the chapter on the sending of the Apostles, when Christ tells them, "You will be led before governors and kings for my sake. . . . But when they deliver you up, do not think of how or what you will speak: for it will be given to you in that same hour what you will speak. For it is not you who speak, but the Spirit of your Father who speaks in you."[66] The prophet is an instrument, God's mouthpiece—but so is the preacher. Indeed the preacher should "efface himself," as Jean Leclercq says, thinking only of the glory of God and the edification of his neighbor.[67] In this regard, the difference between a woman prophet and a male preacher was perhaps as much one of emphasis as of substance.

A discussion by Thomas Aquinas both reinforces this impression and suggests how strong—and complex—was the association between ownership of speech and lineal ordination that excluded unauthorized speakers. He takes the concern with ownership back to its foundations as he analyzes Jesus' words in John 7:16: "My doctrine is not mine, but his that sent me." Aquinas explains that there would be no difficulty if Jesus had said, "The doctrine that I speak is not mine," but his words suggest that his doctrine both is and is not his. Aquinas solves this by saying that "the spiritual origin of doctrine is from God," and thus Jesus' doctrine is his insofar as the Son is one with the Father but is not his insofar as he is a "created soul." In other words, Jesus' doctrine is not his insofar as he is human. Moreover, Aquinas adds, it is because Jesus' doctrine is not his own that it is true doctrine. This is the explanation of John 7:18: "He who speaks from himself, seeks his own glory, but he who seeks the glory of him that sent him, the same is true, and no unrighteousness is in him." God is the sole locus of truth; the validity of the preacher's doctrine derives from its origin in God rather than in himself.[68]

As Alexander of Ashby puts it, "If someone speaks, let him speak as it were not his own words, but the words of Christ, attributing nothing of what is well said to himself but all to him from whom comes all good."[69] Aquinas adds that "it is unrighteousness when a man usurps what is foreign [*alienum*] to him" and insists that anyone who seeks his own glory, rather than God's, is unrighteous—a stricture that the preaching manuals repeat many times.[70]

Although Aquinas's argument particularly considers Jesus, his extension of the point to unworthy preachers makes it clear that his observations have wider application. The insistence that a teacher's words are valid only insofar as they mark his connection to God requires the speaker's displacement of himself. A similar move, of course, helped to make prophecy a valid option for women: it downplayed the speaker's body and offered a guarantee that a woman's doctrine was not her own. But the insistence on "the doctrine *of him that sent me*" recalls the need for institutional sanction, for the preacher's participation in a masculine lineage founded by Christ. Thus the alienation of speech Aquinas insists on (*loqui non a se*) justifies the preacher's position in a lineage even as it puts demands on him. Provided he is not speaking "of himself" he does not "usurp" that which is another's; his disowned speech marks the preacher's personal authority and righteousness and also his claim to be "him whom God has sent," his official and lineal authorization by the church. Women's exclusion from priestly lineage, however, meant that even if their doctrine was God's, their speech, if made public, was always in some sense a usurpation of another's privilege; unlike male preachers, they could not comfortably make reference to "him that sent me."

The male preacher's nonownership of his speech, then, both linked him to and distinguished him from a woman prophet because his depersonalized speech, unlike hers, paradoxically gave him ownership of his status as preacher. From this position, though his doctrine might be God's, he could still refer to "my preaching" and claim both his own speech and its scriptural origins in a way that a woman—limited, at best, to reading, reciting, or exhorting—never could. Moreover, institutional sanction and descent from Christ made it possible for the male preacher's body to disappear, in a sense, into that which it represented. The female body, much more marked as bodily in medieval culture, could not stage such a disappearance, and this cultural visibility made it extremely difficult for women to preach in the Middle Ages.[71] It also helps to make medieval attitudes visible now, to access the problems with the human male bodies that late medieval theorists often obscured by assimilating those bodies into an idealized image of the preacher that emphasized office over person.

This, then, is what Aquinas's discussion does not address: the great equalizer between male and female preachers, their humanness. He prefers simply to ignore or condemn the possibility of a human preacher's mixed motives or his inadequacy to his role, and this precludes any serious consideration of the preacher's self (*se*). Such complex questions, however, are precisely the strength of the preaching manuals. As these texts demonstrate, concerns such as ownership of speech, the place of the physical body in the act of preaching, and the preacher's relationship to both an ultimate source of authority in God and the earthly authorization provided by the institutional church arose not just in relation to women but as fundamentally important matters for all preachers. The attempts at definition, like Aquinas's exegesis, show the fragility of the preacher's claim on the doctrine he conveyed and the fragility of the boundaries of preaching. Lying between the purely charismatic speech of prophecy (the ultimate expression of personal authority) and the purely sacramental speech of priesthood (the ultimate form of official authorization), preaching was a hybrid form. The preacher's speech, and ownership of it, are at issue in ways that the prophet's and the priest's are not, and those questions of ownership make the speaking body peculiarly important.

The Absence of Absolutes

The increasing appearance of solidity in the office of preacher that characterizes the thirteenth century, then, was a response to a crucial weakness, as are many displays of strength. The multiple citations required in preaching, with their concomitant questions about ownership of speech and clerical lineage, emphasized the preacher's body because they foregrounded the physical absence of his (or her) ultimate model. The preacher *re*-presents God or Christ precisely because neither is bodily present. As Gillian Evans puts it, paraphrasing the words of Gregory the Great, "God himself works so closely with preachers that when he was on earth and visible to us the words of preachers were withdrawn . . . but now that he is not present in the flesh they must speak for him."[72] Both the preacher's need and his ability to "cite" Christ derive from this relative absence, an absence that makes it difficult or impossible to guarantee the authenticity of the citation.[73] If preaching were simply a matter of citing the words and actions of Christ—in effect, of acting the "script" of preaching—there would clearly be nothing to prevent *any* virtuous and learned speaker from preaching. Such proliferation, however, was unacceptable. As a late preaching manual puts it, "All preaching is sent from

God, without mediation or by the mediation of angels or men, and it always bears the power of God and represents his person."[74] Preaching by
unauthorized speakers, especially women, disrupts a chain of citations—
textual, personal, and institutional—whose ultimate and immediate refer-
ent is the person of God, and this lineage of authority is intended to
constitute the very basis of preaching. That the final guarantor of that lineage is both present, in the form of his representative, and also absent, and
thus unable immediately to guarantee that representative's appropriateness, is the kernel of the problem, and it is this nexus of absence and presence that returns us to modern speech-act and performance theory.[75]

The usefulness of the categories developed by Austin, Derrida, and
Butler for looking at medieval preaching theory, so far from them in time
and worldview, is no accident, I would argue, as we can see by following
the modern chain of citations. Butler builds on Derrida's work to develop
her theory of performance as unauthored citation; Derrida's concepts of
iterability and citation grow in turn out of his disagreements with Austin's
speech-act theory, particularly the latter's rejection of the idea of actors'
language as "hollow and void." Austin's notion of performative speech is
a reflection on the workings of "ordinary language" that draws on the
work of Ludwig Wittgenstein; and Wittgenstein begins his *Philosophical
Investigations*, which generates that theory, with a quotation from Saint
Augustine's *Confessions*, bringing us full circle to the father of Christian
preaching theory. The idea of "ordinary language," of course, which lies
at the center of Wittgenstein's later philosophy, returns us to one of the
key terms of the preaching debate. In effect, it was Augustine's concern
with the nature of language, its workings in a human context, and its role
in the connection between human and divine that produced both *De doctrina christiana* (the first sustained theoretical approach to Christian
preaching) and the passage of the *Confessions* that drew Wittgenstein's attention. Derrida and Butler examine human communication and the establishment of authority in the context of an absolute absence—that is,
from an atheistic perspective—while the medieval theorists begin from an
assumption that there exists an absolute presence, but both groups come
up against many of the same problems and questions.[76] In each case the
theorists must struggle with how spoken human communication repli-
cates or refuses to replicate the notion of an absolute presence or absence
lying behind it.

We can see this most clearly by turning to the point at which Derrida
takes up Austin's arguments. Somewhat like medieval theorists' defini-

tions of preaching, with their constitutive exclusions of prophecy, Austin's theory of speech-acts requires the exclusion of the imitated, delegated, citational speech of actors. He characterizes this as "non-ordinary" and thus denies it a place in his consideration of performative speech, claiming that "a performative utterance will, for example, be in a peculiar way hollow or void if said by an actor on the stage. . . . Language in such circumstances is in special ways—intelligibly—used not *seriously*, but in many ways parasitic upon its normal use. . . . Our performative utterances, felicitous or not, are to be understood as issued in ordinary circumstances."[77] Derrida, whose discussion of citationality begins precisely from this collapse (as he sees it) in Austin's argument, contends that since any speech-act's ability to function depends on its participation in a chain of citation, such "non-ordinary" speech actually shares its defining characteristic as citation with any other speech-act and thus cannot be bracketed out. Similarly, as has been suggested above, attempts to depict prophecy as an entirely distinct and extraordinary category with no bearing on the preacher's authority are in the end unsustainable, and the theorists' repeated attempts at definition suggest that they were uncomfortably aware of this instability.

Citation may seem to be a red herring, since for Austin citation is what excludes a speech-act from ordinary consideration while for the medieval theorists citation is precisely what makes the preacher's speech-act ordinary. The conflict is only apparent, however; indeed, the ultimate instance of Austin's "true" performative speech might be said to be the priestly, sacramental speech that both authorizes and contrasts with the preacher's speech: "I absolve you"; "I baptize you"; "I now pronounce you husband and wife." In the end both Austin's "infelicitous" utterances and the kinds of speech excluded from the category of preaching are rejected because they are "inappropriate" in that the speaker is in some essential sense not the "owner" of that speech, or perhaps we might more correctly say because it does not "belong" to him or her.

Both Austin and the preaching theorists wish to establish a claim that we can determine who has a right to certain kinds of speech.[78] Here again, however, we encounter the problem of absence, the absence of any absolute and fully expressed meaning, figured by Derrida as the impossibility of "saturating" the context of any communication. For Derrida the kind of plenitude imagined and desired by preaching theorists (and to a lesser extent by Austin) is unavailable: "Given that structure of iteration, the intention animating the utterance will never be through and through

present to itself and to its content. . . . In order for a context to be ex-
haustively determinable, in the sense required by Austin, conscious intention would at the very least have to be totally present and immediately
transparent to itself and to others, since it is a determining center [*foyer*]
of context."[79] In view of the bodily absence of God, whose "conscious intention" they would presumably have regarded as "totally present and immediately transparent to itself," if not invariably to others, preaching
theorists recognized the need for a representative. However, because of
human limitations—whether these are regarded as the result of original
sin or of an unruly unconscious—the human representative, unlike the
one he represents, is not capable of a "conscious intention" that is "totally
present." Given the preacher's human shortcomings, the context of
preaching, like any other human context, could never be "saturable" in
Derrida's terms or, it might be said, controllable.[80]

Ultimately, Christian preaching theory was hoist with its own petard
in regard to the issue of divine and human contexts. Unwilling to allow
any inspired person the title of preacher, and the possibility of generating
imitators, theorists of preaching explicitly displaced preaching from full
participation in the realm of plenitudinous, divine communication. Their
concepts of extraordinary and ordinary authority relegated prophecy to a
different sphere and denied women and laymen access to preaching.[81]
Since women were regarded as equal in soul to men, the justification for
preventing them from preaching could only be that this activity takes
place in the human world and thus requires a certain "privilege over others," as Humbert of Romans put it; hence women, being subject to men
in human society, may not preach.[82] This is also the substance of Thomas
Aquinas's argument against public instruction by women, which relies not
on theological underpinnings, as his discussion of women and ordination
does, but on social norms; he cites the ubiquitous Epistle to Timothy.[83]
Such justifications situate preaching firmly in the context of human hier-
archies and limitations. They exclude women and also tend to diminish
the male preacher's ability to claim direct access to the divine in his
preaching. The preacher, whether female or male, thus becomes subject
to questions about social status, personal morality, and interactive performance; the exclusion of unauthorized speakers by appeal to the human
context inescapably entangles the preacher in the demands of that context. Suspended between authorization and inspiration, between citation
and ownership, the preacher had to assert a claim on his language and office that, in order to function, could only ever be provisional.

Holy Duplicity: The Preacher's Two Faces

> This noble ensample to his sheep he yaf,
> That first he wroghte, and afterward he taughte.
> Cristes loore and his apostles twelve
> He taughte; but first he folwed it himselve. . . .
>
> For though myself be a ful vicious man,
> A moral tale yet I yow telle kan.
> Chaucer, Canterbury Tales

THE PREACHER'S ABSTRACT ABILITY TO FORM part of a clerical lineage was only one part of his task; once established in his role he still needed to demonstrate his ability to perform that role convincingly. The problem is neatly encapsulated in the contrasting preachers of the *Canterbury Tales*.[1] Chaucer's description of the Parson in the *General Prologue* is as much a depiction of the ideal priest as the *Pardoner's Prologue*, later in the same text, is a compendium of a preacher's faults.[2] The two figures differ in almost every possible respect relevant to a preacher—intention, authorization, use of rhetoric, mode of delivery. The Pardoner's very title declares him to be of a dubious caste of preachers who often used trumped-up bulls to justify their self-interested preaching, while the Parson, a parish priest whose concern is all for his flock, has pure intentions and a better and more ancient right to preach than anyone save a bishop.[3] Then there are their styles of preaching: the Pardoner's gesticulations, elaborate rhetoric, and spun-out exemplum are the antithesis of the Parson's sober refusal to rhyme or "glose" in his "myrie tale in prose."[4] What does not differ is the worth of their messages; the Pardoner's theme, "Radix malorum est cupiditas" (the love of money is the root of evils), is no less inherently respectable than the Parson's implicit teaching, "Penitenciam agite" (do penance).[5] But the very different responses they have drawn, both from their fellow pilgrims and from modern readers, amply demonstrate the importance of the messenger to his message. The Parson and the Pardoner encapsulate the central ethical and moral issues that concerned the writers of preaching manuals from the twelfth to the fourteenth centuries, a period when preaching was much in question both within and outside the orthodox church. High on the list of potential problems was the appropriate relationship between the preacher's human body and his spiritual task. Fictional and extreme test cases, the Parson and the Pardoner are, in effect, *exemplum in bono* and *exemplum in malo* of that relationship. They can help to highlight and are themselves illuminated in turn by a discussion of how the preacher's person could contribute to or diminish the "office of holy preaching."[6]

While the problems surrounding the preacher's body and office were becoming increasingly acute in the later Middle Ages, they were by no means new. Conrad Leyser has recently argued that Gregory the Great drew on the ascetic tradition to create the ideal of a ruler whose ability to control his own body and, in particular, the "flux" of his speech demonstrated his ability to manage affairs in the world; this control of speech, Leyser argues, in effect substituted for the sexual temperance or abstinence that was the focus for earlier thinkers.[7] Gregory's concern with "how [one could] safely distinguish speakers of true spiritual wisdom from purveyors of empty falsehoods" is reflected in his assertion, "If a man's life is despised, his preaching will be condemned."[8] The concern with personal morality and Gregory's distrust of the rhetorical display that might disguise "empty falsehoods" were crucial to his attempt to link external power to internal virtue, and they formed a key part of his substantial legacy of advice to later preachers on the practical and spiritual difficulties of their task.[9]

Gregory's arguments on these topics remained central for later theorists of preaching, but they came to be used in a spiritual and institutional climate very different from that in which the sixth-century pope had developed them. The reforms instigated by the other famous Pope Gregory in the eleventh century gave rise to new pressures on the body of the preacher. The desire to return to a vision of the apostolic life as one of poverty and preaching, the focus on the clergy as a group set apart, and above all the need to recapture for the church as a whole a radical sense of *sancta simplicitas* all put increased demands on the clergy to possess, and to display in their words and actions, an impeccable personal morality.[10] To fulfill their office and to reinforce the church's power, preachers required both spiritual excellence and unquestioned authorization, qualities displayed above all in the preacher's person.

That "person," however, was a problematic and increasingly divided concept. As the authors of scholastic and disputation literature of the twelfth and thirteenth centuries moved away from the patristic tendency to focus on personal dignity, they began, as Jean Leclercq says, "to distinguish the person from the function, and they did so in order to emphasize the dignity of the function and the obligation of the person to conform himself to it."[11] The personal virtue that had been the primary repository of the preacher's authority suddenly had to coexist with, and in many cases take second place to, the impersonal and hierarchical power of his official authorization.[12] This shift is linked to the one that Stephen Jaeger sees in this same period, from charismatic body to charismatic text.[13] Such a transition is never a smooth one, as Jaeger notes, and the growing focus on authorization worked against the continuing demand for holy simplicity and, more importantly, against the fact that preachers were, inevitably, charismatic bodies. Discussions aimed at preachers on the relationship of their persons to their task display with particular clarity what Ernst Kantorowicz, discussing another kind of dual body, calls the "eager[ness] to reconcile the duality of this world and the other, of things temporal and eternal, secular and spiritual."[14] Attempts to reconcile these dualities, however, often only reinforced the depth of the gap between them.

A comparison of the textual bodies of Parson and Pardoner begins to outline some possible relationships between the preacher's person and his office. All we know of the Parson's physical presence is that despite the breadth of his parish he visits his parishioners faithfully, in rain and snow and gloom of night, "upon his feet, and in his hand a staf."[15] The depiction suggests a body whose sole meaning derives from its service to a larger task; indeed, there is so little sense of particular embodiment here that, as R. N. Swanson puts it, "It is virtually impossible to bring him to mind as a person . . . any attempt to conjure up a physical presence falls completely flat."[16] The feet perhaps recall the image of preachers as the feet of the church, and the staff in his hand reminds us of his role as shepherd: the Parson's body functions as an abstract reflection of his office.

What a contrast this makes to the Pardoner, whose physicality is so foregrounded, simultaneously excessive and elusive, that it may well dominate our sense of him and certainly interferes with his preaching in ways that preaching theorists would have strongly disapproved.[17] First, there is the doubt about his sexuality: "I trowe he were a geldyng or a mare," the narrator says, expressing an uncertainty that has implications not only for his acceptance among the other pilgrims but for his very ability to occupy the office of preacher.[18] Second, there is the theatrical gesticulation about which he boasts in his prologue: "Thanne peyne I me to strecche forth the nekke, / And est and west upon the peple I bekke, / As dooth a dowve sittynge on a berne. / Myne handes and my tonge goon so yerne / That it is joye to se my bisynesse."[19] This kind of physical display is uniformly condemned in preaching handbooks and contrasts sharply with the Parson's approach: here, it is clear, the preacher's office serves his body rather than vice versa.[20] Finally, of course, the Pardoner's greed, the cupidity that both fuels his preaching and provides its subject, marks the unworthy self-interest that motivates his supposedly spiritual work.[21] If the Parson exemplifies personal authority attained through perfect submission to an institutional structure and ideal, and thus powerfully reinforcing that structure and ideal, the Pardoner emblematizes the capacity of the physical body to destroy both personal authority and institutional authorization.

Alastair Minnis has recently discussed the theoretical and theological aspects of the potential gap between the body as locus of authority and the body as locus of a fallible individual.[22] The aim here is to raise similar questions about the practical performance of preaching. Attempts by the authors of *artes praedicandi* to manage the potentially competing meanings of the preacher's body are all the more informative because they deal with a figure who was not, like a king, in a removed position of divine right nor, like an author, at a distance from his audience, but one who had constantly to perform both his virtue and his authority for a present, and possibly resistant, audience. In establishing the preacher's claim implicitly to represent the church's dignity and authority, preaching theorists often contrast the authorized representative with those excluded from or inappropriate to the office of preaching, such as heretics, laymen, women, and immoral preachers. References to such denigrated categories of persons can help us to understand the importance of the preacher's persona and the vulnerability of an authorization that had to depend upon it.

In the practice of preaching, the bodily effacement implied in Chaucer's textual portrait of the Parson was simply impossible: preaching is a physical performance, and thus the problems raised by the preacher's body had to be addressed. Medieval discussions of the complex concept of persona demonstrate the doubleness inherent in the very activity of preaching, a doubleness that was both essential and potentially devastating to the preacher's activity and role. In their yearning for holy simplicity, for an idealized congruence between the preacher's words and his deeds, his message and his persona, the preaching theorists inadvertently highlighted the preacher's hybridity and his inevitable participation in a world of partialness, appearances, and duplicity.[23]

Persona and Authority

The primary meaning of *persona* according to J. F. Niermeyer's *Lexicon* is "individual, human being," and this seems to be the sense underlying the varied uses of the term in the *artes praedicandi*.[24] The importance both of particularity and of the power and frailty of humanness arises again and again in discussions of the preacher's persona. However, the first definition given by Charles du Cange, "dignitas," is more in line with meanings noted later in Niermeyer, such as "competence, qualification," "someone of a certain standing," "official," and even "parson."[25] The connotations of status and authority suggest that the term *persona* could encompass the possibly conflicting demands of the individual and of his office. Preaching manuals draw on this range of meanings, but their use of the term relates it especially to the human side of the preacher's activity: his interaction with an audience, his status, his body, his actions in the world.

An address to priests by the late twelfth-century bishop and preacher Maurice of Sully begins to illustrate in a practical way the divisions inherent in the concept of persona. Maurice says that the priest's three main responsibilities are a holy life, knowledge, and preaching.[26] He goes on to note that "holy life" means that the priest must cleanse himself "from all bodily and spiritual uncleanness" (*de tote l'ordure de son cors e de s'ame*) by which "his soul might appear ugly and ill-kempt before God, and his person before the world" (*s'ame puet estre malmise e enlaidie devant Deu e sa persone devant le siecle*).[27] The two pairings here are "body and soul" and "person and soul," an imperfect repetition that reflects the multiple meanings of *persona*. "Person" is, first of all, set off against the "soul" that only God sees, and it is imagined as that which the priest, as a prerequisite for preaching, presents to the world. Maurice implies that the two kinds of uncleanness (of soul and body) and the two kinds of presentation (to God and the people) are equivalent, but this of course elides the imperfection of human perception as compared to that of God. God will know how true the preacher's presentation is, but a human audience may not. A key characteristic of persona, then, is that it refers to the preacher's activities and appearance in the world, to external, human communication rather than the preacher's internal connection with God. The pairing of person and soul also suggests, without insisting on it, that the preacher's external presentation to his human audience will reflect his relationship to God, that internal and external purity are linked. However, persona is not only divided from soul and thus put squarely into the arena of human interaction, but is also shown to include both the priest's physical body and his self-presentation. The parallel pairings "soul and body" and "soul and person" suggest that body and persona are intimately linked and that, in Maurice's view, the body [cors] can impair the effectiveness of the preacher's self-presentation, make his person [persone] "ugly" before the people and thus, presumably, detract from his message. The preacher's persona is intimately connected to but not entirely synonymous with his body.

For Maurice, it seems, the emphasis falls on the preacher's appearance before his two audiences, God and people, and persona is imagined as prior to preaching, as part of the basis for the activity. It is also, however, subject to contamination by the preacher's sinful body. Writing for a group whose mission to preach was not in question, parish priests, Maurice focuses his attention on the preacher's moral qualities as the basis for his authority, reflecting to some extent the older ideal of personal dignity rather than the new attention to office.

A different emphasis appears in the work of Humbert of Romans. While Humbert, like Maurice, saw persona as related to both body and status, and as a basis for the practical exercise of the preacher's office before a human audience, his *De eruditione praedicatorum* is more attentive to questions of authorization and legitimacy. It is not surprising that Humbert, as an ecclesiastical official and a member of an order of wandering preachers, shows a strong concern both with maintaining the boundaries of official authorization (boundaries that had at times been drawn against the mendicants) and with a preacher's ability to establish authority before an audience.[28] Taken together, the categories he discusses under the heading "De persona praedicatoris" demonstrate the potential capaciousness of this concept and its suspension between ideas of the physical and the social. Humbert says that, "regarding the person [of the preacher], it should be noted" that he should be of the male sex, not evidently deformed, physically strong, of appropriate age (i.e., not too

young); that he should have "some prerogative over others"; and finally
that he should not be a "contemptible person," by which, Humbert clarifies, he means someone of vicious life.[29] The preacher's person, for Humbert, must both represent and uphold his preeminence over those he
addresses.

The "his" in that sentence is no accident, since Humbert's first category entirely excludes women from the practice of preaching. This exclusion is foundational: above all the preacher must be a man. Humbert
justifies his ruling on a fourfold basis that recapitulates the standard arguments against women preachers.[30] The first reason for women's exclusion
is deficiency of understanding, which Humbert says is more to be expected in women than in men; the second is women's subordinate status;
the third is that if a woman were to preach, her appearance might provoke
men to lust; and finally, women are barred "in memory of the foolishness
of the first woman, of whom Bernard said, 'She taught once, and over-
threw the whole world.' "[31] Like the categories as a whole, this list offers
a combination of body-related and status-related prohibitions, and we
may note that two of Humbert's qualifications for male preachers,
strength and "some preeminence over others," are often used to exclude
women and thus would tend to reinforce his initial ban on female preachers on both physical and social grounds.

While the focus of this initial category might seem to be squarely on
women, all of Humbert's reasons for excluding women have some bearing on men, a fact that is usually made explicit in the text. The first category, lack of intelligence, is one that Humbert claims is more applicable
to women than men. The way he expresses this, however, makes it clear
that women's weakness is relative ("intelligence . . . is not to be expected
in women so much as in men") and thus to some extent undermines it as
a basis for exclusion.[32] The second issue, subordinate status, implicitly recalls women's subjection to men, but as Humbert's more general category of "preeminence" suggests, this too can be grounds for excluding
men as well as women. These categories emphasize women's inadequacy
and weakness, but since both are qualities that men can share, they act as
a reminder that women are only one group of many that were barred from
preaching and undermine women's exceptionally rigid exclusion.

Humbert's third and fourth reasons emphasize not qualities that men
and women might share, but rather women's effect on men. The anxiety
about male lust and the recollection of Eve demonstrate not women's
weakness, but rather their dangerous power. And while these criteria cer-

tainly denigrate the female body as a source of sin and confusion, they implicitly concede that it is male weakness—the ability to be provoked to lust
and Adam's willingness to listen to Eve—that makes women dangerous.
The depiction of women as simultaneously inadequate and threatening to
the office of preacher and the ways in which that inadequacy and threat
implicate men are reminiscent of clerical anxieties about the flesh.[33] Such
a connection is hardly surprising, given the strong medieval association of
flesh and femininity. But the rather elaborate introductory insistence on
women's exclusion raises the suspicion that this approach allows Humbert
to draw attention away from the frailty of the male flesh, and to establish
a solid persona for the preacher, by reiterating the notion that women are
particularly subject to and representative of the weakness that is in fact a
characteristic of all human beings.

Despite this preemptive strike, the categories that follow, with their
imbrication of status and embodiment, cannot but suggest that men, like
women, are immured in physicality. Even their attempts to escape it, via
the establishment of a formal, disembodied authority, depend on the
physicality that men share with women and on the response to their bodies in the physical world. This is what lies behind the prohibition on evident deformity. The attributes of wholeness and masculinity are ones the
preacher needs to be seen to possess in order to establish that he has a
body appropriate to his office. We might think here of the Pardoner, who
seems to feel a need to perform masculinity—perhaps as a way to assert
both his maleness *and* his lack of physical deformity—as well as to proclaim his status and authorization.[34] His physical qualities and his official
qualifications are mutually dependent and equally suspect; they bring each
other and, by extension, the office of preacher into disrepute.[35]

Humbert's last three categories attend less to physical qualifications
than to those of status. The preacher must be of appropriate age, since
Christ did not presume to preach before the age of thirty: here again what
might at first appear to be a physical requirement turns out to be linked
to a question of status and, indeed, to what might be called the ultimate
question of status, the preacher's similarity to Christ. Also, the preacher
must have some prerogative over others "whether in office, or in learning,
or in religion, and so forth," for which reason a layman (like a woman) is
not to preach. Finally, a preacher must not be a contemptible person, lest
his preaching be rejected. Here Humbert cites the standard text from
Gregory the Great: "If a man's life is despised, it is clear that his preaching will be scorned."[36] These last two requirements are presented as

though divorced from embodiment, and remind us that maleness is a necessary but not a sufficient condition for preaching: the preacher must also demonstrate eminence and virtue.

Like those that went before, Humbert's final group of categories emphasizes the preacher's relationship to his audience and the things that may cause them to scorn him or disregard his message, rather than the purely internal qualities that might be necessary for effective preaching.[37] The various subheadings of persona bring together, not to say jumble, the issues of status, authority, authorization, and embodiment, showing the preacher's right and ability to speak as a matter for complex negotiation among him, his congregation, God, and the institutional hierarchy of the church. In these negotiations persona is assumed to precede preaching in some sense and is tacitly regarded as a true reflection of the preacher's internal state. In Humbert's last category, however, we face the troubling prospect of the despicable preacher, a figure who leads us deeper into the complexities of the preacher's persona.

The Body Double

If a man's life is condemned, his preaching will be scorned, Humbert asserts; similarly, as most of the *artes praedicandi* insist, one whose life is admirable will strengthen his preaching.[38] In this context the import of the term *persona* is perhaps best conveyed by Leclercq's assertion that the medieval conception of the preacher's office "excludes . . . all preoccupation with self-interest [*recherche personelle*]."[39] The preaching manuals (and the Pardoner) make it clear that the preacher's "personal" interest in preaching could include anything from desire for adulation, to vainglory, to pure greed: sinful desires that the body could either manifest or hide, promote or suppress. At the same time a good example was a crucial part of preaching. The problem of the preacher's personal relationship to his office had been explored extensively by Thomas of Chobham in the early thirteenth century. In a section of his *Summa de arte praedicandi* titled "On the doubleness of preaching"—that is, on preaching in word and in deed— Thomas moves from the ideal of the preacher as exemplar to the problem of the preacher as sinner. His discussion shows quite clearly how the preacher's physicality is both a benefit and a detriment, an essential element of and a potential danger to his message.[40]

The importance of example, a crucial aspect of a sermon's material as well as its delivery, lies in its inevitable relationship to the physical and the particular, to all the qualities that work against the idealized submergence of the person in the office seen in Chaucer's Parson.[41] It is no accident that that supremely disembodied churchman refuses to use the denigrated, embodied mode of "fables" in his sermon, refuses to speak in the exemplum form that the Pardoner elaborates on so vividly.[42] Not all medieval preachers—indeed, it seems, very few—were as fastidious as the Parson in this regard; exemplary stories were regarded by most as a valuable tool, for the same reasons that made the preacher's personal exemplarity necessary. In one of the many prologues that address the usefulness of similitudes and exempla, Étienne de Bourbon writes that it is necessary that doctrine, like Christ, be "embodied and clothed in flesh" to make it accessible to a lay audience.[43] The image of embodiment and fleshliness carries us right to the idea of the preacher as exemplar; the need to make doctrine visible and palpable that Étienne cites also animates Thomas of Chobham's insistence on the mutual necessity of the preacher's words and deeds. "Every preacher should give a good example [*bonum exemplum*] in his works, and good doctrine in his words," he says, since a good life without preaching is inefficacious.[44] The insistence on preaching both in word and in deed does more, that is, than assert that word and deed must be congruent; it expresses the limitations of words alone in convincingly portraying salvific doctrine. Indeed, Robert of Basevorn seems almost to imply that embodiment is essential to preaching. Regarding God, the first preacher, he says, "He preached frequently through angels who assumed bodies or, as some would have it, some other corporeal likeness which He Himself assumed not in union of substance, but only as its mover, as perhaps he spoke to Adam and many others. . . . And at last He Himself, taking on a human soul and body in the unity of substance came preaching."[45] Even God, it seems, needs a body if he is to preach.

The "unity of substance" of which Robert speaks, of course, was the ultimate instance of doctrine "embodied and clothed in flesh," Jesus Christ. The Incarnation presented doctrine in an accessible form and provided the perfect example for Christians to follow: an embodied human person who fully expressed all the ideals of the faith. As Augustine wrote, "We need a mediator linked with us in our lowliness by reason of the mortal nature of his body, and yet able to render us truly divine assistance for our purification and liberation," and later he says that Christ offered his virtuous humanity as "an example for our imitation."[46] Christ, of course, was an example for all the faithful, but the clergy were supposed to provide an idealized example of appropriate imitation. "Be ye followers of me, even as I also am of Christ," Paul says to the Corinthians, a passage quoted by Thomas of Chobham in his section on doubleness.[47] If Christ's humanity mediates between the heavenly and the earthly, then the preacher, who should be a true reflection of that example, is the mediator at one remove. He too conveys the heavenly by earthly means.

The concept of mediated imitation clearly informs Thomas's treatment of exemplarity and makes visible the demands that this role placed on the preacher, who, Thomas says, "should be like a book and a mirror for his flock, that they may read in the deeds of their leader as in a book, and may see in a mirror what they should do."[48] The numerous exempla collections called *Speculum* . . . (and the many other kinds of books that went under the same title) were intended, as Ritamary Bradley has pointed out, to "show the world what it is and . . . to point out what it should be."[49] Although Thomas is clearly focusing on the latter of these two meanings, the preacher, like his exempla, could illustrate both. The uneasily dual nature of the mirror, a glass in which we see perfection, but see it darkly, is like that of the preacher, an earthly and physical exemplar of an abstract ideal.[50] Just as the exempla used in his sermon clothed doctrine in the flesh of narrative, so the preacher was to clothe a moral ideal in human flesh. The danger, as always, was that the flesh might interfere with the expression of doctrine, rather than facilitating it. For God, whom no "clothing" of flesh can defile, this necessary method carries no dangers, but for the human preacher who followed him it was otherwise.

The preacher's dual allegiance—responsible to God and people, imitating one and imitated by the other—should be internally coherent. But the division introduced by that duality, like the one between words and deeds, could also make the preacher's persona dangerous. One sign of this is the fact that Thomas's concept of the "doubleness" of preaching, which begins by emphasizing the capacity of bodily action to reinforce the preacher's words, quickly turns to the body's potential to undermine those words and to the role of sin in preaching: the bulk of the section on doubleness considers how a preacher should publicize or hide his sins and describes sinful modes of preaching. A certain slippage in Thomas's use of the term *duplex,* twofold or double, helps us to see how immorality and its relationship to the preacher's persona call into question not just the authority of a particular preacher but the nature of preaching itself.

Thomas first uses the term *duplex* to refer to the mutually reinforcing areas of words and deeds: "preaching can only be double" because these two must both be present.[51] As he dissects this concept, however, we begin to see the preacher's "duplicity" as a matter not of beneficial replication but of potentially destructive division. If life and word are not in agreement, "the example killeth what the word giveth life," and rather than reinforcement there is a fatal conflict between the two.[52] This is also the case with the two ways in which a sinner can hide his sin and the two ways in which he can make it public; in each case there is a good and a bad possibility. A positive display of deeds receives no discussion, presumably because it is the situation already discussed in the remarks on exemplarity: if a preacher's life is virtuous, this should be made visible to his audience so that it will reinforce his preaching. The other three possibilities all address the less attractive but apparently, in Thomas's view, more probable situation where the preacher is a sinful man—not extraordinarily sinful, perhaps, but not a straightforward exemplar of virtue.

The sinful preacher, Thomas suggests, has three options. The only positive one is hiding one's sins for the good of others, out of shame before God.[53] Then there are the negative possibilities of displaying one's sins in a bad way or hiding them in a bad way. The first of these is very much what the Pardoner does: he appears not to regret but to glory in his sins; he publicizes them with gusto and élan. Such behavior should be avoided, Thomas suggests, lest the preacher scandalize his flock, making himself a stumbling block to their salvation—as happens with the Pardoner, at least in the context of the *Canterbury Tales*.[54] The other possibility, that of hiding sins in a bad way, brings us to a discussion that links the preacher's doubleness of word and deed with his potential duplicity or hypocrisy as a performer.[55] Thomas speaks harshly of those who "hide their sins in an evil way, that is, under the adornment of virtues [*sub ornamento uirtutum*], and as it were put on their sins like silken garments that they may deceive others and seem beautiful to them."[56] He goes on to compare such preachers to Thamar, in Gen. 38:13–15, who sat at the crossroads in rich clothing like a harlot, and says that "thus do hypocrites act meretriciously, to deceive the sight of those who observe them by an ornate exterior of virtues."[57] Both the emphasis on ornate decoration and the comparison to Thamar create an atmosphere of carnality around what could otherwise be seen as primarily intellectual or spiritual deception. Whereas Humbert of Romans projected onto women the kinds of physical shortcomings that might threaten any preacher, Thomas, by assimilating the hypocritical preacher to a decked-out harlot, suggests that lust and self-display can equally be characteristics of the male preacher. Here we see the dangers of the preacher's physicality: his body is no longer the beneficent double of his doctrine but rather its evil twin, undoing all the good work done by the word.

When Thomas turns to the second half of his initial pairing—the preacher's word or teaching—it becomes clear that physicality and doubleness pose a threat in this realm as well. As we arrive at the section on "the word of preaching" the transformation in the concept of doubleness is complete: like preaching as a whole, the modes of preaching in words are called "duplex." Here, however, doubleness refers not to two halves, capable of working either for or against each other; it speaks rather of division into two mutually exclusive categories, recalling the preacher's possible ways to display his life. The preacher can preach either "for the benefit and use of his neighbors" or "out of desire for earthly gain or the pleasure of human approval"; here again, the Parson and Pardoner line up on opposite sides of a divide.[58] The former category, preaching for the good of others, receives no discussion. The latter is immediately defined as adultery of the Word of God, and those who pursue it are accused of one of four modes of sin: theft, fornication, idolatry, or lying. As with the doubleness of preaching and of the preacher's life, the negative possibilities receive far more attention than the positive ones; it seems that the preacher's personal desires and bodily weaknesses pose a threat that overshadows the beneficial potential of his body.

All four "bad modes" serve the regrettably worldly desires for money, vainglory, and human approval, the self-interest that the *artes praedicandi* universally condemn. The discussions of "fornication" and "idolatry" particularly demonstrate how the preacher's words can be tainted by the demands of his person. Those who "fornicate" in preaching, Thomas says, "luxuriate in the empty words of their own rhetoric" (*luxuriantur in uerbis ponposis eloquentie sue*).[59] The verb *luxuriantur,* which recalls the deadly sin of *luxuria,* or lust, connects with other words in this passage, such as *lasciuia, delectare,* and *dulcedo,* to reinforce the sense of sexual sin evoked by the gratification of personal desires in preaching.[60] The mode linked to "idolatry," on the other hand, returns us to the body and the sense of its own doubleness. "The third way of sinning against the word of God is when [the preacher] commits the same errors that he condemns," says Thomas, and he adds, "This is to build with one hand and destroy with the other."[61] This recapitulation of the words/deeds problem shows the preacher's body, suddenly, as divided not only from the beneficial capabilities of the word but indeed also against itself, as one hand creates what the other destroys.

The preacher, as a creator in both word and deed, must make his two halves work together for his message to be effective. But as the development of Thomas's concept of *duplicitas* in preaching demonstrates, it was not difficult to slip from doubleness as beneficial reinforcement to doubleness as deceptive and destructive division. Divided against himself and from the salvific doctrine he presents, the wicked preacher " 'speaks another's words' ('dicit aliena')," since his behavior makes it clear that the words he speaks cannot truly be his.[62] He breaks the congruence of word and deed that would allow him to be a beneficent exemplar and thus impairs his own authenticity, which is both his claim to be the persona he presents and the source of his authority. In so doing he amply demonstrates the power of the preacher's presence, whose ability to diminish his message only reemphasizes its equally important role in validating that message.

Two-Faced Preachers

Thomas of Chobham recapitulates much of his discussion of the doubleness of preaching later in his text when he considers the issue of persona, a reiteration that demonstrates the link between the problems of self-presentation and morality.[63] An appendix to Humbert of Romans's treatise on Dominican offices makes this connection more explicit, echoing the image of building and destroying used by Thomas: "It is essential that life and teaching should coincide in [the preacher], lest what he builds up with one hand, he destroy with the other. Thus the preacher should present [*praetendere*] humility in his bearing, virtue in his morals, discretion in his words, charity in his zeal for souls, temperance in eating and drinking, and maturity in his actions."[64] The preacher's actions in the world create a persona that must reflect his truly virtuous morals and thus reinforce his capacity to be a preacher, or else fatally undermine it. The unreliability of the preacher's body as an index of his virtue raises a specter of hypocrisy that challenges the very office of preaching—a challenge often conceived in terms of acting.

The dislike of acting was, of course, not invented by Christian preaching theorists; Cicero lamented that orators, "the actors [*actores*] of truth itself," were reluctant to use the persuasive tools afforded by delivery, preferring to leave these to the *histriones*.[65] But the idea of "representing truth" is a complex one, as Christian writers were particularly aware. In his *Soliloquies*, Augustine rejects the provisional truths afforded by acting, saying that "we should, instead, seek that truth which is not self-contradictory and two-faced."[66] Whereas Cicero seemed to envision the ability to use acting techniques without compromising oneself, Augustine, and later preaching theorists, were more alive to the contradictions implicit in the notion of the performer of truth.

What makes these contradictions so problematic, as we have seen, is that it is in such doubleness, such two-facedness, that the very nature and effectiveness of the preacher's role lie. Maurice of Sully suggests that in some sense the preacher is, and must be, two-faced, one face toward God and one toward the people, and later theorists reinforce this notion. Ideally these two faces would be the same; control of speech and moderation of movement would represent cleanliness and orderliness of soul.[67] Such a correspondence would guarantee the visibility of a preacher's wicked life to his audience. Discussions of another aspect of the preacher's self-presentation—not his behavior in the world but the performance of preaching—show why that assumption was so troubling and, not incidentally, why there is such a long-standing antipathy toward acting in preaching theory. Performance in preaching calls forth many of the issues already seen in connection with the preacher's role as exemplar, but it does so in a way that seriously undermines the value of exemplarity as a mode of teaching. Accounts of delivery rework Thomas's notion of beneficial duplicity in a way that makes its dark side more evident, repeatedly showing the divisions in the preacher's self-presentation as places where a gap between appearance and reality might arise.

Alan of Lille, whose *Summa* on the art of preaching is the earliest of the late medieval preaching manuals, discusses the preacher's persona in the following terms: "The preacher should capture the goodwill of his audience by his own person [*a propria persona*] through humility, and by the usefulness of the material he presents, by saying that he proposes to them the word of God that it may bear fruit in their minds, not for any earthly reward, but for their progress and success; not that he may be stimulated by the empty clamor of the crowd, not that he may be soothed by popular favor, not that he may be flattered by theatrical applause; but so that their souls may be formed, and that they should consider not who speaks, but what he says."[68] Alan's language here suggests that the preacher has a complicated relationship to the theatricality of his task: he must create a persona by rejecting the suggestion that he is an actor. The preacher can inspire confidence in his "own" persona specifically by telling his audience that he does not want to seek an actor's rewards (applause, popular favor, earthly gain). This suggests that it is not enough merely to *be* humble; to make his message effective, the preacher must actually *project* his own humility. The ostentatious construction of personal unimportance is essential to his office.[69] Even as he rejects the preacher's association with the actor, then, Alan makes it clear how similar the two roles are. The preacher may—and certainly should—have different goals than the actor, but their methods are strikingly similar.

We may also note here that Alan attempts to evade the problem of persona altogether, but does so in a way that demonstrates the impossibility of such a maneuver. His final note, that the audience should consider "not who speaks, but what he says," does indeed describe the ideal: the message should be important, not the messenger. But like the Parson's body, whose importance consists in its visible submergence in his ecclesiastical role, the expression of this ideal betrays its reliance on that which it claims to discard. For Alan does not just assert that the audience should consider message rather than messenger; instead he says that the preacher should capture the goodwill of his audience (a rhetorical concept) *by telling them* that they should consider not who speaks but what he says. The preacher should use his persona, his presentation of himself, to encourage a disregard for himself as an individual. While on one level the idea of regarding the message rather than the messenger makes sense, on another level the way that message must be conveyed demonstrates the impossibility of such disregard for the personality, individuality, and embodiment of its speaker.

The other reason, of course, that Alan's attempt to minimize the role of the preacher's person is doomed from the start is that in some ways it is extraordinarily important who speaks. If it were not, then anyone speaking the Word of God and promoting a beneficial message could be a preacher: a woman, a layman, a depraved sinner. It is only within the already enclosed world of authorized preachers—those with official sanction, male, undeformed, strong enough, old enough, with a certain prerogative, and living a virtuous life, to use Humbert's requirements—that the messenger is unimportant. The many exclusions necessary before it is possible to emphasize logos over ethos demonstrate sufficiently that the body of the preacher is indeed a crucial aspect of his message.

Alan of Lille's presentation of persona considers it primarily as a verbal performance, albeit one that reflects on the preacher's life. Other texts address persona in terms that insistently return to the preacher's physicality and make clear his disturbing links to the despised figure of the actor. These formulations were sensitive to the ways in which gesture and physical appearance worked to establish the preacher's persona, for better or worse. In a chapter on delivery, for instance, Thomas of Chobham touches on the issues of presentation before an audience raised by Humbert of Romans and Maurice of Sully. Rather tautologically he observes that "it is extremely shameful when a preacher behaves [*se habet*] shamefully in voice, face, or gesture."[70] He goes on to clarify the implications of such behavior, noting that Caiaphas, who stands and furiously addresses Jesus in Matt. 26:62, is rebuked by the Gloss on that passage: "He was angry because he found no place of calumny; by a disgraceful motion of the body he showed the wickedness of his mind."[71] A similar belief in physical gesture as an accurate reflection of inner state must lie behind the many strictures in preaching manuals against "excessive" or "disorderly" gestures: such bodily movements cast doubt on the preacher's control and moderation. Conversely, injunctions to the preacher to preserve restraint and gravity are intended to reinforce the effectiveness of his persona. Thus, the importance of *maturitas* (meaning here, as Margaret Jennings points out, "modestia, gravitas") in a preacher's presentation is noted by Ranulph Higden: "*maturitas* consists in two things, namely, in appropriate motion of the body and in restrained speech of the mouth."[72] Appropriate physical movement reflects an appropriate mental state, reinforcing the preacher's message by reassuring the audience about the nature of his mind and, by extension, the state of his soul.

As Stephen Jaeger has observed, this ideal of a perfect soul in a perfect body, the two reinforcing each other without any gap, appears in a life of Saint Bernard; Bernard's biographer Geoffrey describes the saint as "the first and greatest miracle" that God performed through him, saying that Bernard was "serene of face, modest in his bearing, cautious in speech, pious in action. . . . In his body there was a certain visible grace and charm, which was spiritual and not physical. His face beamed with light, in his eyes there shone an angelic purity and the simplicity of a dove."[73] This depiction reflects, Jaeger argues, an eleventh- and twelfth-century concept of education that was "oriented to the body" and "identifie[d] control of the body with control of the self. . . . The cultivation of external presence is identical with the cultivation of virtue."[74] He suggests that this attitude gradually gave way to a focus on charismatic texts. It is, however, precisely such a conception of the charismatic body that we see in the preaching manuals' insistence on teaching *verbo et exemplo* and on appropriate gesture as evidence of good intentions.

Considering this ideal in light of preaching theorists' ideas of persona helps to clarify why "holy simplicity" was so attractive and yet so unattainable in late medieval preaching. Such simplicity was an ideal of reformist preaching; Peter Damian, for instance, regarded "sancta simplicitas" as characteristic of apostolic preaching, saying that God "[does not] need our grammar to draw men . . . since he sent not philosophers and orators, but simple men and fishermen."[75] Here we see the discomfort with human rhetoric visible from Paul's Epistles onward that still haunted late medieval preaching texts. Humbert of Romans, discussing the preacher's speech, demands "simplicity, without the elaboration of ornate rhetoric."[76] The duplicity inherent in language and the moral neutrality of rhetoric were persistent concerns for practitioners and theorists of sacred oratory. As discussions of delivery show, however, it was not only language but also life that could be double: the preacher's performance demonstrated that both body and words had the capacity to hide the truth as well as display it and thus threatened the ideal correspondence of *persone e ame,* exterior and interior, that holy simplicity demanded.

Preachers' difficulty in fully inhabiting the space of *sancta simplicitas* may in part reflect the fact that, despite the "monachization of priesthood" in the reform period, the preacher's body was inevitably in a situation that made simplicity difficult to achieve.[77] The ideal of monism, the "singleness of heart" that ideally characterizes every true Christian, is one that not accidentally gives its name to monasticism.[78] Precisely because they were performers in the world, preachers were almost by definition unable to access the purity and simplicity that were the monastic ideal; unlike the monk's, the preacher's connection to God had not only to exist but to be publicly displayed. The doubleness inherent in the preacher's persona was inevitably in conflict with *simplicitas.*

Despite these incongruities and challenges preachers were stuck with their charismatic bodies. For them, embodied authority was not subject to supersession by textual authority, precisely because the preacher—a living "book" for his congregation, as Thomas of Chobham put it—conveyed his message via his body. Instead the two modes of authorization existed in uneasy juxtaposition as the demands that the preacher's persona conform to his office intensified. As Jaeger points out, Geoffrey of Clairvaux's life of Bernard "implies a contest between charisma of person and repre-sentation."[79] The problem for preachers was that they were charismatic bodies whose very raison d'être was to be representatives, with the divi-sions that representation inevitably implies.

In the centuries following Bernard's lifetime, preaching theorists still looked to the ideal that he personified and, indeed, to its roots in Gregory the Great's practical admonitions to help them negotiate their dual status as physical presences and spiritual representatives. The Dominican Thomas Waleys, for instance, writing in the first half of the fourteenth century, makes clear the continuing pressure for the preacher's body to convey his spiritual qualities. He cautions, as do many other theorists, against excessive gestures in preaching: a preacher must preserve "due moderation" (*debitam . . . modestiam*) when preaching, and use "appro-priate" (*decentes*) gestures. He warns against bobbing around, nodding the head unduly, whipping from side to side, and waving the arms, saying firmly that "such movements are not appropriate to a preacher."[80] He goes on to say that attention to gesture is important because "if it be-hooves a preacher of the word of God to present himself, at every place and time, so that 'in gait, stance, bearing, and in all his movements he should do nothing that may offend anyone's gaze,' how much more should he preserve these things who shows himself like some star sent from on high and like an angel and messenger fallen from heaven into the presence of the people."[81] Whereas Alan of Lille tries to divorce preaching from act-ing while simultaneously showing how closely related the two are, Thomas Waleys's description suggests that the preacher must use his phys-ical body (gait, stance, bearing, movements) in a way that suggests his spiritual quality. In other words, just as for Alan performance should be used to deny the suggestion of acting, for Thomas the body should be used to elide the preacher's physicality. In each case, it seems, the preacher's self-presentation rests uneasily on his hybrid status as the human messen-ger of a divine message, as an "actor of truth itself."

Thomas Waleys's designation of excessive gesture as "inappropriate" to a preacher raises a final key question. In his manual Thomas of Chob-ham suggests that excessive or disorderly gestures may do more than sim-ply bring the preacher's gravity or modesty into doubt: they may question his very identity as a preacher. He notes that when David wished King Achis to think him stupid he "behaved affectedly, that is, made certain gestures"; by this, Thomas says, we may see clearly that "those who make such gestures in preaching will be considered foolish, and will seem rather

to be actors [*histriones*] than preachers."[82] The emphasis falls on the supposedly inevitable reaction to such behavior, the sense that its "actorli-
ness" will be entirely apparent to the audience and will diminish the
preacher's role to the point of nonexistence. His acting will take over so
thoroughly that his role as preacher will seem "proper" in neither sense of
the word, neither appropriate nor his own. To a certain extent the
preacher's claim to "own" his office is based on his internal fitness for that
office. But since internal fitness, the preacher's spirituality and disinterestedness, is visible only to God, he must make it visible to his audience
through appropriate gestures and behavior in order to assert his identity
as a preacher, and in this assertion there lies always the possibility of deception.[83] If the immoral preacher "speaks another's words," the histrionic preacher seems, as it were, to take on another's body, impairing his
own claims to truth in a way that threatens the very substance of his office.

Maurice of Sully's discussion of *persone e ame* with which we began
shows preachers' awareness of the divisions inherent in persona; the theorists' discussions show why the problem was such a hard one to resolve.
The *duplicitas* that Thomas of Chobham holds up as the true nature of
preaching and the insistence on exemplarity that provides its context attempt to guarantee the authenticity of preaching—but they have a substantial sting in the tail. Wicked deeds cast doubt on the preacher's words,
but once the possibility of acting is introduced, virtuous deeds can do so
as well. The overlapping categories of persona—body, self-presentation,
gesture, deeds—are reminders that if a preacher's body is, as the theorists
implicitly recognize, always an actor's body, then there is no way to know
if he is an "actor of truth itself" or a mere *histrio*. The *artes praedicandi*
suggest that, in preaching at least, holy simplicity was a created rather than
a natural category, belonging to the sphere of *persone* rather than *ame* and
thus subject to the doubleness that plagues human communication. Acting in the world, in both senses, requires the preacher, and the preaching
theorists, to make use and take account of the body. The truth Augustine
desires, the truth that is "not self-contradictory and two-faced," is not an
earthly truth; it is the preacher's heavy task to attempt to convey that singular truth from a position that must always, and inevitably, be double.

The Pardoner, the Parson, and the Audience's Dilemma

Where, then, does this leave us with Chaucer's mirror-image preachers? I suggested above that the body's dangers for preaching can only be rightly understood in the context of the body's contributions to preaching. Similarly the context of holy duplicity suggests that neither Pardoner nor Parson can be completely understood without the other; perhaps no single portrait of a preacher can fully convey the complexities of the office. I began by stressing the Parson's disembodied nature as it contrasts with the Pardoner's excessive physicality, but as I hope the discussion above has suggested, such claims to disinterested abstraction are necessarily suspect. Looking at the Parson and Pardoner together, and in the context of debates on preaching, it is clear that Chaucer has not only embodied a crucial problem in preaching but by that very embodiment re-created for his readers the same dilemmas that preaching theory tried to address.

Those dilemmas appear most strikingly in criticism of the Pardoner. The *Pardoner's Prologue* and *Tale*, as Lee Patterson has noted, "stage many of the issues central to the theological and ecclesiastical debates of late-medieval England," including that of the preacher's morality.[84] A great deal of Pardoner criticism since the middle of the twentieth century—in effect, since the rise of exegetical criticism—has worked to understand his character as it interacts with, comments on, and manifests itself through his ecclesiastical position. Whereas earlier attention to the Pardoner's religious standing often focused on what might be called his external qualities, such as how he exemplifies his profession or the nature of his sermon and its relationship to other sermons, recent work tends to combine this historical approach with an interest in how the Pardoner's psyche is shaped or expressed through exegetical allusions or cultural and religious debates.[85] Given the intensity of religious allusion and structure that shape the Pardoner and his speech, such readings seem entirely appropriate. I would like here to adopt their fruitful attention to religious context, but to look less at the Pardoner's interiority than at how the presentation of his character reflects on "the nature of the cultural authority that produces him," and in particular on the office of preacher.[86] The context of preaching theory, combined with the continuing recognition in modern criticism of the Pardoner as an actor, can suggest some of the reasons why criticism of this character, and its fascination with his interiority, has been so voluminous and so varied.[87]

Chaucer has effectively tempted his readers into a continuing desire to know the truth of the Pardoner by presenting him as one who should, according to his office, be an actor of truth but who insists unrelentingly that his act is all a lie. The dilemmas presented by the embodiment of such a character have entranced critics for the past century, and they have done so, I suggest, because the question about the Pardoner's interiority is one that we are both set up to ask and forever unable to answer. The battles over the relationship between the Pardoner's "inside" and his "outside" arise not solely from differences in modern critical method, but from the very problems with preaching examined here. Chaucer by his depiction of the Pardoner—a depiction to which even the most stalwart opponents of roadside-drama excess concede an undeniable "personality"—has put us in the position of an audience observing the preacher's public perform-ance.[88] Like that audience; we see only the face that looks in our direc-tion. What, if anything, may lie behind it, what "face" the preacher may turn to his creator, and what his intentions may be can only be matters for speculation, but it is speculation that an audience will always engage in.[89] Part of Harry Bailly's fury at the end of the tale may stem from an obscure recognition that, as an audience member, he has been put in an untenable position of uncertainty by one of the very figures who was supposed to provide certainty. He responds by retreating to what he believes he knows about faith—that he will have "Cristes curs" if he listens to the Pardoner's teaching—and by asserting aggressively his own desire literally to get hold of the Pardoner and establish the "truth" about one of that figure's many uncertainties, the nature of his sexual body, in the crudest and most visi-ble way possible.[90]

By "playing" the preacher, then, the Pardoner provides a reminder that all preaching is acting and that as a result our knowledge of the preacher is only ever partial.[91] He may be "strange to himself," as Patter-son's epigraph from Dom DeLillo puts it, but he is also, like every preacher, "strange" to his audience, unknowable and unfathomable. This inescapable strangeness suggests the limitations of the idealized portrait of the Parson, which seems to ask members of the audience to accept a kind of transparency that they know to be false—even as they may wish that it were true. But this is not to say that the Pardoner is in some twisted way more "truthful" than the Parson. Instead it suggests that we must look again at the ideal, wholly simple Parson. In the *General Prologue* it is true that there is little to interrupt readers' view of his transparent truthful-ness.[92] The Parson is an exemplar of holy duplicity, as the *Prologue* insists over and over: his words and deeds are in perfect harmony. And insofar as

that appearance of perfection has been accepted, it has been notably un-
productive of criticism about the Parson as a character precisely because
there seems to be no one there who inflects the message. But this view can
only be sustained if we limit ourselves to the third-person *General Prologue*
portrait. Just as theoretical texts on preaching suggest, the image of a perfectly disembodied exemplar can only be sustained outside the context of
performance. At the points where the Parson ceases to be a third-person
figure characterized by the narrator and speaks in a voice of his own, he inevitably complicates—without necessarily invalidating—his own status as
an ideal.

As Lee Patterson has noted, "the inclusion of the teller with the tale
personalizes the meanings that emerge," and the *Parson's Tale* is not ex-
empt from this phenomenon; the Parson's embodiment, his status as a
character, is sometimes regarded as undermining his message.[93] Patterson
sees the "personalization" of the tales as encouraging "a dramatic reading
that discounts any authoritative significance" and suggests that the *Parson's Tale* only escapes this limitation by transcending the frame narrative
that produces it; it "takes its origin in the very dramatic and realistic context which it will dismiss."[94] As Peggy Knapp points out, however, such a
view involves a paradox: "If [the Parson's] doctrine is true, there need be
no fictions, and yet he formulates this doctrine within a fiction—he *is* a
fiction. Either the unchanging realm (from God's vantage point) of the
revealed Word swallows the flawed, historical, uncertain world of experience, or vice versa."[95] Knapp's point about this paradox is well taken, but
I would argue that there is more room for negotiation than she, or Patterson, allows. The figure of the Parson, in effect, shows that neither the
unchanging realm of authority nor the fluctuating world of experience
does swallow the other; instead, these realms coexist and interact, as they
must do for every preacher.[96] At the end of the *Parson's Tale* the figure of
the individual speaker fades into textuality—but only to give way to the
voice of another speaker, of Chaucer in the Retractions, a reminder that
while the origins of the voice are never guaranteed, it is always a voice that
comes from someone. Preaching is precisely the attempt to bring the unchanging, revealed Word into the uncertain, human world, and the duplicity required of the preacher reflects that disparity. We need not regard
Chaucer's depiction of an idealized preacher as a mere setup for yet another anticlerical critique to argue that it does in the end acknowledge the
impossibility of that single-minded ideal. If the Parson's individuality to
some extent diminishes his capacity to convey authority, that same indi-

viduality, whatever its costs, is simultaneously essential to his existence and effectiveness as a preacher. We can see how physicality both gives and takes away authority in the Parson's speech, the best available proxy for his embodied performance.[97] It is as an audience of his textual speech that we imitate a sermon audience; it is only through language that these characters are present, and only through their speech, as distinguished from the narrator's descriptions of them, that they take on a life of their own. We catch a first glimpse of the Parson as a person, not just an ecclesiastical model, in the *General Prologue* portrait's question, "if gold ruste, what shal iren do?" and its reference to the shame of "a shiten shepherde and a clene sheep," both of which allude to the priest's duty to act as an example.[98] As Jill Mann observes, in the passage as a whole "we realise that once again, it is the character himself who is speaking. It is not the moralist commentator who quotes from the gospel and adds the 'figure' about rusting gold; it is the Parson himself."[99] Such language begins to constitute the Parson as a personality distinct from the abstract ideal of the good priest.

Later instances of the Parson's speech reinforce the hints of his individual character in the *General Prologue*. The epilogue to the *Man of Law's Tale* depicts the Parson's objection to Harry Bailly's swearing, which draws Harry's jocular claim to "smelle a Lollere in the wynd."[100] The Parson's rebuke—itself slightly jocular, reproving without being harsh, as the *General Prologue* had promised—increases our sense of him as an individual, and Harry's mock-accusation points to the specificity of the Parson's response, the way it makes him a potential participant in a recognizable political and religious debate.[101] The Parson may or may not have heretical secrets, but Harry's ability to imagine such a thing, based on the Parson's conversation, is enough to remove the latter from his abstract portrait frame and put him into a world of human interactions. Both Harry and the modern critics who try to break down the Parson's appearance of perfection could be accused of misreading, but in fact their suspicions are an entirely foreseeable response to the presentation of an idealized performer. By making that performer's humanness clear through his individual voice, Chaucer makes it inevitable that such questions will be asked about the Parson, whatever their answers may be.

The Parson's involvement in, and awareness of, a human context can also be seen in his self-presentation in the prologue to his tale. Usually it is his strictures against exempla and alliteration, his rejection of embodied

forms, that draw attention here. Less noticed is his initial address to the
pilgrims, which demonstrates a sensitivity to his audience:

Why sholde I sowen draf out of my fest,
Whan I may sowen whete, if that me lest?
For which I seye, if that yow list to heere
Moralitee and vertuous mateere,
And thanne that ye wol yeve me audience,
I wol ful fayn, at Cristes reverence,
Do yow plesaunce leefful, as I kan.[102]

He begins with an image that personalizes a biblical injunction, the
rhetorical question and first-person form making it almost conversational.[103] The last five lines of this passage alternate between concern for
the audience and concern for the text. The first and third lines address the
audience's willingness to hear; the second and fourth offer what the speaker
can provide (virtuous doctrine, a good will, and reverence for Christ). The
final line combines these areas into "plesaunce leefful," the linking of
what will please the audience with what will benefit them. The address as
a whole is nothing other than a *captatio benevolentiae,* an astute rhetorical move that shows that the Parson is well aware of his need, as Alan of
Lille put it, to "capture the good will of his audience by his own person
through humility, and by the usefulness of the material he presents."[104]
Without questioning the "truth" of his performance of virtue, we may acknowledge that it is inevitably a performance. By creating the Parson as
an embodied character, however sketchily, and by giving him a voice of his
own, Chaucer shows that though he makes very different choices, he is involved in and aware of the same network of audience and performance
that the Pardoner manipulates so skillfully.

What Chaucer's preachers seem at first to present, then, is a study in
holy simplicity versus unholy duplicity, a black-and-white dichotomy, and
on a certain abstract level it remains true that the Pardoner represents an
immoral preacher, the Parson a virtuous one. The context of preaching
theory suggests further possibilities: not just the holy duplicity that
Chaucer's *General Prologue* portrait of the Parson so insistently foregrounds, but unholy simplicity—the Pardoner's single-minded pursuit of
gain, so single that he seems at times to consist only of that quality.[105] Ultimately, however, this opposition also proves too simple; the juxtaposition and the embodiment of polarized abstractions, and the frame in
which they are set, help to show why such dichotomies are unsustainable.

In giving his characters voices of their own, Chaucer disallows our reliance on the voice of the all-knowing creator, on any immediate or transparent access to the truth about any other person, however fictional. Like a preacher's audience, Chaucer's readers may speculate about the speaker's soul, but all we really see is his person, the individual whose specificity and solidity make any claim to transparency—to perfect holiness or perfect unholiness—suspect. No preacher, however virtuous, is an empty vessel through which God speaks, but to understand the beneficial as well as the destructive implications of that fact we need the Pardoner as much as we need the Parson. It is not just that the ideal that the Parson represents can only be perceived, but indeed that it can only exist alongside and interdependent with the counterideal of his troubling, but not simply unholy, colleague.[106] And together they have drawn critical responses that show how we, as readers, still struggle with the problems that face any audience attempting to assess the two-faced truth of public performance.

The traditions of preaching theory that Chaucer drew on in creating his Parson and Pardoner acknowledged and attempted to come to terms with the divisive physicality of preaching, an activity in which the human body that marks the gap between heaven and earth must also become the means of bridging that gap. Persona, imagined as the guarantor of the preacher's authorized status and his connection to God, turns out to be a performance—a performance always capable, as in the Pardoner's case, of spectacular falsity or, more worryingly, of a deception unperceived by the audience. As a result the doubleness of persona and the necessary duplicity of the preacher have the capacity to undermine not only a particular act of preaching or a particular preacher, but the very office. In the face of tensions between visionary and institutional authority, between charismatic body and charismatic text, preaching theorists tried to hold the competing forces together in ways that required them to explore, explicate, and attempt to control the power of the preacher's persona. Their discussions, the best available record of the pressures felt by medieval preachers, give us a certain, admittedly oblique access to the experience of constructing oneself as a person worthy to inhabit "an office more angelic than human."[107]

3

A Manner of Speaking: Access and the Vernacular

Experiencia docet . . .
[Experience teaches . . .]
Proverbial

ALONGSIDE QUESTIONS OF OFFICIAL authorization and self-presentation medieval preachers, like modern ones, had to consider the purely practical aspects of how to get their message across to audiences. Fundamental among these was, of course, the question of language. Unlike modern scholars, medieval preachers seem to have had little interest in the relationship between Latin and vernacular language—or at least little direct record of their musings on this topic has survived.[1] It is thus difficult to know, in most cases, in what language they would have preached, though recent scholarship has suggested that the long-standing notion that Latin sermons were always preached to the clergy and vernacular sermons to the laity, with little or no overlap, may be too simple.[2] Medieval preachers' attention, however, seems to have focused far more on their access to their audiences, an issue that in a larger sense addresses precisely the question of the place of the vernacular in preaching.

The great revival of formal interest in preaching took place before the major debates in England about the vernacular and its appropriate place in religious culture broke out in force, and in general preaching handbooks do not emphasize the question of language.[3] Nevertheless, attentiveness to preachers' discussions of their own language can illustrate how shifting and uncertain the supposed divide between Latin and vernacular really was. Preaching manuals, particularly those by mendicant authors, and discussions of narrative exempla show preachers engaged in a delicate balancing act. Standing between the church hierarchy and the laity in both the mediatory and the liminal senses of the word, preachers required

access to both of those worlds in order to make them accessible to one another. The preaching handbooks, with their complex attention to the
preacher's need both to distinguish himself from and to resemble his
flock, and discussions of exempla, which hovered problematically between
vernacular and Latin modes, show how crucial vernacularity was in establishing a clerical identity that is often seen in opposition to it.

Vernacularity is not the same as popularity, but the Latin term most
preachers used to describe the vernacular suggests that in this context the
two are not unrelated. The word *vernacularis,* while not unheard of, appears far less often than the word *vulgaris* and its offshoots, meaning
"common," "popular," "of the crowd," and so forth.[4] Thus it is sometimes impossible to tell whether a writer is referring to a story *in the vernacular* or merely a *popular* story, a *vernacular* saying or a *common*
saying. This distinction, or lack thereof, is important because vernacularity in preaching has to do not simply with language but with the
preacher's ability to form a connection with his audience, to gain access
to their hearts and minds. Access is often discussed in terms of exclusion—
the need for access implies a prior separation. In preaching, however, access is more a matter of an effective approach, of addressing a given
audience in terms appropriate to their situation. Like many of the sermons
they left behind, most preachers must have been linguistic and cultural
hybrids.[5] Thinking about vernacularity as access helps us to understand
how preachers fashioned themselves as representatives of clerical culture
who maintained their links to the vernacular culture that surrounded
them and that was their first linguistic home.

Talking the Talk: The Preacher's Bridge

The kind of preaching that we think of as vernacular preaching, preaching to "the people" or the laity, was associated throughout most of Christian history with the lower clergy, as Michel Zink has noted, because it
was the lower clergy—below the bishop, that is—who were able to communicate with their flocks in the native, "common" language of the re-
gion.[6] It was perhaps a lack of sufficiently prepared lower clergy that led
to a growing perception, in the eleventh and twelfth centuries, that the
clerical hierarchy was not fulfilling its preaching duties; instead independent, charismatic preachers—some more orthodox than others—sprang
up to fill the gap.

The situation of the Milanese Patarenes, discussed at length by Brian Stock, demonstrates the power of such popular preachers. In an account of the Patarene Landulf Cotta's preaching, the conservative chronicler Arnulf maintains that it was "deliberately 'arranged' for the persuasion of the unsophisticated (*concionatur in populo*)." His description shows a charismatic preacher at work, using the tropes of inadequacy and unlearnedness, youth, inexperience, and so forth—claims that diminish the distance between preacher and audience. As Stock puts it, Landulf "reaches out to the people on their own level, making himself a bridge between the lettered and the unlettered"; he is described as using a kind of call-and-response format and asking the audience to cross themselves: "Both oral and gestural, this revivalist give and take between preacher and audience, which the reduction of the text to Latin undoubtedly tended to suppress, has the effect of welding the two into a single unit." Landulf uses what Stock calls "street language. . . . Although he is not one of the people, he speaks to them as if he were"; this identificatory move, achieved through the preacher's self-presentation and his choice of the "common" language, is apparently essential to his success. As Arnulf sees it, Landulf and Ariald were quick to "pander . . . to the people's tastes (*vulgi mos*)," but it was this very kind of aristocratic, antipopulist disdain that put the institutional church at such a disadvantage in the period before the preaching revival.[7] In such a situation the only hope lay in the work of outstanding preachers of orthodox inclination, and records of preaching for the twelfth century present men such as Bernard of Clairvaux or Robert of Arbrissel, whose charismatic gifts were so great that it was said they could preach in an unknown language and still move their audiences. It was also noted of Bernard, in one of his *vitae,* that he was "lettered among the learned, simple among the simple"—in other words, that he was able to adapt to his audience and the "vulgi mos" in a way that made him a gifted preacher among all kinds of listeners.[8]

Bernard, Robert, and their ilk are exceptional cases; not everyone who preaches to the people is a popular preacher. Faced with the need for more and better ordinary preaching, the church in the late twelfth and early thirteenth centuries pulled itself together and began trying to train people, using in effect the kinds of methods so intelligently exploited by heterodox preachers such as Landulf Cotta. What had come naturally, or gracefully, to a Bernard or a Robert was something that had to be learned by the preachers of the thirteenth century, who needed to be trained both in Latinity (immersion in the scriptural founts of their vocation and un-

derstanding of their institutional position) and in vernacularity (the techniques that would enable them to use their knowledge for the benefit of
all kinds of audiences). In learning to balance Latin and the vernacular,
preachers were in effect learning to establish their own role in a community, and vernacularity was as important in this endeavor as Latinity.

Preachers' mediatory role as "translators" of literate, Latin, clerical
culture for an unlearned, lay, "vernacular" audience can certainly be seen
as one that denied the laity full or independent access to Scripture and to
theological material usually produced in Latin. Opposition to vernacular
translation of Scripture was already an issue in this period, and the famous,
or infamous, idea that the laity are to be presented with truth in simple
form as infants are given milk, because they are not strong enough for
solid food, is frequently featured in preaching manuals.[9] Considered from
the point of view of doctrine, then, the Latin-vernacular relationship in
thirteenth-century preaching seems to recapitulate a hierarchy in which
the laity—*rudes, simplices, illiterati*—were always at the bottom, accorded
no independent will, power, or ability. Even within the preaching manuals, though, we are given reason to question this strict division of the vernacular and Latin and the strict association of these with laity and clergy,
respectively. To understand this problem fully, it is necessary first to develop a more nuanced conception of how preachers thought of their role.
The works of Thomas of Chobham and Humbert of Romans, who shared
a strong interest in effective preaching but wrote for very different groups
of preachers, begin to outline the issues.

Writing primarily for parish priests, Thomas was more concerned
with establishing the preacher's differences from his audience than telling
him how to overcome those differences—an emphasis that no doubt reflects the state of the parish clergy, many of whom were probably hardly
more educated than those they were supposed to instruct.[10] Thomas's
text, which shows a careful attention to the problems of pastoral care, has
little to say about the vernacular in any of its forms. His focus in this area
is on the preacher's need to maintain his position—to establish and present an appropriate persona to his congregation and to keep up the distinctions between himself and them. This is a matter of responsibility as
much as privilege; the preacher owes his audience a good example and
good teaching and must work to provide them. But he should also be
conscious of and maintain his authority. Thomas discusses, for example,
the dangers of excessive humility toward those one has wronged, which
can diminish the preacher's stature, and he warns against preaching in

scruffy clothes or a "habitu laicali."[11] His attitude reflects, it seems, both the popularity of lay and itinerant preaching—in which the preacher's status was not always markedly distinguished from that of his audience—and the beginning of a trend in parochial priesthood in the thirteenth century whereby the priest became increasingly the representative of a larger, diocesan authority, of the church as a whole rather than simply of his own local jurisdiction.[12] In the context Thomas addresses, the priest would have been part of the community to which he preached. He would be known to them—perhaps all too well—and so would not have needed Thomas's, or anyone's, instructions on how to approach them. In this instance the preacher needs to be shown how he can establish, maintain, and display his access to the clerical world of learning and authority in order to make his role in the "popular" world, of which he is clearly a part, an effective one.

In the course of the thirteenth century new modes of preaching arose, distinct from both the charismatic and the parochial. The rise of the Franciscans and Dominicans produced a substantial group of itinerant, trained preachers who would not necessarily be acquainted with the language, customs, and style—in short, with the vernacular—of their intended audiences. It was to such preachers that Humbert of Romans primarily directed his instruction. Because preaching is ultimately a spoken form, the transition from Latin to vernacular involved not simply linguistic translation but the connection with and access to an audience without which any rhetorical exercise is severely impaired. Later complaints about "English Latin" and the mockery of preachers' Latinate speech in works such as Chaucer's *Summoner's Tale* or the morality plays show how much resentment was aroused by preachers, including friars, who failed to learn the "common touch" in their manner of speaking.[13] It is that failure and resentment that the early mendicant handbooks seem designed to avoid. Their approach to the preacher's work of translation indicates that they recognized the interdependence of lay and clerical, Latin and vernacular cultures in the spoken, interactive context of preaching—an attitude that is clearly present in Humbert's text.

In a chapter titled "On the speech of the preacher" (*De loquela praedicatoris*), Humbert addresses, obliquely, the relationship of Latin and vernacular. He first notes the preacher's need to be able to speak clearly, citing the example of Moses and Aaron. His next observation makes reference to Pentecost, and at this point we might expect specific attention to problems of translation and the move from Latin to the vernacular. Humbert's point, however, is less direct. He says that the preacher should have an "abundance" of language: "If the early preachers were given many languages for the purpose of preaching, so that they might have abundant words for everyone," he asks, "how unbecoming is it when a preacher is lacking in words, whether on account of a lack of memory, or a lack of Latinity, or a lack of vernacular speech [or "common speech," *vulgaris loquutionis*], and so forth?"[14] Here Latin and the vernacular appear as equally necessary to the work of preaching; the lack of either handicaps the preacher. This brief indication that "speaking in tongues" is the job of the preacher is the only mention of linguistic issues in the passage; Humbert is interested in the preacher's *language* primarily as an element of the preacher's *speech*.[15] Other desirable qualities he goes on to discuss, apparently equivalent to the importance of ease in various languages, include sonority of voice, a manner of speaking that is easy to follow and well-paced, a simple style, and finally, "prudence in speaking of diverse things to diverse people" (*prudentiam in loquendo diversa diversis*).[16] While such "prudence" is often cited as the reason for speaking simply to the simple, it turns out that what Humbert has in mind is an appropriate message; the audiences he envisions are defined not as lay or clerical but as the good, the wicked, the timid, the wrathful, and so forth.[17] For Humbert, that is, linguistic matters are only one, subsidiary aspect of the preacher's need to make his speech attractive and appropriate to whatever audience he may be addressing.

While Thomas's instructions, then, are for preachers who are already connected to their audiences by language and common experience and who may therefore need to maintain more distance in order to shore up their institutional authority, Humbert writes for those who have the advantage and authority of distance but lack the immediate connection of a parish priest to his flock.[18] In neither case is the linguistic issue of the vernacular much in evidence. What is visible in both texts is an awareness of vernacularity as part of a balance between different kinds of access that are equally necessary to the preacher's task.

The Common Ground of Exempla

The connection between preacher and audience created by vernacularity and the problems this could raise are particularly evident in the preacher's use of exempla and similitudes.[19] It is often noted in preaching manuals and collections of exempla that such "concrete" means of persuasion are particularly appropriate for laypeople. As J.-C. Schmitt says, the form and use of exempla "rest on a veritable anthropology, or at least on the sense that the clergy has of a certain specificity of 'popular' culture. This awareness is the condition of effective preaching: to people who for the most part are considered 'rural,' 'lesser,' 'simple,' 'unlearned,' one must speak of concrete things, 'physicalities,' 'external things,' 'deeds,' without using the subtleties of speculative language."[20] This audience is usually distinguished with clerical loftiness from a more learned audience to whom one may speak directly of higher things.

Many modern readings of the cultural role of exempla strongly emphasize the depth of the divide that the use of example supposedly illustrates. Larry Scanlon has argued that the exemplum was "a narrative enactment of cultural authority" and that, in the context of a sermon to a lay audience, "there is virtually no social permeability between exemplarist and audience. There are simply two distinct groups, the clerical, (*scientes, erudites*) on one side, and the lay (*rudes, simplices*) on the other."[21] Schmitt seems to agree: "The exemplum introduces into the sermon the realistic and agreeable note of a story that in all respects breaks up the general mode of expression in the sermon and seems to establish a furtive complicity between the preacher and his audience. But let there be no mistake: far from being isolated, [the exemplum] is linked to all the other arguments, and the momentary rupture that it introduces reinforces again the ideological function of the sermon, the speech of authority."[22] In both these instances the admission of connection between preacher and audience is subordinated to an assertion of difference that echoes the "rudes, simplices" rhetoric of exempla collections and sermon manuals.

Other scholarly readings, however, remind us that the repeated references in preaching texts to the simple, the unlearned, or the rustic— terms that emphasize the divide between the clergy and their audiences—ignore the fact that exempla, like vernacularity more generally, did reflect a certain connection between the supposedly learned preacher and his supposedly unlearned flock.[23] Schmitt notes that the medieval preacher "finds himself constrained in a sense by the necessities of his 'exemplary' pedagogy to involve himself in the multiple networks of oral narrativity," and David d'Avray points out that the use of "extended comparisons or analogies . . . is one of the mental habits or customs which most influenced the directions which the thinking of preachers followed in the thirteenth century and after."[24] Thus to suggest, as Schmitt does, that the medieval preacher was "constrained" by the need to use exempla is to overlook the ways in which such techniques were at least as much a way to cross the divide between *simplices* and *clerici,* between Latin and vernacular, as a way to maintain it.[25] This is reflected in the fact that preachers, who were of necessity clerics, are certainly not above using concrete instances to make their points; both Thomas's and Humbert's texts are filled with such comparisons. It is worth remembering in this context that not all the clergy were equally learned and that many of them no doubt shared their audiences' cultural interests. Indeed, Caesarius of Heisterbach's famous anecdote about the preacher who woke his drowsing flock with the teaser "There was a certain king, called Arthur" is told of a monastic audience (the monks of Heisterbach).[26] Here the ultimate symbol of *roman*—a worldly genre named for the worldly language in which it was created—is shown to appeal to the "learned" just as he might to the "simple." While the clergy were eloquent on the subject of the laity's reliance on externalities and *historiae,* they themselves were by no means always above such a taste.

If the clergy's use and appreciation of exempla could suggest one important area of convergence between them and the laity, the need for verisimilitude in exempla suggests a further connection. While, on the one hand, the preacher's ability to guarantee his story merely by telling it was a sign of his authoritative status, the story also had to have verisimilitude, a recognizable relation to experience. As Humbert of Romans puts it, "care should be taken that exempla be of sufficient authority [*competentis auctoritatis*], lest they be scorned, and realistic [*verisimilia*], so that they will be believed, and that they contain something instructive [*aliquam aedificationem*], lest they be put forth in vain"; the ultimate requirement for exempla is spiritual usefulness, but authority and verisimilitude are seen as essential to their functioning.[27] As does the preacher, these tales owe a dual allegiance: to the authority that validates them but also to the experience that makes them acceptably "realistic" examples. The former demonstrates the preacher's participation in the learned culture of books and tradition; the latter demonstrates his participation in the vernacular culture he shares with his audience.

Nor is experience at issue only in the content of exempla; it also shapes the preacher's use of them. Jacques de Vitry observes approvingly that some preachers "knew by experience how much benefit the laity and simple people derive from such narrative examples, not only as edification but as relaxation."[28] Jacques's appeal to "experiencia" is not an uncommon move in preaching manuals, where the phrase "experiencia docet" is frequently invoked, particularly in the context of audience-preacher interaction. The observation of the Franciscan Francesc Eiximenis that "familiarity breeds contempt, as experience teaches" neatly combines received wisdom with the claims of personal knowledge.[29] There were certainly plenty of authoritative accounts of how preachers should deal with their flocks, but it appears that in considering the fine points of personal interaction, and the preacher's need to negotiate his status with an audience rather than assuming it, experience was felt to be an equally important teacher. As Siegfried Wenzel has pointed out, "experience" and "authority" as categories of argument in medieval sermons are not in opposition but rather are mutually reinforcing.[30] The authority of experience is not divorced from the world of learning any more than the authority of learning is divorced from the world of experience. The preacher is the medium for both, personifying for his congregation the institutional knowledge and authority that must work through an individual, and through a vernacular.

In addition to the theoretical issues raised by exempla, there was the simple issue of performance. The preacher, unlike most of his congregation, had access to exempla in their "abstracted," usually Latin, form—that is, as elements of collections without any context.[31] It was he who made the transition from the universal to the particular and from Latin to the vernacular. Scanlon notes that the flexibility of exempla as presented in collections, so that they could be used on various occasions, "sets the preacher apart from his audience even as he establishes common ground with them," since it marks his association with a culture that they can only reach through him.[32] But this transition from the general to the specific inevitably involved the preacher in both sides of the equation and demanded his participation in "networks of oral narrativity," his ability not merely to convey doctrine but to make that doctrine live.[33] For an exemplum to be effective, various authors assert, it must be put across well. As Jacques de Vitry says, "proverbs, similitudes and everyday examples [*vulgaria exempla*] . . . cannot be expressed in writing as they can by gesture and word and the manner of speaking, nor do they move or rouse the audience in the mouth of one person as they do in the mouth of another."[34] And Humbert, in *De habundancia exemplorum*, notes that exempla require a style all their own and politely hints that not every preacher is equally good at presenting them: those who "may perhaps not have a pleasing narrative style," he says, "should not give up a means [of teaching] in which they are gifted for one in which they are not."[35] More than some other forms of instruction, the exemplum was a kind of dead letter until the preacher brought it to life.[36] Despite his access to the "abstracted" exemplum, he participated fully and crucially in its transformation into a concrete, embodied form of instruction, and that transformation, if successfully enacted, demonstrated his ability to assimilate to his audience in some way, to speak to them with verisimilitude; like his exempla, he must appear "real."[37]

Thus, although the "rupture" that the exemplum represents in a sermon may ultimately serve to reinforce the ideological import of the rest of the sermon, it exacts a price for doing so. By marking a point of "complicity," as Schmitt puts it, a moment of identification between preacher and audience, the use of exempla implicitly addresses the preacher's relationship to his authority and raises the question of how, and indeed whether, he is set apart from his audience. The same is true of vernacularity more generally: the preacher's ability to address his congregation in the "common language" meant not only his ability to speak French, Italian, or English but also his ability to use exempla, proverbs, and other "common speech" to get his message across. To form a connection the preacher had, to a certain extent, to make himself like his audience—or rather, to acknowledge and exploit his existing likeness to them.

Walking the Walk: The Preacher as Common Man

The ambiguous relationship of the preacher's two allegiances can be seen also in Humbert's *De eruditione,* in a section not on formal preaching but on how to make "private conversation" edifying. In the previous chapter "Against preachers who, in familiar conversation, say useless things [*vana*], as worldly people do," Humbert has been holding forth on the wickedness of "worldly speech" (*linguam mundi*).[38] It is clear that "worldly" here does not equate with the vernacular. While one of Humbert's arguments against worldly speech is that if schoolboys who lapse out of Latin into the vernacular are punished, preachers who lapse into useless speech should be still more severely chastised, another notes that just as preachers "should not abandon heavenly language for earthly [*linguam caelestem propter linguam mundi*], so a Frenchman, wherever he may go, does not easily abandon his own language for another, on account of the nobility of his language and his fatherland."[39] Vernacular speech, then, can be either earthly or heavenly, just as Latin can.[40] The schoolboy example, moreover, implies that worldly speech is the "vernacular" of the clergy, who must be trained into the practice of heavenly speech—a perhaps unintentional equation that acknowledges both the preacher's human fallibility and the constructed, learned quality of his role as preacher.[41]

Although Humbert criticizes "worldly speech," he recognizes that it can be useful at times. His chapter on private conversation emphasizes again the need to consider what, when, to whom, and how one speaks, and it admits that "sometimes one should speak holy words, sometimes tell good exempla, and sometimes even use some secular words."[42] Later he clarifies this need, saying that secular words may sometimes be used "for the purpose of a certain conformity" (*propter quamdam . . . conformitatem*) with the people addressed.[43] If even secular speech is occasionally permitted for good ends, surely the "conformity" with an audience marked by the vernacular—like the "furtive complicity" created by exempla—is one of the preacher's strengths and ultimately one of the things that in turn promotes the audience's imitation of him, their adoption of the preacher's "forma."[44]

This is not to deny that a strong distinction remained, and was promoted, between clergy and laity, Latin and vernacular, learned and unlearned in many cases, or that there was a cultural investment in regarding the laity as simple and unlearned by comparison with the clergy. But even when those seemingly opposed categories were used, they could be deployed in ways that demonstrate the complexity of their relationship. We see this in a sermon delivered by Stephen Langton near the beginning of the preaching revival. The sermon takes as its theme "Attendite uobis et uniuerso gregi" (drawing on Acts 20:28) and instructs its clerical audience on the responsibilities of their office.[45] Partway through the sermon, after an extended discussion of Cain and Abel that gives a biblical rationale for the preacher's responsibility to his flock, Langton changes his approach:

Let me also speak in an everyday manner [*uulgariter*] for those who are more simple [*simpliciores*]: notice with what great veneration simple and unlearned laypeople [*simplices laici et ydiote*] prepare for Easter, with what punishments they afflict their bodies, what fasts, prayers, and vigils; they are ornamented as it were with heavenly pearls, so that they might participate in the Lord's Supper. What Easter is to them, almost any day is to you, and therefore consider carefully by their example what you ought to do, lest what befalls a lying people should befall you.[46]

While this passage clearly makes a distinction between clergy and laity, Langton's use of "simpliciores" and "simplices" in the same sentence seems to imagine clerics who are not so far from their flocks and indeed teaches those clerics with the kind of method—appeal to everyday experience—that was often advocated for laypeople. Moreover he encourages the audience to attend to the admirable example of pious preparation offered by the laity, reversing the more usual injunctions to laypeople that they should imitate the clergy. Langton is sensitive to the diversity of his clerical audience throughout, ending his discourse with the announcement, "I wish to conclude with an everyday example for the simple [*simplices*]" and a brief similitude about a merchant. Here there is a distinct sense of the clergy and laity existing along a spectrum of *simplicitas,* as it were, across which the preacher needs to range in his attempts to reach all of his audience.

The use of vernacular, then, can bring out similarities between clergy and laity as well as marking their differences. And if some writers seem to concede the use of exempla, the vernacular, or other means of connection as a regrettable necessity, there are other descriptions that actively valorize such connection. One of these is the repeated story of the unlearned preacher whose similitudes or exempla are persuasive where the words of a learned preacher were not. Christoph Maier relates one version of this exemplum, about the preaching of the crusade in a village: A papal legate, unsuccessful in persuading the populace, eventually called on the unlearned village priest (*sacerdos simplicissimus scripture et litterature*), who reluctantly agreed to take his place and proceeded to convince almost everyone without use of scriptural authority, "with simplicity by showing a good example" (*simplicitate boni exempli ostencio*). The preacher used the familiar image of threshing and winnowing chaff from grain to tell, as it were, an exemplum involving himself and the other clerics present: the papal legate, he said, had threshed the crowd like grain and prepared them, and it was now his own job to winnow them and find who was chaff and who would go on crusade.[47] As the story shows, the anonymous preacher did a masterful job of including himself and his parishioners in a framework of recognizable experience that was also a manifestation of doctrinal truth (a tactic identical to that used by Stephen Langton with his audience of priests). The papal legate in Maier's exemplum may have been using the vernacular, but clearly he was not speaking the audience's language.[48] The tale also reflects the desire for holy simplicity that is a persistent thread in medieval Christianity and that mitigates the negative aspects of referring to an audience as "simplices."[49]

Conceptions of a preacher's contact with "the people," then, involve style and genre as much as language—the preacher's need not just to speak in the vernacular but to talk the talk with his audience. Other advice offered to preachers extends this need to understand, use, and respect vernacular or "common" modes of communication to the preacher's behavior in the world, his ability to walk the walk as well as talk the talk. In these contexts, as in those that address language and genre, nonclerical culture and nonclerical people are understood to be shrewd and deserving of respect: they may be *simplices,* but they're not stupid.[50] A preacher's good behavior reflects well on the church and maintains his institutional position, but it also gains him the personal respect of his audience, without which all the institutional backing in the world is useless.

Such attention to and respect for the audience seems to be the point of an entertaining passage in an anonymous appendix to Humbert of Romans's work on the offices of the Dominican order. The unknown Dominican writes his instructions for traveling preachers, pointing out that when traveling in pairs they should be polite to one another and not quarrel in front of others, that they should avoid asking for special meals at inns, and so on. He goes on to note that a preacher should "conform himself [*conformet se*] in good customs to those with whom he spends time [*conversatur*]." The first verb here, *conformare,* is the same word Humbert chose when discussing the occasional need for a preacher to use secular language in private communication. What this author has in mind, however, is the table manners of various regions. "In some areas," he writes, "it is rude to drink out of the bowl; to look over the cup while drinking; to slurp soup noisily from your spoon; to lean your elbows on the table; and so on."[51] Such things are not sins, he says, but should be avoided among those who regard them as inappropriate. One of the preacher's responsibilities, then, is to make himself similar to his audience in whatever ways are compatible with his office and with good behavior.

This discussion may seem at first to be a detail, a brief and amusing glimpse of medieval manners that enlivens a list of dry regulations. But of course "table-fellowship," as David Aers has pointed out, has deeper connotations in a Christian context.[52] The attention to reaching the audience, to the use of storytelling, and to familiar conversation recalls the teaching methods of Jesus as represented in the Gospels and thus reiterates the desire to live an apostolic life and to recapture the original teachings and, to some extent, the social modes of early Christianity that characterized much late medieval preaching. This ideal appears as a shap-

ing metaphor in two mendicant works: the *Communiloquium* of the thirteenth-century Franciscan John of Wales and the *Liber de introductione
loquendi,* also known by the name of its first section, the *Liber mensalis,*
by the fourteenth-century Dominican Filippo of Ferrara.[53]

John of Wales begins his florilegium with a prologue observing that
the preacher must know how to edify all of his diverse flock, "not only in
declamatory preaching but in familiar and mutual conversation. . . . And
this is by the example of the savior, who not only preached publicly in
cities and synagogues, but also often offered parables and the words of life
to his hearers at the table."[54] Here the preacher's imitation of Christ is
used not to set him apart from or above his flock, but rather to bring them
closer together in "familiar and mutual conversation." John notes that
such conversation is not only validated by Christ's example but also is
"frequently . . . more effective" than public preaching, emphasizing a
horizontal, egalitarian mode of communication between clergy and laity
rather than a hierarchical, vertical one.

Mutually edifying conversation, then, seems to be John's goal. In
pursuit of that he develops, as his title indicates, the idea of "communiloquium," a term that has a number of connotations. To him it seems primarily to connote universality—that is, the ability to address "omnibus
hominibus"—but in a way that makes that universality a marker of diversity, rather than homogeneity, among the audiences of sermons. As John
says, not all preachers have the leisure to collect the materials necessary for
reaching their varied audiences, so he has compiled "some general observations for the instruction of men according to the variety of their situations."[55] His formulation balances the demands of the universal and the
particular, seeing the audiences of preaching simultaneously as collective
unities, all of whom are to be addressed, and as subgroups and even individuals in need of particular attention. Here the "ability to communicate
across the range of professions and social classes," before it comes to be
seen as the "special" property of the linguistic vernacular, is regarded as a
central aspect of effective preaching in whatever language.[56]

If all potential audiences are seen as one cohesive group, moreover,
preachers are included in that universal community; among those to
whom "shared discussion" is to be addressed are preachers themselves. Although the professional preacher is in one sense a privileged audience of
the work as the imagined speaker of its instructive tidbits, he is also part
of the more general audience that will be drawn into the network of mutually edifying conversations, through the inclusion of texts that address

him in his particular social role. Thus while the work is primarily designed for preachers, its central idea of shared speech, of conversation, implies that a lay interlocutor could instruct the preacher, as well as vice versa.[57] An anecdote about Saint Dominic also suggests this possibility. It tells how, meeting with a foreign religious on the road, he "miraculously obtained the ability to speak [the stranger's] language, so as to enjoy the benefits of a holy conversation."[58] Here the gift of tongues often imagined to privilege the preacher's speech instead benefits the saint as a listener, and the linguistic shift enables interpersonal conversation, rather than preaching. Like this story, and like collections of exempla, the *Communiloquium* does not so much break the language barrier as reimagine it. It depicts preachers simultaneously as a group with special access to instructive speech and as participants in a conversation that requires them to understand that speech in a cooperative rather than a hierarchical mode. John of Wales's original reference to Christ's methods reinforces this, a reminder of a world where, at least before Acts 2, the question of language per se is little in evidence and personal, familiar communication forms the heart of teaching.

Similarly in Filippo da Ferrara's *Liber mensalis* and the larger *Liber de introductione loquendi* from which it is taken, the issue of adapting discourse to one's audience and situation is central. The "stories" that sometimes get short shrift in discussions of preaching are here regarded as the basic material of edifying conversation, whether at the table, standing around the fire, on a ship, walking, or in whatever situation the preacher might find himself. Like the anonymous friar making recommendations for table manners, Filippo sees the preacher's world as one of concrete, everyday interactions. And again "table-fellowship" is the idealized form of such exchanges, forming the starting point for all other modes of interaction between preacher and laity.[59] In his ongoing conversation with "seculares" the preacher has a duty to keep up his end. By doing so he fulfills his vocation and avoids the "wicked silence" (*mala taciturnitas*) criticized by Humbert of Romans, among others.[60] Silvana Vecchio observes that Filippo's book is not so far from the secular "conversation manuals," written by friars as well as by laymen, that began to appear in the fifteenth century.[61] But in Filippo's work there is not yet a definitive turn toward the secular and away from the doctrinal; at this point in the development of mendicant teaching exempla and doctrine, instruction and conversation are held in suspension rather than competition, and all have a place at the table. Like John of Wales, Filippo sees it as the preacher's task to consider the particularities of situation and of person and to adapt himself as required by his circumstances and his audience in order to make his speech as effective as possible.

If we consider the vernacular, then, in its role of the "common," the well-known, the shared or popular aspects of culture, it becomes clearer what medieval preachers might have thought about when they thought about the vernacular. What we may regard as primarily a linguistic aspect of sermon literature was clearly, in its original, lived context, bound up with many other things. The result is that clerical attempts to present Latin and vernacular, clergy and laity as opposed categories are continually undermined by the writers' recognition that they deal with a situation, preaching, in which these categories had to be largely overlapping in order to function.[62] Indeed, considering vernacularity not as a purely linguistic issue but as a matter of the preacher's access to his audience allows us to see that preachers did not so much traverse the imagined space between laity and clergy as embody it; the preacher's very identity as a cleric relied on his ability to participate in the "vernacular."

4

"Mere Words": Gendered Eloquence and Christian Preaching

Et sermo meus et praedicatio mea non in
persuasibilibus sapientiae verbis, sed in ostensione
Spiritus et virtutis.
[And my message and my preaching were not in
persuasive words of wisdom, but in demonstration of
the Spirit and of power.]

1 Cor. 2:4

The seductiveness of the feminine is for the medieval
Christian West virtually synonymous with delusiveness
of language embodied in rhetoric, whose seduction,
that of "mere words, worse than that of empty noises"
(Augustine), recapitulates the original sin—that "she,"
in the words of John Chrysostom, "believed in the one
who professed mere words, and nothing else."
R. Howard Bloch, *Medieval Misogyny and the Invention
of Western Romantic Love*

THE DEEP-SEATED CHRISTIAN MISTRUST OF language posed a significant
problem for medieval preachers. How could "mere words," human eloquence, rightly express a divine message, given rhetoric's involvement in
the worldly snares of spectacle and seduction? The anxiety over the "seductive power of spoken rhetoric" transferred the concern with the
preacher's embodied performance even to the realm of his language, focusing attention on those elements of rhetoric that recalled physical allure
or spectacle: *elocutio*, or style, particularly as it relates to the decorative aspects of language; and delivery (*pronuntiatio* or *actio*), the physical presentation of a speech or sermon.[1] As Jody Enders has observed, "Christian
rhetoricians deplored the dependence of ethical content on a dramatic delivery that had no intrinsic moral identity," but there was no way to cut

the knot: delivery and style are essential to rhetoric, and rhetoric is essential to preaching.[2] Preaching theorists recognized that in conveying their divine message to an audience, especially a lay audience, they had to make that message verbally and performatively attractive; and to do so they needed a pagan art. At the same time the superficial attraction of "mere words" could not be allowed to distract attention from the doctrine they "dressed."

The dangerous virtues of rhetoric as they are formulated in classical and early Christian discussions raise two linked issues: the question of ownership, whether God or the speaker should be regarded as ultimately responsible for a speech's effectiveness; and that of allure, how the feminine associations of rhetorical display might implicate speaker, audience, and their relationship to one another. The patristic "estheticization of gender" had an important influence on preaching theory, and the persistent anxiety about divine and human work in preaching retains certain associations with the discourses of misogyny.[3] But while early Christian treatments of human artistry, like that of Tertullian, see the problems of ownership and sensuality as deeply intertwined, most late medieval preaching theorists worked to dissociate these concepts. Drawing strength from Augustine's recuperation of rhetorical artistry, they deflected attention from its potential for alluring amorality by emphasizing technique and proffering ritualistic apologies for any infringement on God's prerogative of creation. Some handbooks remain anxious about the attractions of rhetoric—strongly associated, in a Christian context, with the feminine—particularly in their discussions of the preacher's effect on and response to his audience. For the most part, however, the late medieval emphasis on the verbal and technical aspects of rhetoric made it possible (as I argue in the next chapter) to displace the sensual implications of persuasion onto other discourses such as hagiography, where their claims on male preachers could be obliquely explored through a consideration of the public speech of women.

Christianity and Rhetoric: The Sins of Artifice

The potential dangers of rhetoric, stemming from its superficiality and its lack of what Enders calls an "intrinsic moral identity," are recognized in rhetorical and oratorical theory from ancient Greece onward. These dangers are especially associated with sophistic rhetoric, against which Plato and others proposed a "philosophical rhetoric" that held an allegiance to truth as well as efficacy; the latter becomes the model for Christian rhetoric.[4] Plato, a fierce critic of oratory's ability to deceive, has Socrates refer in the *Gorgias* to oratory as "pandering" that lures fools "with the bait of ephemeral pleasure."[5] The language implies that eloquence that appeals to an audience is equivalent to sexual allure, a claim that will haunt later accounts of Christian persuasion.[6] In addition to his objection to what Christianity would call worldly pleasure, Plato mistrusted the "dichotomy between speaker and technique" that rhetoric made possible, a dichotomy that was to prove a source of great anxiety for theorists of Christian preaching.[7]

Alongside Plato's denunciation, however, there existed less hostile attitudes, and these too formed part of the Christian inheritance. For Aristotle, "the dichotomy between speaker and technique is unavoidable, not evil, so a good orator simply closes the gap."[8] The argument of rhetoric's moral neutrality is one that Augustine will take up later. As we saw in a previous chapter, the gap between appearance and reality, or between the preacher's rhetoric and his morality, is inevitable.[9] Cicero and Quintilian attempt to close it by "claim[ing] that only a good man can be a good orator," and Gregory the Great makes a similar argument in a Christian context.[10] Other theorists of rhetoric, however, recognized that this attractive solution was not feasible in practice and tried to find other ways of controlling rhetoric's detachability from any moral content. The issue was complicated by the principle, found in both Aristotle and Cicero, that the best artistry is imperceptible as such: the orator "must disguise his art and *give the impression* of speaking naturally and not artificially."[11] If to "speak naturally" means to speak in an unstudied way that supposedly expresses some true interiority rather than an artificial persona, then it could be said that according to Cicero surface should appear to be depth. And if the rhetor's character was good, then form might indeed be continuous with content and the message might match its medium.

In the patristic era, however, such a contingent solution raised persistent anxieties. The deceptive potential of form and surface acquired newly threatening aspects, as Christian thinkers promoted an ascetic vision that associated and denigrated the flesh and the letter.[12] In part such asceticism was a way to distinguish Christian communities from the pagan world that surrounded them, and one might suppose that rhetoric, with its worldly aims and its potential for misuse, would have been abhorrent to the church fathers. Moreover, although rhetoric was not exclusively a

quality of pagan writings, as Augustine demonstrates in *De doctrina christiana,* it was nonetheless strongly associated with pagan literature, not
least by an educational system that saw all literary study as a part of oratorical training, as in the *Institutio oratoria* of Quintilian. As a result attitudes toward classical learning generally were intertwined with concerns
about rhetoric, further tainting its usefulness. Yet most of the early teachers of the church were trained in rhetoric from childhood in a way that inevitably shaped their later thinking, and many of them even taught it.[13]
Thus classical rhetorical thinking and expression were embedded in the
early language of Christianity just as biblical rhetoric was, and the church
fathers' powers of expression certainly aided the early propagation of doctrine. Functional but morally slippery, classical rhetoric raised all kinds of
troubling questions for early Christians trying to make use of a culture
they were also trying to abandon, and this ambivalence carries over into
later Christian preaching.[14]

The most influential patristic discussion of preaching is Augustine's
De doctrina christiana, which set the tone for later works and is quoted,
directly or indirectly, in many late medieval preaching manuals. Before
turning to Augustine, however, it is necessary to look further back to an
author whose battle with paganism was even fiercer and whose tormented
relationship to rhetorical art had echoes throughout the Middle Ages:
Tertullian. Living in the days when Christianity was a minority religion
under threat of extinction by a pagan establishment, he never flagged in
his condemnation of idolatry and all its manifestations, among which he
included pagan literature, the theater, spectacles of Roman society such as
the circus, and feminine clothing and adornment.[15] Such activities and interests were, in his view, quite literally un-Christian, in violation of the
first and second commandments. At the same time, however, Tertullian
was deeply imbued with classical culture and education, which shaped his
thinking and his language to a substantial degree. The simultaneous use
and denigration of pagan art and learning in his writings demonstrates a
struggle that was transmitted, albeit in less intense form, to later Christian
writers.

Tertullian is generally happy to lambaste art of any kind as the product of the fallen angels, a snare for all Christians, and to associate artistic
production with the "daughters of men" who first lured those angels to
earth. For the most part his attacks are on visible instances of idolatry and
surface ornament: clothing, theater, spectacle. When he says that beauty
can only lead to lust, he is talking specifically about *decor corporis.* This su-

perficial allure is particularly associated with women: according to Tertullian the fallen angels, originators of artistry and idolatry, "granted to women as their special and, as it were, personal property these means of feminine vanity," such as jewelry and cosmetics.[16] Although such decorations are, supposedly, no longer proper to Christian women, this is because Christian women are supposed to have abandoned the flesh, not because the superficial has lost its feminine connotations. For Tertullian even pagan literature is associated with physical allure. The mere spectacles of the pagan stage are contrasted with the purity of Christian art: "If the literary accomplishments of the stage delight you, we have sufficient literature of our own . . . and ours are not fables but truths, not artful devices [*strophae*] but plain realities [*simplicitates*]."[17] The fundamental contrast for Tertullian is between that which is single (*simplex*) in its goals and interests and that which is adulterated (or, we might say, sophisticated) by the taint of human artifice.

Tertullian's objections to such artifice are, however, in somewhat bad faith. He makes extensive use of pagan philosophy and rhetorical principles in his writings, and as George Kennedy has observed, he "never directly attacks rhetoric as such."[18] Indeed he makes uninhibited use of it for his diatribes, drawing as much on classical form and style as on the biblical thought and language that pervade his writings.[19] Timothy Barnes goes so far as to say that "philosophy and theology . . . are subordinate to oratory" in Tertullian's writings, adding, "which accounts for [their] effectiveness."[20] Insofar as Tertullian's rhetorical language is artistic, he too participates in the "interpolation" into God's creation that he regards as the hallmark of the devil.[21]

Tertullian's willingness to use pagan rhetoric and even philosophy suggests that there is something specific about the literature of pleasure that he objects to—perhaps the fact that its only appeal is its surface; its interior has nothing to offer.[22] At one point he does make an effort to address the "supervenient status of his own thought upon the superficial" on somewhat similar grounds, imagining a dialogue with a listener who challenges him: " 'You have tried to persuade me with words,' he says, '—a very wise remedy.' But even if speech were silent—impeded by infancy or held back by bashfulness (for life is content even with a tongueless philosophy), my appearance [*habitus*] itself would speak. A philosopher, in short, is *heard* so long as he is *seen*."[23] This faintly bizarre and not particularly convincing defense suggests Tertullian's awareness that his use of rhetoric was in conflict with his condemnation of decoration. What is especially interesting, however, is the idea that the philosopher has no need of speech, that it is superfluous in a way that precisely ratifies its validity. His very appearance—a "natural" one, we must presume, shunning the cosmetic and showing exactly what it is—is the guarantee of his truthfulness in speech. Like the theorists who argued that only a good man could be an effective orator, Tertullian seeks to contain the potential deceptiveness of rhetoric by insisting that it is simply a true outward expression of the inward good.[24]

Tertullian, then, ducks the problematically amoral nature of rhetoric by suggesting that rhetoric used in a good cause will merely reinforce the evident goods of its subject. At another point, however, he seems to put his own persuasive speech in a less positive context, albeit without condemning it. Admitting, as Barnes notes, that *De resurrectione mortuorum* is rhetorical in its structure, Tertullian "somewhat disingenuously imputes [this fault] to his adversaries," saying that "heretics provoke us to speak rhetorically, just as philosophers provoke us to philosophize."[25] The comparison with philosophers philosophizing suggests that there is something specifically heretical about rhetoric—a suggestion that, as we shall see, Alan of Lille also makes in the twelfth century. At the same time Tertullian seems to imply that rhetoric used for beneficial purposes is needed to combat rhetoric used for bad ones, an argument that Augustine would later take up.

Thus, while Tertullian's objections to (effeminate) spectacle and decoration are fierce and unyielding, his approach to rhetoric is more cautious. In most cases he opposes the interpolation of human artifice into divine creation; his ideal is a pure and singular truth that speaks for itself, without intermediary. Ultimately he imagines the possibility of an exterior or medium that would allow its interior to shine through, rather than obscuring it. In this way he is able to condemn the artifice that offends him while making use of that which serves his ends. In effect Tertullian negotiates rhetoric's difficulties mostly by omission, leaving later thinkers such as Jerome and Augustine to make more direct accommodation for pagan culture, despite their reservations. They also, unlike Tertullian, explicitly link rhetoric and femininity—an association they do not originate but do expand, with significant consequences for medieval culture.

Both Augustine and Jerome confess to difficulties in abandoning the pagan literature that, for them, competed with Christian learning. For Augustine, who was, like Tertullian, a teacher of rhetoric before his conversion, this literary double-heartedness seems to have gone hand in hand with a difficulty in abandoning the pleasures of the flesh. As Harry Caplan notes, when Augustine "looks back with misgivings upon the days when, as he says, he 'used to sell the talkativeness that emphasizes victory [*victoriosam loquacitatem vendebam*]' . . . one learns how flagrant he judged this offense to be from the fact that his next words refer to the lustful passion of his early years."[26] To a modern reader the more obvious sin of fornication demonstrates the seriousness of the sin of rhetorical display, but the juxtaposition suggests that for Augustine, leaving behind secular eloquence is essentially equivalent to abandoning his mistress and fleshly love: both represent the world that the Christian must desert. In fact this whole chapter of the *Confessions* (4.2) demonstrates a complex of associations familiar from Tertullian. Augustine begins by talking about his days as a teacher of rhetoric, moves on to discuss his mistress, and ends by saying that one time when he had entered a dramatic poetry contest (*theatrici carminis certamen*) a *haruspex* offered his services to help him win. The association of not just rhetoric but the theatrical performance of rhetoric with pagan rituals of sacrifice and divination recalls Tertullian. Augustine goes on to give the whole issue a metaphorical sexual dimension by saying that though he refused the offer, it was not out of any "chaste reservation" and that his soul, "panting after such fond figments, commit[ted] fornication" against God.[27] This brief chapter, less than two pages long, moves without any sense of disjunction through the sins of rhetoric, sexuality, idolatry, and theatricality, creating a vivid sense of the unholy alliance Augustine perceived among these varied temptations and pitfalls.

In another famous example, when Augustine contrasts the lures of pagan literature with the Christian life, it is Dido he chooses to exemplify that literature: "For what can be more miserable than a wretch that pities not himself; one bemoaning Dido's death, caused by loving Aeneas, and yet not lamenting his own death, caused by not loving of thee, O God . . . ? I did not love thee, and I committed fornication against thee. . . . But the love of this world is fornication against God. . . . But I bemoaned not all this; but dead Dido I bewailed, that killed herself by falling upon the sword."[28] Dido, who killed herself over a quasi-adulterous love affair, is a perfect summation of un-Christian ideals. The fact that a man will bewail her suicide and not his own spiritual death is an ideal example, for Augustine, of the power of language to draw people toward falsehood, away from truth. Like Tertullian, he condemns the *Aeneid* as false; certainly it is an example of *fabulae* and *strophae*, as against *simplicitas christiana*. The

further association of Dido's disastrous fornication with the love of this
world again implies that Augustine shares Tertullian's association between
women, carnality, surface display, and idolatry. Both in his personal life
and in his thought Augustine links feminine sexuality and the snares of
rhetoric.

Like Tertullian, of course, Augustine continued to make use of rhetoric; unlike Tertullian, he chose to address the problem of rhetoric's place
in Christianity directly. *De doctrina christiana* is generally regarded as the
foundation stone of medieval Christian eloquence and has been much
studied in this context.[29] Here I wish to look particularly at Augustine's
justifications of Christian rhetoric, which fall into three main categories:
the theological argument that rhetoric, in its principles, is divinely instituted and thus can be used for good as well as evil; the pragmatic argument that if enemies of Christianity are going to use rhetoric, then so
must Christians; and the "treasures out of Egypt" argument, that pagan
learning can be appropriated to Christian uses. The first two of these continued to be at issue throughout the history of Christian preaching.

The argument that rhetoric should not be condemned since it can be
used for good as well as for evil purposes appears in book 2 of *De doctrina
christiana*, with particular reference to the dialectical aspect of rhetoric, its
argument: "The science of definition, division and partition, although it
may often be employed even in fallacies, is not false itself; neither was it
instituted by men, but was discovered in the reason of things."[30] Augustine later makes the same claim about a speech's effect on the audience:
"Men did not ordain that a demonstration of regard would win over a listener, or that a brief and intelligible narration" would be effective.[31] The
materials and means of rhetoric come from God and were merely discovered by mankind; thus it is impossible that they should work only to evil
purposes. It is interesting that Tertullian uses the inverse of this argument
when he presents and then answers the objection that "the materials [of
idolatry] are from God": "even if the material out of which something is
made is from God it does not therefore follow that every way of enjoying
these things is also of God."[32] All human misuses of divinely given material are forms of idolatry. Augustine offers persuasion *to*, Tertullian persuasion *against*, but for both the relative importance of divine and human
creativity is the essential point. The same desire to distinguish human and
divine roles appears in the much later preaching manuals.

Augustine's second argument is a pragmatic one: it is reckless and
foolish to rely on the unadorned truth of one's message while an adver-

sary is able to make use of rhetoric. His view, clearly set forth in the second chapter of book 4 of *De doctrina,* is worth quoting at some length, considering its later influence:

Since persuasion both to truths and falsehoods is urged by means of the art of rhetoric, who would venture to say that truth, in the person of its defenders, ought to stand its ground, unarmed, against falsehood, so that those who are trying to convince us of falsehoods should know how to induce their listeners to be favorably inclined, attentive, and docile, by means of their preface, while the defenders of truth do not know how to do this? . . . The power of eloquence—so very effective in convincing us of either wrong or right—lies open to all. Why, then, do not the good zealously procure it that it may serve truth, if the wicked, in order to gain unjustifiable and groundless cases, apply it to the advantages of injustice and error?[33]

The idea that eloquence is "set in the middle" and can equally be used for good or bad ends is both the practical basis of Augustine's argument and, as he points out in his discussion of rhetoric's divine origins, the cause of much of the suspicion against it. To argue that rhetoric is bad because it can be used for bad ends is foolish, he says; it can equally be used for good, and should be. But this very neutrality makes it a tool that can easily turn against the cause of Christianity. Furthermore, Augustine's argument suggests that in contemporary perception rhetoric was above all a means of persuading people to bad ends. *De doctrina* is essentially a rehabilitation of an art form, and a successful one, but it is not so successful as to erase all concerns about rhetoric, nor would Augustine have wanted it to do so. As he says, not only rhetoric used to bad ends but even rhetoric without a substantial content should be displeasing to serious people.[34]

The third and most thoroughly successful argument Augustine makes is that pagan learning is like the treasures of the Egyptians that the Israelites took with them on their flight, a tremendously effective analogy. The fact that the Middle Ages, despite some persistent grumbling, never seriously objected to the use of pagan literature is in large part attributable to *De doctrina,* and to this widely quoted passage in particular.[35] Again, in this analogy, Augustine notes that the Israelites did not take the gold "on their own authority" (*auctoritate propria*) but rather by God's command, once more asserting the divine origin and approval of Christian rhetoric. Like the Israelites, the Christians should not take up the idolatrous associations of this "gold" but should carry it off "for the lawful service of preaching the Gospel."[36] The beautiful objects—"vessels

and ornaments of gold and silver, and clothing"—were turned from their
pagan function to one pleasing to God, and Christians can do the same
with pagan learning.[37]

Augustine's analogy of Egyptian gold, then, largely establishes the
medieval attitude toward classical pagan literature. Another significant
analogy appears in the writings of Jerome, who, like Augustine, had difficulty subduing his love of language. His struggle is most famously illustrated by the dream he recounts to Eustochium in which God tells him
that he is "not a Christian, but a Ciceronian."[38] The episode suggests
that, like Tertullian, Jerome felt adherence to pagan culture to be incom-
patible with Christian life. Nonetheless he managed, like Augustine, to
find a means of accommodation, borrowing from Origen a suggestive association between pagan literature and the beautiful pagan bride of
Deuteronomy, who can be made an Israelite only after her hair has been
shorn, her nails clipped, and her garments destroyed. Pagan teaching may
be used, but only when it has been, as it were, chastened by Christian
ideals. If Augustine figures pagan literature as ornamental, Jerome imagines it as feminine.[39]

For both Augustine and Jerome, then, and to a lesser extent for Tertullian there is a clear, though certainly not all-encompassing, association
between rhetoric and femininity. The problem was to shear the pagan aspects from rhetoric to make it serve Christianity, just as, in another discourse, the woman's femininity had to be stripped away before she could
become a "female man of God."[40] In Jerome's example the bride retains
her womanliness, losing only the marks that distinguish her as pagan.
Given the complex of associations between idolatry, pagan spectacle, and
female beauty, however, it is not hard to see how, in patristic thought, re-
moving the pagan taint of rhetoric could imply a process of masculiniza-
tion.

Pagan or not, rhetoric remained a potential threat, its presence coded
in certain words and concepts that persist throughout the history of
preaching. Many of these derive, like so much else in preaching theory,
from book 4 of *De doctrina christiana*. They deal with the attractiveness
of rhetoric, and like rhetoric they seem to have a neutral moral valence for
Augustine. The first of these is *delectare*, "to please," which is Augustine's
standard term for the aim and result of effective rhetoric, as well as being
one of the three objects of the orator, borrowed from Cicero: to teach, to
please, and to persuade.[41] Linked to *delectatio* is the word *suauitas*,
"sweetness," which frequently describes the kind of rhetoric that pleases:

"delectatur [auditor], si suauiter loqueris" (the hearer is pleased if you speak sweetly).[42] *Suauiter,* which can also mean "agreeably, attractively, delightfully," is the word most commonly used by Augustine in this complex of ideas having to do with sweetness, attractiveness, and pleasure.[43] Again, there is nothing inherently wrong about these concepts, but if unaccompanied by valuable content they can become a "pernicious sweetness" (*perniciosa dulcedo*).[44] Attractiveness may be misleading: "the one to guard against is the man whose eloquence is no more than an abundant flow of empty words. His listener is more easily charmed by him in matters that are unprofitable to hear about and, all too frequently, such eloquence is mistaken for truth."[45] It is important, therefore, not to value the *suauitas* of eloquence for its own sake. The inescapability of such attractions, however, is suggested by the fact that *suauitas* and *persuasio*— two of the orator's three central goals of instruction, pleasure and persuasion—share an etymological root that indicates their debt to sensual appeal.

On the one hand, then, on its own eloquence is pleasing but not beneficial; on the other hand, it is necessary for effective communication.[46] This is the dilemma faced by all Christian preachers: how to make use of *suauitas dicendi* without allowing it to become the point of the exercise, without permitting alluring surface to eclipse spiritual content or to draw preacher and audience into an improperly sensual relationship to language or to one another. Augustine suggests that in teaching, "truths made clear give pleasure of themselves because they are true," but he is immediately forced to admit that some hearers' "pampered tastes" make eloquence necessary.[47] And in a passage rebuking those who delight in hearing wickedness, he must finally concede truth's inability to speak effectively for itself: "let truths, not falsehoods, be listened to with pleasure. But this, of course, would be impossible, unless they were expressed attractively [*suauiter*]."[48] Augustine seems a little troubled by this necessity for *suauitas;* he would evidently prefer a world where the unaided beauty of truth could teach, please, and persuade without any need for eloquence. And ideally eloquence should be as artless as possible: "In those places where it [biblical eloquence] happens to be recognized by the learned, such matters are being discussed that the words by which they are expressed seem not to have been sought after by the speaker, but to have been associated naturally with those very matters, as if you were to understand wisdom as going out of her home, that is, the heart of the wise man, and eloquence like an inseparable servant following her even though

unbidden."[49] This passage, which draws on both the Bible and Cicero for
its imagery, also harks back to Tertullian in its wish to see eloquence as
artless, natural, the transparent expression of an inward truth, a desire that
persists into the later history of preaching.

This ideal of a rhetoric that seems naturally, inherently fitted to the
truth of its subject provides another of Augustine's teachings: the importance of decorum. Eloquence must be suited both to the speaker and to
the subject: "we should not call it eloquence if it is not appropriate [*non
congruit*] to the person of the speaker"; moreover, "There is a kind of eloquence . . . which is becoming [*decet*] for men eminently worthy of the
highest authority and manifestly inspired by God. Biblical writers have
spoken with this kind of eloquence; no other kind becomes them [*congruit*], nor is that kind suitable [*nec . . . decet*] for other writers."[50] Similarly, a beneficial eloquence will use words appropriately. The apostle Paul
is said to use clauses with "a most suitable variety" (*decentissima uari-
etate*).[51] On the other hand, a "frothy showiness of style" (*spume[us] uerborum ambit[us]*) that displeases the serious audience is not "fitting" for
important truths.[52] Augustine has a strong sense of appropriateness in
preaching, which requires that language, person, and subject all be in accord, and the ultimate judge of such appropriateness is God, on whose
help the preacher must rely.[53] At the same time even the seemingly aus-
tere requirement of decorum links effective rhetoric once again to the demands of beauty (*decor, decus*).[54]

Although Augustine makes a much stronger argument than does
Tertullian for the Christian use of verbal artistry, then, he continues to
struggle with rhetoric's snares, as the claims of sensual appeal intrude into
every aspect of his subject. The role of divine aid versus human invention,
the issue of surface pleasure versus hidden truth, and the problem of what
is appropriate for a Christian or a Christian preacher remain very much in
evidence.[55] Despite Augustine's best efforts to contain them, they carried
over into later discussions of eloquence in preaching.

Medieval Preaching Manuals and
the Rapprochement with Rhetoric

After *De doctrina christiana* the field of preaching theory lay fallow for almost eight hundred years.[56] The late medieval preaching revival brought
forth, for the first time since Augustine, a demonstrable interest in the sys-

tematic study of preaching; starting in the thirteenth century, "writers were increasingly interested in discussing the form (as distinct from the subject matter) of preaching."[57] The shift from interest in content to interest in form implies a move away from the mistrust of human persuasion expressed by Paul and echoed in the various discourses opposing human artifice and display. As Harry Caplan notes, "The distrust of rhetoric as a profane study was not as anxious in the later period as often in earlier times."[58] Indeed, the elaborate concern of the later medieval preaching theorists for the *forma praedicandi,* as well as the *materia,* reflects their willingness to follow the path of Christian rhetoric laid out by Augustine without excessive hand-wringing about the evils of eloquence. The fear that the medium might overtake its message apparently diminished as Christian preaching developed its own history, lessening its dependence on its pagan heritage.[59] To borrow Rita Copeland's terms, we might say that once preaching had fashioned a stable body of its own out of the homiletic tradition and the theoretical basis provided by Augustine, the threats posed by the permeable and unstable body of rhetoric ceased to be so troubling and became an issue at the margin of preaching rather than at its center.[60]

This relegation of anxiety about rhetoric to the margins is reflected in the preaching manuals' treatment of the most "cosmetic" aspects of rhetoric: style and delivery. These are usually addressed briefly by means of almost ritualistic warnings, concise but seemingly indispensable. Insofar as anxiety about rhetoric persisted, it had become less global and was primarily "distrust for embellished style, because rhetoric was an art of adornment."[61] Nevertheless, the *artes praedicandi* retain a latent fear of rhetoric's perils—its link to worldly beauty, its status as human artistry in potential opposition to the grace of God, its lack of a truth guarantee. And the dangerous allure of artistry, for preacher as much as audience, could still be expressed in terms of the feminine: an anonymous thirteenth-century author warns the preacher "not [to] do as those who are so charmed by logic or grammar as never to be able to part from it, in the manner of the husband who knows not how to leave his wife."[62] Here, however, the fear of the feminine seems, by contrast with the patristic discussions, to be much more metaphorical than actual—in part, perhaps, because many *artes praedicandi* focus on language far more than on speaker or audience, deemphasizing the potential for the sensuality of rhetoric to implicate the preacher's person.

Texts that continue to address the alluring qualities of rhetoric, which do exist in the later period, often associate that allure specifically with the preacher's desire to please his audience for his own benefit rather than theirs. Such associations are particularly visible in some of the earliest of the new wave of preaching manuals. The Benedictine Guibert de Nogent's *Quo ordine sermo fieri debeat,* for instance, written in the late eleventh century, covers briefly everything its author could think of that might be relevant to the preacher's activity. Near the end of his treatise, as he makes his final remarks about the manner of preaching and before moving on to the material, Guibert says that one who preaches with "sincera intentio" and no desire for praise will be the most helpful to his audience and will not lead them astray with "grandi eloquentia" for his own glory. He goes so far as to add that one who "tries to ornament his sayings with a more attractive speech [*venustiore eloquio*]" is an irritant rather than a preacher, and he warns that the disgust such a preacher excites will undo the benefits of even his better teachings.[63] The relatively brief mention of this issue is in line with the custom of the later preaching manuals, but the idea that excessive ornamentation negates both the identity and the efficacy of the preacher demonstrates how strongly Guibert rejected such behavior, and his use of "venustior" suggests, at least etymologically, an association between this reprehensible eloquence and physical, even sexual beauty.[64] These remarks are his last word on presentation in preaching, suggesting the importance he attached to them.

Alan of Lille, writing in the late twelfth century, also demonstrates a concern for the potential improprieties of rhetorical language—a concern more intense than that shown by almost any other of the late medieval *artes praedicandi*. He goes beyond Guibert in seeing the preacher's use of excessive verbal elaboration as appealing not only to his own pride but also to his audience's baser desires, thus linking preacher and audience in a problematic complicity that distracts both from the sermon's true religious purpose. It is perhaps not accidental that Alan's denunciations of rhetorical allure, like those of Tertullian and Augustine, exist alongside an exceptional fondness for elaborate eloquence in his own writings. He begins his *Summa de arte praedicatoria* by comparing preachers to angels and goes on to observe, "First, then, we must see what preaching is, what form it should take—in the surface aspect of its words [*superficiem verborum*] and in the weight of its thoughts [*pondus sententiarum*]."[65] His prologue is primarily dedicated to the first of these, the *superficies verborum* that, like Augustine and Tertullian before him, he recognized as a necessary but dangerous component of preaching, a surface that could lead one astray from the true "weight" of the message.

As his *De planctu Naturae* shows, Alan was intensely aware of the links between language and sexuality, and this awareness is manifested also in his advice on preaching.[66] Like Tertullian, Alan associates excessive verbal artistry with theatricality, effeminacy, and deceit, making it clear that these issues were still very much alive at the beginning of the preaching-theory revival. He says with some force:

> Preaching should not contain jesting words, or childish remarks, or that melodiousness and harmony which result from the use of rhythm or metrical lines; these are better fitted to delight the ear than to edify the soul. Such preaching is theatrical and full of buffoonery, and in every way to be condemned. Of such preaching the prophet says: "Your innkeepers mix water with wine." Water is mingled with wine in the preaching in which childish and mocking words—what we may call "effeminacies"—are put into the minds of the listeners. Preaching should not glitter with verbal trappings, with purple patches, nor should it be too much enervated by the use of colorless words; the blessed keep to a middle way. If it were too heavily-embroidered [the sermon] would seem to have been contrived with excessive care, and elaborated to win the admiration of man, rather than for the benefit of our neighbors, and so it would move less the hearts of those who heard it. . . . Such preaching may be said to be suspect, yet it is not to be wholly condemned, but rather tolerated.[67]

I have quoted this passage at length because it so markedly echoes earlier discussions of the dangers of artistry and surface show. Indeed, Alan might almost be quoting here from Tertullian or, especially, from Jerome, who in *Adversus Jovinianum* warns, "Our sense of hearing is flattered by the tones of various instruments and the modulations of the voice; and whatever enters the ear by the songs of poets and comedians, by the pleasantries and verses of pantomimic actors, weakens the manly fibre of the mind."[68] Preaching that is too sensually attractive will, like the spectacles of the pagan theater, rather delight the senses than inform the soul. It also contains "effeminacies" and may display the excessive coloration and adornment that so disgusted Tertullian in the garments of Christian women.

Like personal decoration, then, rhetorical display is too conspicuously the work of laborious human artistry, an artistry whose aim is to allure the listener, Alan suggests, in a way designed to reward and serve the preacher's person rather than his message. Like Guibert before him, Alan claims that such obvious elaborateness is an impediment to the sermon's

effectiveness, asserting that an overly refined sermon will put off the listener precisely because that listener will see it as being directed toward
human approval, rather than a divine intention. This allows Alan to combine the argument against idolatry with a pragmatic one: excessively artistic sermons are not just wrong; they are also ineffective, so that
(implicitly) a preacher should not even be tempted to use them. The fact
that some preachers (including perhaps Alan himself) clearly *were* tempted
and that their verbal displays are considered problematic because they
merely "delight the ear" or win the "admiration of man" strongly suggests that the audience appeal of such artistry was only too evident. In any
case Alan here associates attractive language and the audience's pleasure
in it with other kinds of sensual allure, suggesting that a sermon too at-
tuned to the desires of its audience can effeminize both speaker and
listener if the preacher does not approach it carefully.[69]

After this initial warning against theatricality and elaborateness in language, the treatise moves on to the *sententia,* rather than the *superficies,*
of preaching and gives relatively little advice on how to use rhetoric right-
fully. Alan does admit the usefulness of pagan literature, citing the authority of the apostle Paul and implicitly placing himself in the
Augustinian camp.[70] In other ways, however, he seems to hark back to the
more censorious attitudes of Tertullian. He even, like his predecessor,
links rhetoric with heresy when he uses the image of mixing water with
wine again later in his text to describe preachers who mix the false with
the true, as heretics (and actors) do.[71] We might note here that heretics
are apt to be associated with specifically seductive language, language
that appeals not to the "manly fibre of the mind" but to the feminized
senses.[72] Once again, though, Alan does not attack rhetoric as such; having pointed out its dangers, he leaves his readers to find their own path.

Most of Alan's contemporaries and successors spend far less energy
on their discussions of the preacher's rhetoric, suggesting a change in focus that emphasized the usefulness of eloquence rather than its dangers.
Alexander of Ashby, "the first preceptive writer in a new approach to the
form of preaching," composed his treatise *De artificioso modo predicandi*
around 1200.[73] As the title suggests, he was considerably less concerned
than his predecessors with the dangers of human artistry; in his prologue
he refers approvingly to the "suauis eloquentia" of his addressee, the
newly elected abbot of the Augustinian canons at Ashby, before com-
mencing his "brief treatise on the artistic labor of preaching [*artificiosa
predicandi industria*]."[74] It is not surprising that Alexander cites, shortly

afterward, the "treasures of the Egyptians" argument to fend off those who might disapprove of his use of pagan teachings; he seems thoroughly to have absorbed the most positive side of Augustine's view of rhetoric. As Georgiana Donavin notes, Alexander's "bold assertions and sophisticated reflections about the employment of classical rhetoric . . . [suggest] that this pedagogy may have a history much older than the Augustinian house at Ashby."[75]

Whatever its history before Alexander's treatise, the history of Christian preaching that follows him tends to echo his relatively untroubled attitude toward eloquence. Responding to an imagined interlocutor who asks why he recommends his listener "to strive for attractive language [*uenustatem uerborum*] in Christian teaching," Alexander claims that Paul, despite his dislike of "persuasive words," "did not prohibit ornate language from being used for persuasion toward useful things, but reprehended those who strove more to say beautiful things than useful ones, to please rather than to benefit."[76] Interestingly, the accusation that Alexander overemphasizes *uenustas uerborum* follows a discussion that addresses not verbal style but rather delivery (specifically the use of a voice and facial expression suitable to one's topic), suggesting how closely these two were related. Other authors, while perhaps sympathetic to Alexander's challenger, treat the issue of decorative language with extreme brevity, minimizing its importance. The anonymous author of the thirteenth-century *Ars concionandi* once attributed to Saint Bonaventure says, "overly ornate speech or eloquence is to be avoided in a sermon" and in support offers a string of quotations mainly from *De doctrina christiana*, with a little Jerome thrown in.[77] A short section on good delivery follows, ending with the Augustinian warning that the preacher "should pray before he speaks."[78] Humbert of Romans also associates delivery and style, in a section on the preacher's speech. After remarks on the preacher's diction, resonance of voice and so forth, Humbert says, "A sermon should be simple, and devoid of all the empty ornaments of rhetoric." He quotes Augustine and Seneca to back up his command, "Leave the ingenious style to art; here it is a question of souls." Augustine was not above treating "minor points" such as meter and figures of speech, but Humbert wants it to be clear that these have their proper, and very limited, place.[79] In all of these cases, while precise attitudes toward style and delivery vary somewhat—with Alexander's being the most positive—the dangers of verbal decoration are given a ritualistic dismissal quite different from Alan's elaborate attack.

Still other texts avoid the problem completely by limiting themselves to the structural, rather than stylistic, aspects of rhetoric. While Alexander of Ashby's text is strongly interested in structure—he is credited with reintroducing the language of classical rhetorical form into medieval preaching—later thirteenth-century authors go beyond him, emphasizing the formal construction of a sermon to the exclusion of almost every other aspect of preaching.[80] They seem to have taken seriously Augustine's claim that "the science of definition, division and partition . . . was not instituted by men, but was discovered in the reason of things," an assertion that simultaneously associates rhetorical creation with divine rather than human creativity and with reason rather than mere pleasure.[81] Freed by this idea, they make definition, division, and partition—along with a number of other rhetorical maneuvers—the backbone of sermon creation, leaving to one side both style and delivery, as well as the ethical concerns that rhetorical persuasion inherently raises. Such *artes* are examples of "technical" rhetoric in the specific sense described by George Kennedy: "Of the three factors in the speech situation identified by Aristotle . . . —speaker, speech, and audience—technical rhetoric concentrates on the speech at the expense of the other two."[82] The result, Franco Morenzoni notes, is that many thirteenth-century manuals, like those of Richard of Thetford or Jean de la Rochelle, "remain practically mute on the subject of persuasion."[83] By emphasizing limited aspects of a sermon's structure—for example, how to elaborate on a scriptural theme—rather than interaction or the effect of speech on an audience, such handbooks avoid any discussion of the relationship between the preacher and his listeners in favor of a depersonalized account of the task of sermon creation.

Although purely technical manuals persisted—and in fact form the majority of the surviving preaching handbooks—*artes* that concerned themselves with the moral implications of the preacher's use of language continued to evince some discomfort with verbal decoration. Ranulph Higden, for example, says in a section of his *Ars componendi sermones* on "righteous intention" (*De intencionis rectitudine*) that the preacher must preach for the appropriate reasons—the glorification of God and the edification of his neighbor—rather than for any personal glory or recompense; furthermore he must preach when it is necessary, without letting fear, favor, or any other worldly concerns hold him back.[84] Higden seems to follow Guibert and Alan in associating the questions of righteous intention and audience response with that of language, since he continues this section by noting that "subtlety [*subtilitas*] in speaking is not always required; sometimes unpolished simplicity is more ed-ifying."[85] *Subtilitas,* like *suauitas,* can have more than one valence in preaching literature, constituting in some instances a characteristic of el-egant discourse. Here, however, Higden implies a less positive connota-tion, for in the next sentence he associates *subtilitas* with the "persuasive words of wisdom" that Paul had rejected. Clearly the warning applies to those who would put too much emphasis on human artistry and audi-ence appeal. The paragraph immediately following confirms this. Hig-den says, "On this account empty fables [*fabulosa vanitas*] and childish scurrility are to be avoided, being irrelevant to salvation and pleasing to the ear rather than to the soul, of which the prophet says: your innkeep-ers mix water with wine . . . unless perhaps [they are used] in that way that Augustine teaches in *De doctrina christiana,* toward the end of Book 2, saying that the sons of Israel carried off the treasures from Egypt so that they might afterward put them to a better use, as Jerome did with the sayings of the pagan philosophers and poets when inveigh-ing against Jovinian."[86] At the beginning he seems to be recalling the passage from Alan of Lille cited above, though he does not mention the work. Apparently the "fabulosa vanitas" that pleases the ears rather than the soul, alluring the listener rather than instructing him, was as much to be deplored in the fourteenth century as the "fabulae" and "strophae" criticized by Tertullian in the second. Moreover, Higden as-sociates this mere surface pleasure precisely with the legacy of classical culture. Things that are externally pleasing may only be used if, as Au-gustine says, they are turned to a higher purpose; what those externally pleasing things might be is demonstrated by the example of Jerome, who used pagan philosophers and poets to make his polemical argu-ments more effective.

The association between empty beauty, pagan learning and literature, and rhetorically colorful language persists, then, and with it the distrust they inspire. Despite their lingering concerns, however, the late medieval preaching manuals follow Augustine in their willingness to study and teach the human contribution to eloquence. Indeed, it sometimes seems that the handbook authors, having cordoned off and rebuked *eloquium ornatum,* feel they have paid their debt of anxiety about rhetoric and are then able to use its structure and terms more comfortably. Only when the focus shifts to the effects of eloquence on an audience—with implications both for their salvation and for the preacher's intentions—do the patristic anxieties reignite.

The Artful Preacher

As Higden's reference to "empty fables" reminds us, the concern with audience response is often cast in terms of *vanitas,* the "mere words" to which Augustine shows his antipathy in the epigraph to this chapter. Such empty showiness was by no means a purely superficial problem. A preacher's desire to use excessive, unedifying ornamentation signals, as various authors point out, his wrongful intention. Francesc Eiximenis elaborates on this point, saying that "there are some, puffed up with the wind of pride and vainglory, tricking out [*meretricantes*] the word of God, who in their windy sermons do not intend any of the aforementioned [virtuous] goals, but rather their opposite, namely glory, personal fame and honor."[87] Evident once again is the association between verbal display and carnal sin, both of which reflect an emptiness or lack of substance that thoroughly undercuts the preacher's efforts. He wants an external reward for himself, not an interior improvement in his hearers, and his attempt to gain this result is cast as a kind of seduction.

Such critiques signaled a divide in preachers' sense of the intended audience of their speech. In developing the "technical qualities and rules which insure a finished and acceptable product," the authors of the *artes praedicandi* naturally raised the question of who was supposed to find that product acceptable.[88] For Cicero and his colleagues there was a simple answer: the audience. In taking up the classical framework, though, the Christian preacher did not take up all its goals. In this case, clearly, a focus on the human audience was insufficient: aiming only to please men led to the kind of theatricality and ineffectiveness the preaching theorists so deplored. As Margaret Jennings points out, the *artes praedicandi* are "constantly ordered to a general end—to bring man closer to God," and the fear of making a product that is more pleasing than profitable to its human audience persists.[89] It is thus not surprising that many preaching handbooks, like the technical manuals discussed above, avoid this trap by deemphasizing the audience's response to the sermon and focusing instead on how the preacher's artistry reflects on his relationship to God.

A version of this tactic can be seen in Thomas Waleys's *De modo componendi sermones.* Waleys's text is striking for its unusually lengthy and detailed attention to delivery, which many manuals seem to associate with an overinvestment in the audience's pleasure, as does Alexander of Ashby's imagined questioner. Here the author seems to have a divided attitude about these issues—or rather his theoretical statements do not precisely match his practice. At the beginning of his treatise he offers a disclaimer about what is to follow: "It should by no means be believed that the word of God ministered to the faithful through the office of preaching is bound by any humanly imposed custom or by any humanly invented rules that are introduced in this work, as though the preacher could not act against them."[90] His suggestions, in other words, are not intended as a challenge to God's entire control of preaching. The idea that human artistry might trespass on God's prerogative as the institutor of preaching is reminiscent of Tertullian's ideas of artifice as an idolatrous "interpolation" into God's work of creation. Though Waleys has a far less negative reaction to this concept than does Tertullian, he wishes to make clear the limits of his merely human rules and to avoid any infringement on the prerogatives of divinity. He later notes that the preacher treats topics "which exceed human capacities" and thus counsels him to begin his sermon with a prayer.[91]

Thomas Waleys, it could be argued, is clear about the sermon's ultimate goals; the fact that he nonetheless writes extensive artistic directions for the preacher simply indicates his belief that human creativity can be helpful if it is not given more weight than it deserves. At the same time the brevity of his disclaimers, when measured against the length and detail of his instructions on delivery, suggests that they may be another form of the requisite caveat against rhetoric: warnings of a danger that everyone knows to avoid. Ranulph Higden, beginning a section on how to draw the audience's attention, had similarly said that "deo inoffenso" he would suggest some tricks for gaining the audience's interest and keeping it.[92] The theorists seem uncomfortably aware that their God is a jealous God and that their power to command an audience infringes, to some degree, on his territory. Yet since God is capable of making any sermon, however humanly weak, effective through grace, there is also a danger that the preacher will abdicate his responsibility for good preaching. *Artes praedicandi* must therefore steer between the two extremes of carelessness and hubris in the preacher, but while they mention the latter they focus their attention on the former. With preaching's intent and history now firmly established, the authors of preaching manuals seem to feel they need offer only a brief reminder that God is the "final cause" of preaching, as Robert of Basevorn puts it, both the ultimate source of the message and the guarantor of the medium's efficiency by his gift of grace to the listeners.[93]

Thus, Thomas Waleys's attempt to frame his discussion in terms of the preacher's debt to God cannot obscure his extensive attention to what the preacher can do to increase his sermon's practical effectiveness. Interestingly, however, and probably in part as a result of his predecessors, Waleys is able to treat the undeniable physical aspects of preaching, which are clearly of great interest to him, without embroiling himself in their moral implications. By emphasizing the pragmatic aspects of style and delivery he distances them from questions of intention, and in so doing he makes a valiant attempt to cut the knot that bound rhetoric so closely to the lure of the flesh. We see this in his division of his first three teachings (*documenta*) from the remaining nine: the initial instructions are that a preacher must not be in a state of mortal sin; that he must preserve a rightful intention, seeking to praise God and edify his neighbor rather than to promote himself; and that he must pray to God, the fount of all wisdom, and ask his help in instructing the audience. "The foregoing teachings," Waleys says, "should be observed secretly by the preacher with regard to himself. Many others, however, should be attended to in public, when he preaches to the people."[94] By this tactic the potentially problematic link between the preacher's personal desires and those of the audience is implicitly severed, leaving Waleys free to discuss the fine points of delivery with considerably diminished concern about their moral implications.

An example of this can be seen in his treatment of decorum. The preacher should use "appropriate gestures" (*motus decentes*), and it is not becoming to him (*non decet*) to speak like a boy reciting his Donatus, without comprehension.[95] Rather than looking at what type of rhetoric befits a particular speaker, as Augustine had done, or at the preacher's internal qualities, as did Gregory the Great, Waleys takes a purely practical view. He does not seem concerned with any moral effect of indecorum, only with the fact that it will, in effect, make the preacher look like an idiot before his audience.[96] A warning that the preacher "should not so attempt to please men in preaching that he pursue the vanity of some who, when attending sermons, praise whatever is fancy" is cast less in terms of the moral dangers than as a matter of snobbery: the preacher should not stoop to gratify the tastes of "such worthless hearers" (*tal[es] van[i] auditor[es]*).[97]

Thus, when Waleys tells the preacher that his task is "to instruct the people and draw them to devotion" (*aedificare populum et ad devotionem allicere*), it may not be surprising that his idea of sweet speech seems to have no problematic overtones. Rather than alluring or ornate language,

Waleys is talking about an "intelligible and attractive manner of speaking" (*modum dicendi intelligibilem et allectivum*), which he has just rather startlingly asserted is a sermon's greatest power.[98] This striking emphasis on medium—and particularly delivery—over message, form over content, suggests that for Thomas Waleys, despite his cautious disclaimer at the beginning, human art is of the utmost importance in preaching and need not carry with it any alarming moral baggage. The result is that he presents an unusually positive view of the power of persuasive allure, suggesting that the preacher's appealing eloquence, particularly if it could be freed from concerns about his moral intentions, might be recognized as beneficial rather than threatening.

Such a solution, of course, was sustainable only if one were prepared to assume the preacher's virtuous interiority, and as has been shown, this was an ideal of which the theorists were, albeit reluctantly, suspicious. As John D. Schaeffer notes, "In Augustine's theory and practice, wisdom and eloquence are synthesized in an extemporaneous oral performance that emerges from the preacher's interiority, that is, from an authentic self formed by doctrine," but both the spontaneity of this performance and its authentic reflection of personal virtue could be perceived only through the preacher's artistry, as Augustine was well aware.[99] Despite these intractable problems, most medieval theorists of preaching came to accept, with varying degrees of comfort, that preaching was a hybrid art, the marriage of divine truth with human eloquence. The increasing willingness to disentangle the threads of idolatry, femininity, and superficiality that ran through rhetoric made it possible to diminish many of the concerns that had absorbed the attention of earlier writers. Avoiding, for the most part, the explosive question of how the preacher's body interacted with his language and how the two jointly might influence an audience, the writers of the *artes praedicandi* were able to achieve a relatively comfortable attitude toward the eloquence they taught. But the anxiety about persuasion and allure, marginalized in technically or linguistically focused accounts of the preacher's rhetoric, returned, as we shall see, in other discourses.

5

Transparent Bodies and the Redemption of Rhetoric

[Nulla] mulier[,] quantumcumque docta et sancta,
praedicare debet.
[No woman, however learned and saintly, ought to
preach.]

Robert of Basevorn, Forma praedicandi

IN MANY CONTEXTS THE IMAGE OF THE woman preacher was used primarily as a limit case for acceptable activity, and considerations of female preachers often seem to function mainly to justify exclusion, as we have seen. A major strand in this justification was the idea of the female body's capacity for dangerous allure, an allure already associated with decoration of all kinds, including rhetorical excess and display. At the same time, however, women's persuasiveness—often depicted in terms similar to those used to characterize rhetoric—was acknowledged to have considerable power. Examples abound in the Bible, and Augustine picks up on the theme when at the end of *De doctrina christiana* he recalls Esther's prayer before her attempt at wifely persuasion as a model for the preacher.[1] The powerful persuasiveness of physical beauty, intimacy, and rhetoric could work to good or ill effect, and the association of these motifs opened the way for an intense investigation, in medieval hagiography, of the body's capacity to further as well as obscure a salvific message. The often feminized notion of persuasion was, as I have suggested above, a subject that many preaching theorists preferred to avoid or at least to underplay; saints' lives offer an avenue for exploring the preacher's embodied, persuasive appeals to his audience in a less threatening context.

Late medieval hagiography and preaching literature demonstrate a widespread enthusiasm for certain famous women preachers coexisting with persistent denunciations of the dangers of women's public speech.[2]

Recent scholarship on medieval hagiography has emphasized, as Theresa
Coletti observes, the ways in which "hagiographic narrative and cultic
practice, far from simply representing a stable, transhistorical realm of
Christian values, participated in crucial ways in the production of social
and political power."[3] Narratives concerning women saints of the early
church, particularly virgin-martyr legends, are excellent instances of this
tendency. From the patristic age to the fifteenth century, retellings of their
stories make appeal to an idealized, radical Christian past even as they explore the most topical and thorny of questions.[4] This phenomenon is
clearly visible in late medieval lives of saints such as Mary Magdalene and
Katherine of Alexandria, which represent both the discomfort with
women's public speech and the ways in which that speech could reflect
and, to some extent, mitigate concerns about embodiment and its role in
the preacher's work. Both favorable discussions of wifely persuasion and
denunciations of women preachers link female beauty and persuasive
speech; in high and late medieval lives of these outspoken saints the pairing appears in concrete form. Their legends helped to neutralize the dangerous allure of the superficial by showing how physical and verbal beauty
could be united to serve, rather than threaten, the greater good of preaching. In Jacobus of Voragine's *Legenda aurea* and its immediate sources
male authors use their female characters to work through how human eloquence is related to its divine subject and how the body of the speaker inflects that relationship.

Feminine Persuasion, Feminine Allure

Women's speech was suspect in medieval culture not, of course, because
of its unimportance but because of its perceived power, for good or ill.
The association of such power with sensual and even sexual appeal is visible across the spectrum of discussions of women's speech, from the most
positive to the most negative. The persistent use of the language of sweetness and attraction in such discourses marks the ways in which rhetoric's
dangerous tendencies were emphasized when persuasion was directly associated with the feminine. It also begins to suggest how male preachers
could be tainted with the sexual overtones of the language of preaching.

   Beginning at one end of the spectrum, we see that even positive discussions of women's persuasive abilities were often couched in terms that
implied their dangerous links to sexual allure. Sharon Farmer, in tracing

the history of attitudes toward women's ability to persuade their husbands to Christian belief and behavior, found that late medieval commentators, particularly pastoral theologians, moved away from patristic views of women's ability to persuade through deeds to propose a more actively verbal role for Christian spouses of unbelievers.[5] Thomas of Chobham, for instance, says in his *Manual for Confessors* that "it should always be enjoined upon women to be preachers to their husbands, because no priest is able to soften the heart of a man the way his wife can."[6] He emphasizes that a wife should speak "alluringly" to her husband "even in the bedroom, in the midst of their embraces."[7] The language of softness and sweetness (*emollire, blande*) and the location of the persuasion hint that there is something specifically feminine and sexual about the kind of persuasion Thomas advocates.

Indeed, words such as "blande," "emollire," "dulcis" are used repeatedly to describe the speech of pious wives in the sources Farmer discusses, suggesting that the "suauitas" that Augustine saw as a suspect but effective quality in preaching could take on a markedly feminine cast.[8] Farmer notes this "association of feminine weakness and seduction with the power of persuasion" and suggests that it sometimes implied a distrust of spoken language, which is inherently exterior and sensual—an echo of the ascetic Tertullian.[9] Farmer argues, however, that as women became more active in lay piety, and more able to give alms, writers such as Thomas of Chobham and Orderic Vitalis broke down the dichotomy between speech that "like woman herself . . . was an enticement, luring the soul away from God" and speech as the medium of a divine message, thus giving a more positive valence to the associations between the feminine, the material, and spoken language.[10] Indeed, many of the words used to describe the speech of these pious wives also appear in the lives of "saintly evangelists"—including women—and in the preaching manuals.[11]

When persuasive women are shown in a less positive context, however, the ambivalent language of sweetness and allure moves quickly toward its more negative connotations. This tendency appears most strikingly in discussions of heretical sects, in which the accusations of sexual license that were a commonplace of the polemical literature merge with the resistance to lay preaching to create the nightmare figure of the "prostitute preacher." Geoffroy of Auxerre, who coined the phrase, calls the women preachers of the Waldensians "curious and verbose" and associates them with Jezebel: verbal sin and sexual sin slide into one another.[12] Another anti-Waldensian polemicist, Bernard of Fontcaude, takes the point one step further and "argues by association, likening the heretical preachers to deceitful women": "Therefore they seduce women and men, acting not in a manly but in a womanly fashion."[13] The emphatic association of heretical speech, sexual seduction, and gender blurring or effeminacy in Bernard's text, as Beverly Kienzle shows, implies the threat of pollution—sexual and doctrinal—that attaches to the inappropriate use of rhetoric.[14]

Discussions of wifely exhortation and denunciations of heretical preaching form the opposite ends of a spectrum dealing with female persuasive language. The links between speech, sexuality, and the feminine are treated more extensively and dispassionately in disputational literature, a discourse closely allied to preaching.[15] Quodlibetal questions on women's preaching bring various arguments to bear, but a key one is the assertion from Ecclesiasticus, used by Thomas Aquinas and many after him, that "women's conversation [*colloquium*] inflames men's desires."[16] In exploring and supporting this idea, orthodox disputants repeatedly use language that recalls the preaching manuals' concern with a male preacher's appropriateness to his office. Henry of Ghent, for example, writing in the late thirteenth century, notes that it is "indecens" for a woman to assume the authority of a preacher, and he later says that a woman who has received grace should teach "according to what is fitting—that is to say, . . . privately."[17] Henry also quotes the *Glossa ordinaria* to support his contention that a woman's "vivacity of speech" will provoke listeners to sin rather than mortifying their sins, saying that Paul's famous injunction "I do not permit a woman to teach" is glossed, "for if she speaks she rather incites [a man] to lust, and he is aroused [*irritatur*]."[18] Guibert of Nogent's *Quo ordine sermo fieri debeat* uses the same verb, *irritare,* to describe a preacher who overemphasizes ornate language and grandiose eloquence. According to Guibert, such a man is an irritant rather than a preacher, forfeiting the very name of preacher and the respect of his audience by his focus on rhetoric.[19] In different ways both the attractive woman and the overeloquent man nullify their own preaching activity: the too-alluring medium undermines the message it carries.

A late fourteenth-century disputation against Lollard women preachers brings this discussion back to the troubled question of heresy but argues its case in language much like that of Henry of Ghent. At his trial before the bishop of Hereford in 1391–93 the Lollard Walter Brut had asserted that it was lawful for women to teach and preach (among other priestly activities). A group of orthodox theologians was gathered to argue the church's case against him; some of their points are preserved in a compiled disputation in British Library MS Harley 31. The anonymous author of this piece particularly favors the argument of Saint Thomas Aquinas, also used by Henry of Ghent, that women's speech would allure men. He writes that "although a woman's beauty, form, and every movement may allure [*alliceant*] a man to lust, the sweetness of her voice and the pleasure of her words do so still more."[20] The idea of *allectio* (allure) tends to appear in the preaching manuals as a quality of exempla and other ornaments or of delivery. Despite their potential dangers, these attractions are seen as eminently capable of drawing the listener to God.[21] In the Harley disputation, though, it is clear that the listener is being lured by the wrong bait, drawn aside into fleshly lust rather than attracted to the Word of God. The author further associates this quality with women in general, rather than "meretrices" only, by the following argument: "If you say that this [condemnation of women's speech] should be understood not of a holy and devout woman but of a deceitful and foolish one, this is false, for, other things being equal, a man should be more attracted [*plus allici debet*] by the beauty and sweet voice of a good woman than a bad one, since he knows that the first would keep faith with him, and the second would not."[22] This effectively closes off any claim that feminine beauty and sweetness, which in other contexts are seen as beneficial aspects of women's supposedly inherent persuasive abilities, can act as a justification for public speech. Indeed, as the text's editors note, this concern with women's allure "is directly presented as the speaker's opinion of the nub of the matter": almost his last words are that a beautiful woman (*mulier pulchra*; ugly women are apparently not at issue) will surely inflame her hearers by the *suauitas* of her speech. *Suauitas* (sweetness or pleasure) is, again, the very characteristic so ambivalently promoted by Augustine in *De doctrina christiana* as the preacher's necessary, though double-edged, tool.[23] Once more, physical beauty is linked to sweet and eloquent speech; the persuasive woman combines these characteristics in a display of verbal and physical "eloquence" that may be *allectivus* but is surely not beneficial.

In all of the discourses discussed above—encouragement of wifely persuasion, denunciation of heretics, debate over the right to preach—the speech of women is seen to interact with, complement, or undermine the language of preachers. Lurking beneath all three discussions is the possibility that women's speech could be imagined as a substitute—or worse, a model—for clerical speech, even if that possibility is fiercely denied.[24]

The imagined relationship between female and clerical speech suggests one reason why upheavals in church structure or practice brought with them anxiety about and argument against women preachers. The reform movements and increased interest in lay piety surrounding Lateran IV in the early thirteenth century, the debate over authorization to preach in the twelfth to fourteenth centuries, the struggle against heresy throughout the later Middle Ages—all of these raise the specter of the woman preacher in different forms. This is most evident in the anti-heretical tracts, where women's activity is often directly at issue—though even here, it seems, women play a role in the polemics disproportionate to their numbers. With regard to disputation literature, Alcuin Blamires and C. W. Marx note that "Henry of Ghent's discussion of these matters owes something to contemporary debate at the University of Paris about the office of preaching, especially to the issue of authority and authorization, which was inevitably fuelling that debate in this period of friction between the friars and the secular clergy."[25] And the interest in feminine persuasion discussed by Farmer appears, as she notes, in the context of a strong concern with pastoral issues and the church's duty to its faithful following on the reforms of Lateran IV. In the later Middle Ages the ever-present threat of women's preaching came into focus most sharply when the institutional church was forced to confront challenges to its primacy or efficacy in serving the flock. Concern about women's preaching seems to be in part simply a symptom of orthodox unease.[26]

Rhetoric Redeemed: Women Preacher Saints

Discussions of feminine persuasion, good or bad, highlight terms and issues that were a persistent concern in preaching generally and demonstrate clerical discomfort with the place of women in the church. Hagiographical texts dramatize those concerns and at the same time work to diminish them by portraying women whose outspokenness is depicted as unquestionably to the church's benefit. I focus here on the vitae of saints who had become popular legends by the late Middle Ages: female martyrs of the early church, particularly Katherine of Alexandria, and Mary Magdalene.[27] These saints exploit and at times almost embody the various troubling elements of persuasive eloquence in a way that both flaunts and neutralizes the persistent anxieties about the place of rhetoric in preaching. Their association with the history of the early church helps to reassert orthodox ideas about when women could be permitted to preach and strengthens the institutional church of the later Middle Ages by reference to its idealized past. Karen Winstead has suggested that the puzzling prevalence of "legends featuring aggressive, sharp-tongued martyrs" in the late thirteenth and fourteenth centuries reflects the fact that "the clergymen who produced and popularized so many of these texts saw the saints as embodiments of *clerical* rather than *feminine* authority."[28] Her point is well taken, but I maintain that it was specifically the feminine qualities of these outspoken women that made them useful in exploring the nature of clerical speech and its need to exercise authority, in part, through attraction.

Jacobus of Voragine's enormously popular *Legenda aurea* forms the basis of the following discussion. Written in the late thirteenth century by a Dominican, it clearly reflects the growth of pastoral and sermon literature that characterized that century.[29] In providing information on saints that preachers could use, Jacobus demonstrated what he found telling or important about various lives. Within his collection the lives of the early women martyrs (many of them virgins) form a coherent group that has numerous features in common with the debate over feminine persuasion and allure discussed above. The emphasis on these women's speech, their beauty, their faith, and the interrelation of all three makes their stories a repeated encapsulation of the conflict between earthly allure and heavenly instruction that characterized preaching. Jacobus's legends of early martyrs set the stage for a consideration of Katherine of Alexandria and Mary Magdalene, whose late medieval vitae, particularly in Jacobus's retellings, offer the fullest exploration of the complex interactions of beauty, eloquence, and divine truth.

Although Jacobus does not refer to every female martyr as a preacher, both their activities and his language suggest that it is appropriate to treat them under this heading.[30] Most of the women are seen and heard standing up to their tormentors in ways that permit them to expound at some length on Christian doctrine and their personal devotion to it. That this activity can be regarded as preaching is suggested by the life of Saint Euphemia. In his introduction to her life, Jacobus says that the saint "made sweet sound with the voice of her preaching."[31] In the life, however, the word *preach* is never used; Euphemia "publicly proclaimed her Christianity" (*Christum publice conf[essus est]*), but we hear none of her words on the subject.[32] She further opposes the tyrant and converts some of those sent to torment her, in typical virgin-martyr fashion. Jacobus's use of the word *praedicare* in his introduction indicates that some or all of these activities qualified, in his mind, as preaching. Since they are the same activities that nearly all the virgin martyrs engage in, it seems reasonable to classify their activities under such a heading. In another instance Saint Cecilia, of whom Jacobus never says in so many words that she preached, is later credited with this activity by Chaucer, who indeed makes quite a point of it in his *Second Nun's Tale*.[33] One further example from Jacobus is that of Saint Felicity, a mother martyr rather than a virgin, who refused, like the virgin martyrs, to worship idols and was tortured and killed along with her seven sons. Jacobus quotes Gregory the Great as saying that "by her believing [she] stood out as a servant of Christ, by preaching became also a martyr of Christ."[34] Again, the only form of preaching that appears in Jacobus's version of her story is her reply to the tormentor.

Even when the word *praedicare* is not used, then, the speech of the women in response to their pagan tormentors is a central focus of the story.[35] In view of this emphasis in the virgin martyrs' and other women saints' lives, it is striking that Jacobus's discussions of the two great founders of preaching orders, Dominic and Francis, contain no reference at all to their eloquence as preachers, their effects on an audience, or their actual words in sermons.[36] That these elements, which are also central in the preaching manuals, appear repeatedly in the lives of the virgin martyrs is due in part, no doubt, to the difference in time; Dominic and Francis are modern saints, and their lives are to some extent less formulaic. Nonetheless it is striking that the saint's performance as a preacher is so much more emphasized in the women's vitae, and the distinction suggests that they offered a more useful site—perhaps because of their very distance in time and place—for working out concerns with preaching than did those of the modern male preacher saints.[37]

Jacobus's depiction of the women's speech and its contexts focuses attention on the battle between the allure of the world and the teachings of Christianity. He picks up the Tertullianesque association of femininity, idolatry, worldliness, eloquence, and sensuality but turns it to a new purpose. Jacobus shows the women preacher saints allying worldly, feminine allure with similarly beautiful speech the better to destroy the idolatrous attraction to verbal or physical beauty for its own sake. In doing so he makes it clear that the relationship between physical beauty, virginity, and idolatry—all central to the virgin-martyr narratives—is significantly less clear-cut than misogynistic tradition would imply and that the desire to separate earthly beauty from sacred persuasion is mere wishful thinking.

The extraordinary emphasis on beauty in the tales of the virgin martyrs has often drawn comment. It is sometimes seen as part of a prurient side to the tales, which are, it is said, voyeuristic stories of the sexual torture and violent death of beautiful young women.[38] While it would perhaps be naive to dismiss the role this kind of attraction played in the stories' popularity, to regard physical beauty primarily in this light is to miss the point of the lives and ignore the way beauty functions in the narrative. The virgin martyr's beauty is in fact fundamental to her mission, and yet paradoxically so. It stands in complex relation to the effectiveness of her speech, both attracting and distracting her listeners. While many of the virgin martyrs deliberately confront their future tormentors, numerous others are harassed merely because a man is attracted by their beauty.[39] However the meeting comes about, the tormentor is often struck with the virgin's beauty, even if he is not her suitor, and it is sometimes implied or stated that this beauty is one of his reasons for listening to her. Observers of the confrontation are often explicitly said to be moved by the virgin's beauty (and often her youth and rank as well), a response that leads them to urge the maiden to comply with the tormentor as a way to preserve that beauty.

Obviously such a response to superficial attractions is one that no virgin martyr worth her salt would put up with for a moment. Thus the physical beauty that has, in some cases, put the virgin into this situation becomes both the occasion for and the substance of her preaching message. To the citizens who grieve at her bodily torment, saying, "Oh, what beauty you have lost by not believing in the gods!," Saint Margaret replies, "This torture of the flesh is the salvation of the soul!"[40] The virgin's lovely appearance attracts her audience's attention and goodwill (in much the way the *captatio benevolentiae* does in classical rhetoric) and is then turned upon them, as it were, to show why such an attraction is to be shunned. Because it so often instigates both the virgin's initial confrontation with authority and her speech during that confrontation, beauty seems to be oddly necessary to her ultimate purpose, which is to bear witness to and die for her faith.[41] Like the preacher's rhetoric, the virgin's beauty is the sweetness that lures a hearer to swallow the bitter medicine, a sweetness that is dangerous only if the hearer does not realize he must move beyond it.[42]

This is emphasized by Jacobus's insistence that the saint's appearance is not "mere" earthly beauty, an empty signifier, but instead serves as an external marker of inner, spiritual beauty and worth. Of Saint Agnes, Jacobus notes that "her face was beautiful, her faith more beautiful."[43] Having told us that Saint Lucy's name means light, and that light is beautiful, he clarifies: "The blessed virgin Lucy possessed the beauty of virginity without trace of corruption."[44] The saint's appearance is simply the external expression of her internal qualities; those who are attracted by it are endangered only through their own lack of understanding.

If beauty is linked to purity in the tales of the virgin martyrs, it is also closely tied to the issue of faith versus idolatry. Beauty may be what brings the virgin martyrs into confrontation with the authorities, but the confrontation almost instantly becomes a religious issue. In the life of Saint Anastasia, the emperor, whose prefect has been foiled by the saint's servants, hands the saint over to another prefect, "with permission to marry her if he could make her sacrifice to the gods"—not unlike the pagan bride of Deuteronomy, except that in this case the woman has substantially more agency.[45] In this instance the virgin's loss of her faith will be followed by the loss of her virginity. At other times the virgin is given the option of which sacrifice to make; another prefect (obviously they were a wicked bunch) tells Saint Agnes, "You have just two choices. Either you will sacrifice to the goddess Vesta, with her virgins, since your virginity means so much to you, or you will be thrown in with harlots and handled as they are handled."[46] In this case, as always, the virgin is readier to take the chance with her bodily virginity than to renounce her faith; no doubt she is in sympathy with Augustine's views on spiritual versus bodily chastity, expressed in the *City of God,* and takes the view that purity of heart makes physical rape meaningless.[47] In a similar case the illustrious though nameless Virgin of Antioch presents an interesting meditation on the choice offered her: "Either the virgin sacrifices to the gods or she is prostituted in a brothel."[48] In the course of her musings she asks, "How can you be a virgin and worship a harlot? How can you be a virgin and love an adulterer? How can you be a virgin if you seek carnal love? It is more meritorious to keep the mind virginal than the flesh. Both are good if possible, but if not possible, let us at least be chaste in God's sight if not in men's."[49] The rhetorical questions associate bodily and spiritual virginity even as they claim to distinguish them, as the virgin puts the decision about whether to give up her faith in purely sexual terms. Pagan idolatry is assimilated to physical lust and adultery, strengthening the link between the virgin's religion and her chastity.[50]

On the one hand, it is not at all surprising that the pagan tormentors should attack the virgin simultaneously on the grounds of virginity and faith: what is virginity but a physical expression of the refusal to "fornicate from God" that Augustine defines as true chastity? The pagans, as imagined by the later Christian author, are quick to recognize the importance of this link—but then, the focus on chastity and continence was a strong defining marker of Christianity in a pagan context.[51] On the other hand, the almost instantaneous move from sexual threat to religious threat, or vice versa, and the association made by the virgins themselves between sexual and religious purity demonstrate the extent to which female bodies could be seen as vessels of religious culture. The powerful link between purity of body and purity of soul made the virgin martyr an ideal expression of a perfectly integrated and unified Christian attitude—a monastic ideal that was being transferred to the priesthood in this period.[52] Since a gap between surface and substance was one of the major anxieties raised by preaching, the "total transparency to the will of God" that these women displayed in their lives and speech was both reassuring and instructive for those developing an ideal of Christian rhetoric.[53]

The integrity of the virgin body may also serve to neutralize the threat posed by the "permeable boundaries" of rhetoric. Rita Copeland has argued that anxiety about rhetoric and particularly about stylistic excess is associated with a fear of effeminacy, most dramatically illustrated in the figure of Chaucer's Pardoner.[54] The virile virgin martyr counteracts such anxieties with the rhetoric of a perfectly intact and impermeable body. Her virginity guarantees the propriety of her rhetoric and prevents it from straying into the kind of excess that could express a gendered threat. At the same time this virginity guarantees the moral worth of her story, whose decorative or rhetorical aspects might otherwise be suspect— as the marked similarities between hagiography (especially in the vernacular) and secular romance suggest.[55]

By linking physical and spiritual beauty, spiritual beauty and virginity, and virginity and perfect Christian faith the virgin-martyr legends invert all the most dangerous attributes of femininity: physical allure, sexual availability, moral inconstancy. The virgin martyr displays these potential threats only to neutralize them by perfectly reversing them, to purify them by emptying them of any chance of imperfect signification. Her earthly beauty is the idealized sign of her spiritual beauty, showing "an immediate and natural relation of signifier and signified," and the linkage continues from there, to be finally guaranteed and validated by her death, which is at once a statement of the impossibility of perfect virginity and a proof that all her signs pointed in the right direction, referred ultimately to a reality beyond the physical.[56] Only by death, by martyrdom, can the virgin finally validate her transparency as a signifier.

This is demonstrated in reverse, as it were, by a miracle of the apostle Saint Andrew. In this episode a bishop takes in and agrees to teach a woman who is young and beautiful; she has been given in marriage to a husband but wants to maintain her virginity, and she asks for his spiritual guidance. The bishop, like a more genial version of the pagan tormentor, "admir[es] her noble origin and her physical beauty as well as her fervor and eloquence" and agrees to teach her.[57] The first suspicious circumstance here, even had we not been told from the beginning that the woman was really the devil, would be that she seeks earthly (and male) help; but this is not in itself a disqualification. Saints such as Cecilia and even Katherine have priestly helpers in their conversions and subsequent religious lives, though usually such helpers are sent, not sought out. The real problem here—the reason that this woman with all the appropriate external markers cannot be a holy virgin—is that she will never be a martyr. She is in the wrong kind of story. The signs that, in the virgin martyr lives, are supposed to indicate instantly a true and constant Christian are here instantly suspicious because a young, beautiful woman is always a suspicious circumstance when she is not actively seeking, and more or less certain to attain, a martyr's death.[58] Our knowledge that the story is not one of martyrdom would tip us off to the problem of the "virgin's" identity even without Jacobus's warning.

Katherine of Alexandria

The virgin martyr's ability to contain and redeem those dangerous characteristics that preaching might share with women (beauty, sweetness, allure) is nowhere more clearly demonstrated than in the figure of Katherine of Alexandria. Her legend, famously, not only raises the familiar issues of beauty and sexual threat but takes on the dangers of preaching directly by making her a skilled rhetor who must debate other skilled rhetors in the interest of the Christian faith. In both the mid eleventh-century Vulgate life of Katherine (the foundation of most later versions) and Jacobus's retelling, typical virgin-martyr characteristics are used intensively to show how an idealized, castigated Christian rhetoric could model that most difficult task, the bodily communication of spiritual truth.

Katherine's story is, briefly, as follows. The beautiful daughter of a wealthy pagan nobleman, she is extensively educated at her father's wish in all branches of learning. She later undergoes a conversion to Christianity and rejects her pagan studies. One day when she is about eighteen, upon hearing the noise of animals being sacrificed in the city, she goes to confront the wicked pagan emperor Maxentius, criticizes his idolatry, and debates with him about Christianity. He is entranced by her beauty and intelligence but infuriated by her religious beliefs, and he calls fifty philosophers to dispute her. The philosophers, at first scornful and incredulous at their task, are quickly converted by Katherine's supernatural skill in debate and undergo mass martyrdom. After the usual tortures, the conversion of the queen and the king's favorite knight, and various proofs of her sanctity Katherine is beheaded and carried to her heavenly reward.

Endowed with all the typical attributes of the virgin martyr—high birth, beauty, perfect faith, constancy—Katherine is credited in addition with extraordinary intelligence and learning. It is her erudition, combined with the great popularity of her cult, that makes her story so relevant for a discussion of preaching. She is, in a sense, the culmination of the virgin martyr tradition, although her learning and the way she uses it make her unusual. Her rhetorical skill, I argue, functions analogously to her beauty: both exist to attract and convince her audience, even as she ostentatiously despises these qualities. The very traits that could have disqualified her from a purely Christian life, pagan learning and physical attractiveness, come instead to mark her utter devotion to that life. Like death, the ultimate renunciation of un-Christian values, the rejection of the worldly goods of beauty and eloquence demonstrates Katherine's sincerity.

The Latin *passio* of Katherine known as the Vulgate was a mid eleventh-century translation from the Greek and survived in two forms, one an abbreviation of the other.[59] These two form the basis of many of the numerous late medieval accounts of her passion (as opposed to her mystical marriage, which derives from another source).[60] The longer version of the Vulgate and Jacobus's legend of Katherine each offer extensive discussions of her learning, rhetoric, and preaching that shed light on the vexed relationships between worldly means of persuasion and their heavenly ends.[61] The Vulgate text says that Katherine's father had her instructed in "studiis liberalibus" from a young age. Katherine, *decenter ornata* with this learning, "could not be overcome by the verbal trickery of sophistical art" (*nulla sophistice artis argutia poterat supplantari*).[62] Already readers see an anxiety regarding the proper use of learning: Katherine is "*appropriately* graced," in an echo of the concern with decorum shown by Augustine and the writers of preaching manuals and the concern with ornament suggested by Guibert of Nogent's very different evocation of language that is *venustior ornata*. Katherine and her rhetoric maintain a proper attitude toward their own ornamental status, unlike the "verbal trickery" that combines all the suspect qualities of pagan learning and eloquence: deception, subtlety, artifice, mere surface. This encomium on Katherine's learning and appropriate use of it to defeat lesser debaters is immediately followed by a sentence beginning, "She, the keeper of her virginity," suggesting an association between her ability to overcome others in argument and her ability to remain a virgin.[63]

When Katherine hears the racket of animal and human noise occasioned by Maxentius's enforced sacrifices to the pagan gods, she inquires about the cause and then goes to confront the emperor, after arming herself with prayer and the sign of the cross. Katherine's first speech to the emperor marks her distinctive use of pagan eloquence. It was suggested above that the virgin martyr's beauty functions as a kind of *captatio benevolentiae*. This is fortunate for Katherine, since she makes no attempt in her speech to arouse goodwill in her hearers. Indeed, her first demonstration of rhetorical skill turns the *captatio benevolentiae* on its head. Rather than salute the emperor's power or goodness, she says, "The dignity of your rank and the path of reason would impel me to offer you greetings, Emperor, if that [worship] which you now give to the cult of demons were turned toward your creator."[64] This refusal to court goodwill demonstrates as strongly as possible her lack of interest in placating the emperor and her disapproval of his religious beliefs. From the start Katherine shows her independence of rhetorical tradition even as she benefits from it.

The speech that follows chastises Maxentius for his foolish idolatry. Her theme is that the most pernicious offense of *temeritas humana* is that it "transfers the honor due to invisible majesty to visible creatures" and that it is not only wrong but also dangerous to offer the worship due to God to his creations, which are inferior to him.[65] The emperor appears to be more struck by her visual than her verbal arguments—"with his gaze fixed on the maiden, he silently considered the beauty of her face and the constancy of her words"—and when he replies he seems to be conflating the two: "These [arguments] you advance would indeed be lovely [*speciosa*], maiden, if they were supported by the power of reason."[66] Katherine's arguments, like her, would be truly attractive to Maxentius if they accorded with pagan beliefs; this, of course, is precisely the kind of loveliness Katherine is determined to reject.

The "fortification" (*munimentum*) of human reason that Maxentius considers lacking in Katherine's argument is as nothing to the power of the cross, with which readers have just seen Katherine *muniens* both heart and tongue. As Maxentius says later, "What could be so absurd, so foreign to human reason" as Christian beliefs?[67] Indeed, human reason is not capable of understanding God; the limitations of human knowledge and learning are one of Katherine's major themes throughout the narrative. She notes that she had teachers "noble enough as regards the empty glory of the world," but since they taught her nothing conducive to salvation, she says, "let all memory of them fall silent."[68] Her opening speech to the philosophers Maxentius gathers to dispute with her contains a lengthy list of pagan authors (Homer, Aristotle, Aesculapius, etc.) whose works she mastered and then cast away from her when she came to know the Gospels. She tells them that although she was so well informed in pagan teachings that she could find no one to equal her, "nevertheless, since they are all empty and foreign to true blessedness, renouncing them entirely I declare myself among you to know nothing other than the one who is true knowledge and the eternal blessedness of believers, my lord Jesus Christ, who said through his prophet, 'I shall destroy the wisdom of the wise and reprove the knowledge of the knowing.' "[69] She has already used this passage from Isaiah to Maxentius in describing her conversion from pagan learning to the knowledge of truth. In that instance she follows it immediately with a comment on the worthlessness of idols.

Despite her ostentatious rejection of pagan learning, Katherine still demonstrably makes use of its tools. If human reason cannot account for God, it can at least refute paganism, she tells Maxentius.[70] Her speech throughout shows that regardless of whence her eloquence derives, it still bears all the marks of classical pagan rhetoric. Katherine, in other words, can beat the pagans at their own game and, in doing so, demonstrate to them that the rules have changed.[71] All the teaching of her pagan masters is as nothing; the sign of the cross and a prayer to God, asking that he put "true and pleasing speech" in her mouth, do more than can the fifty cleverest pagan philosophers of the empire.[72] When the narrator describes the scene with the fifty philosophers, "puffed up with haughty eloquence" (*pomposo eloquentie fastu tumentes*), standing on one side and the virgin, "*fidens in domino*," on the other, it is not hard to tell from his language what he thinks of their relative qualifications, nor what the outcome will be.[73]

Katherine's display of eloquence is indistinguishable in form from the greatest efforts of pagan oratory. In terms of effectiveness it differs only in being more powerful. She renders those who try to dispute with her "speechless" (*elingues*), as Maxentius says, and after a remarkably short time converts all fifty of her opponents. Her success and the manner of it demonstrate that a perfect Christian exposition, drawing only on the power of the Word, is entirely equal to all the efforts of human art. The preacher must trust in God, who says, "When you stand before kings and rulers do not consider ahead of time what or how you will speak, for I will give you mouth and wisdom"—part of Katherine's prayer as she goes to face the philosophers and a not infrequently quoted passage in the preaching manuals.[74] Katherine has all the resources of pagan learning and eloquence at her command but chooses to reject them—and triumphs.[75]

Having disposed of, or rather subsumed, pagan eloquence in the person of the philosophers, Katherine moves on to the fundamental problem of idolatry in her ongoing debates with Maxentius. The issue is raised in particularly obvious form by Maxentius's entirely obtuse offer to make an idol in her image and set it in the city, to be honored by all who pass. This is his idea of a trick (*ars*) that may soften (*emollire*) her virile constancy. Needless to say, he picked the wrong virgin. The debate between him and Katherine on this topic addresses precisely the problem of empty, lifeless, merely external beauty. It allows Katherine to have a great deal of sarcastic fun with his proposal, asking what wonderful material she can be made of that will live and will have eyes that see, ears that hear, and (perhaps most importantly!) a tongue that speaks. Without these, she says, it hardly matters whether she is endowed with feminine beauty or the features of an ape. These are the same limitations, of course, that she has earlier attributed to all the pagan idols: "They are the works of the hands of men; they have eyes and see not, ears and hear not."[76] Indeed, the whole episode enables her to point out the foolishness of idolatry, by means of a reductio ad absurdum, and the utter inferiority of any humanly produced art to the creations of God.[77] She ends by reaffirming not her faith generally but her devotion to Christ as her spouse specifically, reasserting the link between her virginity and her rejection of idolatry. By contrast, in the episode with the philosophers it is her reasoned adherence to the tenets of Christianity, not her virginity, that she emphasizes. As the narrative approaches Katherine's actual martyrdom, her virginity and her role as the spouse of Christ become increasingly important.

That the martyrdom is a triumph she makes clear to Maxentius when he threatens her with it, citing once again her devotion to her spouse and her desire to be an acceptable sacrifice to him. It is typical in the virgin martyr legends—no doubt because of their didactic function—for the virgin to pave the way to her own martyrdom by reaffirming that such a death is a victory rather than a defeat, the culmination rather than the downfall of her resistance to worldly power. In her exemplary virginity and martyrdom Katherine, like other virgin martyrs, makes visible the invisible, God's power and love. In doing so she follows the model of Christ, who was able to "put on a substantial human form . . . through which the invisible could be seen," as Katherine tells the philosophers.[78] The virgin martyr, in her perfection, is the embodiment of an invisible world. When Katherine says to one of the philosophers that "miracles proved by hearing and sight" should "lure" him to the faith (the verb is *allicere*), we may note that she is about to become one of those *miracula auditu et uisu probata*.[79] Even more than this, it is her function and that of every preacher, not just the virgin martyrs, to make the invisible visible, the inaudible audible as best she can to human ears and eyes—while at the same time admitting its essential invisibility, the utter distance between divine and human that makes martyrdom the effective corollary to virginity.

The point about the emptiness of earthly beauty is made forcefully once more. As Katherine is being taken to her martyrdom, the crowd urges her to give in to the emperor: "O form of virgin beauty, o image of sunlike radiance. . . . O maiden worthy of empire . . . do not be careless of the flowering image of your beauty."[80] The focus on her physical attributes, beauty and youth, is striking. Katherine, of course, sets them straight, pointing out that her earthly beauty is like the grass and will return to dust, eaten by worms; her martyrdom is not an ending but a passage into life.[81] Like Christ on his way to crucifixion, she urges them to weep instead for themselves, for whom death will be eternal if they do not follow her message.[82] The beauty that the pagans value and respond to takes on a new, inverted meaning in Katherine's teaching: having used it to attract their attention, she turns that very attraction into a lesson on their errors. The ideal role of physical beauty in Christian preaching, as of rhetoric, is to draw attention to its uselessness.

The Vulgate account, then, associates Katherine with the problematic intersection of eloquence and sexual allure evident both in virgin-martyr legends generally and in discussions of rhetoric. Jacobus's legend, which draws on but abbreviates the earlier version, brings her role as a preacher to the fore, and in so doing demonstrates the saint's ability to defuse the potent combination of allure and persuasion that threatened to undermine preaching. While the Vulgate author depicts Katherine as engaging in two major battles—against pagan learning and worldly eloquence with the philosophers, against idolatry and earthly beauty with the emperor and citizens—he does not emphasize her identity as a preacher, though the word *praedicare* does occur.[83] It is left to Jacobus, a member of the order of Friars Preacher writing in a period when preaching was much more under discussion, to highlight this aspect of her story, making it a lesson to preachers as well as a stirring story for their audiences.

After relating the narrative Jacobus notes that Katherine was remarkable for five things: wisdom, eloquence, constancy, chastity, and privileged dignity. The first two of these are in the proper order for a preacher—wisdom must come before eloquence—and contribute to one another: he points out how her various kinds of "philosophy" appear in her teaching. He does not hesitate to ascribe to her the logic that pertains to "rhetors, dialecticians . . . and sophists," apparently seeing these potentially dubious kinds of knowledge as properly subordinated to her message.[84] He says, secondly, that she had "a most persuasive eloquence in preaching, as is clear from her sermons."[85] This is manifested in three ways: her "most eloquent" (*disertissima*) use of reason to the emperor in attacking the idols, her efficacy in convincing the philosophers, and finally her conversion of the empress and the knight Porphirius. The latter, which is in some ways closest to the activity of a Christian preacher of Jacobus's time, he describes by saying that she had "very sweet and attractive speech, as is clear from Porphyry and the queen, whom she drew to the faith with the sweetness of her speech."[86] Again, the *suauitas* that Augustine advocated is shown to be a most valuable quality in preaching. Indeed, the three activities Jacobus ascribes to Katherine here—reasoning, attracting, and convincing—correspond almost exactly to Augustine's (and Cicero's) three aims: to teach, to please, to persuade.[87]

Eloquence is preceded by wisdom and followed by constancy, two qualities often thought to be fatally lacking in women, a lack that disqualified them from preaching.[88] By flanking the eloquence that had troubling associations to femininity with these two more reassuring qualities, Jacobus guarantees the thoroughly acceptable nature of Katherine's speech. These three qualities—wisdom, eloquence, constancy—are followed by "munditia castitatis," which, as Jacobus observes, Katherine preserved in the midst of things that are usually inimical to chastity, namely "abundant wealth, which softens resistance, opportunity, which invites indulgence, youth, which leans toward licentiousness, freedom, which shakes off restraint, and beauty, which allures."[89] Jacobus notes, that is, the extent to which Katherine in her chastity overcame her dangerous attributes; in her preaching too she overcame qualities (alluring beauty, feminine frailty, inconstant youth, pagan learning) that could have endangered her message.

By her beauty, her virginity, and her constant defense of the faith Katherine embodies the ideal of the virgin martyr whose weaknesses become strengths, her vulnerabilities fortifications, not just for herself but for the Christian faith. By embodying all the elements that could threaten her message and her very Christian identity—youth, beauty, wealth, pagan learning, rhetoric—and then neutralizing them, Katherine, like the other virgin martyrs, becomes the ideal argument for the power of Christianity. Expressing but subsuming these threats, she offers an ideal of Christian preaching, "transparent" to the believing audience and to God.

Mary Magdalene

The other of the two most famous women preacher saints does not by any means fit the virgin martyr model. Mary Magdalene—repentant harlot, *dilectrix Dei,* apostle, contemplative—has an identity arguably more complex than any of the virgin martyrs, save perhaps Katherine.[90] That complexity derived in part from the fact that the figure known to the Middle Ages as Mary Magdalene was actually a composite of three biblical women: Mary the sinner, Mary of Bethany, and Mary Magdalene, the follower of Jesus.[91] As though these roles were not enough for one figure, later legend attributed to her a preaching career in Marseilles.

Although, unlike Katherine, Mary Magdalene had a historical existence, attested to by the Gospels, her preaching activity is equally as legendary, and it rose to prominence at around the same time. Stories concerning her exist from the beginning of the Christian tradition, but it was not until the later Middle Ages that her preaching was routinely a part of the narrative.[92] The roots of her characterization as preacher can probably be found in the Gospels. The episodes in which she poured ointment on Jesus' feet or head (Mark 14:3–9, Luke 7:37–50) were among the most famous and could even be said to be the origin of her cult; in the Gospel of Mark, Jesus tells his companions that "wherever the gospel shall be preached throughout the whole world, this that she has done shall be spoken of in memory of her" (Mark 14:9). Thus the defining act of Mary

Magdalene's love for Jesus is from the beginning linked to the dissemination of the gospel, a fact that might have led later authors to associate her with the work of evangelization. More important, however, is her role as *apostola apostolorum*, when she, showing great constancy, goes to look for Jesus in the garden and subsequently brings the news of his resurrection to the Apostles (John 20:14–18).

The legend by pseudo-Rabanus Maurus—actually a twelfth-century Cistercian work—and Jacobus's thirteenth-century version show how these hints came to be interpreted.[93] "Rabanus" tells of the dispersal of the disciples to the corners of the earth and focuses on the mission of Maximian, Mary Magdalene, and Martha, along with their numerous companions, to Provence. The parceling out of provinces to particular bishops involves only the male contingent, but the author is quite ready to assign a preaching role to Mary and Martha. His description of their activities includes many familiar images and themes. Both Martha and Mary perform miracles to back up their words, offering visible signs of the truth of what they preach. In addition, they are possessed of "admirable beauty of face, virtuous morals, and a prompt and persuasive gift with words," and nearly every listener "was inflamed by the sight of them with love of our Lord the Savior."[94] Their requisite beauty, that is, seems to work to the same effect as that of the virgin martyrs; they are also eloquent and, if not virgins, then certainly of good morals. In short, they have all the requisite characteristics for a woman preacher of the early church.

In the account of Mary that precedes this, the hagiographer gives further details of her preaching. After a lyrical passage describing her intoxication with the "alluring sweetness" (*allectiva dulcedine*) of her beloved while in contemplation, he notes that these delights did not make her forgetful of others. At times, concerned for their salvation, she would set aside contemplative joys and preach to the unbelievers or comfort believers with her "honeyed mind, dropping honeyed words" (*melliflua mente, mellita verba . . . instillans*).[95] This sweetness of speech is understood to derive directly from Mary's relationship to God: she speaks "out of the abundance of her heart" and convinces her hearers by showing them the eyes that wept for Christ and first saw him resurrected, the hair that dried his feet, and so on.[96] Mary's very body becomes a visible sign of her love for Christ and, by extension, of his love and forgiveness of her. "Rabanus" ends his encomium on her preaching and worth by citing the episodes mentioned above. "It was thus fitting," he says, "that just as she was assigned as the apostle of the resurrection of Christ, and the prophet of his ascension, so she should become an evangelist to all the believers in the world."[97] Her mission to the apostles becomes a warrant for a broader mission—one that, the author says, Christ foresaw (and, implicitly, approved) when he said that she would be remembered wherever the gospel was preached.[98] Thus Mary's preaching, which draws on her beauty and eloquence for its effectiveness, is grounded in her personal and even physical knowledge of Jesus, a knowledge that is witnessed by her body and that Jesus linked to her apostolate.

Despite "Rabanus's" warmth in describing the preaching activity of Mary and Martha, that activity is far from central to his account. Indeed, it is largely a corollary to his interest in Mary's role as a contemplative. Jacobus, writing a century or so later, gives much more attention to her mission, although his discussion of it is in the same tradition. In his etymological introduction Jacobus says that Mary can mean "illuminator" and that she is so called "because in contemplation she drew draughts of light so deep that in turn she poured out light in abundance: in contemplation she received the light with which she afterwards enlightened others."[99] The description of her interaction with Jesus during his lifetime is remarkably brief: in just one paragraph, before moving on to the mission to Marseilles, Jacobus runs through an admittedly substantial catalog of the marks of love that Jesus showed her. Clearly his interest lies in the later parts of her *vita* (although he may also have felt that there was little point in expatiating on what was already written in the Gospels).

After arriving in Marseilles, Mary is distressed to see the people worshiping idols; she goes forward and "her manner calm and her face serene . . . with well-chosen words [she] called them away from the cult of idols and preached Christ to them with great constancy [*constantissime*]."[100] The mention of constancy seems somewhat unnecessary in this context, unless the implication is that preaching Christ to a pagan mob is always a risky activity. Jacobus may also, of course, intend to emphasize the Magdalene's lack of feminine inconstancy as a way to indicate, along with her "serenity and discretion," that she preached appropriately. The pagans are quite taken with her; Jacobus says that "everyone was amazed at her beauty, her eloquence, and the sweetness of her speech."[101] He adds that it is hardly surprising that the mouth that kissed the savior's feet should breathe forth the fragrance of the Word better than others. The description of the preacher's eloquence in the language of physical beauty is by now familiar, but it is still striking that Jacobus mentions nothing about the actual substance of her message or her hearers' response to it.[102] All his emphasis is on her eloquence, whose effectiveness is once more linked to her physical contact with Jesus.

This is not the end of the Magdalene's preaching activity; her interactions with the pagan governor of Marseilles and his wife form the next, lengthy section of the *vita*. Here her preaching and teaching activity is clearly central; the word *praedicatio* (or *praedicare*) appears repeatedly.[103] There is also an interesting reference to the kind of feminine persuasion discussed by Sharon Farmer: when Mary wants the governor and his wife to help support the visiting saints, she appears to the wife in a vision and tells her to persuade her husband. In this case the wife fails to do so, but it seems that Mary was aware of the potential for wifely speech in a religious context. The husband, despite various proofs, is unwilling to accept the Magdalene's word for the faith she preaches, and he decides to travel to Rome to visit Peter, whom Mary refers to as "my teacher."[104] His lack of faith, of course, proves unjustified. This point is emphasized by the fact that his wife, who dies in childbirth on the journey, is later revived by Mary and tells him that while he was with Peter in Rome, seeing the holy sights, she was there in spirit with Mary as her guide.[105]

Given the extent to which Mary Magdalene's spiritual power and significance derive from her physical as well as spiritual closeness to Jesus, one might expect her to be a particularly telling example of the relationship between beauty and speech. In fact, this is not especially the case— or at least not in the way one might expect. "Rabanus" makes reference to her beauty primarily in the context of her joint preaching with Martha, where physical beauty is given a high persuasive value. In his discussions of her alone, however, the focus is on how her body signifies her particular relationship to Jesus, rather than on her beauty in the usual sense. Jacobus too prefers to downplay her physical beauty, probably because in this case it retains the negative associations that the virgin martyrs slough off. The snares that Katherine escaped were too much for Mary Magdalene: Jacobus notes that "sensuous pleasure keeps company with great wealth" and that Mary had been known for her beauty and riches but equally for her promiscuity.[106] Given this unhappy history, it is perhaps not surprising that the Magdalene's legends place more emphasis on the beauty of her speech and the meaning of her body than on the beauty of her body—or, indeed, the meaning of her speech. Lacking the virginity that neutralizes the threat of beauty in Katherine of Alexandria, Mary

Magdalene is a more ambiguous example of the function of allure in preaching.

Like Katherine, however, albeit by a different path, she has the qualification of immediate access to Jesus as an inspiration to and guarantee of her speech. Katherine's purity and constancy mark her as the true mystical spouse of Christ, and this intimate relationship thoroughly informs her preaching. Mary Magdalene, to whom this path is not open, reaches the same goal through her attested devotion to and mutually loving relationship with Jesus on earth. In each case a woman's preaching is enabled by the immediacy of her relationship to God, a peculiarly feminine relationship that yields an ideal neither masculine nor feminine: preaching that conveys the Word as transparently as the preacher has received it.

When the pagan philosophers confess to Maxentius that Katherine has converted them, their spokesman describes the effect of her speech. In Katherine, he says, "it is not a living human being that speaks to us, but some divine spirit that stupefied and amazed us with an immortal voice, and converted us so that we would scarcely know how, and would certainly fear, to say anything against that Christ of whom she speaks. For as we heard her preach the name of Christ, the power of his divinity and the service of his cross, our entrails were stirred, our hearts trembled and all the senses of our bodies fled in astonishment."[107] This passage, which expresses metaphorically the grace that works through the preacher, is echoed by Thomas Waleys, who declares that "when the preacher preaches fruitfully and usefully, as he should when his spirit is inflamed, his heart is so immediately joined to the hearts of his listeners that he is aware neither that he has a tongue, nor that his hearers have ears, but it seems to him that his word flows forth from his heart and enters the hearts of his listeners, as it were, without any mediation."[108] Thomas does away with the merely sensual organs, mouth and ears, that may be led astray by the sensual pleasures of rhetoric in preaching, discarding them in favor of an immediate and purely internal communication between the hearts of the preacher and of his listeners, not unlike the purely internal reaction Katherine produces in the philosophers. This is, as it were, the human counterpart of the ideal of God speaking through the preacher without any interference from mere human artifice. Presumably if the preacher is speaking "in fervore spiritus sui," he is in the "inflamed" state recommended by preaching theorists from Augustine onward, a state which marks the true presence of divinity. Thus in Thomas's vision the preacher has closed the circuit. The message runs from God, through the preacher, directly to the listener's heart: the preacher, like the virgin martyrs or Mary Magdalene, has become transparent to his message.

This lyrical vision of artless transparency and immediacy, however, follows Thomas's lengthy and detailed exposition of the human artifice of preaching.[109] Aristotle argued that art's purpose is to make itself invisible; the medium seeks to efface itself, to convey a sense of immediacy. The preacher's art should be subsumed in its message, as Katherine's rhetorical skill is subsumed in her inspired speech. This paradox of artistry that is necessary and yet must be discarded or surpassed is a fundamental problem of Christian preaching.[110] In various ways the women preacher saints help to embody the ideal of the perfectly rhetorical preacher, so perfect that the inside matches the outside without gap, leading to an immediacy possible only through mediation. By presenting both the physical beauty that is related to the dangerous worldly beauties of rhetoric, and also the intimate relationship to Christ that expresses the ideal of unmediated communication with the divine, the female preacher saints point to what is troubling in the activity of a physical human being conveying a divine message. By their perfect transparency to the origin of their message they participate in the kind of paradox that the virgin Mary embodied: female yet virile, public yet chaste, eloquent yet truthful, they collapse all the troubling contradictions that seemingly define them, to become symbols of Christian preaching at its most idealized.[111] Physical beauty was seen as a problem with and for women preachers, but the associations between beauty and eloquence suggest that the issues raised in these saints' lives could have had a much wider application, affecting at least in theory any person, male or female, who tried to convey the Word of God in human speech.

As the threat of paganism receded, theorists of mainstream Christian preaching became less anxious about the uses of rhetoric and its potential dangers. At the same time, however, discourses concerning women's ability or right to display public eloquence took over many of the terms of that anxiety. In a sense, what had been an external, pagan threat potentially imported or perpetuated by the femininity and falsehood of rhetoric became in late medieval Christianity an internal, feminine threat of insubordination, excessive lay devotion, and heresy. The female preacher saints help to contain this threat specifically by embodying it, because the body they bestow on it is beautiful but transparent: its superficial attractions, like those of their pagan learning, lead to the divine truths within. Once the female body and earthly eloquence have served their persuasive purpose, the saints are ready—indeed, eager—to discard them in favor of virile Christian spirituality. These legendary saints were an ideal combination of insider and outsider, pagan converts from a distant period who conveyed an image of extreme Christian purity in the face of extreme pagan threat. By ostentatiously rejecting the external trappings of paganism and femininity that are nonetheless part of her allure, the pagan female other becomes the ideal vessel for Christian doctrine, containing within herself the threats of dangerous beauty and beautiful speech, already castigated, neutralized, and ready for Christian use.

6

The *Alibi* of Female Authority

Docere autem mulieri non permitto, neque dominari in
virum.
[But I do not allow a woman to teach or exercise
authority over a man.]

1 Tim. 2:12

I preche not, syr, I come in no pulpytt.
Margery Kempe, *The Book of Margery Kempe*

IF DISCUSSIONS OF MANY ASPECTS OF preaching—authority, performance,
style, even language—express their concerns about the preacher's humanness through images of fictional or hypothetical women, how did actual
women ever manage to address the church? Strikingly, the debate about
women's claim to authoritative speech formulates itself in many cases
around highly specific notions of place. This can be seen in the reception
of the passage from Timothy noted above. "A woman should not presume to teach," says Gratian's *Decretum*, and the Gloss by Huguccio
adds, "publicly, namely in the church, by ascending the pulpit and making a sermon to the people."[1] The extremely careful definition of place
and activity suggests the author's desire to prevent women's access to a
situation that could allow their speech to be regarded as preaching. His
specificity on this topic reflects the continuing challenges to the definition
and control of preaching in the thirteenth and fourteenth centuries and
indicates an anxiety about containing women's disruptive speech.[2] The
prevalence, as well as the effect, of formulations such as Huguccio's is attested by Margery Kempe's crafty defense against the charge of heresy: if
preaching is to be defined by location, she will make sure to place herself
elsewhere. The fact that Margery was in trouble to begin with, despite her
avoidance of pulpits, shows that the problem is more metaphorical than
physical. It is not, or not exclusively, a woman's actual location in a cleri-

cal space that is at issue, but rather her ability to take up the position of a cleric—in effect, to speak like a preacher.

Like her contemporary Julian of Norwich, Margery lived in the peculiarly fraught religious and political milieu of late medieval England.[3] But the difficulties she faced in moving out of a supposedly feminine private space and into a public, "masculine" world echo those of any medieval woman who attempted to bring together these supposedly dichotomous realms.[4] In spite of all the prohibitions against such activity, there were certain women who did manage to instruct the church publicly, by rewriting the lines drawn to exclude them. Hildegard of Bingen (1098–1179), Birgitta of Sweden (1302/3–73), and Catherine of Siena (c. 1347–80) offer three different but not entirely dissimilar examples. Each approached the interaction of individual experience and institutional authority in ways that both made use of and challenged the exclusion from a public voice foisted upon her by clerical tradition. In doing so, these three women escaped their fixed location within an accepted framework of appropriate female activity and speech. Their strategies anticipate, to some degree, modern feminist treatments of the relationship between experience and authority, and particularly the question of who has a right to speak.

Interestingly, like the discourse that Margery exploited, these modern discussions often frame themselves in terms of place. Diana Fuss's observation that place and self-positioning are central to modern debates over authority and experience alerts us to the appearance of similar themes in the medieval texts.[5] Luce Irigaray, for example, has said that even when women mimic the "place of [their] exploitation by discourse" they are not reduced to that place but rather "remain elsewhere."[6] Irigaray's approach to mysticism and the speech it produces, it has been argued, is one that can serve simply to reassert women's place "beyond the pale."[7] I would agree with Fuss, however, that it marks instead "the simultaneous displacement and *redeployment* of essentialism"—quite an accurate characterization of the strategies of Hildegard, Birgitta, and Catherine, who highlighted their own presumed weakness and femininity precisely as a way to evade the constraints of those characteristics.[8] Irigaray's concept is adopted here not to assert that women *are* elsewhere, but to contend that these particular women were able to make creative use of their exclusion from clerical tradition, whose very insistence on its own boundaries, as Margery Kempe realized, enabled women to give themselves an *alibi*, in Latin, literally an "elsewhere," from which to speak. In doing so, paradoxically, they created a place for themselves within that tradition.[9]

Both in the shared characteristics that enabled these women's speech and in their individual strategies we can see an attentiveness to the competing claims of experiential authority (deriving from the body, from personal interaction, or from immediate, visionary knowledge of God) and clerical authority (deriving from textual knowledge or from a place within a defined, masculine lineage). The competition between charismatic and hierarchical authority was also, of course, a problem for male preachers. But women's strong association with the former and exclusion from the latter meant that in order to preach they had to exploit their claims to experience without being confined by those claims and the stereotypes that accompanied them. The debate examined by Fuss approaches those stereotypes from a slightly different angle, centering on whether men can claim the "authoritative experience" that enables one to "read as (or like) a woman," rather than on how women's bodily experience excludes them from textual authority—a modern twist on the relationship between medieval women visionaries and their admiring male biographers.[10] For the would-be women preachers of the later Middle Ages the question was, instead, how the authority of a woman's experience could be manipulated so as to let her speak like, though never as, a cleric.

Triumfeminate

Hildegard,[11] Birgitta,[12] and Catherine,[13] I argue, form a natural grouping for the study of women's preaching, both by their similarities to one another and by their distinctions from other outspoken women. All three managed, with the support of male clerics, to address the church publicly without being condemned (though they were questioned) for their activity. This sets them apart from more retiring figures such as Elisabeth of Schönau and also from women who were condemned for their speech, such as Marguerite Porete.[14] They were also remarkable for the way in which they combined the active and contemplative lives, an interaction often expressed through preaching. Historically the focus on these women has tended to skew toward either their public, "political" activities or their private, "mystical" ones, though a number of recent studies have begun to correct this division.[15] A consideration of how Hildegard, Birgitta, and Catherine fused their private, experiential knowledge of God with the call to speak out publicly shows them working around such dichotomies. It also demonstrates the persistence of attempts to link bodily experience with women and textual authority with men, a problem that recurs fiercely in modern feminist theory. Hildegard, Birgitta, and Catherine, individually and together, maneuvered between those paired stereotypes, making use of their claims to authoritative experience even as they allied themselves with a textual tradition that worked to exclude them.[16] In doing so they both created a place for themselves within a supposedly masculine preaching tradition and—probably inadvertently—called into question the solidity of that tradition's supposedly self-evident boundaries.[17]

Arguably the most important source of both implicit and explicit authority for all three women was their visionary experience.[18] Such experience offered medieval women one of their few chances to speak out, especially since the visions themselves could address and neutralize the criticisms that might be leveled against feminine authority. While Grace Jantzen has argued that visionary experience was increasingly denigrated in the later Middle Ages, largely on account of its sensual and experiential associations, not to mention its links with women, it is clear that it could nonetheless provide a powerful source of authority, and one that Hildegard, Birgitta, and Catherine all used.[19] The claim of direct access to God was one that could not be lightly set aside, and though all three women found their claims challenged at some point, all three survived the challenges and continued to use their visions as a basis for addressing the church.

At the same time the three women connect in other important ways, forming in a sense three sides of a triangle. First, Hildegard and Catherine of Siena were both lifelong virgins and thus had access to the semisacral power of female virginity.[20] Birgitta, as a widow and mother of eight children, drew more on maternal imagery, bolstered by the powerful figure of Mary. Hildegard and Birgitta were both from aristocratic families and held a high ecclesiastical position as founders of monasteries; the combination of worldly and spiritual power enabled them in ways to which Catherine, a dyer's daughter, did not have access.[21] Finally, and most obviously, Birgitta and Catherine lived in the same century and, more importantly, both worked hard for the return of the papacy from Avignon to Rome during a period of intensive upheaval within the church.[22] Their shared climate and objectives connect the two of them and separate them in important ways from Hildegard, living two centuries earlier in a different milieu.

Indeed, these three figures offer a useful chronological framework, given that Hildegard lived at the beginning of the period that saw a revived interest in preaching as well as a new emphasis on lay spirituality and affective devotion, two trends that strongly influenced women's role in the church.[23] The scholastic and mendicant interest in preaching arose, for the most part, after Hildegard's lifetime, and its impact had largely been absorbed by the mid to late fourteenth century, though new disputations and preaching manuals continued to be written and disputes about women's preaching continued to rage.[24] Thus Birgitta and Catherine reap the harvest—or in some cases the whirlwind—of various important developments in the framework of thought that surrounded women's preaching, and their self-presentations reflect new trends in theology and spirituality that arose during those two centuries. At the same time the reforming spirit of the twelfth century (not to mention its own papal schism) meant that Hildegard, like the other two women, was surrounded by events and attitudes that gave scope for a strong oppositional voice. Ecclesiastical anxiety during her lifetime focused more on church reform and revival than on debates over individual access to the divine, with the result that her role as a woman visionary was perhaps less generally threatening than was that of Catherine or Birgitta.

Voices of Opposition

One major point of similarity between these women, then, is that they all lived in times of upheaval within the church, upheaval reaching even to the papacy, and their public pronouncements and preaching were largely directed against clerical abuses or deficiencies. Kathryn Kerby-Fulton points out that Hildegard, for example, "used her prophetic stance largely in the service of . . . reformist thought" and that, in contrast to her contemporary Rupert of Deutz, she directed her most powerful rebukes to the clergy.[25] Birgitta of Sweden's prophetic call required her to go to Rome, where she was substantially involved in attempts to return the papacy to its original location. And Catherine of Siena, who was commanded to speak primarily out of "love of neighbor," similarly directed much of her public activity toward the papacy's return from Avignon. Like Hildegard, Birgitta and Catherine were strong critics of clerical abuses.[26] It is surely neither accident nor coincidence that these three women, arguably the most powerful public female voices of the Middle Ages, spoke in this context of opposition.

The oppositional stance taken by Hildegard, Birgitta, and Catherine echoes that of the outspoken women of the Bible and of their later Christian counterparts, who offered a new model of the powerful public voice potentially available to women. The virgin martyrs of the early church, whose names and legends remained famous throughout the Middle Ages, had opposed, often fiercely, the pagan rulers of their day, condemning them with fearless, eloquent, and public diatribes that eventually led to their triumphant deaths. While these women were seldom cited as models of female preaching, their lives continued to attract orthodox admiration and possibly to present women with an alternative to silence.[27] The image of the virgin martyr rebuking and confounding the great pagan powers of the earth provided a model for outspoken women that could be invoked in times of crisis, to the benefit of both church and woman prophet. A certain congruence between the church's early days under threat of extinction and its later sense of threat from heretical challenges and internal abuses made available a similarly congruent role for women as the voices of opposition and dissent. Whereas the virgin martyrs challenge the pagan emperors, consuls, and prefects who reject the church's message, Hildegard, Birgitta, and Catherine challenge the popes and prelates who neglect their duties and threaten the church from within. The pagan man's inability or refusal to recognize the virgin's strength, which derives from her physical purity and her devotion to Christ, is confounded and proved wrong, though the virgin loses her life for the greater glory and eventual triumph of Christianity. The later churchmen, adherents of the doctrine rejected by the pagan, recognize the model of the oppositional and divinely approved female voice and do not reject the message of a powerful and orthodox woman. Indeed, as Barbara Newman points out, the clerics challenged by Hildegard, who might have been expected to cite the Pauline injunction against women's public speech, instead welcomed her criticisms, and the same phenomenon can be seen in the *vitae* and letters of Birgitta and Catherine.[28]

Thus, while many factors—clerical protection, strict orthodoxy, recognition by spiritual leaders, high social position, claim to visionary knowledge—protected these women from attack, it seems that there was also a recognized place for women who critiqued the church. In the high and late Middle Ages women's very exclusion from official, hierarchical power offered them a place of opposition, a place outside the clergy from which they could speak to criticize negligence or corruption within the ranks.[29] In fact, criticism of the clergy and especially of the clergy's failure to perform its pastoral functions was a sine qua non of women's public speech. Although once authorized the woman preacher can look to other subjects, the failure of the male clergy is an essential prerequisite for her speech, functioning as both its cause and its subject. The reformist impulses of the later Middle Ages created a climate in which such critical speech was valued, and the twelfth through fifteenth centuries produced many nonlegendary women who took on the role of oppositional voices to the hierarchy—the difference being that now that hierarchy was Christian.

Both in her connection to the days of the early church, via the image of the virgin martyr, and in her use of an oppositional voice, the woman preacher could claim a place outside the existing church hierarchy, could provide herself with an alibi that conferred a special, and always extraordinary, authority. In another sense, however, the continuity of such a tradition, and the near-necessity of such a voice in times of crisis, meant that there *was* a place within ecclesiastical tradition, albeit a provisional and precarious one, for women's speech.[30] Such speech had to be supported by visionary experience and often was not defined as preaching. But its complementarity to clerical work and the speech of preachers suggests that it was possible for women preachers to offer "manifest and public instruction in morals and faith," even if the primary public for such preaching had, of necessity, to be the clergy.[31] The woman preacher's claim to be outside, to be elsewhere, was in fact what allowed her inside, to become part of the tradition.[32]

Even with these prerequisites established, of course, women preachers faced obstacles in their attempt to exercise the "office" of prophet-critic. This is evident in the documents relating to all three women, which record the strategies that they and their supporters used in justifying their right to speak in spite of their gender. The "impediment of sex" from which women suffered can be seen in two particular lines of argument against women's authority to speak: that which founds itself on textual authority, having to do with a biblical mandate and the reading of Scripture; and that which founds itself on personal authority, having to do with the body of Christ.[33] The first of these, textual authority, is the primary axis along which Hildegard makes her case; Birgitta and Catherine, writing in a different spiritual climate, address themselves more to the issue of bodily authority.

Textual Authority, Prophecy, and Hildegard of Bingen

Medieval preaching theorists—and indeed the medieval clergy generally—
were uncomfortable with the idea of nonclerics having access to Scripture,
an attitude that became a matter of intense controversy in the fourteenth
and fifteenth centuries in England. Well before the rise of the Lollards,
however, heretics such as the Waldensians had called for lay access to the
Bible, and it is no accident that this challenge to clerical authorization often coincided with others, such as claims that laymen and women could
preach. Clerical justifications or characterizations of the exclusion often
refer to the veiling of Scripture and the Old Testament parallel of the
veiled ark: laymen are not to pry into the mysteries of Scripture in ways
that could involve a productive (and potentially misleading) interaction of
their own minds with textual authority.

The broad refusal of textual access, and hence authority, to laypeople
in general is intensified in the case of women by a sense of their subordination and also their ritual uncleanness, a problem that comes up in the
Decretum and in the preaching manual by Thomas of Chobham, who
seems to be drawing on Gratian's text.[34] Women's physical bodies gave further dimension to the problems associated with any unauthorized person's
access to textual authority. Ida Raming suggests that the refusal to allow
women to touch sacred vessels reflects "the concept that the chastity and
purity of the *virgo ecclesia* would suffer great injury from a cultic-liturgical
activity of women, a concept which can only be explained by saying that
women are impure creatures . . . or by devaluing them as temptation for
men."[35] The comparison of unclean human women with the idealized and
pure feminine figure Ecclesia both emphasizes the unworthiness of the
former and juxtaposes metaphorical and physical femininity in ways that
could imply same-sex interaction.

Women's exposition of Scripture could also have disturbing erotic
overtones. The idea of the text as something to be acted on from outside
and thus, by a frequent slippage, as a feminized entity is an ancient one
and well attested in medieval literature.[36] And if the "veiled," mysterious
text is seen as feminine, then its interpretation by a woman could be up-
setting. Judith Butler suggests that a tradition going back to Greek philosophy sees the feminine as the "invariably penetrated" and suggests that
"a relation of penetration between two ostensibly feminine gendered positions" might pose a severe threat to the assumed differences between
masculine and feminine.[37] It is worth recalling here that the "women"

who are most often permitted to expound weighty matters in medieval literature—allegorical feminine figures such as Philosophia, Natura, and Raison—are usually expounding *themselves:* that is, the body of knowledge that each explicates is figured as her *own* body (philosophy, nature, reason), and there is thus no juxtaposition of two feminines.[38]

The specific problem, then, seems to be the interaction of the person of a human female, by which I mean both her body and her intelligence, with the words of the Scriptures.[39] It was important to clerics who considered this matter that women's public speech, if permitted at all, should involve no real intersection between the woman and the text. The mere ability to speak the authoritative words of the Bible must not be taken to authorize women's public speech in other contexts, nor may the woman meddle in Scripture by penetrating it with her own understanding or offering her own interpretation of it. Various modes of female speech are seen as permissible, but the limit case, the instance which theoretically is never permissible, is for a woman to address the public, in person, with her own interpretation of the sacred text: in such a case both her place in relationship to a tradition (her claim to participate in an interpretative lineage) and her physical place before an audience are suspect. While a woman may offer moral exhortation or, in some cases, speak as a prophet (though Aquinas would prevent even this, implying that a woman prophet must speak her revelations privately to men), if the biblical text is present she must in some way be absent: either by writing a sermon of her interpretation of Scripture that is then performed by a man or by "absenting" her own intelligence and, as it were, personhood by simply reading the words before her.[40]

Of the women discussed here Hildegard is the one most closely in dialogue with the issues of prophecy and textual authority. The major weapons of the scholastic attack on women's preaching were its marshaling of textual authorities and its claim to pronounce the unified voices of tradition against women as part of the hierarchy, an exclusion whose ineradicable basis was women's subjection, subordination, and potential for pollution. In answer to these methods Hildegard asserts her right to an authoritative voice by, on the one hand, fully inhabiting the positions that she, as a "poor little female," would automatically have been expected to occupy in Christian tradition and, on the other hand, offering a new interpretation of those positions.

The issue of subordination, of feminine frailty, Hildegard co-opts by declaring herself the lowest and humblest of creatures, turning an apparent disqualification into the enabling force of strength-in-weakness.[41] Her famous image of herself as a feather on the breath of God expresses imaginatively her disarming argument that it is the very insubstantiality and smallness of her self that makes her message possible; she is merely the visibly moved signal of a great Mover. She also cites her bodily infirmities to guarantee the truth of her visions, since many of her afflictions are visited on her in response to her refusal, or that of others, to follow the dictates of the living Light.[42] Her physical frailty, one potential argument against women's ability to preach, thus becomes a source of authority.[43] This is expressed obliquely in a famous sermon she preached at Kirchheim, where Hildegard's physical presence remains in the background of the picture, as it were, while the voice of Ecclesia—a "womanly form" like Hildegard but one whose claim to authority is untouched by corporeal weakness—speaks the message.[44] In every instance Hildegard's physical body and its condition are made as nonthreatening as possible but are also used to reinforce her authority.

Hildegard's displacement and diminution of her body are echoed in her disavowal of any personal claim to her knowledge of Scripture. As she says, "In that same [experience of] vision I understood the writings of the prophets, the Gospels, the works of other holy men, and those of certain philosophers, *without any human instruction,* and I expounded certain things based on these, though I scarcely had literary understanding. . . . When these occurrences were brought up and discussed at an audience in Mainz Cathedral, everyone said they stemmed from God, and from that gift of prophecy which the prophets of old had proclaimed."[45] Surely Hildegard would have made the same claim about the gospel homilies she wrote and preached to her nuns: as an expression of her gift of prophecy they derived not from her but from the living Light.[46] At the same time her displacement of herself from the center of the picture never means that she is entirely absent; as the frequent and unsignaled shifting between her voice and that of the living Light makes clear, it is Hildegard's deemphasis of her personal presence that allows that presence to remain.[47]

As the above quotation indicates, Hildegard draws on the tradition of the biblical prophet. This influences the mode of her authorization and also, like her approach to the problem of physicality, allows her to speak from a place subtly different than that expected of her as a woman. The prophet, male or female, was understood to speak not from a written text but from the directly conveyed Word of God. It might be said that where a preacher draws on a text and on his own understanding thereof, the prophet draws on a voice. This distinction is complicated, however, by the fact that messages to prophets and the prophets' own speech are preserved as text in the Bible, and prophetic speech is thus in some way inextricable from a textual mode. The association is echoed in the famous command Hildegard received to "cry out and write."[48] Her prophetic voice relies heavily on the language of the Old Testament prophets, which associates the nontextual voice she receives with a textual tradition.[49] In a sense Hildegard's prophecies and letters are a new Scripture (though she would no doubt have rejected so presumptuous a formulation)—the direct, revealed Word of God conveyed in the recognized, textual language of the prophets and requiring, like any biblical text, exegesis and allegorical interpretation.[50] Hildegard's use of the Old Testament prophets as models associates her voice not with the tradition of female prophets in which even her admirers tended to place her, but instead with a masculine lineage.[51] That model was available to her because prophecy was understood to be unrelated to gender; but by placing herself within it Hildegard claimed for herself a voice other than the feminine one automatically assigned to her. She thus finesses the problem of the woman-text conjunction raised by her indubitable "expounding" of the gospel by incorporating the authoritative textual voice of the prophet into a public voice of her own (in letters and sermons) that overtakes any personal, "feminine" voice she might be supposed to have.

When Hildegard speaks for or from herself, that is, she speaks in the voice of the weak and ailing body, directing focus away from any claim to power or personal authority. While she insisted that she was present to her visions in the sense that she was never asleep or in an ecstasy, she made sure that the origin of her authority was understood to be outside herself. Even when writing her autobiography, she can claim, "I do not speak these words about myself, but true wisdom speaks these things about me."[52] If the concept of text-as-woman could pose problems for a female explicator, Hildegard makes use of it to present herself as text, to subsume her physical persona into her textually authoritative voice.[53] Even when speaking publicly to laity and clergy she could claim in some sense to be elsewhere, to be merely the voiced text explicating itself.

The importance of a textual identification in Hildegard's public speech is strikingly illustrated by the form of her authorization as a public voice. Potential challenges to Hildegard's right to speak are never directly addressed in a vision; instead it is the public reading of her works by Pope Eugenius III in the company of his cardinals, while Hildegard herself is absent, that gives her words their imprimatur. Eugenius's personal interaction with Hildegard's words is emphasized in her *Vita*. As Gottfried of Saint Disibod tells it, the pope specifically asked that Hildegard's writings be *representari*, made present, presumably because they would accurately represent her visions (obviating the need for her to be present). Having received them, Gottfried says, Eugenius, "holding them in his own hands, took on the role of a reciter and . . . publicly read them."[54] The emphasis on Eugenius's holding the text may faintly recall the ceremonial laying on of hands that characterized the rite of ordination, and his public "recital" of a text not his own suggests a kind of inversion of the woman preacher as reciter of a text not her own. Eugenius's conferral of his physical authority on the letters that represent Hildegard is the justification she requires to speak, not just to write, to the world. While some women visionaries (including Birgitta and Catherine) were justified in visions and received a direct call from God to speak in public, Hildegard's indubitable visions were mediated through the clerical hierarchy. By taking the voice of textual authority into her own voice and by founding her claim to speak on the clerical approval of her text, Hildegard creates a form of authorization that simultaneously acknowledges and remakes the framework of authority designed to exclude her. Embracing and embodying the role of the prophet, she finds an alibi for her speech, a place distinct from but recognizable to the masculine, textual, and institutional tradition of the cleric.

Bodily Authority and the Apostolic Role in Birgitta of Sweden and Catherine of Siena

If women reading Scripture raised the question of their access to textual authority, another tradition emphasized the priest's particular access to bodily authority. Women were more likely than men to claim a charismatic, personal authority and to buttress their claims by reference to their bodies, and this tendency only increased as affective devotion gained strength in the later Middle Ages.[55] But the idea that the priest resembled Christ or bore his imprint gave men access to an official, authorized mode of personal and physical authority unavailable to women. Thomas Aquinas focused on the institutional role of the priest and argued that women could not symbolize superiority of office, but he did not explicitly claim that a woman could not physically represent Christ.[56] Another line of thought took exactly this tack, focusing—as did Catherine and Birgitta—

on the physical body of Christ. This is an important part of the argument of Bonaventure, who saw women as simply unable to represent Christ directly.[57] In the first place, women do not have a "natural aptitude" for this order because they cannot receive the tonsure; moreover, only one who bears the image of God can take orders, and man, not woman, bears that image.[58] In the second place, women cannot represent the episcopate, for which ordination prepares one, because the bishop is the husband of the church and a woman cannot be a husband and so cannot be a bishop—a rather bizarre confluence of physical and allegorical gender.[59] Like the arguments against women's assumption of textual authority, this one involves an anxiety about women meddling in affairs in which metaphorical gender makes their physical gender inappropriate.

In preaching, as in ordination, there was a sense that the preacher should imitate Christ not only in spirit but physically, so that Christ's age, his bearing, and even his clothes became models for the preacher.[60] The preacher must not only represent but even resemble his ultimate exemplar—a criterion difficult for any woman, however learned and holy, to meet.[61] In this context the human Christ's masculinity would tend to prevent women from adequately representing him. While Aquinas's insistence that a sacrament should resemble the reality it represents has some bearing here, the focus on the human body of Christ and the link to the specific context of preaching suggest that this is a subtly different approach to the problem.

The increased focus on Christ that we see in Bonaventure's views on women's ordination could both help and hinder women. A fourteenth-century disputation by John Duns Scotus goes even further; he argues that the exclusion of women from the priesthood must have been Christ's will since there is no other obvious reason to exclude women and, indeed, that exclusion is a detriment both to women and to the church.[62] This is an elision of the constructed traditions of Christianity and a direct appeal to Christ's own will that is characteristic of fourteenth-century fideism rather than twelfth- and thirteenth-century scholasticism, but the result is the same: women do not have access to the kind of authority that commissions the male priest or preacher. If a woman speaks publicly, the origin of her words must lie outside the ecclesiastical lineage and outside her, coming directly from God. Because even direct access to God had to be ratified by the clerical establishment, however, it was essentially impossible for a woman to claim any access to public speech that was not mediated by a hierarchy that excluded her.

All three of the women discussed here made use of that hierarchy's essential support. At the same time each resisted or modified the view of God that would have used physical dissimilarity to question her likeness to Christ and by extension her ability to speak as one of his apostolic descendants.[63] Birgitta and Catherine in particular continued in this vein to offer a new version of the embodied masculine lineage that supposedly derived from Christ's male body and perpetuated their exclusion from an apostolic role. Unlike Hildegard's, their authority derives less from a textual tradition and milieu than from an appeal to God in the second person (in both senses)—though of course, in a religion in which the Word is made flesh, such a distinction is far from absolute. And where Hildegard adopted the role of prophet, Birgitta and Catherine took on the roles of both prophets and apostles.[64] Catherine's ability to speak derives directly from her personal relationship to Jesus. Birgitta moves between the modes embraced by the other two women, taking at times a prophetic, biblical voice and at times reporting friendly, almost familial conversations between herself, Jesus, Mary, and other saints. Both she and Catherine have a capacious, personalized view of divine authority that allows them to access its power through precisely the kind of appeals to bodily experience that were often used to contain women and block them from clerical authority. Thus the focus on the body of Christ, despite its disadvantages for women, also created a new mode of spirituality that enabled them to speak authoritatively without directly addressing the troubled issue of textual authorization.

Looking at the initial callings of Birgitta and Catherine, we can see already a significant difference from Hildegard's experience. On one hand, in the two later instances the women's concerns about their ability to convey God's Word are personally addressed by God himself, and they are authorized directly by Him, rather than indirectly by the clerical hierarchy. On the other hand, this sense of being called seems linked for both Birgitta and Catherine to a sense of being part of a new clergy, or perhaps more accurately to a sense of how the concept of the clergy might be enlarged, its lineage made less exclusive.[65] While Birgitta and Catherine, like Hildegard, draw on the sense of an alternative lineage, a tradition elsewhere, they also use that alibi to place themselves as claimants to an existing structure of authority.

Birgitta of Sweden

Birgitta's *Revelations* relate that when she was first addressed by God she saw, much as Hildegard often did, a bright cloud. Unlike Hildegard, she fled in terror, only accepting the truth of the voice she had heard on God's third try, when she saw not simply a bright cloud but also, apparently for the first time, "in it, the likeness of a human being, who said this: 'Woman, hear me; I am your God, who wish to speak with you.' "[66] We may sense a faint exasperation on the part of God here, but there is also an interesting implication of a transition between modes of revelation, from a disembodied presence and voice to the "likeness of a human being." The awesome and unimaginable first person of the Trinity gives way to the more familiar and comprehensible second person.

Christ—for it is indeed he, as the rest of the vision makes clear—then presents Birgitta with a telling image of her place in the spiritual economy, saying that he speaks to her "for the sake of the salvation of others" and that she "shall be [his] bride and [his] channel."[67] The juxtaposition of the two roles, bride and channel, seems neatly to address both the problem of presumption and the question of Birgitta's presence to her message. While the image of a channel implies passivity and the absence of self—a suggestion that Birgitta draws on at times to disavow personal responsibility for her prophetic words—the image of God's bride recalls, rather, Saint Bernard's image of a vessel, one who is fully present to Christ and filled by him.[68] Birgitta thus stands in the lineage of the prophet "spoken through" like a trumpet, but the image is complicated by its association with the charismatic authority conveyed by her intimate personal relationship to God. Like Hildegard, she both exploits and evades feminine stereotypes.

The vision goes on to relate that the devil sinned in three ways, by pride, by desire, and by lust, and says that the great men of Sweden are following in his footsteps. This account, which deals with world history and takes a biblical tone, has a strong prophetic ring to it, but it is also clear that Christ is the speaker and is personally addressing Birgitta, his spouse. This is a very different image than that provided by the awesome voice that hails Hildegard "o homo." Since "kings, princes and prelates" are not recognizing the gift of Christ who, as he reminds Birgitta, came to earth and took on humanity for their sins, he says, "I will gather the poor, the wicked, the minors and the wretched, and with them I will fill up the place of the others, so that my army will not be weakened because of their absence."[69] The gap left by the failure of those who should lead requires a new army to fill it. Birgitta would seem to be one of the poor wretched minors who will make up this army, in yet another version of the strength-in-weakness motif. She thus focuses less on her personal, physical weakness or frailty than on her position in a hierarchy, envisioning a new order that will take the place of the old—if not exactly a new clergy, then something very like it.

Birgitta takes a similarly dual role in her approach to her own writings. The revelations are represented as God's direct words to her, which she conveys as a channel. One of her *Reuelaciones extrauagantes,* however, pays more attention to the actual process of composition and the work that both Birgitta and her interpreters put into making that direct, divine speech comprehensible.[70] In this vision Christ first characterizes himself as a carpenter who builds and decorates a wooden image that is later painted over by his friends with their own colors; just so, he says, he has brought his words from the "forest of [his] divinity" into Birgitta's heart, and his friends, her redactors, have colored and ornamented them in books. Thus far Birgitta is merely the passive location, the "house," where all this activity takes place. Christ goes on to observe, however, that at times Birgitta works over the words she has received: "now you turn them over and over in your mind, now you write and rewrite them, until you come to the proper sense of my words." Just so, he says, his spirit came and went on "evangelists and doctors," so that at times they wrote things they later retracted or emended. Like the evangelists, Birgitta gets the words she speaks and writes from "the infusion of the spirit"—even if those words are later given a fuller explication by others.[71] If Birgitta's heart (*cor*) is the place where revelation occurs, conveying that revelation to the rest of the world still involves her mind (*animus*); she is not only the recipient of the vision but its first interpreter, and as such her role is congruent with that of the evangelists.[72]

The image of Birgitta's heart as a place of fruitful construction is echoed in many physical metaphors that emphasize her relationship with and similarity to Mary.[73] God tells her that she will be the mother of spiritual children as before she was the mother of carnal children.[74] One Christmas Eve, Birgitta experienced a "mystical pregnancy" in which she felt a movement "as if a living child were in her heart turning itself around and around," a movement others could perceive on the outside of her body and that Mary interprets to Birgitta as a sign of her prophetic vocation.[75] Like Hildegard's, Birgitta's body bears witness to the truth of her speech, but here it is maternal metaphors and imagery that give her a sense of authorization and a way to convince others of her authority.

One of Birgitta's surviving Old Swedish meditations brings together the concepts of house, enclosure, lineage, and (implicitly) pregnancy, suggesting that the interaction of these ideas is central to her sense of her calling. The passage, translated by Bridget Morris, says, "Pray for me, apostles and evangelists and all those who were enclosed in the house on the day of Pentecost when you received the Holy Spirit, for what you felt when you received courage to speak. . . . Help me, that by your prayer the same spirit [may deign] to visit my heart and come alight in it and never cease or be quenched. Then I would receive words and deeds to do and speak according to his blessed will."[76] The image of the Apostles enclosed in the house derives, of course, from the gospel passage in Acts 2 but also recalls Birgitta's image of her heart as a house receiving the infusion of the spirit.[77] Like Mary, like the Apostles, Birgitta is the body that "receives" the Holy Spirit and so receives the gift of prophecy *and* the right and duty to speak it. Claire Sahlin points out that "the conception of Christ in his mother's body represented for Birgitta, as for others in the later Middle Ages, the moment when Mary was filled with the wisdom of God and given the gift of prophecy"; Birgitta's *Sermo angelicus* also puts forward the idea that, as Sahlin says, "after the ascension of Christ, Mary was the teacher of the apostles (*magistra apostolorum*), revealing to them all things that they did not completely know about her Son."[78] Here again Mary's intimate personal knowledge of Christ—and perhaps the familiar image of her as part of the Pentecost revelation—associates her, and implicitly Birgitta, with the Apostles' mission to preach. Pregnancy and preaching become linked and available to both men and women cooperatively.[79] And as they do, Mary, who is central to Birgitta's sense of vocation, moves away from the role of the woman who "thought many things in her heart, but spoke few with her mouth" so beloved of opponents of women's preaching.[80] In the *Revelations* she is hardly recognizable as that dutifully silent figure; instead, her intense association with female physicality, and particularly pregnancy, becomes a justification, rather than a substitute, for speech.[81]

Thus where Hildegard emphasized her prophetic visionary authority and requested clerical approval of her desire to make it public, Birgitta uses images of physical fruitfulness and the presence of Christ's humanity to highlight the personal relationship that authorizes both her own public speech and the existence of a new order of those who may speak for

Christ. While Birgitta "stresses that she neither sees nor directly speaks with, nor receives answers from God, Christ, the Virgin or the Devil themselves—these things are only the paraphrases of experiences," the expression of her visions repeatedly presents those personages without insisting on the periphrastic nature of their reported words, and her speech thus has a very different quality than that of Hildegard.[82] Her interactions with the great figures of the Christian faith and her role as a mother, once carnal, now spiritual, allow her to enter the lineage of authority at a point that, while recognizably authoritative, is nonetheless still quite distinct from the clerical hierarchy. She reworks that hierarchy by insisting on the familiar, personal qualities of inspiration and instruction.[83]

Catherine of Siena

Catherine of Siena used many of the same emphases as Birgitta did, though her relationship to the Dominican order gave her a different approach to the issues of lineage and exclusion implicit in women's relationship to clerical office. Catherine's calling had two phases: first, her mystical marriage to Christ, the culmination of her contemplative life; and second, her public mission. In both phases Catherine imitates a predecessor who shares her name, the virgin martyr Katherine of Alexandria, though only in the first phase does her *vita* explicitly note this imitation.[84] The first, legendary Katherine became the bride of Christ in a mystical marriage and shortly thereafter challenged the pagan emperor, disputing with, preaching to, and converting the fifty philosophers he brought to conquer her, all the while disavowing her own exceptional learnedness and claiming that her speech came only from God. For her pains she was martyred—in her eyes, a consummation devoutly to be wished. By invoking this example the biographer Raymond of Capua implicitly places the later Catherine in the powerful virgin-martyr tradition as she begins her own public activity, fitting her into a recognized, quasi-official lineage of women who taught the church. It is worth noting, however, that we do not know whether Catherine herself made this connection; she was, like Hildegard and Birgitta, seemingly more likely to choose masculine models.[85]

    In addition to this relatively familiar lineage Raymond and Catherine, like Birgitta, draw on a more unusual source of strength for women preachers: the Virgin Mary. As noted above, the Virgin was often used by opponents of women's preaching to point out that even the most virtuous of women had not taught publicly, and thus to insist that women's preaching should remain outside the public, official sphere—but at the same time Mary's bearing of the Word was sometimes used by male preachers to characterize their own activity.[86] Both aspects of Mary are evident in the scene in which God calls Catherine to preach publicly. Raymond explicitly assimilates her role to that of the Virgin at the Annunciation, linking the two women and associating Mary's physical bearing of the Word made Flesh with Catherine's bearing of the Word in her apostolate—an association also made with the Apostles at Pentecost, but one that arguably derives extra force from Catherine's own sex.[87] The association with Mary also draws on the powerful doctrine of Christ's Incarnation—that greatest of impossibilities and greatest tenet of the Christian faith—to undergird Catherine's authority as a preacher. The man who questions her right to bear God's Word thus implicitly questions the foundation of his own faith.[88]

Raymond's references to the virgin martyrs and to Mary link Catherine with traditions of feminine authority, but he and apparently Catherine also associated her public activity with a masculine lineage, in ways that can suggest a new understanding of that lineage. Raymond notes that her mystical marriage is a special sign of grace like those given to Saint Paul and to the Apostles, thus linking Catherine to the origins of ecclesiastical preaching.[89] And it seems that Catherine desired to become part of a great masculine tradition: as he calls her to preach, God says, "You should remember how from your childhood the zeal for salvation of souls, which I planted and watered, grew in your heart, so much so that you intended to disguise yourself as a man, and join the Order of Preachers in foreign parts, so that you might be of use to souls," and he observes that she now wears the habit of the Dominicans, the Order of Friars Preacher, as a lay member of that order.[90]

It is worth noting that "zeal for souls"—the concern for the salvation of others that lies at the heart of a preacher's mission—forms Catherine's connection to the Dominican order.[91] Another vision expounds this connection more fully. Catherine sees Christ come forth from God's mouth and Dominic from God's breast and is told that they are alike in being preachers, and moreover that Dominic still preaches through his successors—of whom she no doubt sees herself as one. God then says that Dominic's principal intention in founding his order was concern for souls and adds, "Therefore I say to you that he was to some degree similar to my

natural son in all his acts: and therefore the likeness of his body is shown
to you now, which had a great likeness to the body of my most holy natural and only-begotten son."[92] We may recall here the requirement that
the physical aspect of a sacrament represent the sacred reality. The fact
that Dominic's physical similarity to Christ derives from his interior similarity, his "concern for souls," opens up new possibilities for Catherine.[93]

These possibilities are graphically illustrated in a famous episode early
in Catherine's association with Raymond of Capua. One evening as she
tells him the revelations she has received in the course of the day, Raymond is amazed. He writes,

Within myself I wondered about these matters: Do you think all she says is true?
While I was thus wondering, I was looking at her face as she spoke; suddenly her
face was transformed into the face of a stern man, which, regarding me with a
fixed gaze, terrified me greatly. It was an oval face, of middling age, with a thin,
wheat-colored beard, displaying majesty of aspect, by which he clearly showed
himself to be the Lord: nor could I then see any face there, except that one. And
when, fear-stricken and terrified, throwing my hands in the air, I exclaimed, "Oh,
who is this, who looks at me?," the virgin responded, "He who is."[94]

Like Catherine's vision of Dominic, Raymond's vision of Catherine involves a physical similarity that shows how spiritually congruent the
preacher-prophet is to the source of her message, and how apt a representative of that source. The "zeal for souls" that links Catherine to Christ
and Dominic is expressed as a physical congruence, placing the woman
preacher fully inside the lineage of Christian preaching. Birgitta brings
Mary and Christ together as teachers and connects herself to that lineage
through her similarity to Mary and the Apostles; Catherine and Raymond
continue this expansion of authoritative models by associating the woman
preacher with Christ, as friend and fellow-monk as much as bride.[95] By
collapsing the prophetic and preaching lineages that descend from Christ
into a timeless relationship and even unity between him and herself,
Catherine completes the chain of displacement and replacement that allowed all three women to make use of the authority accorded them by
their bodily experience without being entrapped by the stereotypes associated with that experience.

Making Space

Hildegard, Birgitta, and Catherine each experienced a high level of personal spiritual development before being called to preach. Hildegard, having seen visions from her childhood, did not begin to make them public until her early forties, at which time she first felt compelled to gain the clerical approval that would give her a public voice. Birgitta, whose childhood was also (though in a more conventional way) unusually holy and even at times visionary, did not receive the call to be God's "channel" until after the death of her husband, when she, like Hildegard, was in her early forties. And Catherine, who only lived to be thirty-three, nevertheless had long experience of intimacy with God, culminating in a mystical marriage, before she was given a public mission. This sequence of events demonstrates, and all three women's biographers also stress, the combination of the contemplative and active lives that married the best of the monastic tradition with the new concern for *edificatio proximorum*. As a fourteenth-century preaching manual notes, this was equally an expectation of male preachers: "The preacher, since he is a medium between God and men, and receives from God what he pours forth on men, should attain, or be well-disposed and near to attaining, the perfection of each life, that is, contemplative and active."[96] Hildegard, Birgitta, and Catherine drank from the founts of divine authority as deeply as any male preacher and, like him, drew on resources both experiential and textual, approaching God through book and body. The different roads they took in doing so reflect the varying circumstances that constrained and enabled them, but these varied paths brought these women to places from which they could claim the voice, if not the name, of preacher.

Returning briefly to Margery Kempe, I would like to suggest that the self-positioning and the manipulations of metaphorical place visible in all three of the lives discussed here help us to understand Margery's inability to attain a status like that of Hildegard, Birgitta, or Catherine. To be sure, Margery had personal disadvantages, lacking either the social position of Hildegard and Birgitta or the virginity of Hildegard and Catherine—the latter being, of course, a matter of enormous concern to her. Her historical situation also disadvantaged her since the dangers of heresy and the clerical shortcomings that often formed the basis for women's speech had in early fifteenth-century England become linked to that very speech through fears of Lollardy. On the one hand, these circumstances might, in themselves, have precluded her from taking on a recognized preaching role. On the other hand, Margery certainly claimed visionary authority and managed to attract certain clerical supporters; the fact that she was so nearly able to perform the preacher's role suggests that there was still room for maneuver. Somehow, though, she made a misstep. Despite the canny defense cited at the beginning of this chapter, the fact that she ever came to be accused of preaching is in itself an indication of her incomplete ability to manipulate the various positions available to her, to create a believable alibi.[97]

The Book of Margery Kempe is, as has often been noted, one long attempt to establish its main character's authority and her claim to speak religious discourse.[98] In pursuit of this claim Margery adopts, interestingly, all the feminine models discussed above—Mary, the virgin martyrs, the tradition of exemplary women such as Ecclesia, and even Birgitta—and uses these as the basis for her authority. Her reputation may in part have suffered from this unwillingness or inability to claim a masculine lineage, to short-circuit questions of sex and gender. By contrast, in their ability to displace attention from where they are, the female body itself, to where they supposedly are not, the clerical tradition that they critique, Hildegard, Birgitta, and Catherine show the importance of sleight of hand in the establishment of female authority.[99] Once the subject is clerical misbehavior, on the one hand, and immediate access to God, on the other, the emphasis on embodiment becomes an enabling rather than a disabling quality for women, and the woman preacher is able to shift the terms of debate. So intense is the focus on her visionary experience that the fact that she has taken up a position elsewhere, speaking in the textual mode of a preacher (albeit a textual mode infused with charismatic force), is scarcely noted and the question becomes not whether she may speak but what she has to say. So gracefully do the three women studied here perform their superimpositions and exchanges of categories—female and male, textual and experiential, divine and human, charismatic and hierarchical—that clerical tradition, despite its official suspicions, ultimately accepts their alibi.

7

Sermones ad Status and Old Wives' Tales; or, The Audience Talks Back

Aniles fabulas devita.
[Avoid old wives' tales.]
1 Tim. 4:7

Up stirte the Pardoner, and that anon:
"Now, dame," quod he, "by God and by seint John!
Ye been a noble prechour in this cas."
Chaucer, *Canterbury Tales* 3.163–65

THE PREACHER'S ATTEMPT TO ESTABLISH AN authoritative voice in which he could convey Christian doctrine was always a vexed one, and nowhere is this more clear than in the late medieval genre of the sermon *ad status*. These sermons, which addressed audiences according to their professional or social group, threaten to erode the exceptional and unchallenged privilege of priestly speech precisely by calling attention to that speech as the attribute of one professional class among many. The admirable desire to engage with the audience brings into sharp focus the problems attendant on attempting to maintain preachers as a group set apart from the world, even as their vocation required their participation in it.[1] This conflict is exploited by estates literature, which treats in satirical form the same failings addressed by *ad status* sermons and makes the didactic, critical priestly voice available to nonpriestly speakers while at the same time questioning that voice's claims to disinterestedness. Ultimately, the ways in which these genres bring the preacher's speech down to earth open the door to one vernacular author's creation of a poetic voice: Geoffrey Chaucer's Wife of Bath becomes, in light of the *sermones ad status* and their descendants, both the natural inheritor of clerical privilege and the figure who definitively upends its claims to ultimate authority. The debt of the *Canterbury Tales* to sermon traditions illuminates the problem of the preacher's ties to the world and offers a novel solution, allowing the poet simultaneously to exploit the power and to escape the dangers of exercising authoritative speech. In doing so, Chaucer presents an elaborate exploration of the relationship of speech to the intransigent physicality of the body (figured here as aggressively female) that brings together in very pointed form a great many issues discussed in previous chapters: access to vernacular speech and modes as a counterpart or challenge to clerical discourse; literary lineage and descent; the femininity of persuasion; and perhaps above all, the nature and fragility of the preacher's embodied authority and the ways in which it gets explored through images of women speakers.

Ad status sermons, which address particular audiences according to their moral, social, or, increasingly, professional situations, began to appear in the twelfth century. These sermons reflect the desire for an ordered hierarchy with clear classifications that also characterized the Gregorian reform. At the same time the explicit desire to address the particular characteristics of varied lay audiences requires the preacher to shape his speech to his audience's needs in a way that tended to break down or weaken the boundaries between priest and laity, and the later collections contribute further to the leveling of laity and clergy by making both groups the objects of critique. Estates literature, a satirical counterpart to the *sermones ad status* that characterizes and critiques various social groups according to their professional qualities, profits from and extends the decentering of the clerical voice begun by the sermons. The imagined author or speaker of these satires—some of which take the form of sermons—is no longer necessarily a priest, and the clergy are taken to task with enthusiasm. These satirical works also, not coincidentally, begin to address the problematic associations between clerics and women, one key point where the clergy's claim to unworldliness often foundered. Dyan Elliott has argued that clerical wives' "mixed, hybrid, 'impossible' status [was] ambiguous in a way that reveals the seams in classificatory categories," thus threatening the reformers' desire for "a strict division between clergy and laity."[2] Her astute discussion of this theme in texts on the priesthood is borne out by the irruption of images of women, and of literary forms associated with them, into preaching and estates satire. The recurrence of such forms shows how the association between clerical and female bodies begins to infect clerical speech.

The decentering of the priestly voice that permits the emergence of lay critiques, the leveling of the priestly body with lay bodies, and the overlap of female and clerical voices are all visible in Chaucer's *Canterbury Tales*, written in a political and religious climate in which priestly authority was under increasing stress.[3] Almost thirty years ago Jill Mann showed that the *General Prologue*, rather than being a portrait-gallery drawn from personal experience, was a full-fledged instance of the genre of estates satire.[4] Robert Hanning has recently expanded on Mann's work, offering an illuminating exploration of the ways in which Chaucer, in the *Canterbury Tales*, "appropriates and subverts discourses of estates criticism and confession," particularly in his presentation of the Wife of Bath and the Pardoner, two figures who encapsulate the female and mendicant voices so central to the satirical consideration and lay appropriation of priestly speech.[5] But whereas Hanning sees the preacher who gives rise to confessional and estates discourses as "an authoritative, quasi-prophetic voice thundering, as if from above or outside the human condition, against fallen humanity in its varied, estate-defined manifestations"—a view that the Gregorian reformers would surely have embraced—I argue here that the priestly voice is very much implicated in the interactions of lay and clerical genres, as the role of preacher takes its place alongside other "estate-defined manifestations" of "fallen humanity."[6] Chaucer's treatment of preaching and preachers demonstrates how thoroughly, by his time, the preaching voice had been undermined, and he does so by re-creating the problem of clerical wives in a new guise.

Lynn Staley has observed that fourteenth-century Wycliffite challenges to priestly authority and promulgation of vernacular Scriptures "disturbed the order of society whereby priest topped layperson as man topped woman."[7] Despite attempts to set the clergy apart, *sermones ad status* and estates literature, and the similarly mirrored clerical and lay genres of exemplum and fabliau, repeatedly and almost obsessively returned to the situation where that order collapsed as priest "topped" woman. If we look at the Wife of Bath in the context of estates satires that address clerical concubines, it becomes apparent how the decentering of the priestly voice, and its intimate relationship to the women it tried so hard to exclude, offered Chaucer a way both to create an authoritative voice and to elude the scrutiny of the speaker's body that could bring that voice into question. From the *ad status* sermons, through estates literature, to the *Canterbury Tales* the notion of the preacher as the voice of the laity undergoes shifts and appropriations such that a fundamental distinction—between priests and women, the most authorized and the most unauthorized speakers in a medieval ecclesiastical context—dissolves into a confusion of categories. Ultimately Chaucer can create a priest who is a Wife, and in so doing form his own voice.

Although the developments in the preaching voice and in images of preachers that appear in the genres explored here often display the bad faith inherent in clerical claims to stand outside human society, it is only fair to note that preachers' failings in this regard were to a large extent the result of an understandable inability to become inhuman, as the reformers and theorists of priestly office often seem to advocate. Indeed, the increasing democratization of voice visible in medieval preaching, estates satire, and especially in the *Canterbury Tales* is in part the result of preachers' own best instincts, their desire to connect with every listener. The delegitimation of preaching thus grew not only from preachers' failings, as anticlerical satire or Lollard critique might suggest, but from their own efforts and, in a sense, their own success at their chosen work. To the extent that they fulfilled certain key aspects of their mission by addressing their lay audiences as individuals, they began to unravel their own exclusive claim to be the voice of authority.

Sermones ad Status and the Tongue of the Laity

Several collections of Latin *sermones ad status* survive from the period c.1150–c.1300, and there were many more individual sermons that followed their lead in attempting to address listeners in ways congruent with their particular qualities.[8] These sermons are a late medieval expression of preachers' long-standing acknowledgment that different audiences need to be addressed in different ways, combined with a growing recognition that the "three estates" model of society—those who fight, those who pray, and those who work—was no longer nuanced enough to cope with the increasing complexity of town life and the variety of occupations.[9] The sermons are thus one expression of the preaching revival and the concern for pastoral care that characterizes the church in this period, and they are closely linked to the growth of confessional manuals, with their attentiveness to the particularity of professional sins. Even as they attempt to respond to developments in late medieval society, however, they are caught up in those developments in ways that ultimately lead to a democratization of the preaching voice.

The *sermones ad status* begin to blur the strict division between laity and clergy through what might be called their individualization of the audience. The idea that human beings could be divided into specific professional groups, and addressed in the light of those groups' concerns, implied a kind of corporate identity. Maria Corti has suggested that the *ad status* sermons reflect a desire to order all human beings, including the laity, according to models deriving from the hierarchy of angels and "personae ecclesiasticae" and that one result of the creation and elaboration of these categories is that "the individual owes his own social reality" to the existence of the group to which he belongs.[10] Lay categories thus take up residence in the same hierarchical universe as clerical ones, though they remain ranked below them, and confer upon their members a professional identity that in a sense gives them a public existence. On a more individual level, confessional manuals began in the twelfth and thirteenth centuries to address each penitent according to his or her professional situation, suiting questions about sins to the particular temptations and responsibilities of that profession.[11] In both preaching and confession, as M.-D. Chenu puts it, "the teaching of the Christian life . . . was diversified according to the hearers, the vocations, [and] the states of life, introducing the consideration of the 'subject' into the teaching of the faith."[12] The detailed and concrete conceptions of lay groups that preachers and confessors developed in order to fulfill their pastoral responsibilities were conveyed to the laity as audiences of sermons and as penitents and may well have contributed to a certain solidification of lay identities, on both an individual and a group level. This shift in sermon approaches begins to break down the larger distinctions that had formerly prevailed, such as that one should preach more complex and subtle things to the clergy, simpler and more straightforward ones to the laity, and reflects a more nuanced sense of an audience's needs.[13]

If *sermones ad status* contributed to the formalization of lay identities, they also, in subtle ways, diminished the sense of the clergy as a group set apart and unified within itself that had been promoted since the Gregorian reform. For one thing, the sheer volume of growth in the varieties of labor meant that the "vertical" qualities of medieval society, in which *laboratores* stood below *bellatores* and *oratores*, began to be strained by "horizontal" pressure.[14] The very diversification of trades that made *sermones ad status* useful began to draw energy and attention toward lay society: in order to function, these sermons needed a certain amount of concrete detail and concern for the secular world. Moreover, estates sermons address *all* professional groups, and the clergy are substantially represented. The

placement of clerical ranks in company with other professions, along with
the substantial number of professional handbooks for preachers and confessors produced in this era, reinforces the sense of clergy as workers like
other workers, with a similar need for training and tools of the trade. The
sermons' careful attention to audience also begins to break down any
sense of ecclesiastics as a unified body; as Jacques de Vitry says, "one
should preach differently . . . to prelates, to simple priests, to secular
canons and to clerics."[15] In both their internal diversity and their involvement in the world of work, clerical and lay groups began to resemble one
another.

Although the *sermones ad status* had a certain tendency to level the
priest's or preacher's role with others, they initially upheld the image of
the preacher as one standing above and outside society. Honorius Augustodunensis's *Sermo generalis*, one of the earliest full-fledged instances of
the genre, considers eight groups, each of which has its own little sermon
ending with an exemplum: priests, judges, the rich, the poor, soldiers,
merchants, farmers, and married people.[16] The sermon dealing with
priests reinforces many of the prevailing beliefs about their role. Although
Migne titles this sermon "Ad sacerdotes," the designation proves to be
misleading: priests are not the audience here but rather the subject. In
fact, the sermon is addressed to a lay audience and begins, "We priests
should be your tongue, and expound to you by interpretation all things
that are sung or read in the divine office."[17] This indicates that Honorius
is particularly considering the priest in his role as preacher—indeed, it
suggests that preaching, in its particular guise of expounding Scripture in
the context of the divine office, is the priest's primary responsibility. The
entire sermon continues in this first-person mode: the preacher is actually
telling his audience about himself, rather than about themselves, in a way
that reinforces the difference between his profession and theirs. Honorius
later alludes to the familiar ideas that "whatever we teach in words, we
should demonstrate as in a mirror by our deeds" and that the laity
"should look more to our words than to our works," referring the priest's
authority to God's: "we are the legates of the highest King of all kings,
and bring his commands to you."[18] Such repetition of familiar teachings
emphasizes the authoritative nature of the priest's and preacher's roles,
and the exemplum Honorius recounts at the end of the sermon similarly
focuses on the outstanding dignity of the office, telling of an admirable
priest who "taught the people entrusted to him with fervent zeal." After
a vision of his own impending death in which a multitude of angels prom-

ised to carry him off to heaven, he called his brothers around him, and on the appointed day the angels appeared to fulfill their promise. "Oh beloved, how blessed was the soul that deserved a consort of angels!" Honorius exclaims.[19] The sermon does address the priest's duty to his flock, but it is considerably more emphatic about his exalted status and his links to a celestial hierarchy.[20]

While Honorius's sermon implicitly reinforces the clergy's preeminence, it also introduces a number of motifs whose deployments in the *ad status* sermons and their offshoots would ultimately contribute to the diminution of the preacher's unquestioned authority. Honorius's claim to be "linguam vestram" is the most important of these. Here the priest's speech is imagined to substitute, as it were, for the laity's, and his role as "lingua" is emphasized by the fact that priests are represented not as the audience of this sermon "Ad sacerdotes," but only as its speakers: the priest's is the voice that speaks, and the lay audience's role is to listen. Even in later collections of *sermones ad status* in which priests and other clergy are addressed as audiences (rather than escaping critique, as in Honorius's sermon), the speaking voice is still that of the preacher. But even as Honorius's image deprives the laity of a voice of its own, it foreshadows the lay co-optation of the preacher's voice. Identifying the priest as his audience's tongue has implications for the laity's ultimate ability to speak for itself and, in so doing, to undermine the clergy's monopoly on authoritative speech.

Honorius adopts a lay voice most evidently in the exempla that end each sermon. His use of this form is one way in which he, in keeping with the aims of a "general sermon," suits his address to his audience's everyday concerns: "the speech of teachers should be formed according to the nature of the audience," as Gregory the Great put it.[21] And in exempla like those used by Honorius, the teacher's speech was not only formed to address the audience but indeed took on their voice, however temporarily. Several though not all of his stories involve snatches of dialogue between characters, presumably designed to intensify the story's verisimilitude. Such impersonations—whether in the obvious form of exempla or in more subtle modes—were an established feature of preaching. Gregory the Great, in his *Dialogues,* suggests that impersonation of the laity is fundamental to preaching. He observes at one point that in the book of Ecclesiastes, Solomon "was speaking for many persons and not for himself alone." Solomon's "impersonation" of these many people is designed to bring them "into harmony by the reasoning of the speaker."[22] He must take his audience's character upon himself (*in se personas suscipere*) in order to strengthen them, adopting their views and concerns as his own in order to reach them. Gregory notes at the beginning of this brief section that Ecclesiastes means "the preacher," and he says that this is *because* Solomon takes on the voice of the people.[23] This passage depicts it as the preacher's task to speak "as though he did not speak alone" (*quasi solus locutus non est*), to "[take] on, as it were, the feeling of the disorganized crowd" (*in eo quasi tumultuantis turbae suscepit sensum*). The ultimate goal of his exercise, of course, is the resolution of the "disorganized crowd" into a unified Christian church. The affinity between such impersonation and the impulse behind the *sermones ad status* is suggested by Corti's observation that the sermons "move from general structures, from models of reality constructed on broad unities of signification, in order to apply them to the sensible, empirical world in such a way as to eliminate the disorder, the discordances, and to substitute for them, according to the typical definition of the school of Chartres, the idea of an *ordinata collectio creaturarum.*"[24] In both cases the desire to bring the disorderly world into a unified whole requires recognizing and voicing its diversity and particularity, a voicing that ultimately can resist or escape its doctrinal context.

The danger latent in impersonating a voice in order to neutralize it was recognized by medieval theorists of rhetoric. Gregory's notion that impersonation can assimilate the audience's "sensum," and implicitly its voice, into the preacher's voice is echoed in Geoffrey of Vinsauf's *Poetria nova*, which begins to suggest the means by which the impersonated voice may resist its own absorption. Geoffrey enjoins the figure of Prosopopoeia, or Personification, "To a thing which has no power of speech, give the power lawfully to speak, and let license endow it with tongue."[25] In both impersonation and personification—closely related categories in medieval rhetoric—the authorized speaker gives "license" and "lawfulness" to that which apparently cannot speak for itself, whether this be the "disorganized people" or an inanimate object.[26] While initially that "license" (the same word used of the authorization to preach) is in the gift of the preacher or the orator, the power of speech that he bestows in a delegated fashion can ultimately become the property of the borrowed voice. As Carolyn Dinshaw has argued, "Impersonation depends on both the imagined presence and the simultaneously perceived absence of the character impersonated. When that character is usually silenced, is excluded from or marginalized within society . . . impersonation thus enacts—gives visible and formal expression to—this social condition."[27] While foregrounding marginalization was hardly the aim of the *sermones ad status,* their ability to give "visible and formal expression" to certain lay voices begins to raise the possibility that one day those voices might speak for themselves.

One group that contributed to the diffusion of the priestly voice, albeit while retaining many of its privileges, was the mendicant friars. G. R. Owst picks up the motif of impersonation here, claiming that the friars were "eager to provide the voiceless multitude with voices of their own": his view is that mendicant preachers were the group most likely to have given rise to the satirical religious and political songs of thirteenth- and fourteenth-century England that may be seen as incorporating a lay viewpoint. Owst's utopian vision of mendicant preachers "moving about freely among the dregs of the population, often sharing the peasant's lot when actually out of the pulpit" and helping to "ring in the era of redress from below as well as above" requires caution; the friars did not long retain their dispossessed status to quite that extent.[28] But their "radical social message," their emphasis (at least early in their history) on poverty, and their conflicts with the secular clergy may have made them attractive spokesmen for lay concerns, particularly in the thirteenth century.[29] Moreover, because of the friars' role as popular preachers they were widely regarded as inveterate and undiscriminating tellers of "empty fables," a secular form par excellence. Mendicant preaching manuals are actually quite orthodox in their distinctions between valuable exempla and frivolous stories, but the frequency of the allegation suggests a distaste for the friars' use of lay forms.[30] In separating, even partially, the preaching voice from the visible structures of the institutional church and in adopting "popular" forms in their preaching, the friars contributed to the diffusion of that voice and perhaps to its increasing accessibility to nonclerics.[31]

Estates Satire

If the *sermones ad status* raised, albeit inadvertently, the question of whose voice spoke in preaching, the satirical genre that developed alongside and to some extent from them contributed further to making the preacher's voice only one among many.[32] Estates satire, which, like *ad status* sermons, arose in the twelfth century, equally concerned itself with the specific failings of particular social and professional groups.[33] The earliest

texts are Latin secular poetry, such as the poems of Walter of Châtillon or
some of those in the *Carmina Burana,* but late in the twelfth century and
during the centuries that followed, vernacular works began to appear in
substantial numbers. Although the satires appeared as early as, and perhaps earlier than, the first formal surviving *ad status* collection, the genre's
debt to the sermon tradition is suggested by the fact that a number of estates satires that are explicitly or implicitly labeled as sermons appear in the
thirteenth century and later. The famous *Chessbook* of Jacobus de Cessolis, for instance, is a collection of sermons on the failings of various
groups; the *Bible au Seigneur de Berzé* of the layman Hugues de Berzé was
written as "a sermon on the evils of the time [that would] exhort men of
all classes to seek the good"; and the *Sermones nulli parcentes,* discussed
further below, offer biting, versified guidelines for estates preaching by friars.[34]

While an emphasis on moral reform is still in evidence here, there are
two important shifts. One is the growing tendency to combine that reforming claim with an interest in secular amusement, so that alongside the
works labeled, however satirically, as "sermons," we have *La Bible Guiot,*
by the "Epicurean monk" Guiot de Provins, written "to make his listeners laugh, apparently, and not to reform them," and many other texts in
which the bitter voice of the satirist gives way to a more comic tone.[35] The
other, particularly important change from actual sermons is in the identity of the speaker. Even when Jacques de Vitry, for instance, addresses the
faults of a clerical audience, it is still his own sacerdotal voice speaking the
critique, but the process of leveling begun in the *ad status* collections,
which set priests and bishops alongside other groups to be criticized with
(and often more forcefully than) those others, ends in a situation where
any speaker can adopt sermonic forms. Ultimately the speaking voice can
become not a priestly one but that of a failed monk or a secular poet.[36]

In the text I focus on here, the *Sermones nulli parcentes*—"sermons
that spare no one"—the speaking voice is still a clerical one and, as the title suggests, the work offers an intriguing hybrid of *sermones ad status* and
estates satire.[37] Most religious professions are addressed here as audiences
of sermons rather than as speakers and are given the same kinds of instruction as the lay groups. The exception is the "fratres qui populo
praedicant," who seem to be the work's primary audience: they receive
special placement as the group that is imagined to preach these "sermons"
to the others.[38] As with Honorius's "Ad sacerdotes," however, this text
that seems initially to leave preachers their privileged position as authori-

tative speakers eventually suggests the vulnerability of their claim to that role. Like the debt to impersonation and exempla in the *sermones ad status,* this vulnerability reflects the link between the preacher's voice and that of a "marginal" group, in this case women. But the link begins to lead toward an understanding of the ways in which both preachers and women challenge the categories of estates literature, including implicit distinctions between those who speak and those who listen.

The *Sermones nulli parcentes* begin with an address to the "brothers who go through all the world and circle it, preaching to the ignorant" and praises their exalted sermons on biblical topics.[39] The writer goes on to say that while such sermons are all very well, it is also important to preach "singulariter," individually, to show each person "how he may sincerely please God," echoing the concerns with particularity and moral reform that motivated the *sermones ad status.*[40] The "book of sermons" then begins and speaks first of the religious estates, from the pope, cardinals, patriarchs, and so on, down to nuns, and then turns to secular groups, ending with women.[41] Friars are addressed not in the list of estates but rather at the beginning and end of the poem. They thus take a special place as the purveyors or subjects, rather than the objects, of satire, the only group whose faults are not directly critiqued. They are further set apart as the addressees of the poem's frame, rather than of its "singular" criticisms, and thus are given a kind of universal status that valorizes their claim to be able to speak to all without being addressed by any.[42]

This exalted position is perhaps not surprising if we imagine the writer as one friar addressing others. Somewhat more puzzling is the unusual treatment of women. Whereas most of the individual "sermons" start right in with an address to the chosen group, or at most with an aside that "this is what you should say to X," the sermon to nuns that ends the religious estates begins instead with an address to the friars: "When you come to a cloister of women, attend, I pray, to the command of charity, so that you do not accuse them harshly. I do not say that you should spare them, however, but only that you should behave rather gently, lest you break a vessel of such fragility."[43] The speaker goes on to observe—drawing on a familiar misogynist trope—that "if something is prohibited a woman, it seems to her that she will die if she does not do that thing at once."[44] The "sermon" never switches out of a third-person, antifeminist-observation-of-women mode: that is, it never speaks to women directly but only talks about them.[45] Women are denied the chance to be even the audience of a sermon, much less its speakers. Nonetheless the author exhorts his brothers not to despair of preaching to nuns on account of their faults; to do so is a deviation from the path of charity. One must speak to them "with gentle speech" (*sermone blando*) and try to lead them to glory.[46] The chapter devoted to women in general, the last in the collection, takes a similar tack. The instructions here begin, "Honor women, never accuse them harshly," and the author goes on to note that the world was saved by a woman; that women do not respond well to criticism; that "each of us is, indeed, born of a woman"; and that "we" should thus honor "them."[47] This is followed, once again, by the plea not to break such a fragile vessel but to preach frequently to women in an appropriate manner that takes their weaknesses into account. Women, like nuns, are never addressed directly. The emphasis on the preacher's approach and attitude to his subjects, rather than on those subjects themselves, is striking.

Immediately following the instructions on preaching to women is the final section of the *Sermones* concerning "those friars who preach to the people." The approach here is the reverse of that in the sections on women: the text is entirely in the form of direct address to the author's "brothers" in preaching. They are, notably, the only group in the collection defined as preachers; though patriarchs' duty to preach is mentioned, it is not stressed as their primary function. And because the friars hold an unusual and privileged place in this work, preachers do not come in for the same kinds of criticism as do other groups. Unlike the preceding chapters, this one speaks almost exclusively to what friars *should* do, spending little time on how they fall short of this—with one exception. Toward the end of the passage, having exhorted his brothers always to display "a constant tongue, religious living and infinite charity," the author concludes, "Flee wicked associations with women, lest, God forbid, you should pollute the image of divinity. And if you should hold conversation with them, I beg that only the mouth should speak, and that the hand should not be pressed, for God is not praised in this way."[48] This is the end of the main part of the text; the remaining eight lines consist of a declaration that the work is complete and a prayer to the Virgin Mary.[49] Such a conclusion suggests that the crucial weakness to which friars are subject is women and that the repeated insistence that they should, in charity, preach to women puts them in jeopardy of sexual sin.[50] This, combined with the third-person treatment of women, seems to imply that the moral failings of women are peculiarly transferable and that friars are in especial danger of such contagion.

The conjunction between women and friars in this text, I argue, is no accident. It reflects the anomalous position of both groups in the framework of estates satire and the ways in which they elude or question it, and that challenge to the estates mode helps in turn to clarify the vulnerability of the preacher's voice. Although women and clerics—especially friars—seem at first to hold antithetical positions in estates satire, they are linked by two factors. The first is their very anomaly: each group holds, in a sense, a marked place in these satires. Women's role in estates literature is particularly uncertain since they do not fit neatly into any one of the "three orders" on which that literature is based.[51] They thus form, as Shulamith Shahar has put it, a "fourth estate" and are inserted into late medieval estates satire under various headings: by marital status, by religious calling, and occasionally as members of various other professions.[52] Frequently they are tacked on to the end of the lists of estates (as in the *Sermones nulli parcentes*) in a way that suggests their belatedness and outsider status. The clergy, on the other hand, are in the reverse situation: they are right at the center of estates satire, as both "the estates most frequently and fully treated by satirists"—many estates pieces go through all clerical ranks before turning to the secular ranks, and some address only the clergy—and often, it seems, the creators of the critique.[53] These roles reflect simultaneously a view of the clergy as the most important or eminent group in society, responsible for the moral well-being of others, and also a sense that their high responsibilities make them particularly apt to fall short of what is expected.[54] The contrasting positions of women and friars in estates literature are suggested by each group's unusual relationship to the sermonic voice: friars are the privileged speakers ("we"), women purely the object of speech ("they"); neither is in the standard audience position of "you." The *Sermones nulli parcentes* imply, however, that women's exclusion from the authoritative speaking voice offers no protection to that voice but rather undermines it by calling attention to the susceptibility of its speakers.

The second factor that links women and clerics is the long-standing existence of anticlerical and antifeminist traditions in medieval culture, which shape the characterizations of the late medieval satires. These traditions appear side by side in one of the earliest treatments of either theme in Christian writings, the pastoral Epistles of Paul.[55] The injunctions on clerical and female speech and clerical and female sexual behavior, presented almost simultaneously in the first Epistle to Timothy, prove to have a lasting effect; in the medieval tradition, women and clerics have notably similar failings.[56] Women are accused most commonly of garrulousness, pride, worldliness, sexual promiscuity, gluttony, and being spendthrift.[57] Clerical critiques tend to focus on worldliness and in particular avarice; vainglory; misuse of speech (failure to preach, deception, flattery, and preaching for personal gain are favorite themes); soft living; and sexual misconduct—as well as an overall failure to fulfill their duties.[58] Although presented in different forms, the shortcomings parallel each other: sins related to money and material comfort, to self-indulgence, to pride, to speech, and to sex. The latter two, speech and sex, are particularly important because several sins described as especially characteristic of these two classes, such as greed and pride, are widespread criticisms of many groups. Sins of the tongue and sexual sins thus seem to be outstandingly characteristic of women and clerics. Moreover, as the *Sermones* suggest, there is both overlap among the sins themselves and a constitutive relationship between the sins of women and the sins of clerics: each promotes the other.[59]

The emphasis on and association between sexual and verbal sin, though it appears in critiques of many clerical ranks, is especially typical of antifraternal satire. Accusations of verbal and physical seduction are a staple of antifraternal literature from its inception, drawing on biblical warnings about false prophets and their particular success with women.[60] While the critiques of friars certainly had jurisdictional and ecclesiological underpinnings, they may also have served to solidify the status of other clergy. Rejecting the friars and their associations with women could be one way of disclaiming the links to excluded voices that both enabled and threatened the preacher's speech and returning to that speech its ordered, hierarchical univocality.[61]

Insubordinate Fictions: Satire, Exemplum, Fabliau

Even in a relatively straightforward text such as the *Sermones nulli parcentes,* whose intent seems anything but antifraternal, troubling questions about the friars begin to arise as soon as they are associated with women. But those concerns about friars and women, far from returning control to a more authoritative or unworldly clerical speaker, instead contribute to a growing diversity of voices. As the potential misbehavior hinted at in the *Sermones* becomes the subject of full-fledged satire, it gives rise to an extensive literature of critique whose detailed depiction of female and fraternal shortcomings demonstrates, as do *sermones ad status,* the danger inherent in characterizing particular groups in order to rebuke them more effectively. In characterizing their subjects these texts end up creating characters; in speaking for or as those figures they end by giving them a voice.[62] This effect is most evident in a genre that deploys the stereotypes of antifeminist and anticlerical satire to a nearly obsessive degree: in the corpus of Old French fabliaux almost every other tale depicts the connivances of a lustful priest or friar with a dissatisfied wife.[63] The lively characters of this genre are the epitome of clerical-female complicity, a complicity characterized by the manipulation of speech in the service of sexual appetite.

Fabliaux are by no means a side issue in a discussion of preaching, for they reflect an important debate that has to do precisely with the preacher's control over the voices he borrows. The strictures against *fabulae* that come in the same breath as instructions on the use of exempla, and the fulminations against preachers who misuse narrative, demonstrate how easily an entertaining but morally efficacious story could cross the line—if a line even existed—into vain amusement. Without an appropriate doctrinal context to anchor the exemplum and fill it with meaning, it was capable of being detached and, while perhaps retaining a reputation for moral value, becoming a mere empty tale. The difference between collections of virtuous exempla and of scandalous fabliaux is primarily that the latter have been expanded, "fleshed out," in a way that seems to have happened to exempla in their spoken, sermon context, not in their written form.[64] It was in the course of such expansions that the figures presented in exempla could become full-fledged characters with voices of their own. Many exempla are clearly only a small step from fabliaux, as Marie Anne Polo de Beaulieu's summation of some of Johannes Gobi's exempla shows: "ruse by wife helps lover escape . . . same ruse by pilgrim's wife . . . drunken husband placed in convent" are all fabliau plots redeemed here by their intended didactic context.[65] Thus, although exempla were supposed to be "subordinate" to the preacher's doctrinal point, they always threatened to escape their confines.[66] Once a story or a figure had been given the realistic detail and link to lived experience that made it effective, it could attain a new independence from its context and deliver a message—not only about the preacher's doctrine, but perhaps about the preacher himself—very different from the one he intended.

The potential insubordination of fiction was one problem with exempla in sermons; another was the genre's feminine associations. As early as the Pauline Epistles, which warn against "worldly fables fit only for old

women" (1 Tim. 4:7, sometimes translated as "old wives' tales"), a taste
for useless stories was imagined as a peculiarly female attribute. And anxiety about feminine speech—gossip—runs through preaching manuals,
which reliably repeat injunctions against scurrilous storytelling and show,
in many cases, concerns about overfamiliarity with the laity and with
women in particular.[67] However, even as lay speech, in the form of "fables," threatens the purity of clerical speech, it is regarded as an effective
form of that speech and indeed at times as hardly distinguishable from it.
Larry Scanlon discusses an exemplum that figures the news of Christ's
Resurrection as "rumor," the ultimate in flighty feminine speech; in another instance of such a conflation, misogynist interpretation of the Bible
declared that Mary Magdalene was first told the news of the resurrection
because Christ knew that a woman could not keep a secret.[68] This interpretation denigrates Mary's speech, of course, but it also suggests, as does
the rumor exemplum, that preaching and gossip are ultimately the same
thing.[69] As Silvana Vecchio has pointed out, "eloquence, separated from
wisdom and constancy, was transformed into *garrulitas*": if the preacher's
conduct was not capable of providing an appropriate framework for his
speech, that speech could become indistinguishable from women's chat-
ter.[70]

Both exempla and fabliaux, then, can suggest a troubling similarity
between clerical and lay, especially female, speech. Like the antifeminist
and antifraternal modes of estates satire, moreover, fabliaux bring to life
characters who embody the potential for carnal relationships between
women and clerics. When the preaching voice is filtered through satire,
the result is the creation of figures capable of appropriating the already
destabilized voice of authority. The solidity of antifeminist and antifraternal stereotypes both emphasizes and challenges these groups' unusual position in estates literature. As the women excluded from clerical discourse
and the scapegoated representatives of that discourse are brought together through exempla, fabliaux, and estates satires, they create a potent
combination that ultimately invalidates any voice that would claim to criticize others while escaping critique itself.

Poets, Priests, and Wives: The Chattering Classes

The transformation of "traditional polemic materials into more or less
self-contained dramatic forms" was, as Derek Pearsall has observed, a fa-

vorite technique of Chaucer's, one he employs particularly in his depiction of the friar in the *Summoner's Tale,* and in the Wife of Bath's and Pardoner's *Prologues.*[71] The polemic materials themselves inadvertently invited such treatment, as I have argued above, but Chaucer's use of them goes beyond what previous authors had done. He takes up the bodies and voices imagined by the *sermones ad status* and estates literature—priests and preachers alongside wives—and exploits their dismantling of privileged priestly speech to give voice to his own "Mother Tongue," as Hanning has brilliantly dubbed her.[72] His characterization of the Wife of Bath offers a striking instance of how, in the English vernacular context, the developments in preaching literature discussed above contributed to the creation of an authoritative lay voice.

Chaucer takes from the preaching tradition not only the tools to create a poetic voice but also a warning. Estates sermons and satires focus attention on the body of the preacher in a way that shows how such scrutiny undercuts any claim to disinterested speech, and Chaucer demonstrates how well he understood their lessons. He uses the impersonated voices bequeathed by preaching in a way that both highlights how the speaker, far from standing "above and outside . . . fallen humanity," is implicated in his own critique of it and at the same time ostentatiously evades those critiques himself. He claims to speak only as a reporter or a translator, recognizing that this "delegated" authority will enable him to elude the critiques authority is heir to. The Wife of Bath, I argue, is the perfect vehicle for the expression of Chaucer's inheritances from and challenge to the preaching tradition because she most insistently foregrounds the debt of the preaching voice to the body that produces it and at the same time allows Chaucer to deflect attention from his own persona onto hers.

To create the voices of the *Canterbury Tales,* Chaucer exploited a rhetorical device central to the *sermones ad status,* the doctrine of rhetorical appropriateness.[73] Part of this concept is the idea, noted above, that the preacher's voice should conform itself to his audience. In the *Canterbury Tales* this concern is flipped around: now the voice must fit not the audience but the speaker, although that speaker must in turn, like a preacher, take account of his audience.[74] As Glending Olson has observed, in the rhetorical concept of "circumstances"—the question of to whom, where, when, why, and how one speaks—lies "the conceptual link between the estates tradition . . . and the storytelling."[75] Chaucer goes to great pains to note that "whoso shal telle a tale after a man, / He moot reherce as ny as evere he kan . . . Or ellis he moot telle his tale untrewe, / Or feyne thyng, or fynde wordes newe"; he goes on to justify the license of speech that this entails by claiming the ultimate authority: "Crist spak hymself ful brode in hooly writ, / And wel ye woot no vileynye is it."[76] This allusion simultaneously justifies Chaucer in his role as reporter/author and assimilates the characters who speak "brode" to the ultimate preacher. Thanks to the transformations of *sermones ad status* and estates satire, and the transfers of voice they have effected, the issue is no longer solely the preacher's responsibility to reach his audience but the "reporter's" duty accurately to represent that audience as it talks back.[77]

Chaucer makes a similar move in the lines immediately following those quoted above: "Eek Plato seith, whoso that kan hym rede, / The wordes moot be cosyn to the dede."[78] This principle informs preaching; the insistence that the preacher should reinforce his verbal teachings by his behavior runs through the preaching manuals. But the context here makes it a statement about accurate imitation and faithful representation: about the reporter's responsibility, again, to those whose speech he records (and implicitly to his audience, to give a faithful account).[79] By inverting the conventions that shape the preacher's voice Chaucer diffuses the location of authoritative speech, focusing our attention—as do the genres he draws on—on speaking bodies other than his own.[80] Many of these bodies, particularly those of the Pardoner and of the friar in the *Summoner's Tale*, do their part to undermine the preaching voice through the problematic way in which they claim it. But it is in the *Wife of Bath's Prologue* that we see most clearly the implications and legacy of the sermon tradition that lies behind the *Canterbury Tales*.

Lee Patterson has suggested that the Wife of Bath is "a model for the poet" and later that "the Wife's performance provided Chaucer with an opportunity to represent and defend his own poetic activity."[81] Here I build on Patterson's analysis to suggest some ways in which the Wife's relationship to Chaucer's poetic voice recalls and develops her relationship to the clerical voice she embodies (as the physical representation of its worst nightmares), challenges, and appropriates. That the Wife takes on a clerical voice and practices clerical tricks to justify herself has long been noted, and my concern here is not to replicate or simply reiterate the excellent work that has explored her mimicry of masculine language.[82] Instead, I offer a juxtaposition of the Wife with estates satire on clerics and their concubines in order to permit a "return of the repressed," as Elliott calls the priest's wife. What is repressed here, and what the Wife makes visible, is the clerical voice's allegiance not just to the feminine body but to the very priestly body that the Gregorian reform tried to set apart from human concerns and weaknesses. Considered in this light the Wife is by no means a woman trapped by the prison-house of masculine, clerical language; instead she is the voice in which Chaucer deconstructs that language and its claims to disembodied authority.[83]

The Wife's efficacy emerges with particular clarity when her *Prologue* is considered alongside satirical poems on the wives of priests. These poems complete the transfer of voice begun in the *sermones ad status* and estates satire: instead of the usual approach, in which the wickedness of a group is addressed or lamented by an "outside" voice, these texts—like Chaucer's *Canterbury Tales*—allow the objects of the satire to speak for themselves. The priests are the performers of the satire that critiques them, using their authoritative voices and texts unwittingly to condemn themselves in the first person. Thomas Wright included three such treatments of clerical wives in his collection of poems (falsely) attributed to Walter Map: "De concubinis sacerdotum," "Consultatio sacerdotum," and "De convocatione sacerdotum."[84] The third of these is largely a recapitulation of the second. "De concubinis sacerdotum" and "Consultatio sacerdotum," on which I will focus here, have instructive differences but are both noteworthy for the ways in which their manipulation of the clerical voice foreshadows that of the Wife of Bath.[85]

"De concubinis sacerdotum," which was probably written in the early thirteenth century, consists of a narratorial introduction that suggests that banning clerical wives will simply lead priests to prey on the wives of others.[86] The voice then becomes that of a priest ("Ita quidam presbyter caepit allegare"), who presents a fairly reasoned argument for clerical marriage, based primarily on arguments from the Old Testament and tradition. "The Old Testament teaches us to multiply; nowhere is the New found to prohibit this," he asserts, and rings several changes on this motif.[87] The Wife of Bath, too, is fond of the Old Testament: "God bad us for to wexe and multiplye; / That gentil text kan I wel understonde," she declares, adding later, "Wher can ye seye, in any manere age, / That hye God defended mariage / By expres word? I pray yow, telleth me."[88] The priest in "De concubinis" goes on to ask, "Do soldiers not proceed from soldiers, and kings from kings, to succeed them?," a point picked up by the Wife: "Certes, if ther were no seed ysowe, / Virginitee, thanne wherof sholde it growe?"[89] The clerical speaker even anticipates the Wife's observations about "membres of generacioun" and her "sely instrument":

"The Old Testament, which is the true foundation of our law, teaches us that men and women should know that instrument by which they may have increase of offspring."[90] In a particularly pleasing reversal, the priest in "De concubinis" uses as his final authority Saint Paul himself, noting that it was *after* Paul was carried up to the third heaven, where he learned "many very secret things," that he came back to give moral instruction, including "Let those who wish have their wives."[91] Even the Wife's usage, or rather evasion, of Paul's teachings does not go quite so far in claiming him as an advocate for marriage—and certainly not for clerical marriage.[92]

"De concubinis sacerdotum," like the *Wife of Bath's Prologue*, draws on a long-established marriage debate for its terms.[93] What makes it unusual is its placement of a clerical proponent of the arguments for marriage in a satirical frame in which his claim that "on account of these learned teachings [*dogmata doctorum*] and others, I believe it to be better, and more becoming [*decorum*], that each [priest] should have his own [wife]" undercuts the very concepts that he exploits.[94] Christian doctrine and priestly decorum were widely considered to militate against clerical marriage, not to support it; in reversing their emphasis the poem makes a teasing point about the reliability of clerical authority. It is important to recognize that the priest's position here is not entirely ludicrous. Although the second Lateran Council in 1139 had officially banned clerical marriage, the battle was far from over, even in the wake of Lateran IV's reassertion of the need for clerical celibacy.[95] The difficulties in implementing the decrees made the lecherous priest, as Elliott observes, "a stock figure in the anticlerical arsenal of secular letters."[96] The priest of "De concubinis" is not sufficiently characterized, however, to be called lecherous; his physicality does not undermine his message since he never claims a personal interest in the matter. Although he is a *presbyter* himself, he speaks of the problem of clerical wives in a detached, third-person manner throughout the poem, ultimately declaring that he has spoken for (*pro*) clerics and priests and that they and their wives should say a paternoster for him. This detachment, along with the historical context and the relatively traditional nature of the arguments, diminishes the severity of the satire; it is primarily the narrator's references to Bacchus and Venus, along with the poetic form, that make the priest's careful argument seem dubious.[97]

The tone sharpens and we come still closer to the Wife of Bath in the "Consultatio sacerdotum."[98] Rather than one measured clerical voice presenting impersonal biblical arguments, here there is a babble of clerical speakers—well over twenty in all—offering every possible rationale that comes to mind in order to keep their wives in the face of a prohibition from the "praesul."[99] The speakers range from a "doctor and prelate learned in canon law" through cantor, cellarer, scholastic, and numerous priests. The poem is a veritable compendium of clerical offices, ending with a "monachus praedicator."[100] In this it recalls the tendency of *sermones ad status* to divide and subdivide social groups, and it diminishes the sense of a monolithic clerical class by emphasizing that class's diversity. Nevertheless the clerics here do speak with the single voice that the twelfth and thirteenth centuries desired from their *auctores*. Unfortunately for the proponents of an idealized clergy, what that one voice expresses is a refusal to give up female companionship.

The variety of speakers and the near-total lack of an external narrative voice immediately set this poem apart from "De concubinis sacerdotum"; the distance is emphasized when, early in the poem, a little squabble arises between two of the speakers. An "elder with trembling step" declares that since he's not up to much any more he will not complain if his companion is taken away. A "crafty cantor" objects loudly that this is no reason why everyone else should have to suffer, causing the elder to blush mightily and modify his position to urge discretion before the laity. At this point a cellarer jumps in to observe that since he is currently married to an ugly shrew (*meretrix monocula*) he'll be happy to trade her in for the elder's discarded concubine, an offer that leads to general merriment.[101] There can be no doubt that we are in the sexual-slapstick world of fabliau and that incongruous context highlights the clerical nature of the arguments that are brought to bear.

The clerics in the "Consultatio" use varied tactics to justify themselves, as noted above, and like those in "De concubinis," many reappear in the *Wife of Bath's Prologue*. The first speaker, a "doctor et praelatus" well-versed in canon law, claims that the rule of chastity is a harsh one and that "only angelic life is pure"; another argues scholastically, "No man is obliged to do that which is impossible; you know that modesty is not given to clerics; it is therefore concluded that we should keep our mistresses"; still others simply assert their desire to keep their wives, one going so far as to declare that he would not give her up for God himself.[102] The general tone of the argument, as well as certain particular points, would be familiar to a reader of the *Wife of Bath's Prologue*. We might note particularly that she too uses the scholastic concept of the "impossibile": "For trusteth wel, it is an impossible / That any clerk wol speke good of wyves, / But if it be of hooly seintes lyves."[103] But where the Wife asserts that it is impossible that a cleric should speak well of wives—that is, that the clerical tradition should give any respect to a secular woman—the clerical speaker asserts that the impossibility is not for clerics to speak well of wives, but for clerics to do without them. The juxtaposition of those two claims suggests that the clergy's relationship to their own authoritative language is inflected by their attitudes toward and their relationships with women.

The "preacher monk" who has the last word in the "Consultatio" makes an elaborate scriptural argument whose mode will again ring a bell with any reader of the Wife: "Who knows whether the Creator would wish / that a priest should cease to be a lover of women, / for whom the Savior was placed on the Cross? / Zachary had descendants and a wife, / who gave birth to John, the great son, / the preacher of the whole world's Redeemer; / I do not believe that he sins who preserves this custom."[104] The example of Zachary also appears in "De concubinis," but there Zachary's son John is characterized as the baptizer of Christ; his role as preacher, emphasized here, manages to suggest that just as a lack of wives would mean a lack of virgins, so in the absence of married priests there would be no preachers. The very "thundering" voice that condemns clerical marriage and the other faults of society is dependent in the most fundamental way on the carnal relationship between priests and women.

The preaching monk eventually concludes, in a delightful parody of the entire concept of estates literature, that the pope (depicted here as a married man himself) "laborare rusticos, milites pugnare / jussit, at praecipue clericos amare" ("ordered peasants to work, soldiers to fight, and, especially, clerics to love").[105] No longer is it a cleric's duty to pray for the other two orders; clearly his calling in life is amorous. Women have taken the place of divinely oriented speech, and the priests' (considerable) learning, which should enable them to preach to the populace and improve spiritual welfare, is put in the service of their own carnal desires. In the process the priestly speaker's claim to be disinterested is completely undermined; biblical quotation, scholastic argument, and moral exhortation are exposed as simply other ways of getting what you want.

The Wife of Bath, of course, is well aware of this and fully avails herself of the clerical privileges. If, as the satirical context suggests, those privileges are designed simply to give clerics access to women, why should women not profit as well? She manages simultaneously, moreover, to accuse her husbands of exactly this trick, repeatedly accusing them of "preaching" and of placing themselves in authoritative masculine company (including Saint Paul and the pope), even as she undermines the claim of misogynistic authority to be disinterested.[106] Her repetitions of "Thou seist . . . thou seist" bring the argument back to personal experience, exactly where the text-based antifeminist tradition claims not to be.[107] Both the second-person address and the references to the husbands' diatribes against her remove any suggestion that preaching here is a lofty or elevated form of speech. The Wife points out just how hollow and self-interested the husbands' supposedly authoritative discourse (as they quote Job and "olde Romayn geestes" at her) really is. Susan Signe Morrison has noted the "Thou seist" speeches and observed that "even the Wife admits that husbands preach."[108] I would suggest, though, that the Wife's attribution of preaching to her husbands is by no means an admission; rather it is an accusation. As such, it is of a piece with her satirical adoption of clerical discourse and with the deauthorizing of the name of preacher that is part of Chaucer's project throughout the *Canterbury Tales.*

When the Wife jumps in ahead of the Parson in the tale-telling, then, she does not just displace or temporarily defer his orthodox sermonic voice.[109] Instead her preemptive strike demonstrates that voice's already-existing allegiance or at least susceptibility to the very same kinds of self-interest and carnality that are supposed to characterize women. In the end, according to the Wife and the "Consultatio sacerdotum," all preachers really are is husbands, arguing with or for their wives. As the secular becomes the subject of sermons, and the clerical world the object of satire, the secular world comes to produce literary "subjects" who speak their own sermons, texts that preach themselves in a way that undermines any claim that preaching could be a disinterested or selfless activity. Ultimately those subjects talk back to the preachers who helped to create them, and the audience takes over the preaching voice, providing the final blow to the claim of untouchable authority.

This vernacular attitude is reflected in the use of the word "preche" throughout the *Canterbury Tales:* it almost always refers to an individual's self-interested discourse. The Wife's—and Chaucer's—success in undermining the clerical voice's authoritative claims is suggested by the fact that the Parson, the only figure with the kind of moral qualifications to preach that the church would recognize, never once uses the term to refer to himself. When other characters speak of him as a preacher, the tone is mocking.[110] The Pardoner, by contrast, calls himself a preacher almost obsessively, and the term is also applied to the Summoner's friar numerous times by himself and others.[111] Since both the Pardoner and the Summoner's friar are utterly corrupt in their use of clerical speech, the repeated application of the term to them makes it more an accusation than a badge of honor. The Wife of Bath clearly takes it in this sense as she reports her direct speech to her husbands: "ye preche," "prechestow," she berates them. She never once refers to herself as a preacher—partly, of course, because as a woman she cannot do so without drawing fire, but also because her character's very existence is predicated on the association of preaching with debased and dubious forms of speech.

It is no accident that, among the pilgrims, it is the Friar and the Pardoner, the figures whose language the Wife of Bath most closely approximates and appropriates, who attempt to label and contain her speech by calling her a preacher. They do so both to suggest that, as a woman, she is out of line and to undermine the force of what she says by pointing out its self-interestedness. In doing so, of course, they condemn themselves. "Ye ben a noble prechour in this cas," the Pardoner observes or complains to the Wife.[112] Although his use of the term implies a critique of the Wife—recalling the troubling figure of the woman preacher and here one whose message is decidedly unorthodox—it also points to the sense that every preacher is also an advocate, one who speaks to a particular "case" and whose claim to an authoritative voice deserves no more or less credit than the next speaker's.[113] And the Friar's attempt to put the Wife in her place by suggesting that they should leave "auctoritees" to "prechyng and to scoles of clergye" is equally revealing.[114] He suggests that she is in the wrong mode for the circumstances, but more importantly he is implicitly questioning her right to use "auctoritees" and trying to confine her to a world of "play" and "game" in which her speech does not threaten the clerical monopoly. But it is too late, for the Wife has already claimed this position herself: "myn entente is nat but for to pleye," she asserts.[115] The fact that she is a threat even from the world of "play" indicates the imperfect boundaries between play and seriousness, fabliaux and exempla, women's speech and clerics'.[116] And the Pardoner and the Friar will shortly demonstrate that the Wife's misreadings and self-interested glossing are in fact no worse than their own.[117] Insofar as *preacher* is a term of abuse, they are truly the *noble prechours* in this text.

The "game" world of fabliau, gossip, and parody gives rise to a play of voices that enables new speakers to intervene in the supposedly serious and unified discourse of preaching.[118] The Parson, the Friar, and the Pardoner all, in different ways, try to contain the speech of preaching, to retain the voice of one thundering from above and outside. But they are locking the barn door after the horse has bolted; already, when "Paul" wrote his Epistle to Timothy about clerics and wives, when Tertullian wrote his rhetorically elaborate invectives against the allure of rhetorical fictions, preaching was beholden to old wives' tales, and preachers to women.[119] All the old Wife does is to make this explicit and concrete by displaying in the starkest mirror possible the clerical tendency to tell stories, gloss for one's own profit, and generally use clerical speech for personal ends. The friars are often used in medieval literature to epitomize the moral slipperiness of language, but their status as clerics, however tendentious their alliance with the rest of the ecclesiastical hierarchy, means that their preaching voices can always revert to an orthodox mode. Only by making the clerical voice a female one—by presenting the priest as Wife—can Chaucer sufficiently foreground that voice's unbreakable links to the bodies, clerical and female, that it tries to disavow.

In a world where the ability to speak *for* oneself and *of* others was a mark of power, it was perhaps inevitable that the "chattering classes"—women and preachers—would have a complex relationship to the system of classification by estates and to its authoritative voice.[120] Their position made them both most susceptible to its critiques and most capable of wielding those critiques against others. And it is perhaps not surprising that a vernacular author who adopted elements of both feminine and preacherly speech in creating his own effective and authoritative language should be in an ideal position to exploit a system of classification that he eluded. Chaucer is too clever to leave his person entirely outside his discourse; that privileged position is one the whole *Canterbury Tales*, and especially his preaching characters, shows to be hollow. Instead he makes himself just one more figure among many, the last of the pilgrims—but one whose "estate" is never clearly defined. "What man artow?" Harry Bailly famously asks Chaucer, who, as speaker rather than topic, is the only pilgrim not identified by profession in the *General Prologue*.[121] No wonder Harry was puzzled: among the many categorizations of the estates system, poets are nowhere to be found.

Abbreviations

Abbreviations are provided both for standard collections and for particular works cited frequently throughout the book. In the case of medieval preaching manuals, the most distinctive part of the author's name has been used, whether this is first name, last name, or geographic designation.

AA.SS.	Bollandus, J., and G. Henschenius. *Acta Sanctorum . . .* editio novissima. Edited by J. Carnandet et al. 68 vols. Paris: Palmé, 1863–.
Blamires and Marx	Blamires, Alcuin, and C. W. Marx. "Woman Not to Preach: A Disputation in British Library MS Harley 31." *Journal of Medieval Latin* 3 (1993): 34–63.
CCCM	Corpus Christianorum, Continuatio Mediaeualis. Turnhout, Belgium: Brepols, 1966–.
CCSL	Corpus Christianorum, Series Latina. Turnhout, Belgium: Brepols, 1953–.
Chobham	Thomas of Chobham. *Summa de arte praedicandi.* Edited by Franco Morenzoni. CCCM 82. Turnhout, Belgium: Brepols, 1988.
Dessì and Lauwers	Dessì, Rosa Maria, and Michel Lauwers, eds. *La parole du prédicateur, Vᵉ–XVᵉ siècle.* Nice: Centre d'Études Médiévales, 1997.
EETS	Early English Text Society. London: Trübner et al., 1864–.
Humbert	Humbert of Romans. *De eruditione praedicatorum.* In *B. Humberti de Romanis Opera de vita regulari,* 2 vols., edited by Joachim Joseph Berthier, 2:373–484. Rome: Marietti, 1888–89.
Kienzle and Walker	Kienzle, Beverly Mayne, and Pamela J. Walker, eds. *Women Preachers and Prophets Through Two Millennia of Christianity.* Berkeley and Los Angeles: University of California Press, 1998.
Leclercq	Leclercq, Jean. "Le magistère du prédicateur au XIIIᵉ siècle." *Archives d'histoire doctrinale et littéraire du moyen âge* 21 (1946): 105–47.
PL	Migne, J.-P., ed. *Patrologia cursus completus: Series latina.* 221 vols. Paris: Migne, 1844–1902.

Waleys   Waleys, Thomas. *De modo componendi sermones, cum documentis.* Edited by Thomas-Marie Charland. In Charland, *Artes praedicandi: Contribution a l'histoire de la rhétorique au moyen âge,* 325–40. Paris: J. Vrin, 1936.

Notes

Introduction

1. An introduction to these texts can be found in Marianne G. Briscoe, *Artes praedicandi,* published with *Artes orandi,* by Barbara H. Jaye, Typologie des sources du moyen âge occidental 61 (Turnhout, Belgium: Brepols, 1992). Most of the known *artes* are cataloged in Harry Caplan, *Mediaeval Artes Praedicandi: A Hand-List* (Ithaca, N.Y.: Cornell University Press, 1934) and *Mediaeval Artes Praedicandi: A Supplementary Hand-List* (Ithaca, N.Y.: Cornell University Press, 1936).

2. In *English Preaching in the Late Middle Ages* (Oxford: Clarendon Press, 1993), Helen Leith Spencer makes a similar point in justifying her attention to "radicals and reformers" who might be said to "belong to the fringes of the subject, not its center"; she argues that "these men were engaging, more or less articulately, with some of the most important challenges confronting the Church and society in their day" (14). Spencer's work focuses on preaching in the period c.1370–c. 1500, and the views on preaching studied in the present work thus form the backdrop or tradition drawn on by the preachers she considers. In both cases the study of the periphery has much to say about the center.

3. Although in some cases women's preaching is rejected on purely physical grounds, such as women's putative lack of strength or insufficiently loud voices, most of the arguments are primarily social; hence I use the term *gender* rather than *sex,* although the medieval theorists generally regard women's subordination, inconstancy, and other disqualifying traits as "natural" sexual characteristics.

4. For a discussion of medieval ideas about the body, "the flesh," and their particular relationship to women that touches on many of the same issues considered here, see Karma Lochrie, *Margery Kempe and Translations of the Flesh* (Philadelphia: University of Pennsylvania Press, 1991), 1–55.

5. On the reform movement generally, see Giles Constable, *The Reformation of the Twelfth Century* (Cambridge: Cambridge University Press, 1996). André Vauchez, *The Laity in the Middle Ages: Religious Beliefs and Devotional Practices,* ed. Daniel E. Bornstein, trans. Margery J. Schneider (Notre Dame, Ind.: University of Notre Dame Press, 1993), 97–99, offers a brief discussion of the reform in the context of pastoral developments.

6. Malcolm Lambert, "The Revival of Heresy in the West: The Eleventh Century," in his *Medieval Heresy: Popular Movements from the Gregorian Reform to the Reformation,* 2d ed. (Oxford: Basil Blackwell, 1992), 9–32.

7. Brian Stock, *The Implications of Literacy: Written Language and Models of*

Interpretation in the Eleventh and Twelfth Centuries (Princeton, N.J.: Princeton University Press, 1983), 151–240.

8. On the new developments in this concept in the eleventh and twelfth centuries, see M.-D. Chenu, *Nature, Man, and Society in the Twelfth Century: Essays on New Theological Perspectives in the Latin West*, ed. and trans. Jerome Taylor and Lester K. Little (Chicago: University of Chicago Press, 1968), 202–69; and Herbert Grundmann, *Religious Movements in the Middle Ages: The Historical Links between Heresy, the Mendicant Orders, and the Women's Religious Movement in the Twelfth and Thirteenth Century, with the Historical Foundations of German Mysticism*, trans. Steven Rowan (Notre Dame, Ind.: University of Notre Dame Press, 1995), 7–30.

9. I do not mean, here or elsewhere, to imply that there was no worthwhile preaching in the period leading up to the twelfth century, nor that the clergy were uniformly inadequate to their office; several recent collections that cover preaching throughout the Middle Ages demonstrate the untruth of such a claim. See, for example, Rosa Maria Dessì and Michel Lauwers, eds., *La parole du prédicateur, V^e–XVe siècle* (Nice: Centre d'Études Médiévales, 1997) (hereafter Dessì and Lauwers); Jacqueline Hamesse and Xavier Hermand, eds., *De l'homélie au sermon: Histoire de la prédication médiévale* (Louvain-la-Neuve: Université Catholique de Louvain, Publications de l'Institut d'Études Médiévales, 1993); Thomas L. Amos, Eugene A. Green, and Beverly Mayne Kienzle, eds., De Ore Domini: *Preacher and Word in the Middle Ages* (Kalamazoo, Mich.: Medieval Institute Publications, 1989). The evidence does strongly suggest, however, that for various reasons the preaching of the orthodox clergy in the tenth to twelfth centuries was not fulfilling all the spiritual requirements of the laity, who therefore turned to other sources of religious instruction offered by wandering preachers, hermits, and heretics (not necessarily mutually exclusive groups).

10. Grundmann, *Religious Movements*, 30. See also Richard H. Rouse and Mary A. Rouse, *Preachers, Florilegia, and Sermons: Studies on the* Manipulus Florum *of Thomas of Ireland*, Studies and Texts 47 (Toronto: Pontifical Institute of Mediaeval Studies, 1979), 46–47.

11. For introductions to the issues involved in unlicensed preaching by these various groups, see Beverly Mayne Kienzle, "Preaching as Touchstone of Orthodoxy and Dissidence in the Middle Ages," *Medieval Sermon Studies* 43 (1999): 19–54; John M. Trout, "Preaching by the Laity in the Twelfth Century," *Studies in Medieval Culture* 4, no. 1 (1973): 92–108; and the essays on medieval culture in Beverly Mayne Kienzle and Pamela J. Walker, eds., *Women Preachers and Prophets through Two Millennia of Christianity* (Berkeley and Los Angeles: University of California Press, 1998) (hereafter Kienzle and Walker).

12. This is the case, for instance, with Norbert of Xanten, who founded the Praemonstratensians, and Robert of Arbrissel, who founded the monastery of Fontevrault. On the widespread phenomenon of the "hermit preacher," see Patrick Henriet, "*Verbum Dei disseminando:* La parole des ermites prédicateurs d'après les sources hagiographiques (XIe–XIIe siècles)," in Dessì and Lauwers, 153–85.

13. On Innocent's activities in this realm, see Jane Sayers, *Innocent III:*

Leader of Europe, 1198–1216 (London: Longman, 1994), 125–63, particularly 141–50, and Rosalind B. Brooke, *The Coming of the Friars* (London: George Allen & Unwin, 1975), 79–88. Brooke offers an important reminder of Innocent's less amiable and inclusive activities, particularly his ferocity toward unrepentant heretics (86–87). The classic account of the darker side of ecclesiastical attempts at reform and renewal in this period is R. I. Moore, *The Formation of a Persecuting Society: Power and Deviance in Western Europe, 950–1250* (Oxford: Basil Blackwell, 1990).

14. As Grundmann observes, for example, it was partly the dispersed and wandering character of the Waldensians that made them impossible to incorporate into the orthodox structure of the church (*Religious Movements*, 40–41).

15. The rise of the "pastoral theologians," Paris masters such as Peter the Chanter and Alan of Lille, is another mark of this renewed interest in pastoral care. See Rouse and Rouse, *Preachers*, 48–51; John W. Baldwin, *Masters, Princes, and Merchants: The Social Views of Peter the Chanter and His Circle*, 2 vols. (Princeton, N.J.: Princeton University Press, 1970), and Franco Morenzoni, *Des écoles aux paroisses: Thomas de Chobham et la promotion de la prédication au début du XIIIᵉ siècle* (Paris: Institut d'Études Augustiniennes, 1995).

16. Canon 10 of the council discusses the need for preachers (Norman P. Tanner, ed., *Decrees of the Ecumenical Councils: Vol. I, Nicaea I to Lateran V,* original text established by G. Alberigo et al. [London: Sheed and Ward; and Washington, D.C.: Georgetown University Press, 1990], 239–40).

17. Grundmann, *Religious Movements*, 66–67.

18. Ibid., 44–46, 55–58. Ray C. Petry notes Francis's "undeviating concern that preaching be in accord with the wishes of the properly authorized hierarchy and the liturgical church" ("Emphasis on the Gospel and Christian Reform in Late Medieval Preaching," *Church History* 16, no. 2 [1947]: 77, n. 7).

19. The ferocious resistance that often greeted the friars, like the jurisdictional battles over whether monks could preach, also demonstrates how hotly contested the territory of preaching could be even within the orthodox church. Since my main concern here is how preachers defined themselves in relation (not, I would stress, in opposition) to the laity, I have for the most part avoided extensive comment on these issues. For further discussion, see Yves M.-J. Congar, "Modèle monastique et modèle sacerdotal en occident, de Grégoire VII (1073–1085) à Innocent III (1198)," in *Études de civilisation médiévale (IXᵉ–XIIᵉ siècles): Mélanges offerts à Edmond-René Labande* (Poitiers: Centre d'Études Supérieures de Civilisation Médiévale, 1974), 153–60; M. Peuchmaurd, "Mission canonique et prédication: Le prêtre ministre de la parole dans la querelle entre mendiants et séculiers au XIIIᵉ siècle," *Recherches de théologie ancienne et médiévale* 30 (1963): 122–44, 251–76; M.-M. Dufeil, *Guillaume de Saint-Amour et la polémique universitaire parisienne, 1250–1259* (Paris: Éditions A. et J. Picard, 1972); and Penn Szittya, *The Antifraternal Tradition in Medieval Literature* (Princeton, N.J.: Princeton University Press, 1986).

20. As Étienne Gilson observes, this was perhaps not so much a new response as the revival of an old one; he suggests that "the *devotio moderna*, which owed its novelty to the stand it took against the scholasticism of the thirteenth century,

simply continues an older trend" already present in the twelfth century ("Introduction," in Chenu, *Nature, Man, and Society*, xii).

21. The literature on this subject is vast, but for an introduction see Caroline
Walker Bynum, *Holy Feast and Holy Fast: The Religious Significance of Food to Medieval Women* (Berkeley and Los Angeles: University of California Press, 1987);
John Coakley, "Friars, Sanctity, and Gender: Mendicant Encounters with Saints,
1250–1325," in *Medieval Masculinities: Regarding Men in the Middle Ages*, ed.
Clare A. Lees, with Thelma Fenster and Jo Ann McNamara (Minneapolis: Uni-
versity of Minnesota Press, 1994), 91–110; Anne Savage and Nicholas Watson, *An-
choritic Spirituality: Ancrene Wisse and Associated Works*, Classics of Western
Spirituality (Mahwah, N.J.: Paulist Press, 1991), 15–28; and Vauchez, *Laity in the
Middle Ages*, 73–82, 185–203, 219–29.

22. The close association between women and heresy is a commonplace from
the early days of the church, and its basis in fact has recently been questioned; see
Shannon McSheffrey, *Gender and Heresy: Women and Men in Lollard Communities, 1420–1530* (Philadelphia: University of Pennsylvania Press, 1995). The evidence
seems sufficient, however, to suggest that while women may not by any means
have dominated heretical groups, such groups did in many cases offer them, as
they offered laymen, a new chance to shape their own religious lives. See, for instance, Anne Brenon, "The Voice of the Good Women: An Essay on the Pastoral
and Sacerdotal Role of Women in the Cathar Church," in Kienzle and Walker,
114–33. On attacks against heretical women preachers, see in the same volume Beverly Kienzle, "The Prostitute-Preacher: Patterns of Polemic against Medieval
Waldensian Women Preachers," 99–113.

23. Some of the tensions particularly relevant to women's spirituality are discussed in Grace Jantzen, *Power, Gender and Christian Mysticism* (Cambridge:
Cambridge University Press, 1995).

24. Chenu, *Nature, Man, and Society*, 238.

25. Useful introductions are Yngve Brilioth, *A Brief History of Preaching*,
trans. Karl E. Mattson (Philadelphia: Fortress Press, 1965); and Jean Longère, *La
prédication médiévale* (Paris: Études Augustiniennes, 1983). On preaching as a
rhetorical form, see James J. Murphy, *Rhetoric in the Middle Ages: A History of
Rhetorical Theory from Saint Augustine to the Renaissance* (Berkeley and Los Angeles: University of California Press, 1974); and George A. Kennedy, *Classical
Rhetoric and Its Christian and Secular Tradition from Ancient to Modern Times*
(Chapel Hill: University of North Carolina Press, 1980). On vernacular preaching,
see Michel Zink, *La prédication en langue romane avant 1300* (Paris: Éditions
Honoré Champion, 1976). Jean Leclercq's article *cum documentis*, "Le magistère
du prédicateur au XIIIe siècle," *Archives d'histoire doctrinale et littéraire du moyen
âge* 21 (1946): 105–47) (hereafter Leclercq), is absolutely indispensable for a study
of the preacher's role. Because of the tremendous geographical and temporal
range of the subject, many of the most valuable recent works on medieval preaching are collections of essays, such as Kienzle and Walker; Hamesse and Hermand,
De l'homélie; Dessì and Lauwers; and Amos, Green, and Kienzle, *De Ore Domini*;
see also Beverly Mayne Kienzle et al., eds., *Models of Holiness in Medieval Sermons*
(Louvain-la-Neuve: Fédération Internationale des Instituts d'Études Médiévales,

1996), and Louis-Jacques Bataillon, *La prédication au XIIIe siècle en France et Italie: Études et documents* (Brookfield, Vt.: Variorum, 1993). Older but still useful studies are A. Lecoy de la Marche, *La chaire française au moyen âge, spécialement au XIIIe siècle* (Paris: Librairie Renouard, 1886); G. R. Owst, *Preaching in Medieval England: An Introduction to Sermon Manuscripts of the Period c.1350–1450* (Cambridge: Cambridge University Press, 1926) and *Literature and Pulpit in Medieval England: A Neglected Chapter in the History of English Letters and of the English People* (Cambridge: Cambridge University Press, 1933); and Thomas-Marie Charland, Artes praedicandi: *Contribution a l'histoire de la rhétorique au moyen âge* (Paris: Librairie Philosophique J. Vrin, 1936). Spencer, *English Preaching*, updates Owst in many ways and is particularly useful on the interaction of heretical and orthodox preaching in fourteenth- and fifteenth-century England. Roberto Rusconi, *Predicazione e vita religiosa nella società italiana da Carlo Magno alla Controriforma* (Turin: Loescher, 1981) provides a number of important primary texts, particularly but not exclusively relevant to Italy, in Italian translation, with introductory essays and notes. Important work on sermons in particular (i.e., not necessarily on preaching more broadly) is being done by Nicole Bériou, David d'Avray, and Siegfried Wenzel, among others; see also Beverly Mayne Kienzle, ed., *The Sermon,* Typologie des sources du moyen âge occidental 81–83 (Turnhout, Belgium: Brepols, 2001), a comprehensive collection.

26. As Nancy Partner observed in her introduction to the special 1993 issue of *Speculum,* "The restoration of women to the scene, to every locale and activity, restores a human world where body and mind are inextricably united. . . . If feminism, in its quite specialized role in medieval scholarship, is the energy behind this effort, then it is not only doing justice to medieval women, it is restoring their full humanity to medieval men" ("Introduction," *Studying Medieval Women: Sex, Gender, Feminism* [*Speculum* 68 (1993)], ed. Nancy F. Partner [Cambridge, Mass.: Medieval Academy of America, 1993], 306).

27. Dyan Elliott, *Fallen Bodies: Pollution, Sexuality, and Demonology in the Middle Ages* (Philadelphia: University of Pennsylvania Press, 1999). Recent collections include Jeffrey Jerome Cohen and Bonnie Wheeler, eds., *Becoming Male in the Middle Ages* (New York: Garland, 1997); D. M. Hadley, ed., *Masculinity in Medieval Europe* (London: Longman, 1999); and Clare A. Lees, ed., with Thelma S. Fenster and Jo Ann McNamara, *Medieval Masculinities: Regarding Men in the Middle Ages* (Minneapolis: University of Minnesota Press, 1994).

28. See particularly Miri Rubin, *Corpus Christi: The Eucharist in Late Medieval Culture* (Cambridge: Cambridge University Press, 1991); Sarah Beckwith, *Christ's Body: Identity, Culture and Society in Late Medieval Writings* (London and New York: Routledge, 1996); and David Aers and Lynn Staley, *The Powers of the Holy: Religion, Politics, and Gender in Late Medieval English Culture* (University Park: Pennsylvania State University Press, 1996), especially the first three chapters by Aers.

29. Aers and Staley, *Powers of the Holy,* 17–19, 37.

30. C. Stephen Jaeger, "Charismatic Body—Charismatic Text," *Exemplaria* 9, no. 1 (1997): 117–37.

31. Although scholars interested in the history of rhetoric have at times, un-

derstandably, suggested that some such texts are not *artes* in the strict sense (see, e.g., Charland, *Artes praedicandi,* 19), these works do address the art of becoming and behaving as a preacher, if not the art of sermon construction. I use the terms "*artes praedicandi,*" "preaching manuals," and "handbooks for preachers" interchangeably to refer to all members of the genre.

32. See Dyan Elliott, *Fallen Bodies, passim;* and Rita Copeland, "The Pardoner's Body and the Disciplining of Rhetoric," in *Framing Medieval Bodies,* ed. Sarah Kay and Miri Rubin (Manchester: Manchester University Press, 1994), 138–59.

33. Dyan Elliott, *Fallen Bodies,* 12.

34. G. G. Sedgewick, "The Progress of Chaucer's Pardoner, 1880–1940," *Modern Language Quarterly* 1, no. 4 (1940): 434.

35. Chaucer was highly aware of contemporary debates on preaching, and he uses preachers in various guises to explore his own concerns with the control, ownership, and authorization of speech. See Susan Gallick, "A Look at Chaucer and His Preachers," *Speculum* 50, no. 3 (July 1975): 456–476; Siegfried Wenzel, "Chaucer and the Language of Contemporary Preaching," *Studies in Philology* 73, no. 2 (1976): 138–61; and Sabine Volk-Birke, *Chaucer and Medieval Preaching: Rhetoric for Listeners in Sermons and Poetry* (Tübingen: Gunter Narr Verlag, 1991). Larry Scanlon, *Narrative, Authority, and Power: The Medieval Exemplum and the Chaucerian Tradition* (Cambridge: Cambridge University Press, 1994) and Alan J. Fletcher, *Preaching, Politics and Poetry in Late-Medieval England* (Dublin: Four Courts Press, 1998) also offer substantial discussions of Chaucer's use of ideas and forms drawn from preaching.

Chapter 1

1. "Quidam vero, Felix nomine . . . cum eumdem venerabilem virum Equitium sacrum ordinem non habere conspiceret, et per singula loca discurrere, atque studiose praedicare, eum quadam die familiaritatis ausu adiit, dicens: Qui sacrum ordinem non habes, atque a Romano pontifice sub quo degis praedicationis licentiam non accepisti, praedicare quomodo praesumis? Qua ejus inquisitione compulsus vir sanctus indicavit praedicationis licentiam qualiter accepit, dicens: Ea quae mihi loqueris ego quoque mecum ipse pertracto. Sed quadam nocte speciosus mihi per visionem juvenis astitit, atque in lingua mea medicinale ferramentum, id est phlebotomum posuit, dicens: Ecce posui verba mea in ore tuo; egredere ad praedicandum. Atque ex illo die etiam cum voluero, de Deo tacere non possum" (Gregory the Great, *Dialogorum libri IV,* PL 77:169B).

2. "Nec sufficit alicui dicere quod sit a Deo missus, nisi hoc manifeste ostendat[,] quia hoc solent haeretici dicere" (Robert of Basevorn, *Forma praedicandi,* ed. Thomas-Marie Charland, in Charland, *Artes praedicandi,* 242). This text is translated by Leopold Krul as *The Form of Preaching,* in *Three Medieval Rhetorical Arts,* ed. James J. Murphy (Berkeley and Los Angeles: University of California Press, 1971), 109–215, but translations here are my own unless otherwise noted.

Robert is paraphrasing Innocent III's letter to the people of Metz; see PL 214:697. See also Alan of Lille, "Liber secundus: Contra Waldenses," in *Contra haereticos libri quatuor,* PL 210:377–78: "quidam haeretici. . . . praedicant non missi a superiori praelato, aut a Deo; nam a Deo missos esse non probant eorum opera, nec miracula comprobant."

3. Bruce C. Brasington, "*Non imitanda set veneranda:* The Dilemma of Sacred Precedent in Twelfth-Century Canon Law," *Viator* 23 (1992): 135.

4. As Gratian observes at one point, "divine miracles ought to be admired, not taken as precedents for the judicial procedures of men *(sunt admiranda non in exemplum humane actionis trahenda)*" (quoted in Brasington, "*Non imitanda set veneranda,*" 146). Such a ruling would make Equitius, for example, ineligible as a precedent for lay speech.

5. John O. Ward, "From Marginal Gloss to *Catena* Commentary: The Eleventh-Century Origins of a Rhetorical Teaching Tradition in the Medieval West," *Parergon,* n.s., 13, no. 2 (1996): 109–20, discusses another manifestation of the attempt to control received authority through modern interpretation; the "catena" commentaries he looks at, unlike older forms of glosses, came literally to replace the text they interpreted, rather than simply accompanying it in marginal form.

6. Silvana Vecchio, "Dalla predicazione alla conversazione: Il *Liber de introductione loquendi* di Filippo da Ferrara OP," *Medieval Sermon Studies* 44 (2000): 68–86, 76–77.

7. "Sunt autem tria quae ad hoc specialiter valent: primum est diligens studium, secundum est consideratio modi aliorum praedicatorum, tertium est oratio ad Deum" (Humbert of Romans, *De eruditione praedicatorum,* in *B. Humberti de Romanis Opera de vita regulari,* ed. Joachim Joseph Berthier, 2 vols. [Rome: Marietti, 1888–89], 2:373–484 [hereafter Humbert], 394). This text is translated in Simon Tugwell, ed., *Early Dominicans: Selected Writings,* Classics of Western Spirituality (Mahwah, N.J.: Paulist Press, 1982), 183–325, but translations here are my own unless otherwise noted.

8. "Christus . . . qui omnes, ut credo, modo[s] laudabiles praedicandi in modo suo inclusit, utpote fons et origo boni" (Robert of Basevorn, *Forma praedicandi,* 245).

9. As A. J. Minnis notes, textual authorities "had to conform, in one way or another, with Christian truth" (*Medieval Theory of Authorship* [London: Scolar, 1984], 10). Thus it was impossible that two genuine authorities should contradict each other. Chenu observes that "more and more in the thirteenth century . . . [the masters] formed common opinions (*communis opinio magistrorum*) after a period of free debate," though he points out that this "common opinion" was not beyond question (*Nature, Man, and Society,* 278).

10. The phrase is Marianne Briscoe's in "Some Clerical Notions of Dramatic Decorum in Late Medieval England," *Comparative Drama* 19 (spring 1985): 3; she is speaking here particularly of preachers' aids, though she also notes Gratian's *Decretum* as a product of this trend. See also Simon Forde, "Lay Preaching and the Lollards of Norwich Diocese, 1428–1431," *Leeds Studies in English,* n.s., 24 (1998): 113.

11. Francine Cardman notes, for instance, that some of the disputations on women's ordination acknowledge room for doubt in their pronouncements, which tends to be ignored in later uses of the texts ("The Medieval Question of Women and Orders," *The Thomist* 42, no. 4 [October 1978]: 588–89). In another example, in 1228 Pope Gregory IX made a pronouncement apparently intended to revoke the permission given to the Humiliati to do certain limited kinds of preaching; as Rusconi notes, the fact that the Humiliati are not specifically named "eases the passage of Gregory IX's prohibition into the *corpus iuris canonici,* where it assumes the force of an absolute and definitive prohibition of lay preaching" (*Predicazione,* 107). On the form and development of quodlibetal questions and disputations, see Bernardo Bazàn, John W. Wippel, Gérard Fransen, and Danielle Jacquart, *Les questions disputées et les questions quodlibétiques dans les facultés de théologie, de droit et de médecine,* Typologie des sources du moyen âge occidental 44–45 (Turnhout, Belgium: Brepols, 1985).

12. Beverly Mayne Kienzle and Pamela J. Walker, "Preface: Authority and Definition," in Kienzle and Walker, xiv. See also Darleen Pryds's essay in the same volume: "Proclaiming Sanctity through Proscribed Acts: The Case of Rose of Viterbo," 159–72; and Rosa Maria Dessì and Michel Lauwers, "Introduction: *Praedicatores* et prophètes," in Dessì and Lauwers, 9–19.

13. Forde, "Lay Preaching," 109. See also Alcuin Blamires, *The Case for Women in Medieval Culture* (Oxford: Clarendon Press, 1997), 187, 189, 196.

14. Peter the Chanter, for instance, declares, "Est enim multiplex praedicatio, scilicet: eruditionis, correctionis, exhortationis, excitationis, consolationis, et sustentationis beneficii" (*Verbum abbreviatum,* chap. 6, PL 205:36C). Peter was unusually tolerant of lay preaching, an attitude that suggests some diversity among the clergy on this point; see Philippe Buc, "*Vox clamantis in deserto*? Pierre le Chantre et la prédication laïque," *Revue Mabillon,* n.s., 4 (1993): 5–47. For a more conservative position, see Michel Lauwers, "*Praedicatio—Exhortatio:* L'Église, la reforme, et les laïcs (XIᶜ–XIIIᶜ siècles)," in Dessì and Lauwers, 187–232. See also the assertion of the Paris master Thomas of Bailly (d. 1328) that there are various modes of preaching, in one of which the preacher "predicat motus quadam naturali pietate, qualiter predicare possunt non solum doctores aut prelati sed et quicumque simplices ad officium predicationis specialiter non astricti" (*Quodlibets,* ed. P. Glorieux, Textes philosophiques du moyen âge 9 [Paris: J. Vrin, 1960], 319–20).

15. "Predicacio est publica persuasio debitis loco et tempore pluribus facta ad salutem promerendam" (Ranulph Higden, *The Ars componendi sermones of Ranulph Higden, O. S. B.,* ed. Margaret Jennings [Leiden: Brill, 1991], 5).

16. Of course not all preaching took place during a Mass, nor did every Mass contain a sermon. I am simply trying to formulate a kind of ideal template for preaching. As Lecoy de la Marche says, preaching "avait pour théâtre ordinaire l'église," though again it is clear that, especially in the later Middle Ages, preaching could occur in many places (Lecoy de la Marche, *La chaire,* 226). See also Longère, "Lieux de prédication," in his *Prédication,* 171–76.

17. The use of the term *publice* in prohibitions of unlicensed preaching (an instance of which appears in the disputation by Henry of Ghent published in Al-

cuin Blamires and C. W. Marx, "Woman Not to Preach: A Disputation in British Library MS Harley 31," *Journal of Medieval Latin* 3 [1993]: 53 [hereafter Blamires and Marx]) suggests that in this context the word may have had a specific implicit meaning that denoted the ultimate boundary of permissible activity.

18. *Speculum Christiani: A Middle English Religious Treatise of the 14th Century,* ed. Gustaf Holmstedt, EETS 182 (London: EETS, 1933), 2. The numerous manuscripts of this work usually present the text in Latin as well as English; Holmstedt gives the Latin of this passage on p. 3.

19. It is also worth noting that much of Christ's own preaching would not, even allowing for necessary differences between his social world and the medieval one, have fit this model, a fact which may have made his radical example especially useful for semilicit preachers. Brilioth notes, however, that the "sermon" in the synagogue (Mark 1:21) took place in a liturgical context (*Brief History,* 8–9).

20. As John Hilary Martin points out, questions about the possibility of women's ordination led medieval theologians to "look into the meaning of the sacrament of holy orders, and analyze the natural characteristics of men vis-à-vis women;" clearly, medieval theorists, like Claude Lévi-Strauss, found women "good to think with" (John Hilary Martin, "The Injustice of Not Ordaining Women: A Problem for Medieval Theologians," *Theological Studies* 48, no. 2 [1987]: 306).

21. Rupert of Deutz makes the link between Rom. 10:15 and the clerical lineage explicit in his "Dispute between a Monk and a Cleric about Whether a Monk Should Be Allowed to Preach." The monk says, "The Apostle, speaking of preachers, wrote: 'How can they preach if they are not sent?' Simply, that means that the preacher ought not assume the right to preach on his own authority. But, as Christ said, 'As the Father sent me, so I also send you.' The Father sent Christ, Christ sent the apostles, the apostles send the archbishops, the archbishops send the bishops, and the bishops send the priests, all at the time of ordination" (translated in Joseph M. Miller, Michael H. Prosser, and Thomas W. Benson, eds., *Readings in Medieval Rhetoric* [Bloomington: Indiana University Press, 1973], 196). On the issue of apostolic succession, "une transmission du charisme ministériel de personne à personne," in the early church, see Hermann Hauser, *L'Église à l'âge apostolique: Structure et évolution des ministères,* Lectio divina 164 (Paris: Éditions du Cerf, 1996), 130; and Hans von Campenhausen, *Ecclesiastical Authority and Spiritual Power in the Church of the First Three Centuries,* trans. J. A. Baker (Stanford, Calif.: Stanford University Press, 1969), 149–77.

22. Robert N. Swanson, *Religion and Devotion in Europe, c. 1215–c. 1515* (Cambridge: Cambridge University Press, 1995), 236.

23. Commonly cited women prophets are Miriam (sister of Moses and Aaron—clearly an outspoken family; see Exod. 15); Deborah (Judg. 4); Hulda (4 Kings 22); and Anna (Luke 2). On the relatively broad meaning of *prophecy* in the early church, see Karen L. King, "Prophetic Power and Women's Authority: The Case of the *Gospel of Mary* (Magdalene)," in Kienzle and Walker, 21–41.

24. Gregory the Great, *Dialogorum libri IV,* cols. 165–69, especially 169.

25. This is increasingly the case in the later medieval centuries, when preach-

ing takes on a "quasi-sacramental" character, as Giles Constable puts it ("The Language of Preaching in the Twelfth Century," *Viator* 25 (1994): 135.

26. The preacher's actual performance of identity is considered in more detail in the next chapter; here I focus on the questions of lineage and authority that such a performance raises.

27. Judith Butler, "Performative Acts and Gender Constitution: An Essay in Phenomenology and Feminist Theory," in *Performing Feminisms: Feminist Critical Theory and Theatre,* ed. Sue-Ellen Case (Baltimore: Johns Hopkins University Press, 1990), 277.

28. Judith Butler, *Bodies That Matter: On the Discursive Limits of "Sex"* (London: Routledge, 1993), 244, n. 7.

29. "My communication must be repeatable—iterable—in the absolute absence of the receiver or of any empirically determinable collectivity of receivers. Such iterability . . . structures the mark of writing itself, no matter what particular type of writing is involved" (Jacques Derrida, *Limited Inc,* ed. Gerald Graff [Evanston, Ill.: Northwestern University Press, 1988], 7).

30. He adds, "This citationality, this duplication or duplicity, this iterability of the mark is neither an accident nor an anomaly, it is that (normal/abnormal) without which a mark could not even have a function called 'normal.' What would a mark be that could not be cited?" (Derrida, *Limited Inc,* 12). These concepts are extended to the realm of acts, as well as signs, in Derrida's discussion of Austin.

31. The wandering preachers who caused the church hierarchy such uneasiness in the eleventh and twelfth centuries are a kind of embodied example of such lack of anchorage. In general the church dealt with them by attempting to fix them in space and give them a clear and recognized ecclesiastical lineage, whether as hermits (in "anchorholds") or as members of monastic communities. See the discussions in Brooke, *Coming of the Friars,* 49–59; and Grundmann, *Religious Movements,* 17–21.

32. "Nova quaedam nuper, de quibus miramur non modicum, nostris sunt auribus intimata, quod [quaedam] abbatissae . . . moniales proprias benedicunt, ipsarumque confessiones criminalium audiunt, et legentes Evangelium praesumunt publice praedicare . . . licet beatissima virgo Maria dignior et excellentior fuerit apostolis universis, non tamen illi, sed istis, Dominus claves regni coelorum commisit" (Innocent III, *Nova quaedam nuper,* PL 216:356). There is some question about the authenticity of this letter. While its authorship by Innocent would add to its interest, it is not essential here, since the associations to and arguments about women's activity are part of a larger debate independent of particular speakers.

33. Innocent is by no means unusual in making this association. Numerous texts depict preaching as one of the most fundamental duties of a priest, if not indeed what makes him a priest. Maurice of Sully, for instance, says that three things are required of a priest: a virtuous life, knowledge, and preaching (C. A. Robson, *Maurice of Sully and the Medieval Vernacular Homily: With the Text of Maurice's French Homilies from a Sens Cathedral Chapter MS* [Oxford: Basil Blackwell, 1952], 79).

34. Ida Raming, *The Exclusion of Women from the Priesthood: Divine Law or*

Sex Discrimination?, trans. Norman R. Adams (Metuchen, N.J.: Scarecrow Press, 1976), xiii. On the theological underpinnings of women's exclusion from orders, see A. J. Minnis, "*De impedimento sexus:* Women's Bodies and Medieval Impediments to Female Ordination," in *Medieval Theology and the Natural Body,* ed. Peter Biller and Alastair J. Minnis, York Studies in Medieval Theology 1 (York, U.K.: York Medieval Press, 1997), 109–39.

35. The precise date of this text, Thomas of Chobham's *Summa de arte praedicandi,* is uncertain, but in Franco Morenzoni's edited version (Turnhout, Belgium: Brepols, 1988 [hereafter Chobham]) Morenzoni places it between c. 1216 and c. 1221 (xxxvi–xxxviii).

36. "De mulieribus, autem, dicit apostolus: *mulieres autem in ecclesia docere non permitto, sed si quid ignorent domi uiros suos interrogent.* Possunt tamen abbatisse et priorisse in capitulis suis moniales suas instruere et uitia reprehendere. Sed non licet eis sacram Scripturam predicando exponere. Possunt tamen publice lectiones de apostolo et de legendis sanctorum et etiam de Euuangelio ad matutinas suas legere. Vnde in canonibus ille moniales que hoc officium habent, diaconisse dicuntur. Non licet eis tamen indui sacris uestibus neque legere Epistolam neque Euuangelium ad missam" (Chobham, 58).

37. "Prophetare uocat apostolus scire mentem sacre lectionis et eam populis exponere. Et hoc pertinet ad maiores in ecclesia" (ibid.).

38. "En fait, reprenant une distinction qui au début du XIIIᵉ siècle paraît désormais bien établie, la *Summa* insiste principalement sur l'idée que la prédication n'est consentie aux laïcs que lorsque le verbe *praedicare* est utilisé comme synonyme d'exhorter au bien, alors qu'elle leur est formellement interdite lorsqu'il est pris *dans son acception propre*, à savoir expliquer publiquement le texte sacré" (ibid., xli; emphasis added).

39. "Ita quod de articulis fidei et sacramentis ecclesie non loquentur," quoted in C. H. Lawrence, *The Friars: The Impact of the Early Mendicant Movement on Western Society* (London: Longman, 1994), 24 and n. 19. Gregory IX later revoked this permission; see n. 11 to the Introduction above.

40. "Quamuis igitur multi sint simplices sacerdotes, qui non nouerunt profunda misteria sacre Scripture, dummodo tantum sciant uitia reprehendere et fidem et bonos mores astruere, saltem uerbis simplicibus, non credimus quod dampnabiles sint. Sic enim predicauit Iohannes Baptista . . . Sic enim predicauerunt apostoli" (Chobham, 57).

41. See Thomas of Chobham's discussion of laymen (57–58) and on the possibility of preaching by women, hermits, and others in time of necessity (71–72).

42. "Non est minoris gratiae prophetare, quam docere, immo et prophetarum est docere publice ea quae eis reuelantur, 1 ad Corinth. 14, 'Qui prophetat hominibus loquitur ad aedificationem': mulieribus concessum est prophetare" (Blamires and Marx, 50).

43. "Prophetia data est mulieribus non ad publicam instructionem sed priuatam, et si vt per eam viros doceat, hoc est ex gratia speciali, quae non respicit sexuum distinctionem" (ibid., 53).

44. Thomas Aquinas, *Summa Theologica,* trans. Fathers of the English Dominican Province, 3 vols. (New York: Benziger Brothers, 1947–48), 3:2698,

supp. q. 39, art. 1; Latin text in Thomas Aquinas, *Summa Theologiae*, ed. Institutum Studiorum Medievalium Ottavienensis, 5 vols. (Ottawa: Commissio Piana, 1953), 5:146a–b. Claire L. Sahlin notes that Aquinas believed "the highest form of prophecy" to be that which "is the furthest removed from human knowledge," namely prediction of the future ("Gender and Prophetic Authority in Birgitta of Sweden's *Revelations*," in *Gender and Text in the Later Middle Ages*, ed. Jane Chance [Gainesville: University of Florida Press, 1996], 73). See also Blamires's observation that in the thirteenth century a favorite scholastic technique against the use of prophets as role models for preachers was "to harden a distinction which had been slowly growing in the Church, between prophecy and preaching" (*Case for Women*, 190).

45. See Alcuin Blamires, "Women and Preaching in Medieval Orthodoxy, Heresy, and Saints' Lives," *Viator* 26 (1995): 135–52, especially 142–45; and a disputation by Eustache d'Arras that claims that women such as Katherine and Mary Magdalene are "specialiter electae . . . et privilegiatae" and that they are not "in statu communi mulierum" (Leclercq, 120). See also Brasington, "*Non imitanda set veneranda*," 142–45.

46. On Eustache d'Arras, see Leclercq, 119–20. Robert of Basevorn says, "Praedicator ex exercitio est qui frequenter praedicat . . . nec una praedicatio praedicatorem facit, ut videtur. Unde pro una praedicatione non videtur ut aliquis mereatur aureolam"—though he does concede that a person who preaches once and would have preached more if he could may merit the aureole; he also specifies, however, that "non solum actui praedicandi debetur aureola, sed actui *legitime exercito*" (*Forma praedicandi*, 239; emphasis added).

47. This is essentially the popular argument that persons ordinarily excluded from preaching and other official tasks may take them on when "the harvest is great, but the laborers are few" (Matt. 9:37); see Blamires, "Women and Preaching," 147, and also, e.g., Chobham, 71–72.

48. Leclercq, 131. Robert of Basevorn, similarly, contrasts preachers "ex institutione ordinaria" and preachers "ex commissione," the latter of whom are not required to preach (*Forma praedicandi*, 240).

49. In Leclercq's summation, "de droit ordinaire, la charge de prêcher convient aux curés, non seulement au titre de la coutume, mais parce qu'il leur a été confié sans intermédiaire: car les curés ont été institués immédiatement par le Christ dans la personne des soixante-douze disciples. Le pouvoir qu'ils possèdent, ils le tiennent donc directement du Christ" (Leclercq, 131). See also the further discussion of ordinary and extraordinary license in Leclercq, 134–36, and Thomas Aquinas's description of the role of abbesses, who possess "not ordinary authority, but delegated as it were" (*Summa Theologica*, 3:2698, supp. q. 39, art. 1). "De abbatissis tamen dicitur quod non habent praelationem ordinariam, sed quasi ex commissione" (Thomas Aquinas, *Summa Theologiae*, ed. Institutum Studiorum Medievalium Ottavienensis, 5:146b).

50. Sherry Reames quotes a sermon by Jacobus of Voragine on Katherine of Alexandria, in which he concedes that a very few women have held the office of preacher under special circumstances: "Quamvis enim mulieribus sit inhibitum officium praedicationis, quibusdam tamen sanctis virginibus fuit officium praedi-

candi a Spiritu S. concessum, quadam praerogativa gratiae singularis" (Sherry L. Reames, *The* Legenda aurea: *A Reexamination of Its Paradoxical History* [Madison: University of Wisconsin Press, 1985], 259, n. 20).

51. Blamires, *Case for Women,* 195, n. 103, quoting Hugh of St. Cher, *Postillae* on 1 Cor. 14:34 (Basle, 1504), f. 103v. Forde discusses the relationship between the terms *predicare* and *predicere;* see "Lay Preaching," 110–12.

52. Claire L. Sahlin offers a helpful overview of the meanings of the terms "prophet" and "prophecy" in the Middle Ages in *Birgitta of Sweden and the Voice of Prophecy* (Woodbridge, Suffolk, U.K.: Boydell Press, 2001), 35–44.

53. "Dicitur etiam predicatio quandoque prophetia . . . Prophetare est ea que dicuntur ad populum exponere, et istud est utile, et secundum hoc prophetare est predicare . . . Alio modo dicitur prophetare futura predicere, de quo hic non intendimus" (Chobham, 17); and later, "Prophetare uocat apostolus scire mentem sacre lectionis et eam populis exponere. Et hoc pertinet ad maiores in ecclesia" (58).

54. Minnis, *Medieval Theory,* 136.

55. "Prophetae in sacris Scripturis appellantur videntes. . . . Sic vacantes Scripturis exponentes eas, videntes meritò dici possunt; cùm & ipsi in eisdem literis Prophetae dicantur, Eph. 4. *Et ipse dedit quosdam quidem Apostolos, quosdam autem Prophetas;* Glossa, *Prophetas,* id est, *Scripturarum Interpretes"* (William of St. Amour, *Tractatvs brevis de pericvlis novissimorvm temporvm ex scriptvris svmptis,* ed. Valérien de Flavigny [Constantiae: Ad Insigne Bonae Fidej Apud Alithophilos, 1632], 17).

56. Exod. 4.1–16; for Aquinas's statement, see p. 22 and n. 44 above. Note the striking description God gives Moses: "Ipse [Aaron] loquetur pro te ad populum et erit os tuum; tu autem eris ei in his quae ad Deum pertinent." Philip of Harvengt uses the story of Moses and Aaron to discuss the priest's or preacher's role as a medium between God and the people, and the "magna . . . et praecipua dignitas" of the clergy, in his twelfth-century *De institutione clericorum tractatus sex,* PL 203:758–59.

57. Exod. 7:1–2: "Dixitque Dominus ad Mosen, 'Ecce, constitui te Deum Pharaonis; Aaron frater tuus erit propheta tuus.'"

58. Alexander of Ashby, "Aux origines des 'Artes praedicandi.' Le 'De artificioso modo predicandi' d'Alexandre d'Ashby," ed. Franco Morenzoni, *Studi medievali* 32, no. 2 (1991): 916. The treatise was written for Alexander's abbot, the head of the Augustinian canons at Ashby.

59. Not surprisingly, the Waldensians preferred to define *prophecy* as "not only declaration of future events but also revelation of hidden things, including exposition of the mysteries of the divine word" (Blamires, *Case for Women,* 190, n. 83; see PL 204:808).

60. Birgitta of Sweden, *Life and Selected Revelations,* ed. Marguerite Tjader Harris, trans. Albert Ryle Kezel (New York: Paulist Press, 1990), 86.

61. See Karen Scott, "'This is why I have put you among your neighbors': St. Bernard's and St. Catherine's Understanding of the Love of God and Neighbor," in *Atti del simposio internazionale Cateriniano-Bernardiniano, Siena, 17–20 aprile 1980,* ed. Domenico Maffei and Paolo Nardi (Siena: Accademia Senese degli Intronati, 1982), 281–82.

62. "Nemo dicit baptismus meus sicut evangelium meum et praedicatio mea." The quotation is from a text by the English Franciscan Thomas Docking, published in Leclercq, 110. See also Simon Tugwell's argument that in the course of the twelfth to thirteenth centuries there was a shift in the preacher's use of the Bible such that "the sermon is not simply an exposition of a biblical text" and "the *thema* provides a row of pegs on which to hang the preacher's message, rather than the actual material of the sermon" (*"De huiusmodi sermonibus texitur omnis recta predicatio:* Changing Attitudes toward the Word of God," in *De l'homélie au sermon: Histoire de la prédication médiévale,* ed. Jacqueline Hamesse and Xavier Hermand [Louvain-la-Neuve: Université Catholique de Louvain, Publications de l'Institut d'Études Médiévales, 1993], 161).

63. This was, at least, the orthodox position, though recurrent Donatism, particularly in the later Middle Ages, made it a highly contested point.

64. Stated in Augustine, *De doctrina christiana.* Published with *De vera religione,* ed. Joseph Martin, CCSL 32 (Turnhout, Belgium: Brepols, 1962), prooemium 4–5 (pp. 2–4). But see also Leclercq, e.g., 108: "le fait d'avoir à composer eux-mêmes, désormais, leurs sermons, entraîne pour eux la nécessité d'être instruits"; and on 111: sacred eloquence is "à la fois un don (*gratia eloquentiae*) et un habitus (*exercitium eloquentiae*)." The problem is discussed further by Franco Morenzoni, "Parole du prédicateur et inspiration divine d'après les *Artes praedicandi,*" in Dessì and Lauwers, 271–90; and Thomas-Marie Charland, "Praedicator gratiosus," *Revue dominicaine* 39 (1933): 88–96.

65. "Non enim debet dicere praedicator verba sua, sed verba Domini et quae sibi Dominus administrat," from Nicolas Byard's collection of *Distinctiones,* quoted in Leclercq, 109. Beryl Smalley, *The Study of the Bible in the Middle Ages* (Notre Dame, Ind.: University of Notre Dame Press, 1964), 12, points out that a long-standing tradition saw the interpretation of scripture itself as "a grace or 'charisma,'" with the Holy Spirit speaking through the exegete.

66. Humbert of Romans takes a slightly different view of this matter, noting that "licet praedicationis gratia specialiter habeatur ex dono Dei, tamen sapiens praedicator debet *facere quod in se est,* diligenter studendo circa praedicationem faciendam, ut laudabiliter fiat. . . . Glossa, in Evangelio Matth. 10, in illud quod dicitur: Nolite cogitare quomodo aut quid loquamini: sed Apostoli in praedicatione fuerunt privilegiati: tamen iis qui non sunt privilegiati ita, conceditur praemeditari" (Humbert, 394; emphasis added).

67. Leclercq, 108–9.

68. Thomas Aquinas, *Super evangelium S. Ioannis lectura,* ed. P. Raphelis Cai, 5th rev. ed. (Rome: Marietti, 1952), on John 7:14–18, 4–6.1036–40.

69. "Qui ergo loqui vult utiliter, loquatur humiliter. Si quis loquitur, non quasi suos, sed quasi Christi sermones loquatur, nil sibi in bene dictis attribuens, sed omnia ei a quo est omne bonum" (Alexander of Ashby, "Aux origines," 908).

70. "Iniustitia enim est quod homo usurpet sibi alienum" (Aquinas, *Super evangelium,* on John 7:17–18, 6.1040). The manual of the fourteenth-century Franciscan Francesc Eiximenis offers many examples of the disapproval of preachers' pride in their own words, such as this denunciation: "proh dolor! et quanta est uanitas! quanta fraus in Dei opere! quanta macula in doctrina Christi quod

unus talis truphator, ad ostendendum se sapientem, conculcet et inuoluat imperite diuinas sentencias et confundat uerbum ueritatis, pretermissa diuina reuerencia et utilitate populi et merito personali! o infelix bestia! que sic aspiras ad tui laudem" ("L'*Ars praedicandi* de Francesc Eiximenis," ed. P. Martí de Barcelona, in *Homenatge a Antoni Rubió i Lluch: Miscellània d'estudis literaris històrics i lingüístics* [Barcelona: n.p., 1936], 312).

71. The implications and mechanisms of women's exclusion from preaching are discussed further in Chapters 2, 5, and 6 below.

72. Gillian Evans, *The Thought of Gregory the Great,* Cambridge Studies in Medieval Life and Thought, series 4, v. 2 (Cambridge: Cambridge University Press, 1986), 81, referring to Gregory's *Moralia in Job* xxx.iv.17. Hanna Pitkin's analysis of the concept of representation is helpful in suggesting some of the nuances that can attach to this term and make it difficult for certain persons to take the role of representative ("Representing as 'Acting For': The Analogies," in *The Concept of Representation* [Berkeley and Los Angeles: University of California Press, 1967], 112–43).

73. We may recall here Derrida's insistence that iterability is connected to absence, that the quality of writing as communication with an absent person is in effect a quality of all communication (*Limited Inc,* 4–10). In inspired or charismatic preaching it can be said that the "presence" of God is powerfully felt by preacher and audience alike. Such preaching, however, cannot be regarded as the norm, and preaching manuals hardly address it, since it is something that cannot be taught. Indeed, since charismatic preaching was a mode often ably employed by heretics as well as saints, its peculiarly extraordinary status made it a dangerous topic. Preaching theorists seem to have preferred to remain in the world of "ordinary" preaching.

74. "Sic igitur patet quod vniuersi predicationes mittuntur a deo inmediate et mediate per angelos aut per homines et semper vires dei gerunt et eius personam representant" (Munich Staatsbibliothek Clm 14550 [s. xiv], f. 97ᵛ).

75. In this period, debates over the apostolic life and the real presence in the Eucharist meant that God's presence on earth was at issue in many different ways; the problem of the preacher as his representative is simply another manifestation of that concern. As Dyan Elliott observes, "The increasing emphasis on the material presence of Christ in the sacrament of the altar opened up a huge chasm in the symbolic order, the very emphasis on presence conjuring up anxieties over absence" (*Fallen Bodies,* 106).

76. Rejecting the idea, as Butler says, that there is any "originating will" behind a human performance of authority or identity expresses a (prior and assumed) rejection of *the* originary Will, the Logos (*Bodies That Matter,* 13; see also 226–27). Both Butler's and Derrida's attempts to formulate how this absence works, however, have led to recurrent complaints that they do not deal adequately with what John R. Searle, in his critique of Derrida's reading of Austin, calls "datable singular events in particular historical contexts" (quoted in Derrida, *Limited Inc,* 27). Butler notes that she was led to write *Bodies That Matter* partly in response to the reiterated question "But what about the materiality of the body?," which similarly suggests that her work does not account fully for a certain kind of

presence that readers feel to be part of their experience—just as shortcomings on the part of medieval preachers could point toward the absence of a perfectly available meaning, an absence that their office was intended to remedy but could at times exacerbate.

77. J. L. Austin, *How to Do Things with Words,* ed. J. O. Urmson (Oxford: Clarendon Press, 1962), 21–22.

78. While Austin ultimately abandons his attempt to define and delimit performative speech, recognizing that it, like preaching, has fluid boundaries, he never disavows his claim that actors' speech is "peculiarly" different from other speech.

79. Derrida, *Limited Inc,* 18.

80. A medieval Christian was probably quite able to envision a truly "saturated" context when God was the speaker: saturation seems, indeed, an apt description of the apparent effect of certain mystical experiences. When the communication takes place between two human speakers, however—and even when it is between God and a human being not in a state of ultimate unity with him—difficulties of transmission immediately begin to intrude; thus the impossibility of conveying mystical experience in (human) language, or the inevitable questions of intention, perception, and reception that plague preaching. Here again charismatic preaching or public prophecy might be regarded as a special case, in which the speaker's human presence is perfectly subordinated to the message that speaks through him or her.

81. As Aquinas puts it, discussing why women's demonstrated ability to prophesy does not allow them to preach, "gratia prophetiae attenditur secundum mentem illuminatam a Deo; ex qua parte non est in hominibus sexuum differentia . . . Sed gratias [*sic*] sermonis pertinet ad instructionem hominum, inter quos differentia sexuum invenitur" (Thomas Aquinas, *Summa Theologiae: Latin Text and English Translation, Introduction, Notes, Appendices and Glossaries,* 61 vols. [n.p.: Blackfriars and New York: McGraw-Hill, 1964–81], vol. 45: *Prophecy and Other Charisms (2a.2ae. 171–8),* ed. Roland Potter [n.p.: Blackfriars, 1970], 134).

82. Humbert, 407. Thomas of Chobham similarly disallows an attempt to sideline issues of human status, albeit in a different context. Discussing whether a priest who prays in mortal sin sins mortally in praying, he cites, as an argument contra, the idea that "sacerdos talis est publica persona, nec orat in persona sua, sed in persona ecclesie" but responds, "Sed hec solutio nulla est. Constat enim quod malus sacerdos quando orat propriam habet actionem, et aliquod opus suum facit" (Chobham, 63). The idea of a priest's ownership of his prayer would presumably apply equally strongly to a preacher's ownership of his preaching.

83. "But I do not allow a woman to teach [the Gloss adds, 'in the church'] or to exercise authority over a man, but to remain quiet" (1 Tim. 2:12 cited in Aquinas, *Summa Theologiae,* vol. 45, 134).

Chapter 2

1. All references to the *Canterbury Tales* are from Geoffrey Chaucer, *The Riverside Chaucer,* ed. Larry D. Benson, 3d ed. (Boston: Houghton Mifflin, 1987), unless otherwise noted.

2. Frank V. Cespedes, "Chaucer's Pardoner and Preaching," *ELH* 44 (1977): 1–18, offers an excellent account of the two characters' debt to the pastoral injunctions of the first Epistle to Timothy and the implications of their juxtaposition. On the Parson as an ideal, see Chaucer, *Riverside Chaucer,* 819, and Jill Mann, *Chaucer and Medieval Estates Satire: The Literature of Social Classes and the* General Prologue *to the* Canterbury Tales (Cambridge: Cambridge University Press, 1973), 55–67; for a different view, see Robert N. Swanson, "Chaucer's Parson and Other Priests," *Studies in the Age of Chaucer* 13 (1991): 41–80. Alastair J. Minnis, "Chaucer's Pardoner and the 'Office of Preacher,' " in *Intellectuals and Writers in Fourteenth-Century Europe,* ed. Piero Boitani and Anna Torti (Cambridge, U.K.: D. S. Brewer, 1986), 88–119, demonstrates with great thoroughness that Chaucer knew and was indebted to discussions of preaching—in particular, bad preaching—in his creation of the Pardoner.

3. On the Pardoner's relationship to his historical brethren, see Alfred L. Kellogg and Louis A. Haselmayer, "Chaucer's Satire of the Pardoner," in Kellogg, *Chaucer, Langland, Arthur: Essays in Middle English Literature* (New Brunswick, N.J.: Rutgers University Press, 1972), 212–44; and also the discussion in Mann, *Chaucer,* 145–52.

4. Chaucer, *Canterbury Tales* X.45, 46.

5. "Therfore my theme is yet, and evere was, / *Radix malorum est Cupiditas,*" the Pardoner declares (ibid., VI.425–26). The Parson never explicitly claims a theme, but his statement that the "goode wey . . . is cleped Penitence" sets his tone, and he later quotes the gospel injunction, "Dooth digne fruyt of Penitence" (X.77–81, 115). The question of whether either Parson or Pardoner actually preaches a sermon as such continues to be debated; the *Pardoner's Tale* has the better claim but varies in some notable ways from the traditional understanding of the form. Robert P. Merrix helpfully summarizes the history of and criteria for the argument in "Sermon Structure in the Pardoner's Tale," *Chaucer Review* 17 (1983), reprinted in *Geoffrey Chaucer's the Pardoner's Tale,* ed. Harold Bloom (New York: Chelsea House, 1988), 125–38. Merrix's conclusion, that the tale is indeed a sermon, is strained at points, like most attempts to attach a definite label to this tale or its teller. Other fairly recent discussions include Alan J. Fletcher, "The Preaching of the Pardoner," *Studies in the Age of Chaucer* 11 (1989): 15–35; and Siegfried Wenzel, "Chaucer," and "Notes on the *Parson's Tale,*" *Chaucer Review* 16 (1982): 237–56.

6. "Sanctae praedicationis officium": the phrase appears, among other places, in canon 10 of the Fourth Lateran Council, which attempted to improve the quantity and quality of preaching (Tanner, *Decrees,* 239).

7. C. Leyser, "Masculinity in Flux: Nocturnal Emission and the Limits of Celibacy in the Early Middle Ages," in *Masculinity in Medieval Europe,* ed. D. M.

Hadley (London: Longman, 1999), 103–20. See also Bruno Judic, "Grégoire le Grand, un maître de la parole," in Dessì and Lauwers, 66–71.

8. Leyser, "Masculinity in Flux," 117; "Cujus vita despicitur, restat ut ejus praedicatio contemnatur" (Gregory the Great, *Homiliarum in evangelia libri duo,* PL 76:1119A, hom. 12.1). The *Regula pastoralis,* particularly its first two sections, discusses this idea extensively (Gregory the Great, *Règle pastorale,* ed. Floribert Rommel, trans. Charles Morel, intro. Bruno Judic, 2 vols., Sources chrétiennes 381–82 [Paris: Éditions du Cerf, 1992]).

9. See Cespedes, "Chaucer's Pardoner," 5, on the Pauline roots of this idea. Leclercq, 137–38, notes how important Gregory was for the medieval conception of the "orateur chrétien."

10. On the reform movement generally, see Constable, *Reformation of the Twelfth Century,* particularly his comments on the "tension" produced by the eleventh- and twelfth-century Church's competing desires for withdrawal from and involvement in the world (24–25, 42–43). On developments in the idea of the *vita apostolica* in the eleventh and twelfth centuries, see Chenu, *Nature, Man, and Society,* 202–69.

11. Leclercq, 118–19.

12. The question of how the preacher's person interacts with his office also recalls, of course, the concept of the king's two bodies, a public self and a private self, first elaborated by Ernst Kantorowicz in *The King's Two Bodies: A Study in Medieval Political Theology* (Princeton, N.J.: Princeton University Press, 1957), and recently discussed in another context by Alastair J. Minnis, "The Author's Two Bodies? Authority and Fallibility in Late-Medieval Textual Theory," in *Of the Making of Books: Medieval Manuscripts, Their Scribes and Readers: Essays Presented to M. B. Parkes,* ed. P. R. Robinson and Rivkah Zim (Aldershot, U.K.: Scolar, 1997), 259–79. As Minnis points out, "with the late-medieval secularization of many aspects of society various dualities were to emerge relating to the 'professional' and 'personal' capacities of human beings" (264).

13. Jaeger, "Charismatic Body"; he notes, for instance, that "procedures for electing bishops and abbots change from a system based on charismatic selection (virtue, personal authority, miracle) to one based on bureaucratic selection (canonical procedure formulated in texts and documents)" (125).

14. Kantorowicz, *King's Two Bodies,* 47, quoted in Minnis, "Author's Two Bodies," 264.

15. Chaucer, *Canterbury Tales* I.495.

16. Robert Swanson, "Chaucer's Parson," 41. For a different view, see Eamon Grennan, "Dual Characterization: A Note on Chaucer's Use of 'But' in the Portrait of the Parson," *Chaucer Review* 16 (1982): 195–200.

17. Minnis, "Chaucer's Pardoner."

18. Chaucer, *Canterbury Tales* I.691.

19. Ibid. V.395–99.

20. Cespedes, "Chaucer's Pardoner," 6–7. Cf. the Pardoner's declaration that he shows his sealed letter of authorization "my body to warente" (Chaucer, *Canterbury Tales* VI.338).

21. The "litany of 'I wol'" in the *Pardoner's Prologue,* noted by Charles A.

Owen, Jr., reinforces both the sense of self and the focus on his own will (rather than God's) that mark the Pardoner as an irredeemable instance of immoral preaching (*Pilgrimage and Storytelling: The Dialectic of "Ernest" and "Game"* [Norman: University of Oklahoma Press, 1977], 174).

22. Minnis, "Author's Two Bodies."

23. Carolyn Dinshaw, in her discussion of the Pardoner, offers a similar assessment of the preacher's language (rather than his persona) and its "slippery and mediate nature . . . [which remains] *essentially* partial" (*Chaucer's Sexual Poetics* [Madison: University of Wisconsin Press, 1989], 171–73).

24. "Persona: 1. individu, être humain—individual, man" (J. F. Niermeyer, *Mediae latinitatis lexicon minus* [Leiden: Brill, 1976], 790).

25. Charles du Cange, *Glossarium mediae et infimae latinitatis*, 10 vols., editio nova (Niort, France: L. Favre, 1883–87), 6:283; Niermeyer, *Mediae latinitatis*, 791.

26. Robson, *Maurice of Sully*, 79. This is a fairly standard list; Robert of Basevorn, in his preaching manual, says that the three things a preacher (rather than a priest) must have are "puritas vitae," "competens scientia," and "auctoritas, qua mittatur ab Ecclesia" (*Forma praedicandi*, 241). Purity of life and sufficient knowledge are common to both lists. When the focus is on priesthood, the third requirement is preaching; when it is on preaching, the third requirement is authority (which in preaching could certainly be the authority of a parish priest), suggesting that these two are paired and that, in a sense, preaching is the expression of priestly authority. Preaching manuals frequently share manuscript space with other works on a priest's or preacher's duties and life; see, for example, Paris Bibliothèque Nationale MS. Lat. 3464 (copied 1458), which contains a rather technical *ars praedicandi* alongside several texts in the same hand on a priest's life and duties.

27. Robson, *Maurice of Sully*, 79.

28. On the mendicant controversy, see particularly Dufeil, *Guillaume de Saint-Amour.*

29. Humbert, 406–7.

30. For an extensive consideration of scholastic discussions of women preachers, see Blamires and Marx; on women's teaching, see Nicole Bériou, "The Right of Women to Give Religious Instruction in the Thirteenth Century," in Kienzle and Walker, 134–45.

31. Humbert, 406.

32. "Prima est defectus sensus, de quo non praesumitur in muliere tantum sicut in viro" (ibid.).

33. Robert Swanson points out that fulminations against women in clerical discourse may often reflect a "perceived threat to clerical aspirations to angelic status . . . the danger is not posed by women, but by the clerics' suppressed masculinity" ("Angels Incarnate: Clergy and Masculinity from Gregorian Reform to Reformation," in *Masculinity in Medieval Europe,* ed. D. M. Hadley [London: Longman, 1999], 166).

34. On the Pardoner's performance of masculinity, see his singing (Chaucer, *Canterbury Tales* I.672) and his boast of having "a joly wenche in every toun"

(VI.453); on his possible deformity, note the narrator's remark "I trowe he were a geldyng or a mare" (I.691) and Harry Bailly's threat, "I wolde I hadde thy coillons in my hond" (VI.952), which are often taken together to suggest the Pardoner's possible eunuchry. This would not, of course, be a visible deformity but is also forbidden; see Lev. 21:20. The classic "diagnosis" of the Pardoner as a physical eunuch is W. C. Curry, *Chaucer and the Mediaeval Sciences* (Oxford: Oxford University Press, 1926). Dinshaw discusses the relationship between the Pardoner's performances and his sexuality in *Chaucer's Sexual Poetics*, 157–58.

35. For readings that link the Pardoner's problematic performance to his office, see H. Marshall Leicester, Jr., " 'Synne Horrible': The Pardoner's Exegesis of His Tale, and Chaucer's," in *Acts of Interpretation: The Text in Its Contexts, 700–1600: Essays on Medieval and Renaissance Literature in Honor of E. Talbot Donaldson*, ed. Mary J. Carruthers and Elizabeth D. Kirk (Norman, Okla.: Pilgrim Books, 1982), 25–50; Fred Hoerner, "Church Office, Routine, and Self-Exile in Chaucer's Pardoner," *Studies in the Age of Chaucer* 16 (1994): 69–98; and Scanlon, *Narrative*, 192–205.

36. "Cujus vita despicitur, restat ut ejus praedicatio contemnatur" (Humbert, 407).

37. The preacher's virtue is of interest to Humbert elsewhere, as in "De vita praedicatoris," the first chapter of a section on "Things that are necessary to a preacher" (399–400), but it is clear that for him *persona* is almost entirely an external matter.

38. Humbert of Romans makes this point (400). The need to teach "verbo et exemplo" is insisted on in almost every discussion of preaching that is not exclusively devoted to the construction of a sermon. On the importance of this concept in the age of the preaching revival, see Caroline Walker Bynum, Docere verbo et exemplo: *An Aspect of Twelfth-Century Spirituality*, Harvard Theological Studies 31 (Missoula, Mont.: Scholars Press, 1979).

39. Leclercq, 109.

40. Two recent discussions of doubleness or duplicity are of interest here. In the conclusion to *Christ's Body*, Beckwith discusses "the extreme tensions of ideal and real, of transcendent and immanent played out in the image" of Christ's body (114), and her characterization of the "duplicity" of that and other symbols, "saturated, laden with context, and manipulable out of that context" (112), is reminiscent of many of the problems preachers—imitators, of course, of that ultimate symbol—struggled with in their work. Nicholas Watson explores the more negative valences of "doubleness," particularly as applied to women, as well as the ways in which this concept could be manipulated toward a more beneficent understanding of duplicity, and indeed toward a recognition that "to be human is . . . precisely to be 'double naturelly'" ("'Yf wommen be double naturelly': Remaking 'Woman' in Julian of Norwich's Revelation of Love," *Exemplaria* 8, no. 1 [1996]: 13–25).

41. On the particularity of example, see Carlo Natali, "Paradeigma: The Problems of Human Acting and the Use of Examples in Some Greek Authors of the 4th Century B.C.," *Rhetoric Society Quarterly* 19 (1989): 141–52. On the medieval exemplum, see Claude Bremond, Jacques Le Goff, and Jean-Claude

Schmitt, *L' "Exemplum,"* Typologie des sources du moyen âge occidental 40 (Turnhout, Belgium: Brepols, 1982).

42. "Thou getest fable noon ytoold for me, / For Paul, that writeth unto Thymothee, / Repreveth hem that weyven soothfastnesse / And tellen fables and swich wrecchednesse" (Chaucer, *Canterbury Tales* X.31–34).

43. "Incorporari et carne vestiri" (quoted in Bremond et al., *L' "Exemplum,"* 85). The passage as a whole is eloquent on the need for embodiment in teaching. See A. Lecoy de la Marche, ed., *Anecdotes historiques, légendes et apologues tirés du recueil inédit d'Étienne de Bourbon, dominicain du XIIIe siècle* (Paris: Librairie Renouard, 1877), 4–5.

44. "Debet enim quilibet predicator dare bonum exemplum in opere, et bonam doctrinam in uerbo, quia si bene uiuat et nichil predicet, *quantum prodest exemplo, tantum nocet silentio*" (Chobham, 24).

45. Robert of Basevorn, *The Form of Preaching,* trans. Leopold Krul, in *Three Medieval Rhetorical Arts,* ed. James J. Murphy (Berkeley and Los Angeles: University of California Press, 1971), 126–27; I have modified the translation slightly. The Latin reads, "Frequenter per angelos corpora assumentes praedicavit, vel, ut aliqui volunt, in alia similitudine corporea quam Ipse assumpsit, non in unitatem suppositi sed tantum ut movens, sicut forsan loquebatur Adae et multis aliis. . . . Et tandem Ipse, corpus humanum et animam in unitate suppositi assumens, veniens praedicavit" (Robert of Basevorn, *Forma praedicandi,* 243–44).

46. Augustine, *City of God,* trans. Henry Bettenson (London: Penguin Books, 1984), 9.17, 21. The latter passage is cited in Scanlon, *Narrative,* 9. See also Giles Constable, "The Ideal of the Imitation of Christ," in his *Three Studies in Medieval Religious and Social Thought: The Interpretation of Mary and Martha, The Ideal of the Imitation of Christ, The Orders of Society* (Cambridge: Cambridge University Press, 1995), particularly 169–93.

47. "Imitatores mei estote sicut et ego Christi" (1 Cor. 11:1) (Chobham, 24).

48. "Debet enim predicator esse quasi liber et speculum subditorum ut in operibus prelati quasi in libro legant, et in speculo uideant quid sibi faciendum est" (ibid.). Jill Mann discusses the priest's role as exemplar, including several references to the priest as mirror, in *Chaucer,* 63–65.

49. Ritamary Bradley, "Backgrounds of the Title *Speculum* in Mediaeval Literature," *Speculum* 29 (1954): 100.

50. On the double-edged nature of the speculum image, see Bradley, "Backgrounds," 105, 112. As Sarah Beckwith observes, "the mirror image . . . stresses both identity and difference and it is this tension in the ladder of analogy that provides the necessity for and the means of ascent" ("A Very Material Mysticism: The Medieval Mysticism of Margery Kempe," in *Gender and Text in the Later Middle Ages,* ed. Jane Chance [Gainesville: University Press of Florida, 1996], 202).

51. "Videtur iterum quod non sit nisi duplex praedicatio, scilicet in uita et in uerbo" (Chobham, 24).

52. "Quod uiuificat uerbo occidit exemplo" (ibid.).

53. There is a faint recollection here of Maurice of Sully's "persone e ame," the sense that the preacher is performing for two audiences at once, of whom only one can know the truth of his performance. Compare Thomas of Bailly's obser-

vation that "there are two ways in which a preacher can do or not do what he preaches: a hidden or secret way, and a public or notorious way" (predicantem contingit *dupliciter* facere uel non facere que predicat: uno modo occulte uel secrete, alio modo publice et notorie) (Thomas of Bailly, *Quodlibets,* 320, emphasis added).

54. The Pardoner's self-display and its effects are discussed at length by Minnis; see "Chaucer's Pardoner," especially 111–15, and "Author's Two Bodies," 273–74, where the earlier discussion is briefly recapitulated before being carried into new areas.

55. Erving Goffman, *The Presentation of Self in Everyday Life* (Garden City, N.Y.: Doubleday, 1959) addresses in a modern sociological context many of the issues that arise in medieval discussions of persona, and his reminder that performance does not necessarily indicate insincerity on the part of the performer is salutary; see, for example, his discussion of "cynical" performances as opposed to those that the performer himself believes in (6, 17–21). Which of these the Pardoner presents has, of course, been a disputed question in Chaucer studies. I am grateful to Phil Beck for drawing my attention to Goffman's work.

56. "Quidam . . . malo modo peccata sua abscondunt, scilicet sub ornamento uirtutum, et quasi induunt peccata sua sericis uestibus ut alios decipiant et eis formosi uideantur" (Chobham, 25).

57. "Ita meretricantur ypocrite ut uisus decipiant intuentium per ornatum uirtutum exteriorem" (ibid., 26).

58. "Similiter in uerbo predicationis duplex est modus. Quidam enim predicant ad fructum et ad utilitatem proximorum, alii ad cupiditatem lucri terreni, uel ad uoluptatem fauoris humani" (ibid.).

59. Ibid., 26–27.

60. The long-standing associations between eloquence and sensuality are discussed in Chapter 4 below.

61. "Tertio modo peccatur in uerbo Dei quando ille qui uitia detestatur eadem facit. . . . Hoc est una manu construere, et alia manu destruere" (Chobham, 27).

62. Ann W. Astell, "The *Translatio* of Chaucer's Pardoner," *Exemplaria* 4, no. 2 (1992): 411. She is quoting from Augustine, *De doctrina christiana* 4.29.62. The full passage reads, "The word of God is not another's for those who obey it; on the contrary, he delivers another's words [*dicit aliena*] who, although he speaks well, lives badly. For whatever he says that is good seems to be devised by his own genius, but it is really foreign to his character" (Augustine, *Christian Instruction,* trans. John J. Gavigan [New York: Fathers of the Church, 1947], 233). See the discussion of ownership of speech in Chapter 1 above.

63. Chobham, 68–70. This discussion occurs in the chapter on "Who can and should preach," which also discusses lay preaching and women's preaching, topics on which Thomas's views, though orthodox, are notably liberal.

64. "Unde necesse est ut concordet in ipso vita et doctrina, ne quod per unam manum aedificat, per aliam destruat.

"Praetendat itaque praedicator in habitu humilitatem, in moribus honestatem, in verbis discretionem, in zelo animarum charitatem, in cibo et potu sobrietatem, in agendis maturitatem" (in *B. Humberti de Romanis Opera de vita regulari,* ed. Joachim Joseph Berthier, 2 vols. [Rome: Marietti, 1888–89], 2:369). Jean Gerson uses a similar concept when he describes those whose lives combine the active and the contemplative as, in Valerie Lagorio's words, "heroic *ambidextri,* such as Christ, the angels, apostles, Fathers of the Church, prelates, and pastors" (Valerie Lagorio, "Social Responsibility and the Medieval Women Mystics on the Continent," in *Spiritualität Heute und Gestern: Internationaler Kongress vom 4. bis 7. August 1982,* vol. 2, Analecta Cartusiana 35, ed. James Hogg (Salzburg: Institut für Anglistik und Amerikanistik, 1983), 97.

65. Cicero, *De oratore,* ed. H. Rackham, trans. E. W. Sutton, 2 vols., Loeb Classical Library (Cambridge: Harvard University Press, 1976), 3.215. On the history of hostility to acting, see Jonas Barish, *The Antitheatrical Prejudice* (Berkeley and Los Angeles: University of California Press, 1981); and Jody Enders, *Rhetoric and the Origins of Medieval Drama* (Ithaca, N.Y.: Cornell University Press, 1992), particularly the first chapter.

66. Quoted in Barish, *Antitheatrical Prejudice,* 57; the Latin reads, "Debemus . . . illud verum quaerere, quod non quasi bifronte ratione sibique adversanti" (Augustine, *Soliloquies and Immortality of the Soul,* trans. Gerard Watson [Warminster, U.K.: Aris & Phillips, 1990], *Soliloquies* 2.x, pp. 94–96). As David Lawton notes, the persona of the Pardoner "leaves us with the ancient questions about rhetoric: how can a disguise do other than conceal truth, and what is truth that can be disguised?" (*Chaucer's Narrators* [Cambridge, U.K.: D. S. Brewer, 1985], 36).

67. This is similar to the ideal discussed by Leyser, "Masculinity in Flux."

68. "Praedicator debet captare benevolentiam auditorum a propria persona per humilitatem, et a rei quam proponit utilitate, dicendo, se iis proponere verbum Dei, ut fructum faciat in mentibus eorum, non ad terrenum emolumentum, sed ad provectum et profectum eorum; non quod inanibus vulgi clamoribus excitetur, non quod favorabili aura mulceatur, non quod theatrali applausu deliniatur; sed ut eorum animi informentur, et quod ipsi considerare non debent quis loquatur, sed quid" (Alan of Lille, *Summa de arte praedicatoria,* PL 210:113–14).

69. This reflects Goffman's observation that "while in the presence of others, the individual typically infuses his activity with signs which dramatically highlight and portray confirmatory facts that might otherwise remain unapparent or obscure" (*Presentation of Self,* 30). The effective projection of humility in preaching, it should be noted, takes the form not of excessive self-abasement but of a middle path, moderation in all things. Alan's earlier strictures against theatrical language are followed by an instruction not to use insipid language, and later Thomas Waleys cautions the preacher against either "overly splendid" clothing or "scruffy" clothing (*vilitatem vestium*), saying that "[Christ's] clothing was moderate, for it was neither overly showy nor too contemptible" (*De modo componendi sermones, cum documentis,* ed. Thomas-Marie Charland, in Charland, *Artes praedicandi,* 325–403) (hereafter Waleys). The important thing in each case seems to be that the preacher not draw attention to himself or his external attributes (words, clothing) by any sort of excess; moderation will allow the internal qualities (message, character) to shine through. See Chapter 4 below.

70. "Valde enim inhonestum est cum predicator inhoneste se habet in uoce uel in uultu uel in gestu suo" (Chobham, 302).

71. "Iratus quia non inuenit locum calumpnie; inhonesto gestu corporis ostendit turpitudinem mentis" (ibid.)

72. "Maturitas consistit in duobus, scilicet: in convenienti corporis motu et in modesto oris affatu"; this appears in a section on appropriate performance (*De prolacionis aptitudine*) in Higden, *Ars componendi sermones,* 10.

73. The translation is mostly from Jaeger, "Charismatic Body," 129, with a small addition of mine at the end. The Latin reads, "Serenus vultu, modestus habitu, circumspectus in verbis, in opere timoratus. . . . Apparebat in carne ejus gratia quaedam, spiritualis tamen potius quam carnalis. In vultu claritas praefulgebat, non terrena utique, sed coelestis: in oculis angelica quaedam puritas, et columbina simplicitas radiabat" (*S. Bernardi vita prima*, PL 185:303B–C).

74. Jaeger, "Charismatic Body," 123.

75. "Nec enim Deus omnipotens nostra grammatica indiget, ut post se homines trahat . . . cum . . . non miserit philosophos et oratores, sed simplices potius ac piscatores" (Peter Damian, *De sancta simplicitate,* PL 145:697B; the translation is from Miller et al., *Readings,* 218, n. 2).

76. "Item, simplicitatem sine curiositate ornatus rhetorici"; he goes on to quote Seneca: "A speech that applies itself to truth should be unpolished and simple" (Humbert, 403). See the further discussion on rhetoric in Chapter 4 below.

77. The quoted phrase is Robert Swanson's; see "Angels Incarnate," 162.

78. Rosemary Radford Ruether discusses the concept of monism in "Misogynism and Virginal Feminism in the Fathers of the Church," in *Religion and Sexism: Images of Woman in the Jewish and Christian Traditions,* ed. Ruether (New York: Simon and Schuster, 1974), 153–56. The phrase "singleness of heart" is from Peter Brown, *The Body and Society: Men, Women, and Sexual Renunciation in Early Christianity* (New York: Columbia University Press, 1988), 37. See also Constable, *Reformation of the Twelfth Century,* 8, 20, though he points out that monasticism too shared in the difficult tensions of the reforming period (see, e.g., 34). John of Wales, encouraging the preacher to teach by example as well as words, quotes Gregory's description of a monastic ideal: "what he shows to human eyes in his demeanor he should display [*praetendat*] in his behavior before the eyes of God" (*Summa collationum, sive Communiloquium* [Ulm: Zainer, 1481], f. 18v).

79. Jaeger, "Charismatic Body," 129.

80. "Tales motus praedicatorem non decent" (Waleys, 332).

81. "Si enim praedicatorem verbi Dei omni loco et tempore sic deceat se habere, ut *in incessu, statu, habitu et in omnibus motibus nihil faciat quod cujusquam offendat aspectum,* quanto magis ista servare debet [qui] quasi lumen quodam de supernis emissum et tanquam angelus et nuntius quidam de coelo lapsus in praesentia populi se ostendit" (ibid.). The embedded quotation is from the *Regula Sancti Augustini.*

82. "Legitur de Dauid . . . quod ipse coram rege Achis affectabat, id est gesticulationes quasdam faciebat, quibus simularet se esse stultum. Vnde, manifeste patet quod qui in predicatione tales gestus faciunt, stulti reputantur et magis uidentur esse histriones quam predicatores" (Chobham, 302–3). Thomas's insis-

tence that from this example "it is perfectly clear" (*manifeste patet*) that histrionic gesturing is inappropriate may seem a little overemphatic. Other manuals contain similar warnings against excessive theatricality and hand-waving. Thus, Ranulph Higden cites Hugh of St. Victor's instruction that one "should speak only with the mouth, not gesturing too much with the arms or the hands as advocates do, not moving the head or face in an exaggerated way, nor turning up one's eyes *like a hypocrite*" (*solo ore loquatur non nimis brachia aut manus ostendendo sicut faciunt placitatores, non capud aut visus exagitando, nec oculos* velud ypocrita *invertendo*) (Higden, *Ars componendi sermones,* 10; emphasis added).

83. Humbert of Romans attempts to avoid this pitfall by insisting that the first thing that constitutes the preacher's virtuous life in the human community (*bonitas conversationis inter homines*) is that his life should be good in the eyes of God (*coram Deo*); otherwise, says Humbert, "everything that he displayed outwardly [*totum quicquid exterius praetenderetur*] would be hypocrisy" (457).

84. Lee Patterson, *Chaucer and the Subject of History* (Madison: University of Wisconsin Press, 1991), 420. Alan J. Fletcher has recently stressed the Pardoner's specific significance with regard to heterodoxy in late fourteenth-century England; see "The Topical Hypocrisy of the Pardoner," in his *Preaching, Politics and Poetry,* 266–80.

85. For instances of the earlier mode, see Kellogg and Haselmayer, "Chaucer's Satire," and Coolidge Otis Chapman, "The Pardoner's Tale: A Mediaeval Sermon," *Modern Language Notes* 41 (December 1926): 506–9. Sedgewick, "Progress," is helpful in providing a sense of earlier criticism, as is John Halverson's insightful update, "Chaucer's Pardoner and the Progress of Criticism," *Chaucer Review* 4 (1970): 184–202, which notes the tendency to combine historical and phenomenological approaches (193). Influential considerations of the interaction of a religious worldview with the Pardoner's individual character include Alfred L. Kellogg, "An Augustinian Interpretation of Chaucer's Pardoner," in Kellogg, *Chaucer,* 245–68; Monica McAlpine, "The Pardoner's Homosexuality and How It Matters," *PMLA* 95 (1980): 8–22; Leicester, "Synne Horrible"; Patterson, *Chaucer,* 367–421; and Carolyn Dinshaw, "Eunuch Hermeneutics," in Dinshaw, *Chaucer's Sexual Poetics,* 156–84. Steven F. Kruger's "Claiming the Pardoner: Toward a Gay Reading of Chaucer's Pardoner's Tale," in *Critical Essays on Geoffrey Chaucer,* ed. Thomas C. Stillinger (New York: G. K. Hall & Co., 1998), which begins its consideration of the Pardoner's body from a different perspective than this chapter, touches illuminatingly on many of the same issues; see especially 160–65.

86. Scanlon, *Narrative,* 195.

87. On the Pardoner as an actor, see for example Donald R. Howard, *The Idea of the Canterbury Tales* (Berkeley and Los Angeles: University of California Press, 1976), 347–50; and Halverson's intriguing notion of the Pardoner's performance as a "put-on" ("Chaucer's Pardoner," 194–201).

88. See, e.g., Derek Pearsall, "Chaucer's Pardoner: The Death of a Salesman," *Chaucer Review* 17, no. 4 (1983): 358–65. Although he gives fairly short shrift to the "psychologizing" tendency of modern criticism, "a sport that has no rules," Pearsall acknowledges that "it will not do to push the Pardoner back into the con-

ventional frame of the confession of sin made by an allegorical personification" (358, 360). He argues that there is no "inner consciousness," that the Pardoner is all surface, all performance—one way, of course, of solving the *persone e ame* dilemma, at least in the case of a fictional character. But even so he ultimately concedes that the tale "is still the tale told by the Pardoner, and it is impossible to forget the context in which it is told, and the person who tells it" (363)—an impossibility that applies equally to the performance of preaching.

89. As Sedgewick puts it, "There are, of course, no two opinions about his charlatanism. But there is no final making-up of the mind about the Charlatan himself"; he suggests also that the Pardoner "fuse[d] two elements diametrically opposed: the sermon and narrative which in themselves faced one way, the self-revelation which faced another" ("Progress," 444–45, 448–49). My suggestion is that the Pardoner's two-facedness is to a certain extent symptomatic not just of his own shortcomings but of the very nature of his office.

90. " 'Nay, nay!' quod he, 'thanne have I Cristes curs! / Lat be,' quod he, 'it shal nat be, so theech! / Thou woldest make me kisse thyn olde breech, / And swere it were a relyk of a seint, / Though it were with thy fundement depeint! / But, by the croys which that Seint Eleyne fond, / I wolde I hadde thy coillons in my hond / In stide of relikes or of seintuarie. / Lat kutte hem of, I wol thee helpe hem carie; / They shul be shryned in an hogges toord!' " (Chaucer, *Canterbury Tales* VI.946–55). Such a relic, though false, would at least be demonstrably and definitely false, unlike the distracting and disconcerting half-truths that hang around the Pardoner.

91. As Halverson puts it, "The figure of the Pardoner with which we have to deal is almost entirely an image that the Pardoner himself projects. (Of the 'real' Pardoner we know next to nothing)" ("Chaucer's Pardoner," 196).

92. Eamon Grennan demonstrates that the portrait's narrator deploys a stereotype of the bad priest or preacher to give this good parson specificity, a "physical and moral existence as an individual as distinct from his institutional function," and goes on to argue that the Parson's institutional function derives from and is "subordinate" to his moral nature ("Dual Characterization," 195).

93. Lee Patterson, "The 'Parson's Tale' and the Quitting of the 'Canterbury Tales,' " *Traditio* 34 (1978): 373–74. This view regards the Parson's apparent rejection of embodiment as essentially incomplete and critiques him and his tale by using his own personal existence against him. See, for example, Laurie A. Finke, " 'To Knytte Up Al This Feeste': The Parson's Rhetoric and the Ending of the *Canterbury Tales*," *Leeds Studies in English*, n.s., 15 (1984): 95–105; and Robert Swanson, "Chaucer's Parson," in which he suggests that the Parson is "quite possibly no better than many of his contemporaries in the priesthood" (79).

94. Patterson, "Parson's Tale," 374, 380.

95. Peggy Knapp, *Chaucer and the Social Contest* (New York: Routledge, 1990), 94.

96. On this interaction, see John M. Ganim, *Chaucerian Theatricality* (Princeton, N.J.: Princeton University Press, 1990), 121–23.

97. H. Marshall Leicester, Jr., in "The Art of Impersonation: A General Prologue to the *Canterbury Tales*," *PMLA* 95 (March 1980): 213–24, has rightly ques-

tioned the tendency to equate voice with the presence of a "real" individual in discussing the *Tales* (216). His argument that "the voicing of any tale, the personality of any pilgrim, is not *given* in advance" but "has to be worked out by analyzing and defining the voice created by each tale" (217) is in some sense cognate to the uncomfortable realization in preaching theory that, given the inevitable reliance on persona, the preacher's presence cannot be a guarantor of meaning. In each case the persona that claims to be expressed through the speaking voice is to some degree created by that voice (or, for an actual preacher, by physical self-presentation).

98. Chaucer, *Canterbury Tales* I.500, 504.

99. Mann, *Chaucer*, 66. For other discussions of the Parson's idiosyncratic voice, see Ralph W. V. Elliott, *Chaucer's English* (London: Andre Deutsch, 1974), 148–50, and Patterson, "Parson's Tale," 369.

100. Chaucer, *Canterbury Tales* II.1173.

101. The Parson's idealized qualities are precisely those desired by Lollard imaginings of the good parish priest (see, for example, Knapp, *Chaucer and the Social Contest*, 91–93; and Margaret Aston, *Lollards and Reformers: Images and Literacy in Late Medieval Religion* [London: Hambledon Press, 1984], 16, n. 61), and the way his goodness is established by contrast with the evils of others in the *General Prologue* does suggest a polemical context. But his placement in the tale-telling frame gives him a human specificity that must draw a healthy skepticism about his ability to embody any abstract ideal. J. A. F. Thomson suggests that the use of "Lollere" is ambiguous here and that Harry Bailly views the Parson "more as . . . a Puritan than as . . . a heretic" ("Orthodox Religion and the Origins of Lollardy," *History*, n.s., 74, no. 240–42 [1989]: 42).

102. Chaucer, *Canterbury Tales* X.35–41.

103. Knapp suggests that the Parson's "language is inflected to resemble that of his parishioners" (*Chaucer and the Social Contest*, 45).

104. Alan of Lille, *Summa de arte praedicatoria*, cols. 113–14.

105. For readings that suggest that the Pardoner's unholy simplicity is less simple than it seems, see McAlpine, who calls the Pardoner's avarice a "screen sin" ("Pardoner's Homosexuality," 14); Halverson's warnings against taking the Pardoner at "face value" ("Chaucer's Pardoner," 191, 197); and Lee Patterson, "Chaucerian Confession: Penitential Literature and the Pardoner," *Medievalia et Humanistica*, n.s., 7 (1976), in which he notes that the Pardoner is a little overinsistent on his single-minded pursuit of money (164).

106. Here I would agree with Cespedes's overall point that "*The Canterbury Tales*, taken as a whole, is an open-ended investigation of the protean possibilities between these two positions" (i.e., those of the Parson as unfeasible ideal and the Pardoner as "evil but eloquent"), but I suggest that the "investigation" takes place not just around but within these two characters (Cespedes, "Chaucer's Pardoner," 15). As Kruger notes, "the dilemma of reading that the Pardoner poses for the other pilgrims is never solved; it hangs heavily over many of the tales that follow it"—and over the performances of preachers ("Claiming the Pardoner," 165).

107. "Cum praedicationis officium sit potius angelicum quam humanum" (Waleys, 329).

Chapter 3

1. As Spencer observes, "The English sermon-writers very rarely discussed the problems they encount[er]ed in translating; in common with many other translators of the period, they usually saw no reason to declare that their work was a translation" (*English Preaching*, 123). See also Morenzoni, *Des écoles aux paroisses*, 61, n. 178.

2. This is an old debate, going back to Albert Lecoy de la Marche and Barthélemy Hauréau in the nineteenth century. Their opposing viewpoints—that all preaching to the laity was entirely in the vernacular, all preaching to the clergy in Latin (Lecoy de la Marche) or that some bilingualism would have characterized many, if not most, sermons (Hauréau)—are still under discussion. For instance, Longère in *Prédication* says that "Lecoy de la Marche a sûrement raison" (162), while Giles Constable suggests that recent scholarship would tend to support Hauréau's long-disregarded thesis ("Language of Preaching," 134–42). Constable's excellent article raises many of the issues discussed below, albeit from a slightly different angle, and I am indebted to his formulation of the question. See also Spencer, *English Preaching*, 55–57, 118–33.

3. The fourteenth- and fifteenth-century English context has perhaps been too influential in how earlier material is read, encouraging us, like Trevisa's Lord in the *Dialogue of a Lord and a Clerk*, to "cast . . . the issue of vernacular translation and the politics of access as a social contest" that takes a similarly antagonistic form across times, cultures, and forms of discourse (Jocelyn Wogan-Browne et al., eds., *The Idea of the Vernacular: An Anthology of Middle English Literary Theory* [University Park: Pennsylvania State University Press, 1999], 324).

4. That "popular" does not necessarily mean *vernacular* is implied, for instance, by Thomas of Chobham's observation at one point that "dicitur uulgariter *omne rarum carum*" ("it is commonly said, 'everything rare is precious' "); the fact that "uulgariter" here refers to a rhyming Latin proverb (*omne rarum carum*) suggests that the term can point to a "common" culture that is not linguistically vernacular, or not exclusively so (Chobham, 75). In "The Specific Rationality of Medieval Magic," *American Historical Review* 99 (1994): 813–36, Richard Kieckhefer argues for the existence of a culture common to laity and clergy. It might also be noted that Jacques de Vitry's so-called *sermones vulgares* (his collection of *ad status* sermons) which are preserved in Latin, address groups representing both clergy and laity; the prologue and some of the edited sermons are in *Analecta novissima spicilegii solesmensis, altera continuatio*, vol. 2: *Tusculana*, ed. J. B. Pitra ([Paris:] Typis Tusculanis, 1888), 189–93, 344–461.

5. "Rapid, even instantaneous, transposition from one language into the other must have been a knack that a professional preacher would have acquired with some facility" (Spencer, *English Preaching*, 119).

6. "Prédication du bas clergé, prédication aux simples dans leur langue, utilisation des sources patristiques, ces trois aspects indissolublement liés donnent la définition et la clé de toute la prédication romane. Le recours à la langue vulgaire et sa portée ne prennent leur sens, on le verra, qu'en fonction des deux autres éléments" (Zink, *Prédication*, 89; see his full discussion of this issue, 85–113).

7. Stock, *Implications of Literacy,* 169–70. The section on the Patarenes is on pp. 151–240.

8. Quoted in Constable, "Language of Preaching," 145.

9. The Waldensian attention to scripture in the vernacular, for instance, provoked the wrath of many clerics—not least because this vernacular translation and Bible study often led to preaching; see Lambert, *Medieval Heresy,* 72–74. Humbert of Romans, among many others, uses the "milk for the little ones" metaphor; his discussion is quoted in J.-Th Welter, *L'Exemplum dans la littérature religieuse et didactique du moyen âge* (Paris: Occitania, 1927), 73 n. 13 (cont. from 72).

10. Jean-Claude Schmitt speaks of "poor secular clerics [who were] in reaction against the monastic orders, and whose culture was at least as close to that of the laity as to the Latin culture of the Church" (Bremond et al., *L'*"Exemplum," 162).

11. Chobham, 68–69.

12. See Joseph W. Goering, "The Changing Face of the Village Parish II: The Thirteenth Century," in *Pathways to Medieval Peasants,* ed. J. A. Raftis (Toronto: Pontifical Institute of Mediaeval Studies, 1981), 323–33. Thomas, a former student of Peter the Chanter at Paris, was in a sense a conduit of this larger structure to the lower clergy, just as the preacher was supposed to become a conduit of doctrine to his flock.

13. On "English Latin," see Spencer, *English Preaching,* 118–33.

14. "Item, copiam verborum. Si enim propter praedicationem primitivis praedicatoribus data sunt genera linguarum, ut abundarent verbis ad omnes, quam indecens est cum praedicator habet interdum defectum in verbis, vel propter defectum memoriae, vel propter defectum latinitatis, vel propter defectum vulgaris loquutionis, et hujusmodi?" (Humbert, 402). The concept of "abundantia" in speaking, and particularly in the use of exempla, appears in Jordan of Saxony's *Libellus de initiis Ordinis Praedicatorum,* in which he says that Dominic, wherever he went, "semper aedificatoriis affluebat sermonibus, abundabat exemplis"; the word is repeated by Giovanni of San Gimignano and Arnold of Liège (all three uses are quoted in Vecchio, "Dalla predicazione alla conversazione," 75–76, nn. 27, 29, 30, respectively). Note also the title of Humbert of Romans's collection *De habundancia exemplorum.*

15. Carla Casagrande notes that Aquinas makes a similar association between "grace of speech" and the gift of tongues; see "Le calame du Saint-Esprit: Grâce et rhétorique dans la prédication au XIIIᵉ siècle," in Dessì and Lauwers, 249. As Casagrande observes, "*gratia sermonis* concerne tout le processus communicatif de la prédication," linking preacher and audience (249–50).

16. Humbert, 403.

17. The list is reminiscent of the genre of *sermones ad status,* discussed at more length in Chapter 7 below.

18. This is not to say that the mendicant friars had no anxieties about their authority; the fourteenth-century Franciscan Francesc Eiximenis was very much aware that "omnis familiaritas parit contemptum, secundum quod experiencia docet" ("L'*Ars Praedicandi,*" 307).

19. As Welter's treatment of exempla (exemplary stories) and similitudes

(comparisons from the natural world) shows, the boundaries between these two were somewhat blurry; see, for instance, his *L'Exemplum*, 79. David L. d'Avray, sensibly, treats the various types of illustrations as a coherent group, rather than trying artificially to separate them (*The Preaching of the Friars: Sermons Diffused from Paris Before 1300* [Oxford: Clarendon Press, 1985], 225–35). See also Louis-Jacques Bataillon, "*Similitudines* et *exempla* dans les sermons du XIIIᵉ siècle," in *The Bible in the Medieval World: Essays in Memory of Beryl Smalley,* ed. Katherine Walsh and Diana Wood (Oxford: Basil Blackwell, 1985), 191–205.

20. "La constitution et l'usage des exempla reposent ainsi sur une véritable anthropologie, ou du moins sur le sentiment qu'ont les clercs d'une certaine spécificité de la culture du 'peuple.' Cette prise de conscience est la condition d'une prédication efficace: à des gens qui pour la plupart sont jugés 'agrestes,' 'minores,' 'simplices,' 'rudes,' il faut parler de choses concrètes, 'palpabilia,' 'exteriora,' 'facta,' sans utiliser les subtilités du langage spéculatif (*verba, sententiae*)" (Bremond et al., *L'*"Exemplum," 85).

21. Scanlon, *Narrative,* 34, 67.

22. "L'exemplum introduit dans le sermon la note réaliste et plaisante d'un récit qui rompt à tous égards le mode d'énonciation général du sermon et semble établir entre le prédicateur et son public une furtive connivence. Mais qu'on ne s'y trompe pas: loin d'être isolé, il se relie à tous les autres arguments, et la rupture momentanée qu'il introduit renforce encore la fonction idéologique du sermon, parole d'autorité" (Bremond et al., *L'*"Exemplum," 164).

23. Siegfried Wenzel makes a similar point with regard to the snippets of vernacular songs inserted into many sermons: "Rather than prove a point or formulate the preacher's message, these round out a picture or add color to a story. Undoubtedly they kept the audience awake and created an atmosphere of common experience shared by the preacher and his congregation, much as some preachers today strive for popularity by quoting snippets from *Reader's Digest* or *Godspell*" (*Preachers, Poets, and the Early English Lyric* [Princeton, N.J.: Princeton University Press, 1986], 227–28).

24. Bremond et al., *L'*"Exemplum," 86; d'Avray, *Preaching of the Friars,* 227.

25. Scanlon, similarly, argues that "the discursive concession which the narrative form of the exemplum makes to the laity, and which accounted for its ideological power, will also make it the ideal means for the vernacular appropriation of clerical authority" (*Narrative,* 80). He locates this reappropriation in works such as Chaucer's *Canterbury Tales* and Gower's *Confessio amantis.* I would differ from Scanlon, however, by suggesting that even in the absence of such an active reappropriation the "discursive concession" of exempla implicitly undermined the distinction between clergy and laity.

26. "Audite, fratres, audite, rem vobis novam et magnam proponam. Rex quidam fuit, qui Artus vocabatur"; the abbot then broke off and rebuked his newly attentive audience for their greater interest in secular than in spiritual matters (Caesarius of Heisterbach, *Caesarii Heisterbacensis monachi ordinis Cisterciensis dialogus miraculorum,* ed. Joseph Strange, 2 vols. [Cologne, Bonn, and Brussels: H. Lempertz and Co., 1851], 1:205). A similar accusation is found in the *Sermones de tempore et sanctis* by Odo of Châteauroux, whose audience is not spec-

ified: "Vos potius vigilaretis audiendo de Parcevalle, quia etiam de die et ad horam verbum Domini audire non vultis, vel cum molestia et taedio auditis" (in *Analecta novissima spicilegii solesmensis, altera continuatio*, vol. 2: *Tusculana*, ed. J. B. Pitra [(Paris:) Typis Tusculanis, 1888], 227). Odo's critique reflects the early popularity of Chrétien de Troyes: in addition to this mention of Perceval, he has above complained of his audience's devotion to "figmentis de Arturo compositis et de Herec et Chyges" (227).

27. "Circa exempla vero attendendum est ut sint competentis auctoritatis, ne contemnantur; et verisimilia, ut credantur; et aliquam aedificationem continentia, ne inutiliter proferantur" (Humbert, 467).

28. "Per experientiam noverunt quantus fructus ex hujusmodi fabulosis exemplis proveniat laïcis et simplicibus personis, non solum ad aedificationem, sed ad recreationem" (Jacques de Vitry, *Sermones vulgares*, 192).

29. Eiximenis, "*L'Ars praedicandi*," 307.

30. Wenzel, "Chaucer," 151–52.

31. This translation from the "universal" Latin into the more "particular" vernacular is another instance of the preacher's mediatory status. On Latin and vernacular as universal and particular, see for example Kevin Brownlee, "Commentary and the Rhetoric of Exemplarity: Griseldis in Petrarch, Philippe de Mézières, and the *Estoire*," *South Atlantic Quarterly* 91 (fall 1992): 870–71. But Nicholas Watson, in "Visions of Inclusion: Universal Salvation and Vernacular Theology in Pre-Reformation England," *Journal of Medieval and Early Modern Studies* 27, no. 2 (1997): 145–87, suggests that it is rather the vernacular that is universal; and Étienne de Bourbon makes a strong case for the universality of exempla: "Ipsa siquidem exempla valent ad omnes homines et ad omnem statum et ad omnem materiam, et ad omne malum dissuadendum, et ad omne bonum suadendum et adipiscendum et promovendum, in omni loco et tempore, predicacione et monicione" (Lecoy de la Marche, *Anecdotes*, 12–13).

32. Scanlon, *Narrative*, 66.

33. See here Stock on the role of literate members of "textual communities" and their connection to the illiterate members of those communities; he points out that "non-literates" who were part of textual communities "had already begun to participate in literate culture, although indirectly" (*Implications of Literacy*, 91).

34. "In his verbis, similitudinibus et exemplis adtendendum est, quod non possunt ita exprimi scripto, sicut gestu et verbo atque pronuntiandi modo, nec ita movent vel incitant auditores in ore unius, sicut in ore alterius, nec in uno idiomate, sicut in alio" (Jacques de Vitry, *Sermones vulgares*, 193). The passage is quoted slightly differently in Thomas Frederick Crane, ed., *The Exempla or Illustrative Stories from the* Sermones Vulgares *of Jacques de Vitry* (London: David Nutt for the Folk-Lore Society, 1890), xliii n. (cont. from previous pp.).

35. "Sunt enim multi quibus data est major gracia loquendi per auctoritates, raciones vel interpretaciones vel aliis modis quam per exempla, circa que forte non habet graciosam narracionem et non expedit istis relinquere modum [docendi], in quo habent graciam propter illum in quo non habent" (quoted in Welter, *L'Exemplum*, 72–73, n. 13).

36. Le Goff also notes the strongly oral quality of exempla and their link to performance (Bremond et al., *L'* "Exemplum," 82).

37. This transformation from abstract to particular was to some extent an inevitable feature of vernacular preaching. There are many instances where scriptural and other Latin texts in the third person are translated in surviving sermons not only into the vernacular but also into the second person, reminding us of the personal immediacy of preaching. See, for example, Zink, *Prédication,* 97, where the third-person Latin becomes second-person Old Occitan: "Tunc convertitur . . . Adonc es trastornaz vas Deu."

38. Chapter 39: "Contra praedicatores qui in familiaribus colloquutionibus loquuntur vana, ad modum saecularium." The chapter also demonstrates some suspicion of storytelling: "hoc requiritur ab illo qui et sacerdos et praedicator est, ut nugas vel fabulas os ejus non proferat" (Humbert, 463, 465).

39. "Et ideo cum [praedicatores] vadunt per mundum, non debent dimittere linguam caelestem propter linguam mundi, sicut Gallicus, quocumque vadat, non de facili dimittit linguam propter aliam, et propter nobilitatem linguae suae, et patriae suae"; the section on schoolboys reads, "Item, pueri in scholis, quibus imposita est lex loquendi latinum et non romantium, quando incidunt etiam casualiter in verbum romantium, statim puniuntur cum ferula in confusionem suam: quanto magis digni sunt confusione et poena, illi quorum interest loqui utilia, quando loquuntur vana!" (ibid.).

40. As Vecchio observes, "the distinction between edifying speech and useless speech [*parole vane*] cannot be perfectly mapped onto the distinction between sacred speech and profane speech" ("Dalla predicazione alla conversazione," 79). On the dangers of "vaniloquium" and related failings, see Carla Casagrande and Silvana Vecchio, *I peccati della lingua: Disciplina ed etica della parola nella cultura medievale* (Rome: Istituto della Enciclopedia Italiana, 1987), 425–39.

41. A later vernacular work, the *Pore Caitif,* makes a similar point from a different angle. As Nicholas Watson puts it, one of the lessons of this text is that "the 'clergy' that really needs to be learned (whether by vernacular readers or clerics) is not Latin, but holiness" ("Conceptions of the Word: The Mother Tongue and the Incarnation of God," *New Medieval Literatures* 1 [1997]: 108).

42. Chapter 40: "In hujusmodi loquutionibus quandoque dicenda sunt verba sancta, quandoque exempla aliqua bona recitanda, quandoque etiam aliqua verba saecularia referenda" (Humbert, 466).

43. "Circa verba vero saecularia, si quandoque dicantur, propter quamdam cum hominibus conformitatem, tamen cavendum est ne talia dicantur quae sint longe a verbis Dei" (ibid., 467).

44. Stock cites the Patarene Landulf "asking like Saint Paul that his listeners imitate him (*imitatores mei estote*)," a request that puts him in an exalted, apostolic mode but at the same time suggests that his listeners can attain a similar "way of life" (*forma nostra*) (*Implications of Literacy,* 170).

45. Phyllis B. Roberts, "Master Stephen Langton Preaches to the People and Clergy: Sermon Texts from Twelfth-Century Paris," *Traditio* 36 (1980): 258–59. Roberts dates the sermon to c. 1180–1207, probably toward the end of that period.

46. "Vt etiam uulgariter loquar propter simpliciores, adtendite cum quanta ueneratione simplices laici et ydiote preueniunt diem Pasche. Quantis castigationibus corpus affligunt, ieiuniis, orationibus, uigiliis; quasi celestibus margaritis ornati, ut Dominice mense possint interesse. Rursum quod eis est dies Pasche, hoc est fere quelibet dies, et ideo quicquid facere debeatis, saltem ex eorum exemplo perpendite, ne accidat uobis quod populo preuaricanti" (ibid., 262).

47. Christoph Maier, *Preaching the Crusades: Mendicant Friars and the Cross in the Thirteenth Century* (Cambridge: Cambridge University Press, 1994), 122. This exemplum is one variant of a popular type, whose history is discussed in Scanlon, *Narrative*, 31–32.

48. Filippo da Ferrara's *Liber de introductione loquendi*, which gives advice to preachers on how to talk beneficially outside of preaching contexts, notes that "interdum magni clerici deficiunt in verbis quando non precogitaverunt" and encourages them to have a stock of conversational gambits on hand (which his work offers to provide) (Vecchio, "Dalla predicazione alla conversazione," 69, n. 7).

49. See Watson, "Conceptions of the Word," on kenosis, the theological underpinning of the notion of holy simplicity.

50. Francesc Eiximenis warns his fellow preachers of the audience's perspicacity and marvels at their forbearance, writing, "Vident tamen seculares multos predicatores sic scandalosos, sic male edificantes eos in uerbis et factis, quod mirum est, et specialiter gracia Dei in hoc mirabiliter operatur, quia seculares non lapidant eos tanquam capitaliter puniendos"; the notion that bad preachers only escape being stoned to death by the miraculous grace of God seems to indicate a healthy respect for lay audiences, whose disgust is seen as entirely justified (Eiximenis, "L'*Ars praedicandi,*" 307–8).

51. "Item, in bonis consuetudinibus conformet se his cum quibus conversatur. Verbi gratia, in aliquibus regionibus indecens est de scutella bibere; ultra scyphum, dum quis bibit, respicere; potagium de cochleari ut sonus audiatur sorbere; mensae cubitis incumbere, et similia. Quae quamvis peccata non sint, tamen vitanda sunt propter honestatem, apud eos qui talia reputant indecora" (in *B. Humberti de Romanis Opera de vita regulari,* ed. Joachim Joseph Berthier, 2 vols. [Rome: Marietti, 1888–89], 2:370).

52. Aers and Staley, *Powers of the Holy,* 38.

53. John of Wales, *Summa collationum*. There are numerous early editions, one of which (Strasburg, 1489) has been reprinted (Yorkshire: S. R. Publishers, 1964). The *Communiloquium* was probably composed around 1265–70, according to Jenny Swanson, *John of Wales: A Study of the Works and Ideas of a Thirteenth-Century Friar* (Cambridge: Cambridge University Press, 1989). There is as yet no readily available edition of Filippo of Ferrara's work, which was composed in the second quarter of the fourteenth century, though a critical edition is in progress (Vecchio, "Dalla predicazione alla conversazione," 68–69, n. 5).

54. "Predicator euangelicus . . . sedula diligentia studere debet vt sciat omnes instruere doctrinaliter & ammonere efficaciter, non solum in predicatione declamatoria, sed in collatione familari & mutua. . . . Et hoc exemplo saluatoris, qui non solum predicabat publice in ciuitatibus et synagogis, sed etiam in mensis, parabolas et verba vite frequenter auditoribus proponebat" (John of Wales, *Summa col-*

lationum, f. 18r). I have modernized puncutation and capitalization and have silently expanded abbreviations in transcribing this text.

55. John of Wales, *Summa collationum,* 19v.

56. Wogan-Browne et al., *Idea of the Vernacular,* 329.

57. Vecchio discusses Humbert's treatment of the idea that the extension of "verba aedificatoria" to certain kinds of secular speech opens a teaching role to others than the clergy ("Dalla predicazione alla conversazione," 80). The impression of such interchange is strengthened by the fact that John of Wales draws heavily on classical sources for his teachings, so that much of the advice or wisdom his book contains is, from a Christian perspective, "secular" in origin. Jenny Swanson notes that even in citing Augustine he draws mostly on the saint's "classical lore and *exempla*" (*John of Wales,* 18).

58. The incident comes from the *Vita* of Costantino of Orvieto and is cited in Vecchio, "Dalla predicazione alla conversazione," 75, n. 27.

59. "Having put in the first book those things that may be told [*recitari*] at the table, now in this second book we include those things that can be said while you are standing at the fire with people . . . note that all the stories included in the first book can also be told when you are at the fire" (Vecchio, "Dalla predicazione alla conversazione," 83, n. 52).

60. See Casagrande and Vecchio, *Peccati,* 441–53. "Mala taciturnitas" is Scylla to the Charybdis of "vaniloquium" or "multiloquium."

61. Vecchio, "Dalla predicazione alla conversazione," 81–83.

62. As Constable says, "the very term Latin was used more broadly in the Middle Ages than it is today. . . . It should be used in apposition, not in opposition, to vernacular, which it frequently resembled" ("Language of Preaching," 136–37).

Chapter 4

1. Sharon Farmer, "Persuasive Voices: Clerical Images of Medieval Wives," *Speculum* 61 (1986): 541.

2. Enders, *Rhetoric,* 30. See also Copeland, "Pardoner's Body," 146.

3. The phrase is R. Howard Bloch's; see *Medieval Misogyny and the Invention of Western Romantic Love* (Chicago: University of Chicago Press, 1991), 37–63.

4. Kennedy, *Classical Rhetoric,* 55; on sophistic rhetoric, see 25–40 and especially the section on the second sophistic, 37–40; for Plato's opposition to sophistry, see 41–85, particularly the section on the *Gorgias.* See also Murphy, *Rhetoric,* 60.

5. Quoted in M. L. Stapleton, *Harmful Eloquence: Ovid's* Amores *from Antiquity to Shakespeare* (Ann Arbor: University of Michigan Press, 1996), 2.

6. Although Christian rhetors looked primarily to public or civic eloquence for their models—when they looked for such models at all—the fact that "persuasion . . . often accompanies love (*erôs*) in art and religion as well as in literature" in the classical world no doubt contributed to eloquence's suspect character

(Nicolas P. Gross, *Amatory Persuasion in Antiquity: Studies in Theory and Practice* [Newark: University of Delaware Press, 1985], 16). See also Erik Gunderson's observation that "sex is indissociable from oratory. . . . The scandal is in giving pleasure, in pandering, in betraying the orator's destiny as a 'manly' man" (*Staging Masculinity: The Rhetoric of Performance in the Roman World* [Ann Arbor: University of Michigan Press, 2000], 178).

7. Stapleton, *Harmful Eloquence,* 2. Gunderson notes that "against this self-mastery and discipline [characteristic of idealized rhetorical training] the rhetorical theorists pit wanton pleasures," a contest that recurs in later Christian discourses (*Staging Masculinity,* 5).

8. Stapleton, *Harmful Eloquence,* 3. See Kennedy, *Classical Rhetoric,* 33, for a similar argument about Isocrates.

9. See the discussion in Chapter 2 above.

10. Kennedy, *Classical Rhetoric,* 33. See Quintilian, *Institutio oratoria,* trans. H. E. Butler, 4 vols. (London: William Heinemann, 1920), 2:xx, 4–9. On Gregory the Great, see Murphy, *Rhetoric,* 293. Alcuin made a similar attempt to "confine delivery to a Christian context of moral excellence"—without success, Jody Enders notes (Enders, *Rhetoric,* 33–34).

11. Stapleton quoting Aristotle, in *Harmful Eloquence,* 2–3, emphasis added; on Cicero, see p. 4.

12. On the particularly misogynistic versions of this asceticism, see Marcia L. Colish, "Cosmetic Theology: The Transformation of a Stoic Theme," *Assays* 1 (1981): 3–14; and Bloch, *Medieval Misogyny,* 37–63. On early Christian attitudes toward the physical more generally, see Brown, *Body and Society.*

13. For an in-depth investigation of one example, see Robert Dick Sider, *Ancient Rhetoric and the Art of Tertullian* (Oxford: Oxford University Press, 1971). On the Church Fathers' rhetorical education, see Murphy, *Rhetoric,* 55; and Kennedy, *Classical Rhetoric,* 146. This was not only a patristic phenomenon; the eleventh-century reformer Peter Damian, author of a treatise on "holy simplicity," had been a teacher of rhetoric before his conversion. See Karl F. Morrison, "Incentives for Studying the Liberal Arts," in *The Seven Liberal Arts in the Middle Ages,* ed. David L. Wagner (Bloomington: Indiana University Press, 1983), 33–34.

14. For an extensive discussion of the early Christian negotiations with pagan culture, see Murphy, *Rhetoric,* 46–63, to which my treatment here is indebted. On the development of preaching in the early Church and its relationship to rhetorical tradition, see Kennedy, *Classical Rhetoric,* 135–49.

15. Peter Brown has described how Saint Paul "crammed into the notion of the flesh a superabundance of overlapping notions," a superabundance that Tertullian takes over (Brown, *Body and Society,* 48).

16. Tertullian, *The Apparel of Women,* in Tertullian, *Disciplinary, Moral and Ascetical Works,* trans. Rudolph Arbesmann, Emily Joseph Daly, and Edwin A. Quain (New York: Fathers of the Church, 1959), 119; "Illi . . . angeli qui . . . proprie et quasi peculiariter feminis instrumentum istud muliebris gloriae contulerunt" (Tertullian, *La toilette des femmes (De cultu feminarum),* ed. and trans. Marie Turcan, Sources chrétiennes 173 [Paris: Éditions du Cerf, 1971], 48).

17. Tertullian, *Spectacles,* in Tertullian, *Disciplinary, Moral and Ascetical*

Works, 104; "Si scaenicae doctrinae delectant, satis nobis litterarum est . . . nec fabulae sed ueritates, nec strophae sed simplicitates" (Tertullian, *Les spectacles* [*De spectaculis*], ed. and trans. Marie Turcan, Sources chrétiennes 332 [Paris: Éditions du Cerf, 1986], 314).

18. Kennedy, *Classical Rhetoric,* 147.

19. Sider, *Ancient Rhetoric.*

20. Timothy David Barnes, *Tertullian: A Historical and Literary Study* (Oxford: Clarendon Press, 1985), 210.

21. Tertullian contrasts God as *inventor* with the devil as *interpolator:* "Non ergo hoc solum respiciendum est a quo omnia sint instituta, sed a quo conuersa. Ita enim apparebit cui usui sint instituta, si appareat cui non. Multum interest inter corruptelam et integritatem, quia multum est inter institutorem et interpolatorem" (*Les spectacles,* 90).

22. On Tertullian's use of pagan learning, see Barnes, *Tertullian,* 196, 205–10.

23. "Sermone, inquit, me suasisti, medicamine sapientissimo. Verum, etsi eloquium quiescat, aut infantia subductum aut verecundia retentum (nam et elingua philosophia vita contenta est), ipse habitus sonat. Sic denique auditur philosophus dum videtur" (Tertullian, *De pallio,* in Tertullian, *Opera,* 2 vols., CCSL 1–2 [Turnhout, Belgium: Brepols, 1954], 2:750; my translation). The passage is also translated and discussed in Bloch, *Medieval Misogyny,* 42 and 218, n. 29. The subject under discussion here, strangely enough, is the philosopher's pallium—a piece of clothing—as a kind of speech act, in what would seem to be a piling up, rather than a dispersal, of decorative modes of communication.

24. He tries a similar tactic with female appearance: "tanta enim debet esse plenitudo eius [i.e., pudicitiae] ut emanet ab animo in habitum et eructet a conscientia in superficiem" (Tertullian, *La toilette des femmes,* 164).

25. "Ita nos rhetoricari quoque prouocant haeretici, sicut etiam philosophari philosophi" (Tertullian, *De resurrectione mortuorum* 5.1, in Tertullian, *Opera,* 2:926, quoted in Barnes, *Tertullian,* 209, n. 4).

26. Harry Caplan, "Classical Rhetoric and the Mediaeval Theory of Preaching," in *Historical Studies of Rhetoric and Rhetoricians,* ed. Raymond F. Howes (Ithaca, N.Y.: Cornell University Press, [1961]), 76–77.

27. "Sed hoc quoque malum non ex tua castitate repudiavi, deus cordis mei. . . . talibus enim figmentis suspirans anima nonne fornicatur abs te?" (Augustine, *Confessions,* trans. William Watts, 2 vols., Loeb Classical Library [Cambridge: Harvard University Press, 1977], 4.2, pp. 151, 150).

28. "Quid enim miserius misero non miserante se ipsum et flente Didonis mortem, quae fiebat amando Aenean, non flente autem mortem suam, quae fiebat . non amando te, deus. . . ? . . . amicitia enim mundi huius fornicatio est abs te . . . et haec non flebam, et flebam Didonem extinctam ferroque extrema secutam" (Augustine, *Confessions* 1.13, pp. 39–41, 38–40).

29. See Kennedy, *Classical Rhetoric,* 153–60; and Murphy, *Rhetoric,* 56–64.

30. Augustine, *Christian Instruction,* trans. John J. Gavigan (New York: Fathers of the Church, 1947), 2.35.53, p. 107; "Item scientia definiendi, diuidendi atque partiendi, quamquam etiam rebus falsis plerumque adhibeatur, ipsa tamen

falsa non est neque ab hominibus instituta, sed in rerum ratione comperta" (Augustine, *De doctrina,* 69).

31. Augustine, *Christian Instruction* 2.36.54, p. 108; "Neque hoc ab hominibus institutum est, ut caritatis expressio conciliet auditorem aut ut facile, quod intendit, insinuet breuis et aperta narratio et varietas eius sine fastidio teneat intentos" (Augustine, *De doctrina,* 70).

32. Tertullian, *Apparel of Women,* in Tertullian, *Disciplinary, Moral and Ascetical Works,* 127.

33. Augustine, *Christian Instruction* 4.2.3, p. 169; "Nam cum per artem rhetoricam et uera suadeantur et falsa, quis audeat dicere, aduersus mendacium in defensoribus suis inermem debere consistere ueritatem, ut uidelicet illi, qui res falsas persuadere conantur, nouerint auditorem uel beneuolum uel intentum uel docilem prooemio facere, isti autem non nouerint? . . . Cum ergo sit in medio posita facultas eloquii, quae ad persuadenda seu praua seu recta ualet plurimum, cur non bonorum studio comparatur, ut militet ueritati, si eam mali ad obtinendas peruersas uanasque causas in usus iniquitatis et erroris usurpant?" (Augustine, *De doctrina,* 117). This recalls Cicero's lament that orators have abandoned delivery to the *histriones;* see Chapter 2 above.

34. Augustine speaks here of "that attractiveness of style, which certainly does not teach falsehoods, but ornaments trifling and perishable truths with a frothy showiness of style" (*Christian Instruction* 4.14.31, pp. 196–97).

35. In "Classical Rhetoric," Caplan notes three quotations that express "the dominant attitude to pagan erudition": this one from Augustine, the "marriage law" in Deut. 21:10–13 drawn on by Saint Jerome (discussed below), and Prov. 9:1, "Wisdom has built her house, she has hewn out her seven pillars," the seven pillars being interpreted as the liberal arts (77).

36. Augustine, *Christian Instruction* 2.40.60, p. 113; "Ad usum iustum praedicandi euangelii" (Augustine, *De doctrina,* 74).

37. Augustine, *Christian Instruction* 2.40.60, p. 112; "uasa atque ornamenta de auro et argento et uestem" (Augustine, *De doctrina,* 73). In the *Confessions,* Augustine uses a similar image when discussing rhetoric's ability to be used well or badly: he says that "verbis autem ornatis et inornatis, sicut vasis urbanis et rusticanis utrosque cibos [i.e., truth or deception, wholesome or unwholesome food] posse ministrari" (5.6, p. 224). Compare the much later argument of Thomas of Bailly that a bad man can produce good doctrine, just as worthless ground can produce precious gold; thus, "sicut aurum eligitur, terra relinquitur, sic et nos debemus doctrinam accipere et mores relinquere" (*Quodlibets,* 323). Taken together, the passages demonstrate the consistency of this imagery and remind us of the image of both preacher and language as vessels for a divine message.

38. "Mentiris, ait, Ciceronianus es, non Christianus: ubi enim thesaurus tuus, ibi et cor tuum (Matth. 6.21)" (Jerome, *Ad Eustochium [Epistola 22* (Letter 22)*],* PL 22:416).

39. Eugene F. Rice, Jr., *St. Jerome in the Renaissance* (Baltimore: Johns Hopkins University Press, 1985), 5–6; the discussion is in Jerome's Letter 70. Dinshaw discusses Jerome's analogy in *Chaucer's Sexual Poetics,* 22–25.

40. I borrow the phrase from Gillian Cloke, *This Female Man of God: Woman*

and Spiritual Power in the Patristic Age, AD 350–450 (London: Routledge, 1995). On the ideal of virginal "virility" for Christian women, see Barbara J. Newman, *From Virile Woman to WomanChrist* (Philadelphia: University of Pennsylvania Press, 1995), 3–6.

41. The concept, though not always in the same words, appears repeatedly in Cicero's works. In his translation of Augustine's *De doctrina,* John Gavigan offers a list of references, including *Orator* 21.69; *De oratore* 2.27.115, 2.28.121, 2.77.310; and *Brutus* 49.185 (Augustine, *Christian Instruction,* 193, n. 1).

42. Augustine, *De doctrina* 4.12.27, p. 135.

43. Augustine uses *suauis* in other, less positive contexts: he found the heretic Faustus "hominem gratum et iucundum verbis, et ea ipsa, quae illi solent dicere, multo *suavius* garrientem"; and he speaks later of Faustus's "eloquium . . . seductorium" (Augustine, *Confessions* 5.6, pp. 222, 226; emphasis added).

44. Augustine, *De doctrina* 4.5.8, p. 121.

45. Augustine, *Christian Instruction* 4.5.7, p. 173; "Qui uero affluit insipienti eloquentia, tanto magis cauendus est, quanto magis ab eo in his, quae audire inutile est, delectare auditor et eum, quoniam diserte dicere audit, etiam uere dicere existimat" (Augustine, *De doctrina,* 120).

46. Augustine, *De doctrina* 4.5.8, p. 121: "Qui enim eloquenter dicunt, suauiter, qui sapienter, salubriter audiunt."

47. Augustine, *Christian Instruction* 4.12.28, p. 194; 4.13.29, p. 195; "[Uera] per se ipsa, quoniam uera sunt, manifestata delectant," but "Propter eos . . . quibus fastidientibus non placet ueritas, si alio quocumque modo, sed si eo modo dicatur, ut placeat et sermo dicentis, datus est in eloquentia non paruus etiam delectationi locus" (Augustine, *De doctrina,* 136).

48. Augustine, *Christian Instruction* 4.14.30, p. 196; "Uera tamen dicantur et iusta, non iniqua libenter audiantur; quod utique non fieret, nisi suauiter dicerentur" (Augustine, *De doctrina,* 137).

49. Augustine, *Christian Instruction* 4.6.10, pp. 176–77; "Et in quibus forte locis agnoscitur a doctis, tales res dicuntur, ut uerba, quibus dicuntur, non a dicente adhibita, sed ipsis rebus uelut sponte subiuncta uideantur; quasi sapientiam de domo sua, id est, pectore sapientis procedere intellegas et tamquam inseparabilem famulam etiam non uocatam sequi eloquentiam" (Augustine, *De doctrina,* 122–23).

50. Augustine, *Christian Instruction* 4.6.9, p. 175; "Nec iam dicenda est eloquentia, si personae non *congruit* eloquentis, ita est quaedam, quae uiros summa auctoritate dignissimos planeque diuinos *decet.* Haec illi locuti sunt nec ipsos *decet* alia nec alios ipsae; ipsis enim *congruit*" (Augustine, *De doctrina,* 122; emphasis added).

51. Augustine, *Christian Instruction* 4.7.13, p. 179; *De doctrina,* 125.

52. Augustine, *Christian Instruction* 4.14.31, p. 197; *De doctrina,* 137.

53. Augustine, *Christian Instruction* 4.15.32, p. 198; *De doctrina,* 138–39.

54. Gunderson, *Staging Masculinity,* notes a similar tension in Cicero's *De oratore:* "The pleasure of [the orator's] pleasantness . . . must be hard and rugged, not sweet and like an overripe fruit" (205). See also his discussion of *decet, decor,* and *decus* (207).

55. In addition to the passages from book 2 cited above in notes 31, 36, and 37, see 4.15–16.32–33, which argues that although the effect of preaching comes from God, this does not absolve human preachers from responsibility for their task. John D. Schaeffer discusses this aspect of Augustine's thinking in "The Dialectic of Orality and Literacy: The Case of Book 4 of Augustine's *De doctrina christiana*," *PMLA* 111 (October 1996): 1133–45.

56. Gregory the Great's *Pastoral Care*, though extremely influential, addressed primarily the moral and doctrinal aspects of preaching rather than its technical ones; see Murphy, *Rhetoric*, 292–97, and Gillian Evans, *The Thought of Gregory the Great*, Cambridge Studies in Medieval Life and Thought, ser. 4, vol. 2 (Cambridge: Cambridge University Press, 1986), 75–86. On the gap between Augustine and the later theorists, and some possible reasons for it, see Murphy, *Rhetoric*, 297–300. On the medieval preaching manuals, see Briscoe, *Artes praedicandi*.

57. Murphy, *Rhetoric*, 311.

58. Caplan, "Classical Rhetoric," 76.

59. On the development of the "homily" form of preaching, see Murphy, *Rhetoric*, 298–99, and Kennedy, *Classical Rhetoric*, 136–38. The essays in Amos, Green, and Kienzle, *De Ore Domini*, particularly those by Green, Amos, and Lawrence T. Martin, are also useful for their discussion of preaching in the "non-theoretical" period.

60. Copeland, "Pardoner's Body." Also relevant here is Virginia Burrus's intriguing point that the "emerging Christian rhetoric of masculinity" in the fourth century "illumines the competitive rhetorical economy within which it seeks to usurp the privileged maleness of the classical discourse" ("Reading Agnes: The Rhetoric of Gender in Ambrose and Prudentius," *Journal of Early Christian Studies* 3, no. 1 [1995], 29). Having successfully achieved the position of "privileged maleness," however, later Christian discourse found itself, in turn, plagued by the recurrence of feminized qualities, which it attributed to that same, now-vanquished classical discourse.

61. Caplan, "Classical Rhetoric," 79. Kennedy suggests that the great weakness of Augustine's *De doctrina christiana* was that it "encouraged the identification of rhetoric with style" already present in ancient rhetoric (*Classical Rhetoric*, 159).

62. Quoted in Caplan, "Classical Rhetoric," 78–79.

63. "Irritat qui talis agnoscitur, non praedicat, quia quo dicta sua venustiore ornare conatur eloquio, tanto acriore astantium pectora ad contemptum (proh dolor!) etiam eorum quae bene ab eo dicuntur, et maxime sui ipsius vexat fastidio" (Guibert de Nogent, *Quo ordine sermo fieri debeat*, PL 156:30).

64. In his memoirs, which he modeled on Augustine's *Confessions*, Guibert follows his exemplar in his harsh assessment of poetry: as he studied pagan poetry, he says, his "mind was led away by these enticements of a poisonous license" and he was "snared . . . by the wantonness of the sweet words" of the poets; the language and attitude clearly echo Augustine and again show the persistence of his views into the later Middle Ages (Guibert of Nogent, *Self and Society in Medieval France: The Memoirs of Abbot Guibert of Nogent*, ed. John F. Benton, trans. C. C. Swinton Bland and John F. Benton, Medieval Academy Reprints for Teaching [Toronto: University of Toronto Press, 1984], 87).

65. Alan of Lille, *The Art of Preaching*, trans. Gillian R. Evans, Cistercian Studies Series 23 (Kalamazoo, Mich.: Cistercian Publications, 1981), 16; and "Primo ergo videndum est, quid sit praedicatio, et qualis esse debeat quoad superficiem verborum, et pondus sententiarum," in *Summa de arte praedicatoria,* col. III.

66. See Jan Ziolkowski, *Alan of Lille's Grammar of Sex: The Meaning of Grammar to a Twelfth-Century Intellectual* (Cambridge, Mass.: Medieval Academy of America, 1985). Alan's sense of the sexual implications of rhetorical language echoes that of the classical rhetoricians; see Gunderson, *Staging Masculinity.*

67. Alan of Lille, *Art of Preaching*, 18–19; "Praedicatio enim in se, non debet habere verba scurrilia, vel puerilia, vel rhythmorum melodias et consonantias metrorum, quae potius fiunt *ad aures demulcendas,* quam ad animum instruendum, quae praedicatio *theatralis est et mimica,* et ideo omnifarie contemnenda, de tali praedicatione dicitur a propheta: Caupones vestri miscent aquam vino (Isa. 1). . . . In illa praedicatione est aqua vino mista, in qua puerilia et scurrilia verba, et animos quodammodo *effeminantia* ponuntur: *praedicatio enim non debet splendere phaleris verborum, purpuramentis colorum,* nec nimis exsanguibus verbis debet esse dejecta, sed 'Medium tenuere beati.' Quia, si nimis esset *picturata,* videretur *nimio studio excogitata,* et potius *elaborata* ad favorem hominum quam ad utilitatem proximorum, et ita minus moveret animos auditorum. . . . Talis autem praedicatio potest dici suspiciosa, non tamen contemnenda, sed sustinenda" (Alan of Lille, *Summa de arte praedicatoria,* cols. 112–13; emphasis added).

68. Bloch, *Medieval Misogyny,* 33; "Rursum auditus vario organorum cantu, et vocum inflexionibus delinitur: et carmine poetarum et comoediarum, mimorumque urbanitatibus et strophis, quidquid per aures introiens, virilitatem mentis effeminat" (Jerome, *Adversus Jovinianum* 394, PL 23:297B). The passage as a whole moves from acting, feminine beauty, and decoration to poetry and the allure of rhetoric to sweet smells, appropriate for "dissolute people and lovers."

69. Thomas of Chobham makes a similar point when he describes a kind of preaching "dangerous both to preacher and to audience," which aims more for "the pleasure of wanton ears [*aurium prurientium*]" than spiritual edification (Chobham, 18). There is an echo here of 2 Tim. 4:3: "the time will come when they will not endure sound doctrine, but wanting to have their ears tickled [*prurientes auribus*], they will accumulate for themselves teachers in accordance to their own desires."

70. "Poterit etiam ex occasione interserere dicta gentilium, sicut et Paulus apostolus aliquando in Epistolis suis philosophorum auctoritates interserit" (Alan of Lille, *Summa de arte praedicatoria,* col. 114).

71. "Unde de falsis praedicatoribus dicitur: Caupones nostri miscent aquam vino. Aquam enim vino miscent, qui falsa cum veris praedicant, ut haeretici faciunt; item qui verbum pro favore humano vendunt, ut hypocritae" (ibid., col. 183).

72. The locus classicus for this is the description in 2 Tim. 3:6 of "those who enter into households and captivate weak women weighed down with sins, led on by various impulses," which the Middle Ages frequently read as a warning against heretics (or friars); see Chapter 5 below.

73. Murphy, *Rhetoric*, 314.

74. Alexander of Ashby, "Aux origines," 902, 903.

75. Georgiana Donavin, " 'De sermone sermonem fecimus': Alexander of Ashby's *De artificioso modo predicandi*," *Rhetorica* 15, no. 3 (summer 1997): 284.

76. "Dicet aliquis: quod mones nos in doctrina Christiana uenustatem uerborum querere? Videtur esse contra apostolum, qui in quodam loco ait: non in persuasoriis uerbis. Ad hoc responderi debet quod non prohibet ibi apostolus ornatu uerborum uti ad utilia persuadenda, set eos ibi reprehendit qui magis student pulcra dicere quam utilia, placere pocius quam prodesse" (Alexander of Ashby, "Aux origines," 908). The division of "useful" from merely "beautiful" rhetoric was one of the most effective aspects of Augustine's legacy to the Middle Ages. Alastair J. Minnis notes its appearance in another context, Henry of Ghent's prologue to his *Summa quaestionum ordinariarum*, which treats the question of the proper place of verbal style in Christian teaching. Henry comes to a conclusion similar to that of many preaching theorists; as Minnis notes, "Having warned against putting style before substance, with the formidable support of Augustine, Henry apparently feels that he can then proceed to make a measured defence of literary elegance" ("Medium and Message: Henry of Ghent on Scriptural Style," in *Literature and Religion in the Later Middle Ages*, ed. Richard G. Newhauser and John A. Alford [Binghamton, N.Y.: Medieval & Renaissance Texts & Studies, 1995], 220).

77. "Cavenda sunt in sermone nimis ornata eloquia vel eloquentia" (Pseudo-Bonaventure, *Ars concionandi*, in *Doctoris seraphici S. Bonaventurae... Opera omnia*, 10 vols., ed. Collegium S. Bonaventurae [Ad Claras Aquas (Quaracchi): Collegium S. Bonaventurae, 1882–1902], 9:15).

78. "Item attendendum est secundum Augustinum, 'ut non sit prius dictor quam orator' " (ibid., col. 16).

79. Humbert of Romans, *Treatise on Preaching*, ed. Walter M. Conlon, trans. the Dominican Students, Province of St. Joseph (London: Blackfriars Publications, 1955), 43–44; "Circa loquelam ejus notandum est quod debet habere . . . simplicitatem sine curiositate ornatus rhetorici. . . . Aliae artes ad ingenium pertinent: hic negotium animarum agitur" (Humbert, 402–3). Humbert also, however, makes an interesting comparison between the preacher's need for "pulchritud[o] conversationis" and women's physical beauty, saying that "another thing [the preacher needs] is zeal, as is clear from women, who give a great deal of energy to achieving beauty in their adornment. And in the same way, holy men should work to achieve beauty in their behavior" (459, my translation).

80. On Alexander's use of classical terminology, see Donavin, "De sermone," 279–82; and Murphy, *Rhetoric*, 314–17.

81. Augustine, *Christian Instruction* 2.35.53, p. 107.

82. Kennedy, *Classical Rhetoric*, 16. He is describing the strand of Greek rhetoric that gave rise to the tradition of rhetorical handbooks, including ultimately the *artes praedicandi* themselves.

83. Morenzoni, *Des écoles aux paroisses*, 237.

84. Higden, *Ars componendi sermones*, 7–8.

85. Ibid., 8: "non semper requiritur dicendi subtilitas set quandoque plus edificat simplex ruditas."

86. "Item in hac parte declinanda est fabulosa vanitas aut puerilis scurilitas tam quam impertinens ad salutem pocius aurem quam animam demulcens, de quo propheta ait: caupones vestri miscent aquam vino . . . nisi forsan eo modo quo docet Augustinus, de doctrina christiana libro 2, versus finem dicens quod filii Israelis abstulerunt preciosa de Egipto ut ea postmodum meliori usui coaptarent, sicut fecit Ieronimus invehendo contra Iovinianum dicta philosophorum et gentilium poetarum" (ibid.).

87. "Sed sunt nonnulli uento superbie et uanaglorie inflati, meretricantes uerbum Dei, qui in suis uentosis predicacionibus nullum finem de predictis intendunt, sed pocius repugnantem scilicet gloriam, fama propriam et honorem" (Eiximenis, "L'*Ars praedicandi*," 306).

88. The quoted phrase is Margaret Jennings's; see Higden, *Ars componendi sermones*, xv, n. 20.

89. Ibid.

90. "Nullatenus est credendum quod verbum Dei praedicationis officio fidelibus ministrandum alligetur consuetudini alicui humanitus introductae seu regulis humano ingenio adinventis quae in hoc opero inseruntur, quasi contra eas praedicatori agere non liceat" (Waleys, 329).

91. "Cum igitur praedicator, non de rebus minimis sed de maximis, et quae excedunt humanum ingenium, sit acturus, omnino expedit ut precetur ad auxilium divinitatis, plus confidens in divino auxilio quam in proprio ingenio" (ibid., 331).

92. Higden, *Ars componendi sermones*, 32. This section (*De auditorum alleccione*) is taken almost verbatim from Robert of Basevorn, who says, "Debet enim praedicator, *quantum secundum Deum potest,* allicere animos auditorum ut reddat eos benevolos ad audiendum et retinendum" (*Forma praedicandi*, 260). The section primarily treats the use of exempla, encouraging the preacher to find something "subtile et curiosum" to get the audience's attention.

93. Robert of Basevorn, *Forma praedicandi*, 234. On the balance between grace and personal effort, see Charland, "Praedicator gratiosus," 88–96.

94. "Praemissa autem documenta observanda sunt a praedicatore secretius quoad seipsum. Multa autem alia servare debet in publico, dum praedicat ad populum" (Waleys, 331).

95. Ibid., 332, 334.

96. Waleys claims to have seen some whose gestures are so excessive "that they seemed to have entered into [*inisse*], or rather to have run mad into [*insanisse*], a duel with someone, to the extent that they themselves, along with the pulpit in which they stood, would have crashed to the ground had not others held them up" (ibid., 332). And those who babble their sermons, he alleges, will have their listeners saying, "He never composed this sermon he's giving, he got it from someone else" and "He's reciting to us as a little boy would recite" (334). The tone is clearly one of ridicule rather than moral opprobrium.

97. "Nonum documentum est, ut videlicet praedicator non conetur sic hominibus in praedicando placere ut sequatur aliquorum vanitatem qui frequentantes sermones ea quae sunt curiositatis commendant. . . . Et sine dubio a talibus vanis auditoribus vix aliquid commendatur nisi sapiat vanitatem. Sed non expedit

praedicatorem talium auditorum laudibus aut vituperiis commoveri" (ibid., 336–37).

98. "Maxima virtus sermonis quoad ipsius effectum . . . est modus pronuntiandi et dicendi" (ibid., 332); the previous quotations are from 332 and 333, respectively. The latter assertion, which seems surprising in a Christian context, is more or less a quotation from Quintilian: "the nature of the speech that we have composed within our minds is not so important as the manner in which we produce it" (*Institutio oratoria* 11.3.2, cited in Enders, *Rhetoric,* 21).

99. Schaeffer, "Dialectic of Orality," 1137.

Chapter 5

1. "[The preacher] should pray that God will put a good sermon into his mouth. For, if Queen Esther, who was about to speak before the king in behalf of the temporal well-being of her nation, prayed that God would put 'a well-ordered speech' in her mouth [Esther 14:13], how much more should he pray to obtain such a gift who is laboring 'in the world and in teaching' [1 Tim. 5:17] for the eternal well-being of men?" (Augustine, *Christian Instruction* 4.30.63, pp. 234–35).

2. This fascination on the part of orthodox authors is all the more intriguing in view of the fact that during this period heretical groups were calling upon these same saints—figures such as Katherine of Alexandria and Mary Magdalene—as models for women's preaching and were being roundly denounced for doing so. See Blamires, "Women and Preaching," 135–52, and Katherine Ludwig Jansen, "Maria Magdalena: *Apostolorum Apostola*," in Kienzle and Walker, 68–69.

3. Theresa Coletti, "*Paupertas est donum Dei:* Hagiography, Lay Religion, and the Economics of Salvation in the Digby *Mary Magdalene,*" *Speculum* 76, no. 2 (2001): 337. On the continuing currency of saints' *vitae,* see also Brasington, "*Non imitanda set veneranda,*" 142–43.

4. See, for example, the discussions by Burrus, "Reading Agnes," 25–46; Karen Winstead, *Virgin Martyrs: Legends of Sainthood in Late Medieval England* (Ithaca, N.Y.: Cornell University Press, 1997); Brigitte Cazelles's introduction to her edited book *The Lady as Saint: A Collection of French Hagiographic Romances of the Thirteenth Century* (Philadelphia: University of Pennsylvania Press, 1991); and Sheila Delany, *Impolitic Bodies: Poetry, Saints, and Society in Fifteenth-Century England* (Oxford: Oxford University Press, 1998).

5. Farmer, "Persuasive Voices," 528. She notes that this new emphasis reflects the increasing interest in pastoral responsibilities in the late twelfth and early thirteenth centuries (526–29). On the pastoral theologians, see Baldwin, *Masters, Princes, and Merchants,* esp. 1:xi–xii, 34–43, 107–16.

6. Quoted in Farmer, "Persuasive Voices," 517.

7. "Mulieribus tamen semper in penitentia iniungendum est quod sint predicatrices virorum suorum. Nullus enim sacerdos ita potest cor viri emollire sicut potest uxor. . . . Debet enim in cubiculo et inter medios amplexus virum suum blande alloqui" (ibid., n. 1).

8. On *suauitas*, see Chapter 4 above. Bernadette Paton, *Preaching Friars and the Civic Ethos: Siena, 1380–1480*, Westfield Publications in Medieval Studies 7 (London: Centre for Medieval Studies, Queen Mary and Westfield College, University of London, 1992), illustrates the persistence of such language in descriptions of wifely persuasion, citing the late fifteenth-century Franciscan Cherubino da Siena's advice to a wife to "admonish an erring husband 'dolcemente e piacevolmente,' sweetly exhorting him to sin no more" (218).

9. Farmer, "Persuasive Voices," 539–40.

10. Ibid., 542. On Thomas, see also Jacqueline Murray, "Thinking about Gender: The Diversity of Medieval Perspectives," in *Power of the Weak: Studies on Medieval Women,* ed. Jennifer Carpenter and Sally-Beth MacLean (Urbana: University of Illinois Press, 1995), 9–12.

11. Farmer, "Persuasive Voices," 540.

12. Beverly Mayne Kienzle, "The Prostitute-Preacher: Patterns of Polemic against Medieval Waldensian Women Preachers," in Kienzle and Walker, 101.

13. Ibid., 104. The quotation is from Bernard of Fontcaude, *Adversus Waldensium sectam liber,* PL 204:821: "Seducunt ergo mulieres, viros, non viriliter sed muliebriter agentes" (quoted in Kienzle, "Prostitute-Preacher," 111, n. 27).

14. Kienzle, "Prostitute-Preacher," 104–5. Tertullian also emphasizes the link between rhetoric and heresy, as between femininity and rhetoric; see Chapter 4 above. Bernard seems almost to echo Tertullian when he calls the seduction of men by the words of women the "ar[s] pristina" of the devil (*Adversus Waldensium sectam,* col. 826, quoted in Kienzle, "Prostitute-Preacher," 112, n. 34).

15. The university triad of "lectio, disputatio, praedicatio" meant that disputation was an expected precursor of and preparation for preaching; see Smalley, *Study of the Bible,* 196–213. For an example and brief explication of the triad, see Peter the Chanter's *Verbum abbreviatum,* PL 205:25.

16. Blamires and Marx, 41. This article reproduces the text of Henry of Ghent's *quaestio* "On Whether Woman Should be a Teacher of Theology" (*Summa quaestionum ordinariarum,* bk. 1, art. 11, ques. 2) and presents the newly edited text of a late fourteenth-century *quaestio* "On Whether Women May Preach," from MS Harley 31.

17. "Secundum quod decet—scilicet . . . priuate" (in Blamires and Marx, 54).

18. "Mulier . . . viuacitatem sermonis non habet ad mortificandum, sed magis prouocandum peccata, et ideo super illud, 'Docere mulierem non permitto,' dicit Glos. 'Si enim loquitur magis incitat ad luxuriam, et irritatur'" (ibid., 52).

19. "Irritat qui talis [a preacher for glory or gain] agnoscitur, non praedicat, quia quo dicta sua venustiore ornare conatur eloquio, tanto acriore astantium pectora ad contemptum (proh dolor!) etiam eorum quae bene ab eo dicuntur" (Guibert of Nogent, *Quo ordine sermo fieri debeat,* PL 156:30).

20. "Licet pulcritudo, forma, et omnis gestus mulieris alliceant hominem ad libidinem, maxime tamen dulcedo vocis et complacencia verborum" (Blamires and Marx, 58).

21. See, e.g., Higden's discussion "De auditorum alleccione," on how to keep listeners entertained (*Ars componendi sermones,* 32–34).

22. "Si dicis hoc intelligi non debere de muliere sancta et deuota sed mere-

trice et fatua, hoc falsum est quia, ceteribus paribus, plus allici debet vir pulcritudine et vocis dulcedine mulieris bone quam male quia scit quod prima conseruaret sibi fidem et secunda non" (Blamires and Marx, 59).

23. Ibid., 47, 63.

24. Helen Solterer, *The Master and Minerva: Disputing Women in French Medieval Culture* (Berkeley and Los Angeles: University of California Press, 1995), addresses the similar contest between the speech of women and of authoritative men in secular literature. As she points out, "there is an implicit conflict between the unaccountable verbal power of women and the masters' standard" (54), and the exploration of that conflict, like the representation of women in preaching discussions, helps to explore larger questions about the authority of the clerical voice.

25. Blamires and Marx, 44. See also Leclercq on the increasing interest in the office of preacher in the thirteenth century (119–32). One of the texts included in this section is a disputation by Eustache d'Arras on the legalistic issue of whether a woman who preached merited the aureole of the doctor (he decided in favor, albeit with reservations; see 119–20).

26. Winstead makes a similar point with regard to virgin-martyr legends in the social world of thirteenth- and fourteenth-century England: "It is surely no coincidence that these narratives flourished at a time when traditionally sanctioned social relations were being contested and renegotiated" (*Virgin Martyrs,* 105). And Burrus observes that "the popularity of tales of virgin martyrs [in late antiquity] coincides chronologically with the articulation of a distinctly sacramental episcopal authority" ("Reading Agnes," 45).

27. On the development of virgin-martyr legends in the high and late Middle Ages, see Winstead, *Virgin Martyrs.* Victor Saxer, *Le culte de Marie Madeleine en occident: Des origines à la fin du moyen âge,* 2 vols. (Auxerre: Publications de la Société des Fouilles Archéologiques et des Monuments Historiques de l'Yonne; Paris: Clavreuil, 1959), is still the authority on the overall development of the cult of Mary Magdalene, but now see also Katherine Ludwig Jansen, *The Making of the Magdalen: Preaching and Popular Devotion in the Later Middle Ages* (Princeton, N.J.: Princeton University Press, 2000), which looks particularly at mendicant responses and popular devotion to the saint in the later Middle Ages.

28. Winstead, *Virgin Martyrs,* 101.

29. Winstead discusses Jacobus's work in the context of the pastoral revival and other *abbreviationes* of saints' lives (ibid., 64–66). On the likelihood that the *Legenda aurea*'s primary audience was a clerical one (as its Latin form would suggest), see Reames, *Legenda aurea,* 85–87. Andrew Galloway points out that a sermon cycle by Jacobus was also extremely popular in late medieval England ("Marriage Sermons, Polemical Sermons, and *The Wife of Bath's Prologue:* A Generic Excursus," *Studies in the Age of Chaucer* 14 [1992]: 9).

30. On the problems with accepting an overly narrow definition of preaching, see Chapter 1 above.

31. Jacobus of Voragine, *Legenda aurea, vulgo historia Lombardica dicta,* ed. Th. Graesse (Dresden and Leipzig: Libraria Arnoldiana, 1846); translated by William Granger Ryan as *The Golden Legend: Readings on the Saints,* 2 vols. (Princeton, N.J.: Princeton University Press, 1993). The quotation is from *Golden*

Legend, 2:181. The Latin reads, "Suavis enim sonus fit . . . beata Eufemia fecit Deo dulcem sonum cum voce praedicationis" (*Legenda aurea,* 620).

32. Jacobus of Voragine, *Legenda aurea,* 620.

33. Blamires has suggested that Chaucer may have been being deliberately provocative by insisting (especially in the vernacular) on the word *preche,* which is perfectly possible given the time and circumstances when the *Canterbury Tales* were written and prevailing anxieties about Lollards and unauthorized preaching (Blamires, "Women and Preaching," 151).

34. Jacobus of Voragine, *Golden Legend,* 1:364. Interestingly, the text of Gregory's sermon reads, instead, "by her believing she stood out as a servant of Christ, and by preaching was made Christ's *mother*": "credendo exstitit ancilla Christi, et praedicando facta est *mater* Christi" (Graesse, *Legenda aurea,* 396, has "martir"). The reading "mater" is required by the rest of the sermon, whose theme is Matt. 12:46–50, on Christ's "mother and brothers" (Gregory the Great, *Homiliarum,* PL 76:1087). This is obviously not the Felicitas who was martyred with Perpetua, though it seems that her name may have mistakenly become attached to a story usually associated with the mother of the Maccabees. I am indebted to Barbara Newman for drawing my attention to this point, and to Jane Beal for finding Gregory's sermon.

35. Winstead notes that hagiographers of Jacobus's time moved away from the earlier tendency to emphasize the virgin martyrs' devotion and instead "celebrated the exploits of a charismatic heroine who defies society and humiliates her adversary" (*Virgin Martyrs,* 65). The defiance and humiliation almost always involve presenting the saint's public speech in some form.

36. For Saint Francis, see Jacobus of Voragine, *Golden Legend,* 1:186–93, *Legenda aurea,* 204–13. For Saint Dominic, see *Golden Legend,* 2:44–58, *Legenda aurea,* 466–83.

37. Another possible point of comparison would be the early male martyrs, also often virgins. While they participate in many of the same actions as the female virgin martyrs, their physical appearance and virginity receive far less emphasis, and their preaching, while important, is less of a dominant element in their stories. See, for instance, the stories of Saint Andrew (Jacobus of Voragine, *Golden Legend,* 1:13–21), Saint Thomas (1:29–35), and Saint Stephen (1:45–50). The legend of the unfortunate Saint James the Dismembered (2:343–46) has many details in common with his female counterparts, some of which are noted below, but his preaching takes the form of a running commentary—almost a gloss—on his own dismemberment, and the focus is thus rather different.

38. See, for instance, Cazelles, *Lady as Saint.*

39. Among those whose beauty attracts attention through, as it were, no fault of their own are Saint Agnes (Jacobus of Voragine, *Golden Legend,* 1:101–4), the virgin of Antioch (1:250–54), Saint Petronilla (who manages to die before being martyred; 1:315), and Saint Margaret (1:368–70).

40. Ibid., 1:369.

41. As Copeland says, "Rhetoric cannot deny or suppress the force of body as appearance, for it operates through the persuasive appeal of appearance" ("Pardoner's Body," 146). The virgin martyrs both illustrate and subvert this "force of body."

42. The genre of hagiography itself, like rhetoric, aims "to offer something that is moral and edifying but at the same time pleasant and entertaining" (Copeland, "Pardoner's Body," 150); the lives of the women preachers offer a lesson on balancing these two aims, both in their form and in their content.

43. Jacobus of Voragine, *Golden Legend*, 1:102. Compare Saint James the Dismembered, who was "noble by birth and yet more noble by his faith" (2:343). Apparently nobility is the masculine equivalent of beauty, though many female virgin martyrs have both. (Saint James was married.)

44. Ibid., 1:27.

45. Ibid., 1:44.

46. Ibid., 1:102.

47. Augustine, *City of God* 1.16, p. 26: "It must be firmly established that virtue, the condition of right living, holds command over the parts of the body from her throne in the mind, and that the consecrated body is the instrument of the consecrated will; and if that will continues unshaken and steadfast, whatever anyone else does with the body or to the body, provided that it cannot be avoided without committing sin, involves no blame to the sufferer."

48. Jacobus of Voragine, *Golden Legend*, 1:251.

49. Ibid., 1:251. "Nam quemadmodum virgo, si meretricem colas, quemadmodum virgo, si adulterum diligas, quemadmodum virgo, si amorem petas? Tolerabilius est mentem virginem quam carnem habere. Utrumque bonum, si liceat, et si non liceat, saltem non homini castae, sed Deo simus" (Jacobus of Voragine, *Legenda aurea*, 274). The last sentence is reminiscent of Augustine's argument about eloquence versus wisdom in *De doctrina christiana*. See also Burrus, "Reading Agnes," in which she quotes Agnes's declaration (in Prudentius's fourth-century version of her life) that "You may stain your sword with blood as you will—but you will not stain my limbs with carnal lust" (35).

50. Peter Brown points out that the association of idolatry with sexual sin is already strongly present in Saint Paul, and he argues that in Paul's view, "by committing the supreme anomaly of worshipping created things rather than their Creator, pagans had brought upon themselves every kind of sexual anomaly" (*Body and Society,* 51; cf. Rom. 1:24–27). On the particular developments and connotations of the idea of virginity in the Middle Ages, see Clarissa W. Atkinson, " 'Precious Balsam in a Fragile Glass': The Ideology of Virginity in the Later Middle Ages," *Journal of Family History* 8 (1983): 131–43; and John Bugge, *Virginitas: An Essay in the History of a Medieval Ideal* (The Hague: Martinus Nijhoff, 1975).

51. Brown, *Body and Society,* 60. He notes that "strict codes of sexual discipline were made to bear much of the weight of providing the Christian Church with a distinctive code of behavior" and furthermore that "outsiders could admire [continence] as a form of physical heroism equivalent to the observed capacity of Christians to face down the chill fear of death" (60).

52. Ruether discusses this idealized congruence in "Misogynism and Virginal Feminism," 153–56. She points out that monism can either be seen as nonsexual and purely spiritual or be assimilated to maleness, so that femaleness becomes associated with body rather than spirit; Augustine takes the latter view, which

strongly influences later Christian images of women. On the "monachization" of the priesthood, see Robert Swanson, "Angels Incarnate,"160–77.

53. Brown, *Body and Society*, 37. He is discussing here a characteristic of Jewish communities around the time of Jesus' life but one that clearly carries over into Christianity.

54. Copeland, "Pardoner's Body."

55. See Cazelles, *Lady as Saint*.

56. The quoted phrase comes from Bloch, *Medieval Misogyny*, 99; he is speaking specifically of the relationship between virginity and perfect signification.

57. Jacobus of Voragine, *Golden Legend*, 1:19.

58. Burrus offers a similar example, noting that Ambrose of Milan in his fourth-century *De virginibus* "must succeed in obscuring the awkward narrative fact of [Paul's preaching companion] Thecla's triumphant survival of persecution"; he does so, Burrus argues, by juxtaposing Thecla's story with that of the martyred virgin of Antioch, whose tale immediately follows that of Thecla, and thus providing the "necessary fatal conclusion" ("Reading Agnes," 31).

59. S. R. T. O. d'Ardenne and E. J. Dobson note that "the main ingredients of the story [of Saint Katherine] are already present in a brief (probably summarized) version included in the *Menologium Basilianum,* a collection of legends compiled for the emperor Basil I, who died in 886" (*Seinte Katerine, Re-Edited from MS Bodley 34 and the Other Manuscripts,* ed. S. R. T. O. d'Ardenne and E. J. Dobson, EETS [n.s.] 7 [Oxford: Oxford University Press for EETS, 1981], xiv). The Greek and Latin legends are collected in Giovanni Battista Bronzini, *La leggenda di S. Caterina d'Alessandria: Passioni greche e latine* (Rome: n.p., 1960).

60. William MacBain cites fourteen that survive in Old French alone (*De Sainte Katerine: An Anonymous Picard Version of the Life of St. Catherine of Alexandria,* ed. William MacBain [Fairfax, Va.: George Mason University Press, 1987], vii).

61. The Vulgate text is reproduced in MacBain's *De Sainte Katerine* but also in d'Ardenne and Dobson's edition of the Middle English *Seinte Katerine*. Here I use the latter, which provides a critical text with variants.

62. *Seinte Katerine*, 148.

63. "Illa, custos uirginitatis sue" (ibid., 148).

64. "Salutationem tibi, imperator, proferre nos et ordinis dignitas et rationis via premonebat si hec ista qua cultibus demonum exhibes . . . creatori tuo impenderes" (ibid., 149).

65. "Honorem inuisibilis maiestatis ad uisibiles transferat creaturas" (ibid., 150).

66. "Visu in virginem defixo, vultus ipsius claritatem et verborum constantiam tacitus considerabat. . . . 'Speciosa quidem hec ista forent, o virgo, que asseris si rationis munimento fulcirentur' " (ibid., 151).

67. "Quid enim tam absurda, et ab humana ratione tam alienum" (ibid., 152).

68. "Liberalium artium non ignobiles doctores, quantum ad inanem mundi gloriam, habui, de quibus, quia nichil michi quod esset conducibile ad beatam uitam contulerunt, tota hec eorum memoria silescat" (ibid., 155).

69. "Tamen quia vana sunt omnia et a vera beatitudine aliena, hec ista pen-

itus abrogans iudico me inter vos nichil aliud scire nisi hunc qui est vera scientia et credentium beatitudo sempiterna, dominum meum, Ihesum Christum, qui dixit per prophetam: Perdam sapientiam sapientium et intellectum intelligentium reprobabo" (ibid., 162–63). Pagan philosophy, like gaudy dress or human ingenuity, is "alien" to a true Christian. Reames observes that the potential for Katherine's example to be used by heretics led Jacobus, in one of his sermons, to suggest that "the special efficacy of her preaching was due, not to the wisdom infused by God, but to her background in all the liberal arts"; the fact that this approach "revers[es] the priorities of the legend itself" reflects the ambiguity in Katherine's legend and in her own use/rejection of rhetoric (Reames, *Legenda aurea*, 105).

70. "Desine talia predicare que nulla valent ratione comprobari" (cease to preach these things [i.e., pagan beliefs], which cannot be proved by reason) (*Seinte Katerine*, 153).

71. As Katherine puts it, "Est speciosa uictoria aduersarium telis suis, uelut propriis laqueis, irretire" (ibid., 169).

72. "Sermonem rectum et bene sonantem" (ibid., 159).

73. Ibid., 161.

74. "Dum steteritis ante reges et presides nolite precogitare quomodo aut quid loquamini, ego enim dabo vobis os et sapientiam" (ibid., 159). Though not a precise quotation, this corresponds to Mark 13:9–11 and Luke 21:12–15.

75. Whether that learning is entirely absent during her speech, and perfectly compensated for by divine inspiration, or whether it forms part of her own abilities that the inspiration works through is never discussed and is ultimately undecidable.

76. See Ps. 115:4–7.

77. She says, for example, that though the emperor's human subjects may be frightened into worshiping the statue, no such jurisdiction will apply to the birds of the air, who will sit on her head and leave their filthy dung on her face (*Seinte Katerine*, 175–76). Katherine, whose amusement the narrative repeatedly describes (e.g., "uirgo, in risum paulo excitata," 174), is obviously aware of the humorous side of her conflict with Maxentius.

78. "Substantiuam hominis formam induere . . . per quam inuisibilis uideri . . . potuisset" (ibid., 165).

79. "Alliciunt auditu et uisu probata rerum miracula" (ibid., 168).

80. "O . . . forma uirginei decoris, o solaris species candoris. . . . O uirgo digna imperio . . . ne negligas pulchritudinis tue uernantem speciem" (ibid., 190).

81. "Transitus ad uitam" (ibid. 190–91).

82. See Luke 23:27–29. Saint James the Dismembered follows the same model: "When some people wept out of compassion for him, he said: 'Don't weep for me, but mourn for yourselves, because I go on to life, while eternal torment is your due!'" (Jacobus of Voragine, *Golden Legend*, 2:344).

83. *Seinte Katerine*, 171.

84. "Rhetores et dialecticos . . . [et] sophistas" (Jacobus of Voragine, *Legenda aurea*, 796; cf. *Golden Legend*, 2:340).

85. "Eloquentiam facundissimam in praedicando, sicut patet in suis praedica-

tionibus" (Jacobus of Voragine, *Legenda aurea,* 796, my translation; cf. *Golden Legend,* 2:340).

86. "Eloquentiam . . . suavissimam in attrahendo, sicut patet in Porphyrio et in regina, quos eloquii sui suavitate ad fidem attraxit" (Jacobus of Voragine, *Legenda aurea,* 796; my translation; cf. *Golden Legend* 2:340).

87. Augustine, *De doctrina christiana* 4.12.27, p. 135. See the discussion in Chapter 4 above.

88. See, for example, Blamires and Marx, 41.

89. Jacobus of Voragine, *Golden Legend,* 2:341; "Affluentia resolvens, opportunitas inducens, juventus lasciviens, libertas effrenans, pulchritudo alliciens" (Jacobus of Voragine, *Legenda aurea,* 796). Of these qualities, it must be said, "pulchritudo alliciens" receives the most emphasis in the story. In demonstration of this quality Jacobus cites his earlier description of her: "speciosa valde et incredibili pulchritudine omnium oculis admirabilis videbatur" (797).

90. In fact, she was sometimes a virgin as well; Barbara Newman notes a later medieval tradition that claimed the Magdalene had been "re-virginized" through penitence and contemplation (*From Virile Woman to WomanChrist,* 176–77).

91. In addition to Saxer, *Culte de Marie Madeleine,* and Jansen, *Making of the Magdalen,* see Susan Haskins, *Mary Magdalen, Myth and Metaphor* (London: HarperCollins, 1993); and Nicole Bériou, "La Madeleine dans les sermons parisiens du XIIIe siècle," *Mélanges de l'École Française de Rome: Moyen Âge* 104, no. 1 (1992): 269–340.

92. Jansen, "Maria Magdalena," offers a short discussion of the cult's development, with particular reference to Mary's preaching; see 57–67.

93. The pseudo-Rabanus legend is printed in Étienne Faillon, ed., *Monuments inédits sur l'apostolat de Sainte Marie-Madeleine en Provence,* 2 vols. (Paris: Chez l'Éditeur, 1848); Faillon takes Rabanus to be the actual author.

94. "Vultu veneranda venustas, honestas in moribus, in verbis promptissima gratia ad suadendum . . . [omnis] ab earum facie inflammaretur Domini Salvatoris amore" (ibid., 543).

95. Ibid., 541. The combination of active and contemplative lives was an important thread in late medieval mysticism and, of course, in preaching. On the mystical tradition, see Lagorio, "Social Responsibility," 95–104.

96. "Ex abundantia cordis" (Faillon, *Monuments,* 541; cf. Matt. 12:34).

97. "Oportet igitur ut sicut anastasis Christi apostola destinata est ad apostolos, et ascensionis ejus prophetissa, sic et credentium in toto orbe, fieret evangelista" (Faillon, *Monuments,* 542).

98. Ibid., 542.

99. Jacobus of Voragine, *Golden Legend,* 1:375.

100. Ibid., 1:376—I have modified the translation slightly; "Vultu placido, facie serena, lingua discreta eos ab ydolorum cultura revocabat et Christum constantissime praedicabat" (Jacobus of Voragine, *Legenda aurea,* 409).

101. "Admirati sunt universi prae specie, prae facundia, prae dulcedine eloquentiae ejus" (ibid., my translation; cf. *Golden Legend,* 1:377). Compare Odo of Canterbury, beloved of audiences for "the sweetness of both his person and his words," quoted in Spencer, *English Preaching,* 9.

102. Ryan translates the above words as "her beauty, her eloquence, and the sweetness of her message" (Jacobus of Voragine, *Golden Legend,* 1:377), but to render *eloquentia* as *message* seems problematic. As it is, the emphasis on the form of her speech over its content is striking.

103. Blamires notes this repeated usage of *praedicare.* He also observes that "Mary's apostolic career was not merely an academic matter, and indeed vernacular hagiographers underlined her preaching function" ("Women and Preaching," 143–44).

104. Jacobus of Voragine, *Golden Legend,* 1:377. This makes it particularly galling that when things go wrong on the journey the husband blames Mary Magdalene, saying, "Unhappy me, that on your advice I set out on this journey!" (378)—a claim the narrative does not support.

105. Ibid., 1:379.

106. Ibid., 1:375.

107. "Non animalis homo loquitur, sed divinus quidam spiritus qui sane haud mortale sonans nos in stuporem et admirationem adeo convertit ut ad injuriam ipsius Christi de quo loquitur aliquid dicere aut penitus nesciamus aut omnino formidemus. Nam ut christi nomen et divinitatis ejus potentiam simulque crucis ipsius ministerium predicari ab ea audivimus *confusa sunt viscera, corda nostra tremuerunt et omnes corporis sensus stupendo aufugerunt*" (*Seinte Katerine,* 171; emphasis added).

108. "Quando praedicator fructuose praedicat et utiliter, sicut debet dum est in fervore spiritus sui, cor suum ita cordibus auditorum immediate conjungitur quod nec se linguam, nec auditores aures, habere percipit, sed videtur sibi quod quasi absque omni medio de corde suo in corda auditorum verbum suum influit et procedit" (Waleys, 336).

109. See his numerous "documenta" on such matters as clothing, voice, verbal style, and gesture (ibid., 331–40).

110. Casagrande elucidates the competing claims of rhetoric and grace in "Le calame du Saint-Esprit," 251–53; see also Morenzoni, "Parole du prédicateur," in the same volume, 271–90, and Charland, "Praedicator gratiosus," 88–96.

111. It is interesting in this context that a favorite example of a "necessary sign," that is, one whose meaning is not subject to interpretation, is, according to Cicero and to Quintilian after him, "If a woman bear a child, she has lain with a man." The Incarnation is thus a violation of classical sign theory; it denies what seems an obvious truth in order to assert a truth more fundamental, somehow guaranteed by its very paradoxicality.

Chapter 6

1. "Mulier . . . docere non presumat . . . publico, scilicet in ecclesia ascendendo pulpitum, et faciendo sermonem ad populum" (quoted in Buc, "*Vox clamantis,*" 15, n. 31). An anonymous fourteenth-century disputation cites an almost identical prohibition in the late thirteenth-century *Rosarium super Decretum* of

Guido de Baysio: "mulieres in conuentu publico scilicet in ecclesia ascendendo pulpitum, id est, faciendo sermonem ad populum non presumant" (quoted in Blamires and Marx, 61–62).

2. Compare Thomas of Chobham's specification, "In general, it is true that neither a layman nor a woman can preach *publicly, that is, in church*" (Generaliter autem, uerum est quod nec laicus nec mulier predicare potest *publice, scilicet in ecclesia*) (Chobham, 57; emphasis added). Canon law makes a similar demand but without the specific focus on place: "Mulier, quamuis docta et sancta, uiros in conuentu docere non presumat" (*Corpus iuris canonici,* ed. E. Friedberg, 2d ed., 2 vols. [Leipzig: Bernhard Tauchnitz, 1879–81; repr. Graz, 1959], Part 1, Dist. 23, c. 29, 1:86). This text is Robert of Basevorn's authority for his dictum that "[nulla] mulier, quantumcumque docta et sancta, praedicare debet" (no woman, however learned and saintly, ought to preach) (Basevorn, *Forma praedicandi,* 242); see the epigraph to Chapter 5 above.

3. Julian, whose *Revelation of Divine Love* led her to struggle with her own claims to authority, has been the subject of some of the most interesting recent work on women's approaches to authorization; see particularly Watson, "Yf women be double naturelly," 1–34, and Lynn Staley, "Julian of Norwich and the Late-Fourteenth-Century Crisis of Authority," in David Aers and Lynn Staley, *The Powers of the Holy: Religion, Politics, and Gender in Late Medieval English Culture,* (University Park: Pennsylvania State University Press, 1996), 107–78, which touches on a number of other authoritative women in the period, including those studied here.

4. Lynn Staley characterizes Julian's short text of the *Revelations* as "an *act,* a deliberate and courageous move . . . into a public arena where she could be held accountable for her words," and the long text as "even more careful and more audacious: she leaves the bedroom filled with women to enter a distinctly masculine preserve" ("Julian of Norwich," 117). Both in its emphasis on (metaphorical) place and in its attention to the deliberateness of Julian's actions, Staley's description is relevant for the activities of the women discussed in this chapter.

5. "It is by no means insignificant that nearly every piece in the [1987] volume *Men in Feminism* . . . manifests a preoccupation with the question of place, specifically with the problem of where men stand in relation to feminism" (Diana Fuss, "Reading like a Feminist," *differences* 1, no. 2 (1989): 83.

6. Luce Irigaray, *This Sex Which Is Not One,* trans. Catherine Porter with Carolyn Burke (Ithaca, N.Y.: Cornell University Press, 1985), 76. Irigaray discusses mysticism and its relationship to female speech directly in *Speculum of the Other Woman,* trans. Gillian C. Gill (Ithaca, N.Y.: Cornell University Press, 1985), 191–202.

7. Beckwith, "Very Material Mysticism" critiques Irigaray's discussion of mysticism in *Speculum* for its "(mystificatory) association [between women and mysticism] that again places 'woman' beyond the pale" (201).

8. Fuss, "Reading like a Feminist," 80.

9. Compare here Lochrie's note that in studying Margery Kempe she has "tried to pursue that 'something else' " that Jean Gerson saw in women's spirituality but also has worked to show that there is a place for Margery's "difference

within rather than without medieval culture" and that Margery is not simply a "maverick" (Lochrie, *Margery Kempe,* 228, 205). Amy Hollywood, *The Soul as Virgin Wife: Mechthild of Magdeburg, Marguerite Porete, and Meister Eckhart* (Notre Dame, Ind.: University of Notre Dame Press, 1995) similarly argues for women as part of a broader spiritual tradition, rather than as anomalies.

10. As John Coakley has noted in his study of relationships between thirteenth-century friars and holy women, the difference between official, clerical authority and the "privileged, unique" relationship to the divine available to certain women was both visible and at times humbling to the friars, bringing them face to face with "some of the limits of their official authority"; Coakley points out, however, that ultimately these relationships left the friars' authority undiminished and in some ways even strengthened it ("Gender and the Authority of Friars: The Significance of Holy Women for Thirteenth-Century Franciscans and Dominicans," *Church History* 60, no. 4 [1991]: 452). The modern critical debate on experiential authority that lies behind Fuss's article "Reading like a Feminist" includes Peggy Kamuf, "Writing like a Woman," in *Women and Language in Literature and Society,* ed. Sally McConnell-Ginet, Ruth Borker, and Nelly Furman (New York: Praeger, 1980), 284–99; Jonathan Culler, "Reading as a Woman," in *On Deconstruction: Theory and Criticism After Structuralism* (Ithaca, N.Y.: Cornell University Press, 1982); and Alice Jardine and Paul Smith's edited collection *Men in Feminism* (New York: Methuen, 1987), particularly Robert Scholes's article "Reading Like a Man," 204–18.

11. There has recently been an explosion of interest in the sibyl of the Rhine. To begin with, see especially the work of Barbara Newman, including *Sister of Wisdom: St. Hildegard's Theology of the Feminine* (Berkeley and Los Angeles: University of California Press, 1987); "Three-Part Invention: The *Vita S. Hildegardis* and Mystical Hagiography," in *Hildegard of Bingen: The Context of Her Thought and Art,* ed. Charles Burnett and Peter Dronke (London: The Warburg Institute, 1998), 189–210; and "Hildegard and Her Hagiographers: The Remaking of Female Sainthood," in *Gendered Voices: Medieval Saints and Their Interpreters,* ed. Catherine M. Mooney (Philadelphia: University of Pennsylvania Press, 1999), 1–22, as well as her edited work *Voice of the Living Light: Hildegard of Bingen and Her World* (Berkeley and Los Angeles: University of California Press, 1998), especially the articles by Newman, John van Engen, Constant Mews, and Kathryn Kerby-Fulton. See also Kathryn Kerby-Fulton and Dyan Elliott, "Self-Image and the Visionary Role in Two Letters from the Correspondence of Elizabeth of Schönau and Hildegard of Bingen," *Vox benedictina* 2 (1985): 204–23; and Beverly Mayne Kienzle, "*Operatrix in vinea Domini:* Hildegard's Public Preaching and Polemics against the Cathars," *Heresis* 26–27 (1996): 43–56.

12. On Birgitta of Sweden, see Tore Nyberg's introduction to Birgitta of Sweden, *Life and Selected Revelations,* 13–51. Particularly relevant to the issues discussed here is the work of Claire L. Sahlin; see especially *Birgitta of Sweden;* "Gender," 69–95; and "The Prophetess as Preacher: Birgitta of Sweden and the Voice of Prophecy," *Medieval Sermon Studies* 40 (autumn 1997): 29–44. See also Ingvar Fogelqvist, *Apostasy and Reform in the Revelations of St. Birgitta,* Bibliotheca

Theologiae Practicae 51 (Stockholm: Almqvist and Wiksell International, 1993), especially 70–72, 151–72.

13. On Catherine of Siena, see Raymond of Capua, *Vita beatae Catherinae senensis,* AASS April III, 861–968, translated by Conleth Kearns as *The Life of Catherine of Siena* (Dublin: Dominican Publications and Wilmington, Del.: M. Glazier, 1980). Also see the work of Karen Scott, including " 'This is why," 279–94; "Urban Spaces, Women's Networks, and the Lay Apostolate in the Siena of Catherine Benincasa," in *Creative Women in Medieval and Early-Modern Italy,* ed. E. Ann Matter and John Coakley (Philadelphia: University of Pennsylvania Press, 1994), 105–19; and "St. Catherine of Siena, 'Apostola,' " *Church History* 61 (March 1992): 34–46. Scott's work on Catherine, like Sahlin's on Birgitta, is by no means the only recent work on this saint, but it is the best introduction to the issues addressed here. For a brief, helpful account of all three women's lives and contexts, see Valerie M. Lagorio, "The Medieval Continental Women Mystics: An Introduction," in *An Introduction to the Medieval Mystics of Europe,* ed. Paul E. Szarmach (Albany: State University of New York Press, 1984), 184–93.

14. Elisabeth of Schönau, a contemporary and protégée of Hildegard of Bingen, wrote sermons but never preached herself; see Newman, "Three-Part Invention," 209, and *Sister of Wisdom,* 36–37. Marguerite Porete's *Mirror of Simple Souls* (*Le mirouer des simples ames*) contained theological views that came to be regarded as heretical; she was burnt at the stake in 1310. See Peter Dronke, *Women Writers of the Middle Ages: A Critical Study of Texts from Perpetua (d. 203) to Marguerite Porete (d. 1310)* (Cambridge, U.K.: Cambridge University Press, 1984), 217–28, for a discussion of her life and her book. Porete is also discussed in Watson, "Yf women be double naturelly," 2–7.

15. On the tendency toward a skewed focus, see Newman, *Sister of Wisdom,* xvi, and Denise L. Despres, "Ecstatic Reading and Missionary Mysticism: *The Orcherd of Syon,*" in *Prophets Abroad: The Reception of Continental Holy Women in Late-Medieval England,* ed. Rosalynn Voaden (Cambridge: D. S. Brewer, 1996), 141–44. See also Lagorio, "Social Responsibility," 95–104, for a thorough consideration of the combination of the active and contemplative in the lives of medieval women mystics.

16. It is important to raise a caveat here about the extent to which strategies expressed in the works that come down to us from these three women can be seen as their own. As Sahlin says, "It is not usually possible to separate completely the voice of Birgitta from those of her confessors in the *Revelations;* their voices usually blend in a collaborative effort to convey what they believed to be the divine word—the voice of God—revealed through Birgitta" (*Birgitta of Sweden,* 33). I believe this to be the case for all three women and would only stress that such a view is in no way intended to diminish their agency in shaping the strategies that gave them access to a public voice. See also Rosalynn Voaden, *God's Words, Women's Voices: The Discernment of Spirits in the Writing of Late-Medieval Women Visionaries* (York, U.K.: York Medieval Press, 1999), 2–3.

17. Fuss notes the "intractableness of the privileged terms 'men' and 'feminism' " in the debate she discusses, observing that "each in effect erect[s] a defense against the incursions of the other" ("Reading like a Feminist," 88).

18. On medieval women visionaries' understanding of the source of their authority, see André Vauchez, "Female Prophets, Visionaries, and Mystics," in his *Laity in the Middle Ages,* 219–29, especially 220–21; Ulrike Wiethaus, ed., *Maps of Flesh and Light: The Religious Experience of Medieval Women Mystics* (Syracuse, N.Y.: Syracuse University Press, 1993); and Newman, *Sister of Wisdom,* 34.

19. Grace Jantzen, " 'Cry Out and Write': Mysticism and the Struggle for Authority," in *Women, the Book, and the Godly: Selected Proceedings of the St. Hilda's Conference, 1993, Volume 1,* ed. Lesley Smith and Jane H. M. Taylor (Cambridge, U.K.: D. S. Brewer, 1995), 67–76. Jantzen argues in particular that there was an increasing distrust of visions, especially their sensory elements, in the thirteenth and fourteenth centuries. See also Voaden, *God's Words,* 41–72.

20. Franco Gori suggests that virginity had a kind of sacramental and sacerdotal character in early medieval Christianity: "La verginità esprime esistenzialmente una funzione sacerdotale: la vergine, come il sacerdote, è unita a Dio con vincolo particolare" (Ambrose, *Verginità e vedovanza,* ed. Egnatius Cazzaniga and Franco Gori, trans. Franco Gori, Opere morali 2; Sancti Ambrosiani episcopi Mediolanensis opera 14 [Milan: Biblioteca Ambrosiana, 1989], 52). See also Atkinson, " 'Precious Balsam,' " 131–43.

21. On Hildegard, see Newman, *Sister of Wisdom,* 13, 35; and Dronke, *Women Writers,* 201. On Birgitta, see her *Life and Selected Revelations,* which, as the book's editor Marguerite Tjader Harris notes, "show her contacts with many leaders of the church and of secular power" (2).

22. On Birgitta's and Catherine's political activities, see Jo Ann McNamara, "The Rhetoric of Orthodoxy: Clerical Authority and Female Innovation in the Struggle with Heresy," in *Maps of Flesh and Light: The Religious Experience of Medieval Women Mystics,* ed. Ulrike Wiethaus (Syracuse, N.Y.: Syracuse University Press, 1993), 23; on Catherine, see Noële M. Denis-Boulet, *La carrière politique de Sainte Catherine de Sienne (Étude historique)* (Paris: Desclée, de Brouwer, & Cie., [1939]).

23. On these trends see, for example, Vauchez, *Laity in the Middle Ages,* and Grundmann, *Religious Movements.*

24. For a thorough account, see Blamires and Marx. The issue is also discussed in Jansen, "Maria Magdalena," 67–80.

25. See Kathryn Kerby-Fulton, "Prophet and Reformer: 'Smoke in the Vineyard,' " in *Voice of the Living Light: Hildegard of Bingen and Her World,* ed. Barbara Newman (Berkeley and Los Angeles: University of California Press, 1998), 72, 77–80.

26. This is one subject addressed in Birgitta's initial call to speak out in public; Christ criticizes the "princes and prelates" who do not care for him (Birgitta of Sweden, *Life and Selected Revelations,* 19–20; Birgitta of Sweden, *Revelaciones, Book I, with Magister Mathias's Prologue,* ed. Carl-Gustaf Undhagen [Uppsala, Sweden: Almqvist and Wiksell, 1977], 237–38). On a visit to the Holy See in Rome, Catherine demonstrated her awareness of the extreme wickedness of the court and noted the strong contrast this presented with the ideal image it should convey (Raymond of Capua, *Vita beatae Catherinae,* 884).

27. See Chapter 5 above. Thomas of Chobham, 71, offers an unusual instance

of orthodox attention to the virgin martyrs in the context of preaching. See also Blamires, *Case for Women,* 184–98; and Jocelyn Wogan-Browne, *Saints' Lives and Women's Literary Culture c. 1150–1300: Virginity and Its Authorizations* (Oxford: Oxford University Press, 2001), 223–26.

28. Barbara Newman, " 'Sibyl of the Rhine': Hildegard's Life and Times," in *Voice of the Living Light: Hildegard of Bingen and Her World,* ed. Newman (Berkeley and Los Angeles: University of California Press, 1998), 21.

29. As Caroline Walker Bynum puts it, women "emerged . . . as . . . a 'prophetic' or 'charismatic' alternative" to male preaching, and "criticism of corrupt clergy was—in the eyes of both women and men—the special role of religious women" (*Fragmentation and Redemption: Essays on Gender and the Human Body in Medieval Religion* [New York: Zone Books, 1992], 136). While this formulation perhaps makes too rigid a distinction between the "alternative" roles of preacher and prophet, it is clear that criticism of the clergy was central to women's public voice. McNamara, whose military metaphor I borrow here, takes a less optimistic view of women's role: "At best, these women were irregulars in relationship to the professional troops of the clergy" ("Rhetoric of Orthodoxy," 9).

30. Vauchez points out that "saintly women became the last resort of the Church in the crisis that was shaking theological systems and institutions," but he sees this as a role limited to the specific conditions of the late fourteenth century and one that had no lasting effect or influence (*Laity in the Middle Ages,* 236); I would argue that in fact these women are drawing on a long tradition of being the "last resort."

31. "Predicatio est, manifesta et publica instructio morum et fidei, informationi hominum deserviens, ex rationum semita, et auctoritatum fonte proveniens" (Alan of Lille, *Summa de arte praedicatoria,* 111).

32. Butler discusses the way an "excluded and illegible domain"—here, we might say, the problematic and only semiexistent realm of women preachers— "haunts the . . . [intelligible] domain as the spectre of its own impossibility, the very limit to intelligibility, its constitutive outside" (*Bodies That Matter,* xi). Irigaray suggests that in mystical experience, "the distinction between inside/outside [is] transgressed"; in turn this ineffable dissolution of boundaries leads to a more visible and expressible one, as mysticism becomes "the only place in the history of the West where woman speaks and acts so publicly" (*Speculum,* 192, 191).

33. See. Minnis, "*De impedimento sexus,*" 109–39, on the theological arguments against women's ordination, many of which apply also to women's preaching.

34. Thomas of Chobham writes, "It is not permitted [for deaconesses] to put on sacred vestments nor to read the Epistles or the Gospels at mass on account of the uncleanness of menses that frequently happens to them [*inmunditiam menstruorum que sepe eis accidunt*], and on account of the danger of lust, lest priests or other clerics upon seeing them might burn with lust for them" (58). Here both the woman's own uncleanness and her potential to provoke uncleanness on the part of her male audience are used to exclude her.

35. Raming, *Exclusion,* 10.

36. On the feminized text, see Dinshaw, *Chaucer's Sexual Poetics,* 9–24. As

she puts it, allegorical interpretation can be seen as "undressing the text—unveiling the truth, revealing a body figuratively represented as female" (21). See also Susan Gubar, " 'The Blank Page' and the Issues of Female Creativity," in *Writing and Sexual Difference,* ed. Elizabeth Abel (Brighton, U.K.: Harvester, 1982), 73–93; and Staley, *Powers of the Holy,* 123–24. Such imagery is a reminder that all three of the women discussed here, like a great many medieval women saints, were themselves "interpreted" and presented textually by their male confessors, disciples, or admirers.

37. Butler, *Bodies That Matter,* 51. This remark is part of Butler's larger discussion of the ancient association of the feminine with matter and the masculine with form. Drawing on Aristotle, Butler discusses the issue of matter (Greek *hyle*) and the shape given to that matter by a stamp (*schema*), which Aristotle sees as the indissociable body and soul, and she questions the idea that the feminine is always that which takes on form, never that which gives form to something else. Aquinas's treatment of ordination, interestingly, draws on a similar image from Aristotle, describing the character conferred upon the new priest as an indelible mark that enables him to confer this imprint on others (Thomas Aquinas, *Summa Theologica,* trans. Fathers of the English Dominican Province, 6 vols. [London: Burns, Oates & Washbourne, (1914–42)], supp. q. 35, art. 2, 5:13–14). See also his more general discussion of character in *Summa Theologiae. Latin Text and English Translation, Introduction, Notes, Appendices and Glossaries,* 61 vols. (n.p.: Blackfriars; New York: McGraw-Hill, 1964–81), vol. 56: *The Sacraments (3a. 60–5),* ed. David Bourke (n.p.: Blackfriars, 1975), 3a. q. 63, 76–99.

38. Sarah Kay explores, however, the way these figures put pressure on the association of women with carnality and men with intellect ("Women's Body of Knowledge: Epistemology and Misogyny in the *Romance of the Rose,*" in *Framing Medieval Bodies,* ed. Sarah Kay and Miri Rubin [Manchester: Manchester University Press, 1994], 211–35).

39. As Lochrie points out, this problem in preaching is part of a far wider phenomenon: "The intersection of woman's body and her speech is a crucial problem in any analysis of late medieval piety" (*Margery Kempe,* 1).

40. This seems to be the point of Thomas of Chobham's specification, discussed above in Chapter 1, that women may read scripture but may not expound upon it (58).

41. Newman, *Sister of Wisdom,* 34–37.

42. See, for instance, the account of the illness she suffered while she was reluctant to make her visions public, or the one that struck her when her move to the Rupertsburg from her original monastery, Saint Disibod's, was opposed (Monica Klaes, ed., *Vita sanctae Hildegardis,* CCCM 126 [Turnhout, Belgium: Brepols, 1993], 8, 10–11).

43. Humbert of Romans says, for example, that "expedit [praedicatorem] habere vires corporales, ut possit vigilias in studendo, clamorem in praedicando, labores in discurrendo, penuriam in indigentiis, et hujusmodi multa sustinere, sicut fecerunt Apostoli" (Humbert, 407).

44. "In lecto egritudinis diu iacens . . . uidi, uigilans corpore et animo, pulcherrimam imaginem muliebrem formam habentem" ("Lying for a long time in

my bed of sickness . . . I saw, while wakeful in body and soul, a most beautiful image in womanly form") (Hildegard of Bingen, *Epistolarium,* ed. Lieven Van Acker, 2 vols. to date, CCCM 91–91A [Turnhout, Belgium: Brepols, 1991, 1993], 2:333; my translation). The letters have been translated by Joseph L. Baird and Radd K. Ehrman as *The Letters of Hildegard of Bingen,* 2 vols. to date (Oxford: Oxford University Press, 1994, 1998); this is letter 149r, 2:92–94. The rest of the sermon recounts Ecclesia's appearance and her message, coming back at the end to Hildegard, "paupercula feminea forma" (poor little feminine form). The vision—and thus the sermon—takes place in the frame of Hildegard's own bodily weakness.

45. Dronke, *Women Writers,* 145, emphasis added; "In eadem visione scripta prophetarum, ewangeliorum, et aliorum sanctorum, et quorumdam philosophorum, sine ulla humana doctrina intellexi, ac quedam ex illis exposui, cum vix noticiam litterarum haberem ∴ . Hec ad audienciam Moguntine ecclesie allata cum essent et discussa, omnes ex deo esse dixerunt, et ex prophecia quam olim prophete prophetaverant" (232).

46. The sermons are not yet available, although Beverly Mayne Kienzle is preparing an edition. In a striking instance of changing valuation, a recent work celebrating female mysticism says rather dismissively that "Hildegard is more exegete, preacher and teacher than visionary, and a rather prim and proper one at that" (Monica Furlong, *Visions and Longings: Medieval Women Mystics* [Boston: Shambhala, 1996], 35); Hildegard, one feels, would be most surprised. This modern example suggests the extent to which definitions of preaching and visionary experience are in the eye of the beholder.

47. The translators of Hildegard's letters note both her self-displacement and her intermingling of voices (*Letters of Hildegard,* 14); see also Newman, *Sister of Wisdom,* 26–27. Sara S. Poor observes of a similar situation that "the only time it is 'right' for a woman writer to claim a general readership in this context is when no one knows she's there"; she is discussing the transmission of Mechthild of Magdeburg's writings ("Mechthild von Magdeburg, Gender, and the 'Unlearned Tongue,'" *Journal of Medieval and Early Modern Studies* 31, no. 2 [2001]: 238).

48. "Clama ergo et scribe sic," from the "Protestificatio" that introduces Hildegard's *Scivias,* ed. Adelgund Führkötter and Angela Carlevaris, 2 vols., CCCM 43–43A (Turnhout, Belgium: Brepols, 1978), 6.

49. For examples of Hildegardian echoes of the prophets, see Newman, *Sister of Wisdom,* 25–26.

50. Hildegard at times provides a gloss or exegesis of her own visions and at other times leaves them in their uninterpreted form. See the *Letters,* e.g., 36–37, letter 5, in which Hildegard explains her biblical imagery of mountains and valleys, and Klaes, *Vita,* e.g., 20. Though Hildegard did not claim scriptural status for her texts, others were happy to do so for her. Newman, in "Hildegard and Her Hagiographers," notes that some commentators called Hildegard's works "canonizati" and claimed they were numbered "inter sacras scripturas" (9–10).

51. Some commonly cited female prophets are Miriam (Exod. 15), Deborah (Judg. 4), Hulda (4 Kings 22), Elizabeth (Luke 1), and Anna (Luke 2). Hildegard is compared to various of these women by her correspondents (see *Letters,* 2:17,

91, 157) but does not use these models herself. Sahlin points out that Birgitta of Sweden's *Revelations*, too, tended to associate her with the male prophets of the Bible, though some of her followers preferred to associate her with female prophets ("Gender," 75).

52. "Et ego uerba hec non dico de me, sed uera sapientia dicit ista de me et sic loquitur ad me: 'Audi, o homo, uerba hec et dic ea non secundum te, sed secundum me et docta per me hoc modo dic de te'" (Klaes, *Vita*, 22).

53. Newman makes a similar point from a different angle: "potent cultural taboos gave no woman the right to speak *about* God, as male theologians and preachers did, unless she could also speak *for* him in the visionary-prophetic mode" ("Three-Part Invention," 193). See also Staley's discussion of how Julian "applies the (male) tools of intellective authority to the (female) matter of experience," breaking down the common binary modes of thinking that separated text and interpreter, experience and intellect, female and male (*Powers of the Holy*, 139). Sara S. Poor, "Cloaking the Body in Text: The Question of Female Authorship in the Writings of Mechthild von Magdeburg," *Exemplaria* 12, no. 2 (2000): 417–53, discusses the fascinating relationship of the physical and the textual in the writings of a visionary who, like Julian, propagated her teachings in writing rather than in person.

54. "Ea manibus propriis tenens ipseque recitatoris uice functus . . . publice legit" (Klaes, *Vita*, 9). For a discussion of Gottfried's intentions in this scene, see Newman, "Hildegard and Her Hagiographers," 7–8. An interesting parallel appears in Thomas of Celano's *vita* of Saint Clare of Assisi, in which he says that the exceptional privilege of poverty granted to her order was written by Innocent III with his own hand ("pontifex ipse . . . sua manu conscripsit") (*Vita S. Clarae*, AASS August II, 757–58, c. 14). The woman's marginally acceptable behavior requires the validation of the masculine papal body. The passage on Saint Clare is cited and discussed in Grundmann, *Religious Movements*, 65, 295, n. 148.

55. On this subject see, for instance, Bynum, *Fragmentation*, 151–79, 181–238.

56. See Kari Elisabeth Børresen, *Subordination and Equivalence: The Nature and Rôle of Woman in Augustine and Thomas Aquinas*, trans. Charles H. Talbot, rev. ed. (Washington, D.C.: University Press of America, 1981), 242.

57. Cardman notes the distinction between Aquinas's arguments and Bonaventure's and points out that Bonaventure admitted that his position against the ordination of women was only "probabilior," not absolute, though he pointed out that it was supported by many authorities ("Medieval Question," 589–90). Bonaventure says that "In hoc enim Sacramento persona, quae ordinatur, significat Christum mediatorem; et quoniam mediator solum in virili sexu fuit et per virilem sexum potest significari: ideo possibilitas suscipiendi ordines solum viris competit, qui soli possunt *naturaliter repraesentare* et secundum *characteris susceptionem* actu signum huius ferre. Et ista positio probabilior est et multis auctoritatibus Sanctorum potest probari" (Bonaventure, *Commentaria in quatuor libros sententiarum magistri Petri Lombardi*, vols. 1–4 of *Doctoris seraphici S. Bonaventurae . . . Opera omnia*, ed. Collegium S. Bonaventurae, 10 vols. [(Quaracchi): Collegium S. Bonaventurae, 1882–1902], 4:650).

58. On the increasing interest in the "physical" image of God, as opposed to simply the spiritual image, see Newman, *Sister of Wisdom*, 91–93.

59. For Bonaventure's arguments, see *Commentaria*, 4:649.

60. Waleys says, for instance, that "vilitatem tamen magnam in vestibus non video suadere, quia nec de Christo legimus quod magnam vilitatem servaverit in vestibus" (331).

61. In his semisacramental character the preacher needs to exhibit what David Bourke has called "the capacity of a physical thing to signify a spiritual one [in this case, Christ] in virtue of an underlying resemblance to it" (Aquinas, *Summa Theologiae: Latin Text and English Translation*, 56:xvii).

62. Cardman, "Medieval Question," 591; see also Martin, "Injustice," 303–10.

63. Hildegard's reworking of the potentially problematic focus on the male body of Christ is discussed in Newman, *Sister of Wisdom*, 92–93.

64. Scott, "St. Catherine of Siena"; Sahlin, "Prophetess," 30. Sahlin notes, however, that though Birgitta's *Revelations* clearly depict her as a prophet, they never refer to her as one, perhaps because it would have been "too presumptuous" ("Gender," 73).

65. This is, of course, a version (albeit an orthodox and nonaggressive one) of the ongoing attacks on the clerical hierarchy that grew out of the ecclesiastical reform movement and provided a raison d'être for many heretical sects. See Grundmann, *Religious Movements*, 7–30, 222.

66. Birgitta of Sweden, *Life and Selected Revelations*, 78; cf. Birgerus Gregorius, "Legenda Sancte Birgitte," in *Canonization Proceedings of St. Birgitta*, ed. Isak Collijn (Uppsala, Sweden: Almqvist & Wiksells Boktryckeri, 1946), 19.

67. Birgitta of Sweden, *Life and Selected Revelations*, 78; "Non loquor propter te solam sed propter salutem aliorum . . . tu eris sponsa mea et canale meum" (Birgerus Gregorius, "Legenda Sancte Birgitte," 19).

68. On the meaning of this image, see Birgitta of Sweden, *Life and Selected Revelations*, 237, n. 2. Scott discusses Bernard's concept of the preacher as vessel rather than channel ("This is why," 281–82).

69. Birgitta of Sweden, *Life and Selected Revelations*, 20. The Latin reads, "Quia reges et principes et prelati ex beneficiis meis me cognoscere nolunt, ut ad me veniant, ego pauperes, debiles, infantes et miserabiles personas congregabo, quibus loca eorum repleam, ne in exercitu meo ob eorum absenciam aliquis sit defectus" (Birgitta of Sweden, *Revelaciones, Book I*, prologue 39, 238). The image used here echoes the parable of the wedding feast (Luke 14:16–24), reinforcing Birgitta's role as bride. I am indebted to Barbara Newman for pointing out the connection.

70. See Sahlin, "Gender," 86, n. 7.

71. Birgitta of Sweden, *Revelaciones extravagantes*, ed. Lennart Hollman, Svenska Fornskrift-sällskapet, ser. 2, Latinska Skrifter 5 (Uppsala, Sweden: Almqvist and Wiksells Boktryckeri, 1956), 165–66.

72. Sahlin notes that Birgitta's *Revelations* associate her exclusively with male prophets, rather than female ones ("Gender," 75). Her vita, too, tends to prefer comparisons to male prophets, though she is compared to women in other regards. See for instance Birgerus Gregorius, "Legenda Sancte Birgitte," 12 (Moses), 19 (Isaiah), 24 (Ezekiel), etc. Birgitta also receives consolation at one point from

Saint Denis, who reminds her of his missionary work in France and says that God has given her into his hands because he wants to be known throughout the world (Birgerus Gregorius, "Legenda Sancte Birgitte," 18).

73. On Birgitta's "imitatio Mariae," see Claire L. Sahlin, "The Virgin Mary and Birgitta of Sweden's Prophetic Vocation," in *Maria i Sverige under tusen år: Föredrag vid symposiet i Vadstena 6–10 oktober 1994*, ed. Sven-Erik Brodd and Alf Härdelin (Skellefteå, Sweden: Artos, 1996), 227–54, and *Birgitta of Sweden*, 123–68; and Joan Bechtold, "St. Birgitta: The Disjunction between Women and Ecclesiastical Male Power," in *Equally in God's Image: Women in the Middle Ages*, ed. Constance S. Wright, Julia Bolton Holloway, and Bechtold (New York: Peter Lang, 1990), 94–95.

74. Sven Stolpe, ed., *Birgitta: På Svenska, in English, auf Deutsch* (Borås, Sweden: Bokförlaget Legenda, 1973), 62.

75. Sahlin, *Birgitta of Sweden*, 82–83; the quotation is from Birgitta of Sweden, *Revelations, Book VI*, ed. Birger Bergh (Stockholm: Almqvist and Wiksell International, 1991), 145.

76. Quoted in Sahlin, *Birgitta of Sweden*, 46. The emendation is mine; the original translation by Bridget Morris, "same spirit *is worthy to*" seems problematic in the context, and one suspects a confusion such as that which can arise from the Latin "dign[at]us est."

77. Acts 2:1–2: "Et cum conplerentur dies pentecostes erant omnes pariter in eodem loco, et factus est repente de caelo sonus tamquam advenientis spiritus vehementis et replevit totam domum ubi erant sedentes."

78. Sahlin, *Birgitta of Sweden*, 96, 97; the latter quotation makes reference to *Sermo angelicus* 19.12–13.

79. Beverly Mayne Kienzle notes that "bearing the Word" and references to Mary also feature in discussions of men's preaching ("Maternal Imagery in the Sermons of Hélinand of Froidmont," in *De Ore Domini: Preacher and Word in the Middle Ages*, ed. Thomas L. Amos, Eugene A. Green, and Kienzle [Kalamazoo, Mich.: Medieval Institute Publications, Western Michigan University, 1989], 94–96).

80. Kienzle in "Prostitute-Preacher" notes the use of this theme by both Geoffrey of Auxerre and Bernard of Fontcaude in their anti-Waldensian polemics (103, 105, respectively). See also Henry of Ghent, who says that it is shameful for women to teach men, "unless it is a woman gifted with special grace, as was the blessed virgin, who taught the apostles in silence" (Blamires and Marx, 53). Innocent III makes a similar point in his bull *Nova quaedam nuper*, in which he notes that not even Mary was given the power of the keys (PL 216:356).

81. It is unusual in the Middle Ages, as Sahlin points out, for Mary to be presented "as a model or inspiration for women's religious authority," most authors preferring to emphasize her role as "the exemplar of humble obedience and submission" (*Birgitta of Sweden*, 104).

82. Stolpe, *Birgitta*, 71.

83. The implication that Birgitta fulfills a role parallel to that of the clerical descendants of Christ is strongly reiterated in the statement of Matthias of Linköping that her revelations were "more astonishing than that by which Christ

appeared in the flesh. The latter displayed a carnal exterior to carnal eyes, the former shows God and man to spiritual eyes. . . . In the latter He Who wandered the
earth revealed the divine in the human, but in the former He Who reigns in
heaven reconciles the human with the divine" (Stolpe, *Birgitta,* 63; the Latin text
is in Birgitta of Sweden, *Revelaciones, Book I,* prologue 21–23, pp. 234–35). But the
tension or competition between the physical and intellectual expressed here seems
to work against Birgitta's style of prophecy.

84. Raymond of Capua, *Life of Catherine of Siena,* 107.

85. Both Catherine and Raymond do associate Catherine with Mary Magdalene, including her preaching activity (Jansen, *Making of the Magdalen,* 275–77).

86. See n. 81 above. In this context it is interesting to note that in the work
of Thomas Aquinas, according to Børresen, "the traditional theme of [Mary's]
spiritual fruitfulness, compared to that of the Church, is absent. The Church is not
the spouse or the mother; she is the extension and continuation of Christ's human
nature, and His instrument in the work of the redemption. Christ acts through
His Church as Head of the mystical body" (*Subordination and Equivalence,* 235).
This omission removes two potent models for women by cutting the link between
the bodily bearing of the Word and the (female) bearing of the word in women's
preaching, and by making Ecclesia, the Church, an instrument of the male Christ
(as the priest is) and not a female figure in her own right, like the "womanly form"
who appears to Hildegard. By "disappearing" these female personifications and
their generative roles, Aquinas makes it more difficult for women to find a place
in the preaching tradition.

87. Raymond of Capua, *Life of Catherine of Siena,* 113 (on Catherine's "spiritual motherhood") and 116 (on her assimilation to Mary). A letter written after
the death of Birgitta by one of her supporters "asserts that it was only fitting for
Christ to reveal himself to the woman Birgitta, since her revelations, like the Virgin Mary's motherhood, reverse the effects of Eve's disobedience" (Sahlin,
"Prophetess," 33).

88. Thus, God responds to Catherine's fear that "propriety forbids a woman
to mix so freely with men" and her misgivings about a public role "in words like
those of the archangel Gabriel when he said: 'No thing shall be impossible with
God' " (Raymond of Capua, *Life of Catherine of Siena,* 116).

89. Ibid., 108.

90. "Memor esse debes, quomodo ab infantia zelus salutis animarum, me
seminante simul et irrigante, crevit in corde tuo, in tantum quod proponebas te
fingere masculum, et ignotis in partibus ordinem praedicatorum intrare, ut possis
utilis animabus effici: et ex hoc, quem nunc habes, habitum tanto cum fervore
desiderasti" (Raymond of Capua, *Vita beatae Catherinae,* 892).

91. "Zelus animarum" seems to have been a favorite Dominican concept. Étienne de Bourbon, for instance, refers to "ille tantus zelotypus animarum salutis,
beatus pater noster Dominicus" (Lecoy de la Marche, *Anecdotes,* 13; quoted in
Vecchio, "Dalla predicazione alla conversazione," 75, n. 26).

92. Raymond of Capua, *Vita beatae Catherinae,* 913.

93. In this context it should be noted that virgins, including female virgins,
were seen as having a particular similarity to Christ. See two sermons quoted by

Carolyn Muessig, "Prophecy and Song: Teaching and Preaching by Medieval Women," in Kienzle and Walker, 157, nn. 30, 31, which speak of the "conformita[s]" and "similitud[o] expressa" of virgins to Christ.

94. "Intra me cogitavi in quibusdam; Putasne sint omnia vera quae dicit? Dumque sic cogitarem, et in faciem loquentis intenderem; subito facies ejus transformata est in faciem viri barbari, qui me fixis oculis intuendo, nimium terruit: eratque facies oblonga, aetatis mediae, non prolixam habens barbam coloris triticei, majestatemque praeferens in aspectu, ex que se manifeste Dominum ostendebat: nec aliam pro tunc ibi faciem discernere poteram, praeter illam. Cumque pavefactus et territus, erectis circa humeros manibus, exclamarem: O quis est, qui me respicit? Respondit virgo: Ille, qui est" (Raymond of Capua, Vita beatae Caterinae, 884).

95. "Our Lord would even recite the Psalms with her as they walked to and fro in her room, like two religious or two clerics reciting their Office together" (Raymond of Capua, Life of Catherine of Siena, 104).

96. "Nam predicator, cum sit medium inter Deum et homines, et a Deo recipiat quod hominibus refundit, perfeccionem vtriusque vite, contempl[atiue] scilicet et actiue, debet attingere vel esse in bona et proxima disposicione" (Paris, Bibliothèque Nationale MS. Lat. 14909, f. 125v).

97. As Beckwith notes, "Margery is simply too intransigently present" for critics of her mysticism ("Very Material Mysticism," 199). It is not my intention to replicate that criticism but only to suggest that it was in part her strong presence—as difficult for contemporaries as for modern interpreters—that made it impossible for her to displace attention from herself as she would have needed to do to achieve a stable public voice. At the same time Margery was by no means entirely unsuccessful in her project; as the quotation with which I began shows, she was extremely inventive in her attempts to authorize her own speech. She certainly attained more of a public voice than most women of her time would even have aspired to and along the way offered repeated, sharp challenges to clerical assumptions about who had the right to speak to (and for) whom. Wendy Harding offers an excellent discussion of the "dialogic" qualities of Margery's Book and the ways in which it "undoes some of the hierarchical dualities invoked to maintain a masculine authority" (Wendy Harding, "Body into Text: The Book of Margery Kempe," in Feminist Approaches to the Body in Medieval Literature, ed. Linda Lomperis and Sarah Stanbury [Philadelphia: University of Pennsylvania Press, 1993], 170, 177).

98. For an extensive discussion, see Lynn Staley, Margery Kempe's Dissenting Fictions (University Park: Pennsylvania State University Press, 1994). See also Sarah Beckwith on Margery and her critics in "Problems of Authority in Late Medieval English Mysticism: Language, Agency, and Authority in The Book of Margery Kempe," Exemplaria 4, no. 1 (1992): 171–99.

99. Voaden's chapter headings in God's Words implicitly acknowledge this issue: the one on Birgitta is titled "The Lady Vanishes"; the one on Margery is subtitled "The Woman Who Would Not Go Away."

Chapter 7

1. The competing emphases on things that set the clergy apart, such as celibacy, and on their need to connect with the laity through preaching, as well as the increasing importance of confession, which contributed to both distance and proximity, are all visible in the decrees of the Fourth Lateran Council; see particularly decrees 10, 14, and 21 in Tanner, *Decrees,* 239–40, 242, 245. Canon 11 of Lateran III was even more severe on the subject of clerical celibacy (ibid., 217); the Lateran IV formulation leaves some room for differing observances in different regions. Jo Ann McNamara discusses the movement toward clerical celibacy, especially its effect on perceptions of gender, in "The *Herrenfrage:* The Restructuring of the Gender System, 1050–1150," in *Medieval Masculinities: Regarding Men in the Middle Ages,* ed. Clare A. Lees with Thelma S. Fenster and McNamara (Minneapolis: University of Minnesota Press, 1994), 3–29.

2. Dyan Elliott, *Fallen Bodies,* 83.

3. See Knapp, *Chaucer and the Social Contest,* 45–94; and the essays in Aers and Staley, *Powers of the Holy.*

4. Mann, *Chaucer.*

5. R. W. Hanning, " 'And countrefete the speche of every man / He koude, whan he sholde telle a tale': Toward a Lapsarian Poetics for *The Canterbury Tales,*" *Studies in the Age of Chaucer* 21 (1999): 31.

6. Ibid., 42. As he observes, the "preaching office, buttressed by ecclesiastical legislation that set the clergy apart from the laity in dress and behavior" was the creation that "constructed" the monumentally authoritative voice he describes, but he does not explore the fragility of that construction. In an argument that complements the one presented here, Galloway offers an illuminating exploration of how the Wife's voice and arguments build on those of marriage sermons (a subset of the sermons *ad status*) and in so doing "unravel . . . the authority of preaching from within, as it were" ("Marriage Sermons," 13).

7. Aers and Staley, *Powers of the Holy,* 128.

8. The collections are those by Honorius Augustodunensis and Alan of Lille in the twelfth century, and Jacques de Vitry, Humbert of Romans (OP), and Guibert de Tournai (OFM) in the thirteenth. (John of Wales's [OFM] thirteenth-century *Communiloquium* concerns itself with examples and authorities appropriate to particular groups but does not attempt to characterize those groups in any systematic way, unlike the *ad status* collections.) On the genre, and particularly the collections by Honorius, Jacques, and Humbert, see Carolyn Muessig, "Audience and Preacher: *Ad Status* Sermons and Social Classification," in *Preacher, Sermon, and Audience,* ed. Muessig (Leiden: Brill, 2002), 255–76. I am grateful to Dr. Muessig for sharing this work with me before its publication. David d'Avray observes that "major *ad status* collections are few in number" but suggests that these few may have "provided all the specific sermons that were needed" (*Preaching of the Friars,* 127–28). It is also possible, of course, that as professional and social stereotypes became more commonplace it was easier for preachers simply to adapt generalized discourses to specific audiences.

9. Constable discusses the variety of notions of "orders of society" in me-

dieval culture, including the tripartite model emphasized here, and also notes the increasing pressure on such models in the late Middle Ages (*Three Studies,* 251–341).

10. Maria Corti, "Structures idéologiques et structures sémiotiques dans les *sermones ad status* du XIIIe siècle," in *Archéologie du signe,* ed. Lucie Brind'Amour and Eugene Vance (Toronto: Pontifical Institute of Mediaeval Studies, 1982), 148.

11. See Jacques Le Goff, "Trades and Professions as Represented in Medieval Confessors' Manuals," in *Time, Work & Culture in the Middle Ages,* trans. Arthur Goldhammer (Chicago: University of Chicago Press, 1980), 107–21; and D. W. Robertson, Jr., "The Cultural Tradition of *Handlyng Synne,*" *Speculum* 22 (1947): 162–85.

12. M.-D. Chenu, *L'éveil de la conscience* (1969), 45, quoted in Constable, *Three Studies,* 329. Le Goff makes the similar point that the new confessional approaches contributed to "personalization . . . within a larger process of socialization" ("Trades and Professions," 114).

13. Sermon authors and writers of preaching handbooks often begin from this existing principle ("give milk to the small, bread to the greater") and then move into the finer distinctions of status; see, for example, Jacques de Vitry's citation of 1 Kings 17:17: "Jesse ait ad David filium suum, ut acciperet polentam et panes et formellas casei, et misit ut visitaret fratres suos. Per polentam, de qua plures fiunt cibi parvulis, intelligitur simplex doctrina; per panes solida, quae competit adultis; per formellas casei exempla perficiendi consilia, quae pertinent ad perfectos" (*Sermones vulgares,* 189).

14. Corti, "Structures idéologiques," 149. Carlo M. Cipolla argues that in this period "in the cities, a horizontal arrangement emerged, characterized by cooperation among equals" (*Before the Industrial Revolution: European Society and Economy 1000–1700,* 3d ed. [New York: Norton, 1993], 121).

15. "Aliter enim praedicandum est . . . praelatis, aliter simplicibus sacerdotibus, aliter canonicis saecularibus et aliter clericis" (Jacques de Vitry, *Sermones vulgares,* 191).

16. Honorius Augustodunensis, *Sermo generalis,* PL 172:861–70. This is part of his larger collection of model sermons, the *Speculum ecclesiae,* PL 172:813–1108.

17. "Nos sacerdotes debemus linguam vestram esse, et cuncta quae in divinis officiis canuntur vel leguntur vobis interpretando exponere" (ibid., col. 861).

18. "Quae autem verbis docemus, speculum nos factis exhibere debemus" (ibid., col. 861D); "Ideo magis ad verba nostra quam ad opera, karissimi, respicere debetis" (862C); "Legati summi Regis omnium regum sumus, ejus mandata vobis referimus" (862C).

19. "Praesul quidam ferventi studio plebem sibi commissam docebat" (ibid., col. 863A); "O karissimi, quam beata anima quae meruit angelorum consortia!" (863B).

20. Carolyn Muessig points out that the *Sermo generalis* depicts the ideal priest as having monastic virtues, reflecting Honorius's status as a "monk-priest" and further emphasizing his distance from his lay audience ("Audience and Preacher," 258–59).

21. "Pro qualitate igitur audientium formari debet sermo doctorum, ut et ad

sua singulis congruat." The instruction comes from Book 3 of Gregory's *Regula pastoralis,* which is devoted to the "great diversity" required in preaching to various audiences, but the groups are mostly defined by their moral or psychological tendencies and Gregory hardly addresses professional or social classifications (*Règle pastorale,* prologue to book 3, 2:258). Jacques de Vitry quotes the first part of this instruction in the prologue to his *Sermones vulgares,* 190–91. Jacques was an enthusiastic teller of exempla; see Crane, *Exempla.* Humbert of Romans also quotes Gregory in *De eruditione praedicatorum,* the theoretical discussion that precedes his collection of *ad status* sermons (422); the sermons appear in Maxima Bibliotheca Veterum Patrum 25 (Lyons, 1677), 456–567.

22. English citations are from Gregory the Great, *Dialogues,* trans. Odo John Zimmerman, Fathers of the Church 39 (New York: Fathers of the Church, 1959), 193. The relevant passage in Latin reads, "Hic igitur liber idcirco concionator dicitur, quia Salomon in eo quasi tumultuantis turbae suscepit sensum, ut ea per inquisitionem dicat, quae fortasse per tentationem imperita mens sentiat. Nam quot sententias quasi per inquisitionem movet, quasi tot in se personas diversorum suscipit. Sed concionator verax velut extensa manu omnium tumultus sedat, eosque ad unam sententiam revocat, cum in ejusdem libri termino ait: *Finem loquendi omnes pariter audiamus: Deum time, et mandata ejus observa; hoc est enim omnis homo.* Si enim in libro eodem per locutionem suam multorum personas non susceperat, cur ad audiendum loquendi finem secum pariter omnes admonebat? Qui igitur in fine libri dicit: *Omnes pariter audiamus,* ipse sibi testis est quia in se multorum personas suscipiens, quasi solus locutus non est" (*Dialogorum libri IV,* PL 77:324). This idea is akin to that proposed by Saint Paul when he said, "Factus sum infirmis infirmus, ut infirmos lucrifacerem" (1 Cor. 9:22); see Augustine's discussion in *De opere monachorum,* cap. 11, par. 12, in *L'ascétisme chrétien: De continentia, De sancta virginitate, De bono viduitatis, De opere monachorum,* Oeuvres de Saint Augustin 3, ed. J. Saint-Martin, 2d ed. (Paris: Desclée, de Brouwer & Cie., 1949), 346–50.

23. The point is immediately reinforced when Gregory's disciple Peter makes use of impersonation and Gregory responds, "In doing this [impersonating the weak in order to instruct them], you deserve greater respect, because you are thereby imitating the practice of an outstanding preacher" (*Dialogues,* 196); "In hac re amplius venerari debes, in qua morem egregii praedicatoris imitaris" (*Dialogorum libri IV,* col. 325).

24. Corti, "Structures idéologiques," 147.

25. Geoffrey of Vinsauf, *The New Poetics,* trans. Jane Baltzell Kopp, in *Three Medieval Rhetorical Arts,* ed. James J. Murphy (Berkeley and Los Angeles: University of California Press, 1971), 50; the Latin reads, "Cui nulla potentia fandi, / Da licite fari donetque licentia linguam" (Geoffrey of Vinsauf, *Poetria nova,* in *The Poetria Nova and Its Sources in Early Rhetorical Doctrine,* ed. and trans. Ernest Gallo, De Proprietatibus Litterarum Series Maior 10 [The Hague and Paris: Mouton, 1971], 38).

26. Technically speaking, prosopopoeia, or personification, is not exactly the same thing as impersonation, or ethopoeia, but as Henrik Specht shows, the two are often confused or overlap in rhetorical manuals: "in classical rhetoric and

grammar as well as in parts of medieval poetics the figure of 'personification' proper is often defined [as but] a variation of a subdivision of a larger rhetorical form, comprising '*impersonation*' (that is, the attribution of speech to a historical, legendary, or fictitious *character*) as well as 'personification' proper. This comprehensive rhetorical form is treated under a variety of names, including *prosopopoeia, conformatio, sermocinatio, fictio personae, ethopoeia,* and *adlocutio*" (" 'Ethopoeia' or Impersonation: A Neglected Species of Medieval Characterization," *Chaucer Review* 21 [1986]: 13, n. 3).

27. Dinshaw, *Chaucer's Sexual Poetics,* 154.

28. Owst, *Literature,* 220. Over time, as Owst suggests, discussing particularly the events and attitudes that attended the Rising of 1381, "the Orders grew suspicious or disdainful of inflammatory writings in the vulgar tongue," and as they became more institutionalized, like many radical groups, they lost their claim to or interest in a popular voice (221).

29. The quoted phrase is Lee Patterson's; he is discussing the *Summoner's Tale,* in which the friars are depicted as having fallen away from their ideals and become "hopelessly, laughably corrupt," thus uniting against themselves the rural society that they may once, as Owst suggests, have championed (Patterson, *Chaucer,* 319). For the mendicant emphasis on an apostolic life of preaching and poverty and the conflicts between friars and seculars, see for example d'Avray, *Preaching of the Friars,* 43–47, 49–50, and Lawrence, *Friars,* 152–65, on the secular-mendicant controversy in particular.

30. Note for example the extreme dislike manifested in Francesc Eiximenis's preaching manual—and seemingly shared by many others, given all the sources he quotes—of vainglory, showing off, and "trufas vel fabulas," which suggests that like their detractors the Franciscans were well aware of the temptations of the crowd ("L'*Ars Praedicandi*," 301–40). The distaste runs throughout the text; the phrase "trufas vel fabulas" is on 325.

31. Scanlon, *Narrative,* discusses friars and pardoners "as distinguished from the older, more established and more locally oriented parochial and monastic clergy." He sees them, however, as representatives of the "international Church of the later Middle Ages" (148) and suggests that the Pardoner, despite his precise mendicant characteristics, is used primarily to explore "the general relation between the doctrinal and the lay" (192).

32. The first complete book on the genre is Ruth Mohl, *The Three Estates in Medieval and Renaissance Literature* (New York: Columbia University Press, 1933), which took the three orders of society to be its ruling concept, as her title indicates. For Mohl, the defining characteristics of estates literature were an effort at completeness in enumerating the estates; a sense of their divinely ordained origins and importance to social cohesion; distress at the orders' falling away from their duties; and suggestions about how to redress this dereliction (6–7). Mann, *Chaucer,* contains a helpful treatment of the genre (3–10) and a valuable list of many of its surviving exemplars (app., 297–312). Mann considers works that treat only one or a few groups as estates satire, though Mohl prefers to focus on those that aim at "completeness." Here I follow Mann, whose "less rigid" definition of estates literature can be found on pp. 3–4.

33. Although both sermons to and satires on various social groups existed before the twelfth century, the number, interrelationships, and consistent style of late medieval versions of each genre mark them as, at least, a new version of an existing phenomenon. The earliest text Mann mentions is from the tenth century, but her appendices demonstrate that the satires exploded in number during the twelfth to fourteenth centuries.

34. Mohl, *Three Estates,* 31, 39, 23–24. The *Chessbook* by Jacobus of Cessolis, a Dominican friar, can be found in Ferdinand Vetter, ed., *Das Schachzabelbuch Kunrats von Ammenhausen . . . nebst den Schachbüchern des Jakob von Cessole und des Jakob Mennel* (Frauenfeld, Switzerland: J. Huber, 1892). The Latin text is printed as a running footnote to Konrad von Ammenhausen's text, which is numbered by columns rather than pages; the Latin is on the pages of cols. 25–834. The "Bible" of Hugues de Berzé, written probably in the second quarter of the thirteenth century, is not particularly satirical in tone (see comments by the editor on p. 25) but is of interest for the way its lay author claims an authoritative voice: "Ainsi ne puet nus hons avoir / En ce siecle bien son voloir. / Ainsi com je sai sermoner, / Qui ne sui ne clers ne letrés / Ne je ne trai autorités, / Fors de tant que je sai e voi / . . . E si me devroit on mieux croire / C'un hermite ne c'un provoire, / Car j'ai le siecles molt parfont / Cerchié e aval e amont"; here the knowledge of the world that the preacher cultivated to reach his flock is claimed as the natural property of the lay author, rather than of the more unworldly religious figures (*La "Bible" au seigneur de Berzé,* ed. Félix Lecoy [Paris: Librairie E. Droz, 1938], ll. 385–91, 401–4).

35. Mohl, *Three Estates,* 37.

36. See here Scanlon, *Narrative,* 192–205. Martha Bayless makes the important point, however, that anticlerical satires or other works that critiqued the church in some way—many of which were indeed written by clerics—need not be taken as dangerously subversive of the church (*Parody in the Middle Ages: The Latin Tradition* [Ann Arbor: University of Michigan Press, 1996], 177–78).

37. The *Sermones nulli parentes* exist in a unique manuscript that also, intriguingly, contains a German version of the text; both are edited by Theodor von Karajan in "Buch der Rügen," *Zeitschrift für Deutsches Alterthum* 2 (1842): 6–92. Karajan dates the Latin text to c. 1220, shortly after the crowning of Frederick II (6–7), and the German one to 1276 or 1277, based on a reference to "Pope John," presumably John XXI (12); the manuscript itself is from the early fifteenth century (6–7). See also Mohl, *Three Estates,* 23–24.

38. The final chapter, 28, is titled "De ipsis fratribus qui populo praedicant" (*Sermones nulli parentes,* p. 44).

39. "Fratres, mundum qui transitis / totum atque circuitis / praedicantes imperitis" (*Sermones nulli parentes,* ll. 1–3).

40. "Fratres, non vos reprehendo, reverenter haec dicendo / . . . sed videtur vos debere / singulariter docere, / quisque qualiter sincere / deo poterit placere" (ibid., ll. 73–80).

41. The ordering here is fairly standard, particularly in the placement of clergy before laity and men before women; see Mann, *Chaucer,* 6.

42. This recalls the common idea of Latin as a universal language, as against the particularity of vernaculars; see Chapter 3 above.

43. "Dum ad claustrum veniatis / feminarum, intendatis, / precor, nutu caritatis, / ut non dure arguatis. / non dico tamen, ut parcatis, / sed ut mitius agatis, / ne contingat, ut frangatis / vas tantae fragilitatis" (*Sermones nulli parcentes,* ll. 549–56).

44. "Si qua re prohibeatur / mulier, ei videatur, / nisi hoc perficiatur, / ipsa statim moriatur" (ibid., ll.561–64). On this well-established view of women's disobedience and contrariness, see for example Alcuin Blamires, ed., *Woman Defamed and Woman Defended: An Anthology of Medieval Texts* (Oxford: Clarendon Press, 1992), 121, 145–46.

45. As Mann observes, "The duties and failings of the estate of women are often seen from the standpoint of the male moralist . . . the whole of the chapter on women in the *Sermones* [*nulli parcentes*] is occupied in defining the attitude men should adopt toward them" (*Chaucer,* 121).

46. "Ergo nec inproperando / nec quidquam eis imperando / loquimini sermone blando, / omne malum detestando, / boni qualiter gaudebunt, / cum in gloria manebunt, / mali quomodo dolebunt, / quoniam sine fine flebunt" (*Sermones nulli parcentes,* ll. 601–8).

47. "Mulieres honoretis, / numquam dure arguetis" (ibid., ll. 993–94). The section on women is ll. 993–1036.

48. "Mulieres fugiatis, / in societate pravitatis / ne, quod absit, polluatis / imaginem divinitatis. / quibus si confabulatur, / peto solum os loquatur / et non manus comprimatur, / nam sic deus non laudatur" (ibid., ll. 1073–80). Compare the deathbed warning of Saint Dominic to his brothers to "avoid mingling with women such as could cause suspicion, and particularly with young women, since they are especially alluring and able to entangle souls not yet purified in the fire," in chap. 92 of Jordan of Saxony's *On the Origin of the Order of Preachers,* quoted in Brooke, *Coming of the Friars,* 174.

49. The movement from women's wickedness to their potential for outstanding goodness (as exemplified by Mary) that this work depicts is, of course, typical of medieval discussions of women; see Blamires, *Woman Defamed.*

50. Coakley suggests that the mendicant orders' disinclination to take pastoral responsibility for convents was based "not merely on conventional monastic suspicion of excessive association with women, but also a concern not to drain their energy from the preaching which, as it happened, was the very activity that brought them into contact with women in the first place"; here women are imagined as being in competition with the mendicants' duty to preach, a conflict to which I will return below ("Gender and the Authority of Friars," 446). That friars were particularly concerned with their pastoral duties toward women is evident from works such as Eiximenis's *Libre de les dones* (c. 1388), which considers women at various life stages (maidens, widows, etc.) as well as religious women, or the sermons by Humbert of Romans, Guibert de Tournai, and Étienne de Bourbon collected in Carla Casagrande, ed., *Prediche alle donne del secolo XIII* (Milan: Bompiani, 1978).

51. The *Sermones nulli parcentes* acknowledge women's precarious position; the preface to the work takes pains to point out that every degree is addressed, from pope to cleric and emperor to peasant, and adds that "neither nuns nor other

women are forgotten" (*tam monialibus quam aliis mulieribus non oblitis,* p. 15). Mann, *Chaucer,* 121, makes note of women's outsider status in the genre; see also Corti, "Structures idéologiques," 150, and Constable, *Three Studies,* 259–61. Constable points out, however, that there are models of the social order, such as those focusing on marital status (the married, the continent, widows, etc.), in which women are much less marginal (252).

52. Shulamith Shahar, *The Fourth Estate. A History of Women in the Middle Ages,* trans. Chaya Galai (London: Methuen, 1983). See particularly the introduction, 1–10, where Shahar discusses women's place in the estates model and the *ordines* model that preceded it. Women as members of professions are particularly represented in Langland's *Piers Plowman,* though Mann notes how unusual this is (*Chaucer,* 214, n. 13).

53. The quotation is from Mann, *Chaucer,* 17.

54. As Thomson notes, "criticism of worldly attitudes among supposedly other-worldly individuals is the very stuff of satire" ("Orthodox Religion," 52). At the same time the clergy's internal sense of responsibility should not be forgotten and is clearly evident in sermons to priests and preachers throughout the period. They recognized that their position made them natural targets and were no easier on themselves than on others.

55. Mann discusses the "independent traditions" that inform the treatment of some classes in estates satire (*Chaucer,* 106). See Blamires, *Woman Defamed,* for examples of misogynistic medieval texts. On medieval anticlericalism, see John van Engen, "Late Medieval Anticlericalism: The Case of the New Devout," in *Anticlericalism in Late Medieval and Early Modern Europe,* ed. Peter A. Dykema and Heiko A. Oberman (Leiden: Brill, 1993), 19–52. Beginning in the thirteenth century there is also a notably ferocious antifraternal tradition that exists apart from, though it is borrowed by, estates literature. The fount of this is William of St. Amour's vitriolic attack on the mendicants, *De periculis novissimorum temporum,* and the phenomenon as a whole is discussed thoroughly in Szittya, *Antifraternal Tradition.*

56. The first Epistle to Timothy treats, in remarkably short space, such topics as failings of clerical speech (1 Tim. 1:3–7); the high demands on clerical behavior, including sexual behavior (1:9–10, 3:1–10); the apparel and appropriately subordinate behavior of women (2:9–15, 3:11); and suspect widows, whose characteristics include idleness, wantonness, and garrulity (5:5–13). As Hanning observes, based on the criteria set out here the Wife of Bath and the Pardoner are "Pauline nightmares" ("And countrefete the speche," 54); see also Cespedes, "Chaucer's Pardoner and Preaching," 1–18, on the importance of the pastoral epistles for the characters of Pardoner, Parson, and, to a lesser extent, Wife; and see Sarah Disbrow, "The Wife of Bath's Old Wives' Tale," *Studies in the Age of Chaucer* 8 (1986), 63–64, on the Parson as a Pauline ideal.

57. Bloch, *Medieval Misogyny,* gives an extensive account of women's stereotyped failings; see especially 13–35. Blamires, *Woman Defamed,* offers lengthy index entries on "deception," "lust," and "speech, women's."

58. See Mann's list of characteristic shortcomings of friars (*Chaucer,* 225, n. 65) and her discussions of Monk (17–37), Friar (37–54), and Parson (55–67), in the

last of which the failings of the profession are indicated inversely through the Parson's idealized qualities. The Monk's misuse of speech is not discussed, since preaching and teaching were not part of his ordinary professional duties.

59. Mann discusses the links between friars' "persuasive speech" and their womanizing (*Chaucer*, 37–40). See also Szittya, *Antifraternal Tradition*, 53–54 (on the friars' perversion of speech) and 59–60 (on friars and women).

60. The foundational antifraternal text is 2 Tim. 3:1–6, which warns against the dangers of the "last days," in which will appear "those who enter into households [*qui penetrant domus*] and captivate weak women [*seducunt mulierculas*] weighed down with sins, led on by various impulses." *Mulierculas* is also the term used for clerical concubines in canon 11 of the Third Lateran Council (Tanner, *Decrees*, 217).

61. Szittya discusses William of St. Amour's argument that friars threaten to break down the "ecclesiastical economy" of the church through their "infinite and unfixed number" (*Antifraternal Tradition*, 47).

62. The outstanding example here is Jean de Meun, whose embodiment and voicing of antifeminist stereotypes (in La Vieille) and antifraternal ones (in Faus Semblant) was a key source for Chaucer's Wife and Pardoner (Guillaume de Lorris and Jean de Meun, *Le roman de la rose*, ed. Daniel Poirion [Paris: Garnier-Flammarion, 1974], ll. 12385–14548 [La Vieille], 11003–12096 [Faus Semblant]).

63. The emphasis on adulterous triangles in fabliau is discussed in Per Nykrog, *Les fabliaux*, 2d ed., Publications romanes et françaises (Geneva: Droz, 1973). The most recent edition of the fabliaux is Willem Noomen and Nico van den Boogard, eds., *Nouveau recueil complet des fabliaux*, 10 vols. (Assen, Netherlands: Van Gorcum, 1983–98); see also Anatole de Montaiglon, ed., *Recueil général et complet des fabliaux des XIIIᵉ et XIVᵉ siècles imprimés ou inédits*, 6 vols. (Paris: Librairie des bibliophiles, 1872–90), which contains some texts omitted in the *Nouveau recueil*.

64. Fritz Kemmler, *'Exempla' in Context: A Historical and Critical Study of Robert Mannyng of Brunne's 'Handlyng Synne'* (Tübingen, Germany: Gunter Narr Verlag, 1984), 74. See also Jacques de Vitry's implication, discussed in Chapter 3 above, that written collections of exempla are dead letters, useful only when they are animated by the preacher's presentation.

65. Marie Anne Polo de Beaulieu, "Exempla: A Discussion and a Case Study; II. *Mulier* and *Femina*: The Representation of Women in the *Scala celi* of Jean Gobi," in *Medieval Women and the Sources of Medieval History*, ed. Joel T. Rosenthal (Athens: University of Georgia Press, 1990), 56.

66. Thus, Robertson depicts exempla as "subordinate to the doctrine which they illustrate" ("Cultural Tradition of *Handlyng Synne*," 162), and Scanlon points out that clerical culture tended to see narrative as "a subordinate form characteristic of lay culture and open to clerical exploitation," though he acknowledges the instability of that subordination (*Narrative*, 194). See also Walter J. Ong's comments about the role of fiction in preaching, in "Gospel, Existence, and Print," *Modern Language Quarterly* 35, no. 1 (1974): 69; and Alexander Gelley, ed., *Unruly Examples: On the Rhetoric of Exemplarity* (Stanford, Calif.: Stanford University Press, 1995), on the tensions inherent in the use of examples.

67. On overfamiliarity, see, e.g., Humbert, 463–66, and the Dominican Constitutions, which say that traveling preachers "shall avoid being intimate with any dubious companions" (Tugwell, *Early Dominicans,* 467). Both the Epistle to Timothy, which denigrates "Profanas et aniles fabulas" ("worldly fables fit only for old women": 1 Tim. 4:7), and Saint Ambrose, who refers at one point to "Aniles . . . fabulae, ac vulgi opiniones," show that old wives' tales were associated not just with women but also with the "vulgar crowd" more generally. The Ambrose passage, from the *Hexaemeron* (PL 14:204), is quoted in Disbrow, "Wife of Bath's Old Wives' Tale," 62.

68. Scanlon, *Narrative,* 59. Christine de Pizan suggests that this claim regarding Mary Magdalene was current in her time: "I heard some foolish preachers teach that God first appeared to a woman because He knew well that she did not know how to keep quiet, so that this way the news of His resurrection would spread more rapidly" (*The Book of the City of Ladies,* trans. Earl Jeffrey Richards [New York: Persea Books, 1982], 28). Blamires, *Woman Defamed,* notes the use of this antifeminist motif in the *Lamentations of Matheolus* and in Langland's *Piers Plowman* (294, n. 47). Disbrow observes that Augustine at one point felt moved to "attack . . . an unnamed scriptural commentator who applied the label 'old wives' tales' to the written word of the prophets," and that he himself also refers to "tales that failed to present the Old Testament itself in a way that was meaningful to Christians" as old wives' tales; both examples suggest the difficulties of keeping authoritative bibical speech strictly separated from "profane" speech (Disbrow, "Wife of Bath's Old Wives' Tale," 64, 66).

69. In a somewhat similar way, the Wife of Bath says of her "gossib" that "She knew myn herte, and eek my privetee, / Bet than oure parisshe preest, so moot I thee!" (Chaucer, *Canterbury Tales,* III.531–32). Here gossip takes the role of confession and the female friend (like some friars) takes the place of the parish priest.

70. Silvana Vecchio, "Les langues de feu: Pentecôte et rhétorique sacrée dans les sermons des XIIe et XIIIe siècles," in Dessì and Lauwers, 263. As she notes, however, any notion that the preacher could claim to rule on the legitimacy of "profane" speech from an elevated position was under severe threat in this period from the voices of other professions, and the insistence on his exalted status no doubt reflects an uneasy awareness of that threat (266–69).

71. Derek Pearsall, *The Canterbury Tales* (London: George Allen & Unwin, 1985), 222. Mann notes that estates depictions of friars and pardoners have extensive overlaps and that "the stereotypes of the two classes develop from the same basis," including the character of Faus Semblant in the *Roman de la Rose*—himself derived from antifraternal stereotype (*Chaucer,* 278, n. 22).

72. Hanning, "And countrefete the speche," 53.

73. Jacques de Vitry, for example, insists in the preface to his *Sermones vulgares,* "In his igitur non solum quibus, sed qualiter, quando, quo fine et qualia proponuntur, praedicator diligenter attendat" (191). The issue of "who, what, when, where, why" is a concern of all preaching but becomes especially central in *ad status* sermons.

74. A voice appropriate to the speaker is, of course, in itself a rhetorical con-

cept and one discussed in the preaching manuals; see the account of Augustine's notion of decorum in Chapter 4. The persona created by the preacher's choices about language and self-presentation is, in a sense, yet another character.

75. Glending Olson, "Rhetorical Circumstances and the Canterbury Story-telling," in *Studies in the Age of Chaucer, Proceedings No. 1, 1984: Reconstructing Chaucer*, ed. Paul Strohm and Thomas Heffernan (Knoxville, Tenn.: New Chaucer Society, 1985), 215.

76. Chaucer, *Canterbury Tales* I.731–36, 739–40.

77. Jean de Meun and Boccaccio make similar excuses, as noted by F. N. Robinson, editor of the first edition of the "Riverside Chaucer," *The Complete Works of Geoffrey Chaucer* (Boston: Houghton Mifflin, 1933), 770. Olson, "Rhetorical Circumstances," points out Boccaccio's use of the concept (211–12). We might note that the press, the modern chattering class—to whom Chaucer's claim to be a reporter assimilates him—is also a "fourth estate": like women and preachers, they do not have an obvious or stable place in an estates framework.

78. Chaucer, *Canterbury Tales* I.741–42.

79. On responsibility and Chaucer's play with this concept, see Hanning, "And countrefete the speche," 46–47.

80. Barrie Ruth Straus discusses the passages quoted above and their place in Chaucer's undermining of the claim to "absolute authority and univocal truth" ("The Subversive Discourse of the Wife of Bath: Phallocentric Discourse and the Imprisonment of Criticism," in *Chaucer: Contemporary Critical Essays*, ed. Valerie Allen and Ares Axiotis [New York: St. Martin's Press, 1996], 126–44).

81. Patterson, *Chaucer*, 286, 289.

82. On the Wife's debts to preaching discourse, see especially Galloway, "Marriage Sermons." Susan Signe Morrison gives a useful, brief account of read-ings that see the Wife's use of "masculine strategies of power, such as glossing" as "simply weaken[ing] her own stance" and then provides a corrective ("Don't Ask, Don't Tell: The Wife of Bath and Vernacular Translations," *Exemplaria* 8, no. 1 [1996]: 106–9). Patterson, *Chaucer*, discusses her deployment of clerical modes in her "sermon joyeux" (307–13).

83. Straus, "Subversive Discourse," explores Chaucer's diffusion of authority from a feminist viewpoint, while Susan Morrison, "Don't Ask, Don't Tell," ad-dresses many of the same issues in the context of translation debates and Lollardy. By referring to the Wife as Chaucer's voice, I do not intend to dismiss or erase the character's importance as a feminine or lay figure in her own right but rather to complement readings such as those of Straus and Morrison by showing how her status as a woman and a layperson makes her, paradoxically, the ideal figure to rep-resent a preacher. See, on this point, Galloway, "Marriage Sermons," especially 28–30.

84. Thomas Wright, ed., *The Latin Poems Commonly Attributed to Walter Mapes* (London: Printed for the Camden Society by John Bowyer Nichols and Son, 1841), 171–73 ("De concubinis sacerdotum"), 174–79 ("Consultatio sacerdo-tum"), 180–82 ("De convocatione sacerdotum"). Each poem is cited hereafter by title and line number. The three poems are treated as a group by Paul Lehmann, *Die Parodie im Mittelalter* (Stuttgart: Anton Hiersemann, 1963), 112–16, who dis-

cusses their possible historical referents. Hans Walther, *Initia carminum ac ver-suum Medii Aevi posterioris Latinorum. Alphabetisches Verzeichnis der Versanfänge mittellateinischer Dichtungen,* 2d ed., Carmina Medii Aevi posterioris Latina I/1 (Göttingen: Vandenhoeck & Ruprecht, 1969), lists these texts and variants on them by incipit; I here adopt the titles used by Wright for the sake of convenience. Walther's compilation shows that there are two major subsets of this form: "Clerus et presbyteri nuper consedere" (the "Consultatio sacerdotum"), which exists in seven variant forms, usually with differing numbers of clerics (items 2929, 5014, 14460, 16011, 19433, 20322, and 20325); and "Rumor novus Angliae" ("De convocatione sacerdotum"), of which Walther lists two versions (items 12337 and 16929). Wright's "De concubinis sacerdotum," which begins "Prisciani regula penitus cassatur," appears in Walther as item 14734.

85. It is not my intention to suggest that these poems were in any sense di-rect sources for the Wife's *Prologue*; the citations and arguments they present, like hers, go back to Jerome's debate with Jovinian and beyond. What these late me-dieval texts particularly share is their expression of those arguments through the voices of characters personally implicated in the discussion, rather than those ob-serving or offering advice from an external standpoint.

86. Wright suggests that "De concubinis" was probably written shortly after the Fourth Lateran Council, a supposition supported by the poem's complaint that "Non est Innocentius, immo nocens vere, / qui quod Deus docuit studet abolere; / jussit enim Dominus foeminas habere, / sed hoc noster pontifex jussit prohibere" (ll. 29–32; for Wright's speculation, see *Latin Poems,* p. 171 n.). The reference seems clearly to be to the fourteenth canon of the Fourth Lateran Council, which forbade clerical "incontinence" (Tanner, *Decrees,* 242).

87. "Gignere nos praecepit Vetus Testamentum, / ubi Novum prohibet, nusquam est inventum" ("De concubinis" ll. 33–34). See also ll. 37–40 (God cursed those who had not produced generations) and l. 56 ("qui non gignerant omnes erunt rei").

88. Chaucer, *Canterbury Tales* III.28–29, 59–61. Alcuin Blamires notes the possibly heretical implications of arguments based on "Crescite et multipli-camini," as well as the currency of arguments about clerical celibacy in late four-teenth-century England ("The Wife of Bath and Lollardy," *Medium Aevum* 58, no. 2 [1989]: 231–34).

89. "Nonne de militibus milites procedunt? / et reges a regibus qui sibi suc-cedunt?" ("De concubinis" ll. 41–42); Chaucer, *Canterbury Tales* III.171–72.

90. "Nobis adhuc praecipit Vetus Testamentum, / quod nostrae jam legis est verax fundamentum, / ut mares et foeminae sciant instrumentum / tale, per quod habeant prolis incrementum" ("De concubinis" ll. 45–48; cf. Chaucer, *Canterbury Tales* III.115–34).

91. "Paulus coelos rapitur ad superiores, / ubi multas didicit res secretiores, / ad nos tandem rediens, instruensque mores, / suas, inquit, habeant quilibet ux-ores" ("De concubinis" ll. 61–64).

92. Chaucer, *Canterbury Tales* III.77–94; see, e.g., "I woot wel that th'apos-tel was a mayde; / But natheles, thogh that he wroot and sayde / He wolde that every wight were swich as he, / Al nys but conseil to virginitee" (III.79–82).

93. On antimarriage arguments, see Peter Brown, *The Body and Society: Men, Women, and Sexual Renunciation in Early Christianity* (New York: Columbia University Press, 1988), passim; Bloch, *Medieval Misogyny*, 13–35. Important medieval sources for the Wife's *Prologue* can be found in Blamires, *Women Defamed*; these include selections from Jerome, *Against Jovinian* (63–74; the full text is available in *Adversus Jovinianum*, PL 23:221–352), Walter Map, "Valerius to Ruffinus, Against Marriage" (103–14), and Jehan le Fevre, *Lamentations of Matheolus* (177–97).

94. "Propter hoc et alia dogmata doctorum, / reor esse melius, et magis decorum, / quisque suam habeat, et non proximorum, / ne incurrat odium vel iram eorum" ("De concubinis" ll. 65–68).

95. Lehmann, for instance, notes that the ban on clerical wives was reiterated on numerous occasions in England during the thirteenth century, suggesting less than perfect compliance (*Parodie*, 115).

96. Dyan Elliott, *Fallen Bodies*, 117. See her discussion of clerical celibacy and the "return" of the priest's wife in the context of debates over the Eucharist, 116–18.

97. For Bacchus and Venus, see "De concubinis" ll. 13–16.

98. Lehmann argues for a date around 1200 for the "Consultatio." He points out that the villain of the piece is not the pope (as in "De concubinis") but an unnamed "praesul," suggesting perhaps an episcopal order (*Parodie*, 115–16).

99. The importance of their numbers is demonstrated by the fact that several of the variants of this poem begin by specifying them: e.g., "Duodecim presbyteri nuper consedere," "Quindecim presbiteri," "Triginta presbiteri," "Viginti presbiteri" (Walther, *Initia carminum*, items 5014, 16011, 19433, 20325). There is even an eighteenth-century revision in which the council consists of "Viginte Jesuite" (20322).

100. This preacher-monk is highly questionable on two counts: monastic preaching was the subject of frequent jurisdictional battles in this period, and the fundamental requirement of monastic celibacy contrasts oddly with his brilliant sophistry in favor of clerical concubines. Either or both of these may have contributed to his having the final word in this topsy-turvy poem.

101. "Hinc est gradu senior tremulo sic fatus: / 'Ego credo, domini, quod sum fascinatus; / vult removere famulam meam praelatus; / impotens ut praelio, ero contentatus.' / Audit cantor callidus, ergo sonat cum clamore: / 'Quid si vos supponere non estis in valore, / vultis ergo reliquos privare hoc vigore?' / confusus est senior magno cum rubore. / Ergo suum votum sic caepit emendare: / 'Nolo, cantor domine, coquam alienare, / ad tempus ob laicos placet occultare; / ut possimus praesulis jussis obviare.' / Ait cellarius: 'Non potest hoc transire; / me regit una bestia, sinerem salire, / sed meretrix monocula renuit abire; / cum senioris coqua cuperem cambire.' / Tunc in consistorio omnes corrisere, / 'En! Noster cellarius non est stultus vere'" ("Consultatio sacerdotum" ll. 21–38).

102. "Vita sola angelica est pura," "Consultatio sacerdotum" l. 20; "Vir ad impossibile nullus obligatur; / clero pudicitia scitis quod non datur, / retinere famulas ergo concludatur" (ll. 50–52); "vult [praesul] quod meam deseram pro suo mandato: / ego nunquam deseram etiam pro Deo beato" (ll. 75–76).

103. Chaucer, *Canterbury Tales* III.688–90. The Wife's use) of the concept is noted in Patterson, *Chaucer,* 313.

104. "Quis scit, an hoc hominum cupiat Creator, / ut sacerdos mulierum desinat esse amator, / pro quibus est positus in cruce Salvator? / Zacharius habuit prolem et uxorem, / quae Johannem genuit, filium majorem, / praedicentem totius mundi Redemptorem; / non credo quod peccat, servans istum morem" ("De concubinis" ll. 146–52).

105. "Consultatio sacerdotum" ll. 171–72.

106. On Saint Paul, see Chaucer, *Canterbury Tales* III.341, 346; on the pope, III.420.

107. As Bloch has argued, "the discourse of misogyny is always to some extent avowedly derivative; it is a citational mode whose rhetorical thrust displaces its own source away from anything that might be construed as personal or confessional" (*Medieval Misogyny,* 47). See also Susan Schibanoff, "The New Reader and Female Textuality in Two Early Commentaries on Chaucer," *Studies in the Age of Chaucer* 10 (1988), on the Egerton glossator of the Wife's *Prologue,* whose "calm, detached mien of scholar-bibliographer" collapses as he gets into a textual shouting match of competing authorities with the Wife (79–80). Galloway points out that recent work on the Wife has often addressed "the human motives, ideologies, and contexts behind what would otherwise appear to be . . . impersonal 'auctorite,'" and demonstrates how her adaptations of the language and themes of marriage sermons contribute to this project ("Marriage Sermons," 3, 19).

108. Susan Morrison, "Don't Ask, Don't Tell," 115.

109. If we believe that the Shipman's interruption in the epilogue to the *Man of Law's Tale* (Chaucer, *Canterbury Tales* II.1163–90) was originally intended for the Wife of Bath—as its claims that "my joly body schal a tale telle" and "ther is but litel Latyn in my mawe" might suggest (II.1185, 1190), and as has often been argued—then it seems that it was important to Chaucer that the Wife should interrupt the Parson, since that is what the Shipman does here, and again by using preaching terms in a disrespectful way: "heer schal he nat preche; / He schal no gospel glosen here ne teche" (II.1179–80). The terms are similar to those in which the Friar later rebukes the Wife as he attempts to recapture the authority of preaching. Patterson discusses the Wife's displacement of the Parson in *Chaucer,* 315, 316; but while he sees the Parson's voice as, ultimately, "so authoritative that it comes to include the tones of the author himself" (316), I would argue that the Wife's interjection of herself and her tale deliberately links her voice to those of both Parson and author, and that Chaucer intended it to do so.

110. Only Chaucer the narrator refers positively to the Parson as a preacher (in the *General Prologue*). Intriguingly, the figure who is most often referred to as "preaching" in a positive sense is Saint Cecilia, in the *Second Nun's Tale* (Chaucer, *Canterbury Tales* VIII.342, 375, 539).

111. The Pardoner uses the words "preche" or "predicacioun" to refer to his own speech at Chaucer, *Canterbury Tales* VI.329, 345, 393, 401, 407, 414, 424, 427, 433, 439, 443, 461, 915, and the narrator uses the term of him in the *General Prologue* (I.712); the friar of the *Summoner's Tale* is characterized by these terms at III.1712, 1714, 1716, and 2282 and refers to his own "prechyng" and "predica-

cioun" at III.1818 and 2109, respectively. The repetition of forms of "preche" three times in six lines at the beginning of the tale by the narrating Summoner, whose aim is to undermine the Friar, argues strongly for a negative interpretation of the term in itself: given what follows, it is clearly intended here to create an unfavorable impression of the friar in the tale.

112. Chaucer, *Canterbury Tales* III.165. The nature of this interruption has been variously interpreted. Arthur K. Moore, "The Pardoner's Interruption of the *Wife of Bath's Prologue*," *Modern Language Quarterly* 10 (1949), sees it as "recognition and approval" (50); Hanning as "mock praise" ("And countrefete the speche," 54); and Patterson suggests that the Pardoner responds to the Wife as "both professional colleague and sexual challenge" (*Chaucer,* 308). Whatever his tone, the fact that the Pardoner is responding to the Wife's assertion of her claim on her husband's body, and that he immediately adds, "I was aboute to wedde a wyf; allas! / What sholde I bye it on my flessh so deere?" highlights the link between marriage and preaching on which the Wife's speech plays.

113. These issues are explored in comic form in "Gilote et Johane," a fabliau-like text that presents two women preachers whose theme is always one and ever was: the pursuit of carnal love. The text is discussed in Carter Revard, "Gilote et Johane: An Interlude in B.L. MS. Harley 2253," *Studies in Philology* 79 (1982): 122–46. One character observes that a friar "de son art / preche al pueple et foute de sa part" (preaches artfully to the people and screws around on his own behalf), echoing the Pardoner's implication that preaching is always in the service of someone ("Gilote et Johane," ll. 266–67, quoted in Revard, 125). On another text in this vein, see Patterson, *Chaucer,* 307.

114. Both Susan Morrison, "Don't Ask, Don't Tell," 97, and Scanlon, *Narrative,* 146, address this passage, using it to open up discussions of authoritative language and of lay claims to that authority. See also Schibanoff's discussion of the "professional rivalry" created by the Wife's claim to textual authority—in this case, a rivalry with the glossators of her text ("New Reader," 84).

115. Chaucer, *Canterbury Tales* III.192.

116. As Straus notes, the Wife's claim that she is only playing seems at first to be a disclaimer, a return to "woman's place." She goes on to observe, "Under the guise of knowing her place, however, the Wife proceeds to transgress it" ("Subversive Discourse," 529).

117. Graham Caie's discussion of fifteenth-century "corrective" glosses to the Wife's *Prologue* seems to imply that her "gross perversion" of Scripture is peculiar to her carnal, feminine, literal reading and fails to acknowledge the widespread depiction of such glossing and creative exegesis as a clerical failing; the friar of the *Summoner's Tale,* for instance, is as guilty in this regard as the Wife (Graham D. Caie, "The Significance of the Early Chaucer Manuscript Glosses [with Special Reference to the *Wife of Bath's Prologue*]," *Chaucer Review* 10, no. 4 [1975]: 350–60). Blamires, "Wife of Bath," similarly imagines Chaucer "laughing up his sleeve at her exegetical limitations" (236). But Schibanoff, "New Reader," finds the glosses on the Wife's *Prologue* less sweepingly negative and judgmental than Caie suggests, and Lawrence Besserman, "*Glosynge Is a Glorious Thyng:* Chaucer's Biblical Exegesis," in *Chaucer and Scriptural Tradition,* ed. David Lyle Jeffrey

([Ottawa]: University of Ottawa Press, 1984), 65–73, considers the Wife's glossing in relation to the friar's and suggests that Chaucer's view of the Wife's exegesis may not be as condemnatory as criticism has sometimes implied. See also Lawton, *Chaucer's Narrators*, 22, on the potential for over-reading the pilgrims' "ironic" misuses of Scripture.

118. See Laura Kendrick's remark that "the target the fabliaux truly aim to bring down—if only temporarily and playfully, in fiction—is not a genre, but repressive authority in general" (*Chaucerian Play: Comedy and Control in the* Canterbury Tales [Berkeley and Los Angeles: University of California Press, 1988], 98–99). The Friar and Pardoner rightly fear, however, that the effects may not be so temporary after all.

119. On the long history of *aniles fabulas,* see Disbrow, "Wife of Bath's Old Wives' Tale," 61–64.

120. Compare the rebuke given to Margery Kempe when she criticized the archbishop of York, who was questioning her: when he accused her of being a "ryth wikked woman," she said, "Ser, so I her seyn þat ȝe arn a wikkyd man"; after a little more repartee, a "gret clerke wyth a furryd hood" chided her, "Pes, þu speke of þi-self & late hym ben" (*The Book of Margery Kempe,* ed. Sanford Brown Meech and Hope Emily Allen, EETS o.s. 212 [London: Oxford University Press for EETS, 1940], 125).

121. Chaucer, *Canterbury Tales* VII.695.

Bibliography

MANUSCRIPTS

Munich Staatsbibliothek Clm 14550 (s. xiv).
Paris Bibliothèque Nationale MS. Lat. 3464 (s. xv).
Paris Bibliothèque Nationale MS. Lat. 14909 (s. xiv).

PRIMARY WORKS

Alan of Lille. *The Art of Preaching*. Translated by Gillian R. Evans. Cistercian Studies Series 23. Kalamazoo, Mich.: Cistercian Publications, 1981.
———. *Contra haereticos libri quatuor*. PL 210:305–430.
———. *Summa de arte praedicatoria*. PL 210:109–98.
Alexander of Ashby. "Aux origines des 'Artes praedicandi.' Le 'De artificioso modo praedicandi' d'Alexandre d'Ashby." Edited by Franco Morenzoni. *Studi medievali* 32, no. 2 (1991): 887–935.
Ambrose. *Verginità e vedovanza*. Edited and translated by Franco Gori. Opere morali 2; Sancti Ambrosiani episcopi Mediolanensis opera 14. Milan: Biblioteca Ambrosiana, 1989.
Aquinas, Thomas. *Summa Theologiae: Latin Text and English Translation, Introduction, Notes, Appendices and Glossaries*. 61 vols. N.p.: Blackfriars and New York: McGraw-Hill, 1964–81.
———. *Summa Theologiae*. Edited by the Institutum Studiorum Medievalium Ottavienensis. 5 vols. Ottawa: Commissio Piana, 1953.
———. *Summa Theologica*. Translated by the Fathers of the English Dominican Province. 3 vols. New York: Benziger Brothers, 1947–48.
———. *Super evangelium S. Ioannis lectura*. Edited by P. Raphelis Cai. 5th rev. ed. Rome: Marietti, 1952.
Augustine. *Christian Instruction*. Translated by John J. Gavigan. New York: Fathers of the Church, 1947.
———. *City of God*. Translated by Henry Bettenson. London: Penguin Books, 1984.
———. *Confessions*. Translated by William Watts. 2 vols. Loeb Classical Library. Cambridge: Harvard University Press, 1977.
———. *De doctrina christiana*. Published with *De vera religione*. Edited by Joseph Martin. CCSL 32. Turnhout, Belgium: Brepols, 1962.
———. *De opere monachorum*. In *L'ascétisme chrétien: De continentia, De sancta*

virginitate, De bono viduitatis, De opere monachorum. Oeuvres de Saint Augustin 3. Edited, translated, and introduced by J. Saint-Martin. 2d ed. Paris: Desclée, de Brouwer & Cie, 1949.

———. *Soliloquies and Immortality of the Soul.* Translated by Gerard Watson. Warminster, U.K.: Aris & Phillips, 1990.

Birgerus Gregorius. "Legenda Sancte Birgitte." In *Canonization Proceedings of St. Birgitta,* edited by Isak Collijn. Uppsala, Sweden: Almqvist & Wiksells Boktryckeri, 1946.

Birgitta of Sweden. *Life and Selected Revelations.* Edited by Marguerite Tjader Harris. Translated by Albert Ryle Kezel. New York: Paulist Press, 1990.

———. *Revelaciones, Book I, with Magister Mathias's Prologue.* Edited by Carl-Gustaf Undhagen. Uppsala, Sweden: Almqvist and Wiksell, 1978.

———. *Revelaciones, Book VI.* Edited by Birger Bergh. Stockholm: Almqvist and Wiksell International, 1991.

———. *Revelaciones extravagantes.* Edited by Lennart Hollman. Uppsala, Sweden: Almqvist and Wiksells Boktryckeri, 1956.

Bonaventure. *Commentaria in quatuor libros sententiarum magistri Petri Lombardi.* Vols. 1–4 of *Doctoris seraphici S. Bonaventurae . . . Opera omnia,* edited by the Collegium S. Bonaventurae. 10 vols. Ad Claras Aquas [Quaracchi]: Collegium S. Bonaventurae, 1882–1902.

Bronzini, Giovanni Battista, ed. *La leggenda di S. Caterina d'Alessandria: Passioni greche e latine.* Rome: n.p., 1960.

Caesarius of Heisterbach. *Caesarii Heisterbacensis monachi ordinis cisterciensis Dialogus miraculorum.* Edited by Joseph Strange. 2 vols. Cologne, Bonn, and Brussels: H. Lempertz & Co., 1851.

Casagrande, Carla, ed. *Prediche alle donne del secolo XIII.* Milan: Bompiani, 1978.

Charland, Thomas-Marie. Artes praedicandi: *Contribution a l'histoire de la rhétorique au moyen âge.* Paris: Librairie Philosophique J. Vrin, 1936.

Chaucer, Geoffrey. *The Complete Works of Geoffrey Chaucer.* Edited by F. N. Robinson. Boston: Houghton Mifflin, 1933.

———. *The Riverside Chaucer.* Edited by Larry D. Benson. 3d ed. Boston: Houghton Mifflin, 1987.

Christine de Pizan. *The Book of the City of Ladies.* Translated by Earl Jeffrey Richards. New York: Persea Books, 1982.

Cicero. *De oratore.* Edited by H. Rackham. Translated by E. W. Sutton. 2 vols. Loeb Classical Library. Cambridge: Harvard University Press, 1976.

Crane, Thomas Frederick, ed. *The Exempla or Illustrative Stories from the* Sermones Vulgares *of Jacques de Vitry.* London: David Nutt for the Folk-Lore Society, 1890.

Damian, Peter. *De sancta simplicitate.* PL 145:695–704.

De Sainte Katerine: An Anonymous Picard Version of the Life of St. Catherine of Alexandria. Edited by William MacBain. Fairfax, Va.: George Mason University Press, 1987.

Eiximenis, Francesc. "L'*Ars Praedicandi* de Francesc Eiximenis." Edited by P. Martí de Barcelona. In *Homenatge a Antoni Rubió i Lluch: Miscellània d'estudis literaris històrics i lingüístics,* 301–40. Barcelona: n.p., 1936.

Faillon, Étienne, ed. *Monuments inédits sur l'apostolat de Sainte Marie-Madeleine en Provence.* 2 vols. Paris: Chez l'Éditeur, 1848.

Friedberg, E., ed. *Corpus iuris canonici.* 2d ed. 2 vols. Leipzig: Bernhard Tauchnitz, 1879–81.

Geoffrey of Vinsauf. *The New Poetics.* Translated by Jane Baltzell Kopp. In *Three Medieval Rhetorical Arts,* edited by James J. Murphy, 27–108. Berkeley and Los Angeles: University of California Press, 1971.

———. *Poetria nova.* In Ernest Gallo, *The* Poetria Nova *and Its Sources in Early Rhetorical Doctrine.* De Proprietatibus Litterarum Series Maior 10. The Hague and Paris: Mouton, 1971.

Gregory the Great. *Dialogorum libri IV.* PL 77:149–430.

———. *Dialogues.* Translated by Odo John Zimmerman. Fathers of the Church 39. New York: Fathers of the Church, 1959.

———. *Homiliarum in evangelia libri duo.* PL 76:1075–1312.

———. *Règle pastorale.* 2 vols. Edited by Floribert Rommel, translated by Charles Morel, with an introduction and notes by Bruno Judic. Sources chrétiennes 381–82. Paris: Éditions du Cerf, 1992.

Guibert of Nogent. *Quo ordine sermo fieri debeat.* PL 156:21–32.

———. *Self and Society in Medieval France: The Memoirs of Abbot Guibert of Nogent.* Edited by John F. Benton. Translated by C. C. Swinton Bland and John F. Benton. Medieval Academy Reprints for Teaching. Toronto: University of Toronto Press, 1984.

Guillaume de Lorris and Jean de Meun. *Le roman de la rose.* Edited by Daniel Poirion. Paris: Garnier-Flammarion, 1974.

Higden, Ranulph. *The* Ars componendi sermones *of Ranulph Higden, O. S. B.* Edited by Margaret Jennings. Leiden: Brill, 1991.

Hildegard of Bingen. *Epistolarium.* Edited by Lieven Van Acker. 2 vols. to date. CCCM 91–91A. Turnhout, Belgium: Brepols, 1991, 1993.

———. *The Letters of Hildegard of Bingen.* Translated by Joseph L. Baird and Radd K. Ehrman. 2 vols. to date. Oxford: Oxford University Press, 1994, 1998.

———. *Scivias.* Edited by Adelgund Führkötter and Angela Carlevaris. 2 vols. CCCM 43–43a. Turnhout, Belgium: Brepols, 1978.

Honorius Augustodunensis. *Sermo generalis.* PL 172:861–70.

Hugues de Berzé. *La "Bible" au seigneur de Berzé.* Edited by Félix Lecoy. Paris: Librairie E. Droz, 1938.

Humbert of Romans. *De eruditione praedicatorum.* In *B. Humberti de Romanis Opera de vita regulari,* edited by Joachim Joseph Berthier, 2 vols. 2:373–484. Rome: Marietti, 1888–89.

———. *De modo cudendi sermones.* Maxima Bibliotheca Veterum Patrum 25 (Lyons, 1677), 456–567.

———. *Treatise on Preaching.* Edited by Walter M. Conlon. Translated by the Dominican Students, Province of St. Joseph. London: Blackfriars Publications, 1955.

Innocent III. [Letter to the people of Metz.] PL 214:695–98.

———. *Nova quaedam nuper.* PL 216:356.

Jacobus of Cessolis. *See* Vetter.

Jacobus of Voragine. *The Golden Legend: Readings on the Saints.* Translated by William Granger Ryan. 2 vols. Princeton, N.J.: Princeton University Press, 1993.

———. *Legenda aurea, vulgo historia Lombardica dicta.* Edited by Th. Graesse. Dresden and Leipzig: Libraria Arnoldiana, 1846.

Jacques de Vitry. *Sermones vulgares* [selected]. Edited by J. B. Pitra. In *Analecta novissima spicilegii solesmensis, altera continuatio* II, Tusculana, edited by J. B. Pitra, 188–93, 345–461. [Paris:] Typis Tusculanis, 1888.

Jerome. *Ad Eustochium (Epistola 22).* PL 22:394–425.

———. *Adversus Jovinianum.* PL 23:221–352.

John of Wales. *Summa collationum, sive Communiloquium.* Ulm: Zainer, 1481.

Kempe, Margery. *The Book of Margery Kempe.* Edited by Lynn Staley. TEAMS Middle English Texts Series. Kalamazoo: Medieval Institute Publications, Western Michigan University, 1996.

Klaes, Monica, ed. *Vita sanctae Hildegardis.* CCCM 126. Turnhout: Brepols, 1993.

Lecoy de la Marche, A., ed. *Anecdotes historiques, légendes et apologues tirés du recueil inédit d'Étienne de Bourbon, dominicain du XIIIᵉ siècle.* Paris: Librairie Renouard, 1877.

Miller, Joseph M., Michael H. Prosser, and Thomas W. Benson, eds. *Readings in Medieval Rhetoric.* Bloomington: Indiana University Press, 1973.

Montaiglon, Anatole de, ed. *Recueil général et complet des fabliaux des XIIIᵉ et XIVᵉ siècles imprimés ou inédits.* 6 vols. Paris: Librairie des Bibliophiles, 1872–90.

Noomen, Willem, and Nico van den Boogard, eds. *Nouveau recueil complet des fabliaux.* 10 vols. Assen, Netherlands: Van Gorcum, 1983–1988.

Odo of Châteauroux. *Sermones de tempore et sanctis* [selected]. Edited by J. B. Pitra. In *Analecta novissima spicilegii solesmensis, altera continuatio* II, Tusculana, edited by J. B. Pitra, 188–343. [Paris:] Typis Tusculanis, 1888.

Peter the Chanter. *Verbum abbreviatum.* PL 205:23–560.

Philip of Harvengt. *De institutione clericorum tractatus sex.* PL 203:665–1206.

Pseudo-Bonaventure. *Ars concionandi.* In *Doctoris seraphici S. Bonaventurae . . . Opera omnia,* edited by the Collegium S. Bonaventurae, 10 vols. 9:8–21. Ad Claras Aquas [Quaracchi]: Collegium S. Bonaventurae, 1882–1902.

Quintilian. *Institutio oratoria.* Translated by H. E. Butler. 4 vols. London: William Heinemann, 1920.

Raymond of Capua. *The Life of Catherine of Siena.* Translated by Conleth Kearns. Dublin: Dominican Publications and Wilmington, Del.: M. Glazier, 1980.

———. *Vita beatae Catherinae Senensis.* AASS April III. 861–967.

Robert of Basevorn. *The Form of Preaching.* Translated by Leopold Krul. In *Three Medieval Rhetorical Arts,* edited by James J. Murphy, 114–215. Berkeley and Los Angeles: University of California Press, 1971.

———. *Forma praedicandi.* Edited by Thomas-Marie Charland. In Thomas-Marie Charland, Artes praedicandi: *Contribution a l'histoire de la rhétorique au moyen âge,* 231–323. Paris: Librairie Philosophique J. Vrin, 1936.

S. Bernardi vita prima. PL 185:225–466.

Seinte Katerine, Re-Edited from MS Bodley 34 and the Other Manuscripts. Edited by S. R. T. O. d'Ardenne and E. J. Dobson. EETS 7. Oxford: Oxford University Press, 1981.

Sermones nulli parcentes, in "Buch der Rügen." Edited by Theodor von Karajan. *Zeitschrift für Deutsches Alterthum* 2 (1842): 14–45; full article pp. 6–92.

Speculum Christiani: A Middle English Religious Treatise of the 14th Century. Edited by Gustaf Holmstedt. EETS 182. London: EETS, 1933.

Tanner, Norman P., ed. *Decrees of the Ecumenical Councils: Vol. I, Nicaea I to Lateran V.* Original text established by G. Alberigo, et al. London: Sheed and Ward and Washington, D.C.: Georgetown University Press, 1990.

Tertullian. *Disciplinary, Moral and Ascetical Works.* Translated by Rudolph Arbesmann, Emily Joseph Daly, and Edwin A. Quain. New York: Fathers of the Church, 1959.

———. *Opera.* Various editors. 2 vols. CCSL 1–2. Turnhout: Brepols, 1954.

———. *Les spectacles (De spectaculis).* Edited and translated by Marie Turcan. Sources chrétiennes 332. Paris: Éditions du Cerf, 1986.

———. *La toilette des femmes (De cultu feminarum).* Edited and translated by Marie Turcan. Sources chrétiennes 173. Paris, Éditions du Cerf, 1971.

Thomas of Bailly. *Quodlibets.* Edited by P. Glorieux. Textes philosophiques du moyen âge 9. Paris: J. Vrin, 1960.

Thomas of Celano. *Vita S. Clarae.* AASS August II.

Thomas of Chobham. *Summa de arte praedicandi.* Edited by Franco Morenzoni. CCCM 82. Turnhout, Belgium: Brepols, 1988.

Tugwell, Simon, ed. *Early Dominicans: Selected Writings.* Classics of Western Spirituality. Mahwah, N.J.: Paulist Press, 1982.

Vetter, Ferdinand, ed. *Das Schachzabelbuch Kunrats von Ammenhausen . . . nebst den Schachbüchern des Jakob von Cessole und des Jakob Mennel.* Frauenfeld: J. Huber, 1892.

Waleys, Thomas. *De modo componendi sermones, cum documentis.* Edited by Thomas-Marie Charland. In Thomas-Marie Charland, Artes praedicandi: *Contribution a l'histoire de la rhétorique au moyen âge,* 325–403. Paris: Librairie Philosophique J. Vrin, 1936.

William of St. Amour. *Tractatvs brevis de pericvlis novissimorvm temporvm ex scriptvris svmptis.* Edited by Valérien de Flavigny. Ad Insigne Bonae Fidej Apud Alithophilos, 1632.

Wright, Thomas, ed. *The Latin Poems Commonly Attributed to Walter Mapes.* London: Printed for the Camden Society by John Bowyer Nichols and Son, 1841.

SECONDARY WORKS

Aers, David, and Lynn Staley. *The Powers of the Holy: Religion, Politics, and Gender in Late Medieval English Culture.* University Park: Pennsylvania State University Press, 1996.

Amos, Thomas L., Eugene A. Green, and Beverly Mayne Kienzle, eds. De Ore

Domini: *Preacher and Word in the Middle Ages.* Kalamazoo: Medieval Institute Publications, Western Michigan University, 1989.

Astell, Ann W. "The *Translatio* of Chaucer's Pardoner." *Exemplaria* 4 (1992): 411–28.

Aston, Margaret. *Lollards and Reformers: Images and Literacy in Late Medieval Religion.* London: Hambledon Press, 1984.

Atkinson, Clarissa W. " 'Precious Balsam in a Fragile Glass': The Ideology of Virginity in the Later Middle Ages." *Journal of Family History* 8 (1983): 131–43.

Austin, J. L. *How to Do Things with Words.* Edited by J. O. Urmson. Oxford: Clarendon Press, 1962.

d'Avray, David L. *The Preaching of the Friars: Sermons Diffused from Paris Before 1300.* Oxford: Clarendon Press, 1985.

Baldwin, John W. *Masters, Princes, and Merchants: The Social Views of Peter the Chanter and His Circle.* 2 vols. Princeton, N.J.: Princeton University Press, 1970.

Barish, Jonas. *The Antitheatrical Prejudice.* Berkeley and Los Angeles: University of California Press, 1981.

Barnes, Timothy David. *Tertullian: A Historical and Literary Study.* Oxford: Clarendon Press, 1985.

Bataillon, Louis-Jacques. "*Similitudines* et *exempla* dans les sermons du XIIIe siècle." In *The Bible in the Medieval World: Essays in Memory of Beryl Smalley,* edited by Katherine Walsh and Diana Wood, 191–205. Oxford: Basil Blackwell, 1985.

———. *La prédication au XIIIe siècle en France et Italie: Études et documents.* Brookfield, Vt.: Variorum, 1993.

Bayless, Martha. *Parody in the Middle Ages: The Latin Tradition.* Ann Arbor: University of Michigan Press, 1996.

Bazàn, Bernardo, John W. Wippel, Gérard Fransen, and Danielle Jacquart. *Les questions disputées et les questions quodlibétiques dans les facultés de théologie, de droit et de médecine.* Typologie des sources du moyen âge occidental 44–45. Turnhout, Belgium: Brepols, 1985.

Bechtold, Joan. "St. Birgitta: The Disjunction between Women and Ecclesiastical Male Power." In *Equally in God's Image: Women in the Middle Ages,* edited by Constance S. Wright, Julia Bolton Holloway, and Joan Bechtold, 88–102. New York: Peter Lang, 1990.

Beckwith, Sarah. *Christ's Body: Identity, Culture and Society in Late Medieval Writings.* London and New York: Routledge, 1996.

———. "Problems of Authority in Late Medieval English Mysticism: Language, Agency, and Authority in *The Book of Margery Kempe.*" *Exemplaria* 4, no. 1 (1992): 171–99.

———. "A Very Material Mysticism: The Medieval Mysticism of Margery Kempe." In *Gender and Text in the Later Middle Ages,* edited by Jane Chance, 195–215. Gainesville: University Press of Florida, 1996.

Bériou, Nicole. "La Madeleine dans les sermons parisiens du XIIIe siècle." *Mélanges de l'École Française de Rome: Moyen Âge* 104, no. 1 (1992): 269–340.

————. "The Right of Women to Give Religious Instruction in the Thirteenth Century." In Kienzle and Walker, 134–45.

Besserman, Lawrence. "*Glosynge Is a Glorious Thyng:* Chaucer's Biblical Exegesis." In *Chaucer and Scriptural Tradition,* edited by David Lyle Jeffrey, 65–73. [Ottawa]: University of Ottawa Press, 1984.

Blamires, Alcuin. *The Case for Women in Medieval Culture.* Oxford: Clarendon Press, 1997.

————. "The Wife of Bath and Lollardy." *Medium Aevum* 58, no. 2 (1989): 224–42.

————. "Women and Preaching in Medieval Orthodoxy, Heresy, and Saints' Lives." *Viator* 26 (1995): 135–52.

————, ed. *Woman Defamed and Woman Defended: An Anthology of Medieval Texts.* Oxford: Clarendon Press, 1992.

Blamires, Alcuin, and C. W. Marx. "Woman Not to Preach: A Disputation in British Library MS Harley 31." *Journal of Medieval Latin* 3 (1993): 34–63.

Bloch, R. Howard. *Medieval Misogyny and the Invention of Western Romantic Love.* Chicago: University of Chicago Press, 1991.

Børresen, Kari Elisabeth. *Subordination and Equivalence: The Nature and Rôle of Woman in Augustine and Thomas Aquinas.* Rev. English ed. Translated by Charles H. Talbot. Washington, D.C.: University Press of America, 1981.

Bradley, Ritamary. "Backgrounds of the Title *Speculum* in Mediaeval Literature." *Speculum* 29 (1954): 100–115.

Brasington, Bruce C. "*Non imitanda set veneranda:* The Dilemma of Sacred Precedent in Twelfth-Century Canon Law." *Viator* 23 (1992): 135–52.

Bremond, Claude, Jacques Le Goff, and Jean-Claude Schmitt. *L'*"Exemplum." Typologie des sources du moyen âge occidental 40. Turnhout, Belgium: Brepols, 1982.

Brenon, Anne. "The Voice of the Good Women: An Essay on the Pastoral and Sacerdotal Role of Women in the Cathar Church." In Kienzle and Walker, 114–33.

Brilioth, Yngve. *A Brief History of Preaching.* Translated by Karl E. Mattson. Philadelphia: Fortress Press, 1965.

Briscoe, Marianne G. *Artes praedicandi.* Published with *Artes orandi,* by Barbara H. Jaye. Typologie des sources du moyen âge occidental 61. Turnhout, Belgium: Brepols, 1992.

————. "Some Clerical Notions of Dramatic Decorum in Late Medieval England." *Comparative Drama* 19 (spring 1985): 1–13.

Brooke, Rosalind B. *The Coming of the Friars.* London: George Allen & Unwin, 1975.

Brown, Peter. *The Body and Society: Men, Women, and Sexual Renunciation in Early Christianity.* New York: Columbia University Press, 1988.

Brownlee, Kevin. "Commentary and the Rhetoric of Exemplarity: Griseldis in Petrarch, Philippe de Mézières, and the *Estoire.*" *South Atlantic Quarterly* 91 (fall 1992): 865–90.

Buc, Philippe. "*Vox clamantis in deserto?* Pierre le Chantre et la prédication laïque." *Revue Mabillon,* n.s., 4 (1993): 5–47.

Bugge, John. *Virginitas: An Essay in the History of a Medieval Ideal.* The Hague: Martinus Nijhoff, 1975.

Burrus, Virginia. "Reading Agnes: The Rhetoric of Gender in Ambrose and Prudentius." *Journal of Early Christian Studies* 3, no. 1 (1995): 25–46.

Butler, Judith. *Bodies That Matter: On the Discursive Limits of "Sex."* London: Routledge, 1993.

———. "Performative Acts and Gender Constitution: An Essay in Phenomenology and Feminist Theory." In *Performing Feminisms: Feminist Critical Theory and Theatre,* edited by Sue-Ellen Case, 270–82. Baltimore: Johns Hopkins University Press, 1990.

Bynum, Caroline Walker. Docere verbo et exemplo: *An Aspect of Twelfth-century Spirituality.* Harvard Theological Studies 31. Missoula, Mont.: Scholars Press, 1979.

———. *Fragmentation and Redemption: Essays on Gender and the Human Body in Medieval Religion.* New York: Zone Books, 1992.

———. *Holy Feast and Holy Fast: The Religious Significance of Food to Medieval Women.* Berkeley and Los Angeles: University of California Press, 1987.

Caie, Graham D. "The Significance of the Early Chaucer Manuscript Glosses (with Special Reference to the *Wife of Bath's Prologue*)." *Chaucer Review* 10, no. 4 (1975): 350–60.

Caplan, Harry. "Classical Rhetoric and the Mediaeval Theory of Preaching." In *Historical Studies of Rhetoric and Rhetoricians,* edited by Raymond F. Howes, 71–89, 387–91. Ithaca, N.Y.: Cornell University Press, [1961].

———. *Mediaeval Artes Praedicandi: A Hand-List.* Ithaca, N.Y.: Cornell University Press, 1934.

———. *Mediaeval Artes Praedicandi: A Supplementary Hand-List.* Ithaca, N.Y.: Cornell University Press, 1936.

Cardman, Francine. "The Medieval Question of Women and Orders." *The Thomist* 42 (October 1978): 582–99.

Casagrande, Carla. "Le calame du Saint-Esprit. Grâce et rhétorique dans la prédication au XIIIᵉ siècle." In Dessì and Lauwers, 235–54.

———, ed. *Prediche alle donne del secolo XIII.* Milan: Bompiani, 1978.

Casagrande, Carla, and Silvana Vecchio. *I peccati della lingua: Disciplina ed etica della parola nella cultura medievale.* Rome: Istituto della Enciclopedia Italiana, 1987.

Cazelles, Brigitte, ed. *The Lady as Saint: A Collection of French Hagiographic Romances of the Thirteenth Century.* Philadelphia: University of Pennsylvania Press, 1991.

Cespedes, Frank V. "Chaucer's Pardoner and Preaching." *ELH* 44 (1977): 1–18.

Chapman, Coolidge Otis. "The Pardoner's Tale: A Mediaeval Sermon." *Modern Language Notes* 41 (December 1926): 506–9.

Charland, Thomas-Marie. "Praedicator gratiosus." *Revue dominicaine* 39 (1933): 88–96.

Chenu, M.-D. *Nature, Man, and Society in the Twelfth Century: Essays on New Theological Perspectives in the Latin West.* Introduction by Étienne Gilson. Edited and translated by Jerome Taylor and Lester K. Little. Chicago: University of Chicago Press, 1968. Contains selected essays from *La théologie au douzième siècle* (Paris: J. Vrin, 1957).

Cipolla, Carlo. *Before the Industrial Revolution: European Society and Economy 1000–1700.* 3d ed. New York: Norton, 1993.

Cloke, Gillian. *This Female Man of God: Woman and Spiritual Power in the Patristic Age, AD 350–450.* London: Routledge, 1995.

Coakley, John. "Friars, Sanctity, and Gender: Mendicant Encounters with Saints, 1250–1325." In *Medieval Masculinities: Regarding Men in the Middle Ages,* edited by Clare A. Lees with Thelma S. Fenster and Jo Ann McNamara, 91–110. Minneapolis: University of Minnesota Press, 1994.

———. "Gender and the Authority of Friars: The Significance of Holy Women for Thirteenth-Century Franciscans and Dominicans." *Church History* 60, no. 4 (1991): 445–60.

Cohen, Jeffrey Jerome, and Bonnie Wheeler, eds. *Becoming Male in the Middle Ages.* New York: Garland, 1997.

Coletti, Theresa. *"Paupertas est donum Dei:* Hagiography, Lay Religion, and the Economics of Salvation in the Digby *Mary Magdalene." Speculum* 76, no. 2 (2001): 337–78.

Colish, Marcia L. "Cosmetic Theology: The Transformation of a Stoic Theme." *Assays* 1 (1981): 3–14.

Congar, Yves M.-J. "Modèle monastique et modèle sacerdotal en Occident, de Grégoire VII (1073–1085) à Innocent III (1198)." In *Études de civilisation médiévale (IXᵉ–XIIᵉ siècles): Mélanges offerts à Edmond-René Labande,* 153–60. Poitiers: Centre d'Études Supérieures de Civilisation Médiévale, 1974.

Constable, Giles. "The Language of Preaching in the Twelfth Century." *Viator* 25 (1994): 131–52.

———. *The Reformation of the Twelfth Century.* Cambridge: Cambridge University Press, 1996.

———. *Three Studies in Medieval Religious and Social Thought: The Interpretation of Mary and Martha, The Ideal of the Imitation of Christ, The Orders of Society.* Cambridge: Cambridge University Press, 1995.

Copeland, Rita. "The Pardoner's Body and the Disciplining of Rhetoric." In *Framing Medieval Bodies,* edited by Sarah Kay and Miri Rubin, 138–59. Manchester: Manchester University Press, 1994.

Corti, Maria. "Structures idéologiques et structures sémiotiques dans les *sermones ad status* du XIIIᵉ siècle." In *Archéologie du signe,* edited by Lucie Brind'Amour and Eugene Vance, 145–63. Toronto: Pontifical Institute of Mediaeval Studies, 1982.

Culler, Jonathan. "Reading as a Woman." In *On Deconstruction: Theory and Criticism After Structuralism.* Ithaca, N.Y.: Cornell University Press, 1982.

Curry, W. C. *Chaucer and the Mediaeval Sciences.* Oxford: Oxford University Press, 1926.

Delany, Sheila. *Impolitic Bodies: Poetry, Saints, and Society in Fifteenth-Century England.* Oxford: Oxford University Press, 1998.

Denis-Boulet, Noële M. *La carrière politique de Sainte Catherine de Sienne (Étude historique).* Paris: Desclée, de Brouwer, & Cie., [1939].

Derrida, Jacques. *Limited Inc.* Edited by Gerald Graff. Translated by Samuel We-
ber. Evanston, Ill.: Northwestern University Press, 1988.

Despres, Denise L. "Ecstatic Reading and Missionary Mysticism: *The Orcherd of
Syon.*" In *Prophets Abroad: The Reception of Continental Holy Women in Late-
Medieval England,* edited by Rosalynn Voaden, 141–60. Cambridge: D. S.
Brewer, 1996.

Dessì, Rosa Maria, and Michel Lauwers, eds. *La parole du prédicateur, Vᵉ–XVᵉ siècle.* Nice: Centre d'Études Médiévales, 1997.

Dinshaw, Carolyn. *Chaucer's Sexual Poetics.* Madison: University of Wisconsin
Press, 1989.

Disbrow, Sarah. "The Wife of Bath's Old Wives' Tale." *Studies in the Age of
Chaucer* 8 (1986): 59–71.

Donavin, Georgiana. " 'De sermone sermonem fecimus': Alexander of Ashby's *De
artificioso modo predicandi.*" *Rhetorica* 15, no. 3 (summer 1997): 279–96.

Dronke, Peter. *Women Writers of the Middle Ages: A Critical Study of Texts from
Perpetua (d. 203) to Marguerite Porete (d. 1310).* Cambridge: Cambridge
University Press, 1984.

du Cange, Charles. *Glossarium Mediae et Infimae Latinitatis.* Editio nova. 10 vols.
Niort, France: L. Favre, 1883–87.

Dufeil, M.-M. *Guillaume de Saint-Amour et la polémique universitaire parisienne,
1250–1259.* Paris: Éditions A. et J. Picard, 1972.

Elliott, Dyan. *Fallen Bodies: Pollution, Sexuality, and Demonology in the Middle
Ages.* Philadelphia: University of Pennsylvania Press, 1999.

Elliott, Ralph W. V. *Chaucer's English.* London: Andre Deutsch, 1974.

Enders, Jody. *Rhetoric and the Origins of Medieval Drama.* Ithaca, N.Y.: Cornell
University Press, 1992.

Evans, Gillian. *The Thought of Gregory the Great.* Cambridge Studies in Medieval
Life and Thought, series 4, vol. 2. Cambridge: Cambridge University Press,
1986.

Farmer, Sharon. "Persuasive Voices: Clerical Images of Medieval Wives." *Speculum* 61 (1986): 517–43.

Finke, Laurie A. " 'To Knytte Up Al This Feeste': The Parson's Rhetoric and the
Ending of the *Canterbury Tales.*" *Leeds Studies in English,* n.s., 15 (1984):
95–105.

Fletcher, Alan J. "The Preaching of the Pardoner." *Studies in the Age of Chaucer*
11 (1989): 15–35.

———. *Preaching, Politics and Poetry in Late-Medieval England.* Dublin: Four
Courts Press, 1998.

Fogelqvist, Ingvar. *Apostasy and Reform in the Revelations of St. Birgitta.* Bibliotheca Theologiae Practicae 51. Stockholm: Almqvist and Wiksell International, 1993.

Forde, Simon. "Lay Preaching and the Lollards of Norwich Diocese, 1428–1431."
Leeds Studies in English, n.s., 24 (1998): 109–26.

Furlong, Monica. *Visions and Longings: Medieval Women Mystics.* Boston: Shambhala, 1996.

Fuss, Diana. "Reading like a Feminist." *differences* 1, no. 2 (1989): 77–92.

Gallick, Susan. "A Look at Chaucer and His Preachers." *Speculum* 50, no. 3 (July 1975): 456–76.

Galloway, Andrew. "Marriage Sermons, Polemical Sermons, and *The Wife of Bath's Prologue:* A Generic Excursus." *Studies in the Age of Chaucer* 14 (1992): 3–30.

Ganim, John M. *Chaucerian Theatricality*. Princeton, N.J.: Princeton University Press, 1990.

Gelley, Alexander, ed. *Unruly Examples: On the Rhetoric of Exemplarity*. Stanford, Calif.: Stanford University Press, 1995.

Goering, Joseph W. "The Changing Face of the Village Parish II: The Thirteenth Century." In *Pathways to Medieval Peasants,* edited by J. A. Raftis, 323–333. Papers in Mediaeval Studies 2. Toronto: Pontifical Institute of Mediaeval Studies, 1981.

Goffman, Erving. *The Presentation of Self in Everyday Life*. Garden City, N.Y.: Doubleday, 1959.

Grennan, Eamon. "Dual Characterization: A Note on Chaucer's Use of 'But' in the Portrait of the Parson." *Chaucer Review* 16 (1982): 195–200.

Gross, Nicolas P. *Amatory Persuasion in Antiquity: Studies in Theory and Practice*. Newark: University of Delaware Press, 1985.

Grundmann, Herbert. *Religious Movements in the Middle Ages: The Historical Links between Heresy, the Mendicant Orders, and the Women's Religious Movement in the Twelfth and Thirteenth Century, with the Historical Foundations of German Mysticism*. Translated by Steven Rowan. Notre Dame, Ind.: University of Notre Dame Press, 1995.

Gubar, Susan. " 'The Blank Page' and the Issues of Female Creativity." In *Writing and Sexual Difference,* edited by Elizabeth Abel, 73–93. Brighton, U.K.: Harvester, 1982.

Gunderson, Erik. *Staging Masculinity: The Rhetoric of Performance in the Roman World*. Ann Arbor: University of Michigan Press, 2000.

Hadley, D. M., ed. *Masculinity in Medieval Europe*. London: Longman, 1999.

Halverson, John. "Chaucer's Pardoner and the Progress of Criticism." *Chaucer Review* 4 (1970): 184–202.

Hamesse, Jacqueline, and Xavier Hermand, eds. *De l'homélie au sermon: Histoire de la prédication médiévale*. Louvain-la-Neuve: Université Catholique de Louvain, Publications de l'Institut d'Études Médiévales, 1993.

Hanning, R. W. " 'And countrefete the speche of every man / He koude, whan he sholde telle a tale': Toward a Lapsarian Poetics for *The Canterbury Tales*." *Studies in the Age of Chaucer* 21 (1999): 29–58.

Harding, Wendy. "Body into Text: *The Book of Margery Kempe*." In *Feminist Approaches to the Body in Medieval Literature,* edited by Linda Lomperis and Sarah Stanbury, 168–87. Philadelphia: University of Pennsylvania Press, 1993.

Haskins, Susan. *Mary Magdalen, Myth and Metaphor*. London: HarperCollins, 1993.

Hauser, Hermann. *L'Église à l'âge apostolique: Structure et évolution des ministères*. Lectio divina 164. Paris: Éditions du Cerf, 1996.

Henriet, Patrick. "*Verbum Dei disseminando:* La parole des ermites prédicateurs d'après les sources hagiographiques (XI^c–XII^c siècles)." In Dessì and Lauwers, 153–85.

Hoerner, Fred. "Church Office, Routine, and Self-Exile in Chaucer's Pardoner." *Studies in the Age of Chaucer* 16 (1994): 69–98.

Hollywood, Amy. *The Soul as Virgin Wife: Mechthild of Magdeburg, Marguerite Porete, and Meister Eckhart.* Notre Dame, Ind.: University of Notre Dame Press, 1995.

Howard, Donald R. *The Idea of the Canterbury Tales.* Berkeley and Los Angeles: University of California Press, 1976.

Irigaray, Luce. *Speculum of the Other Woman.* Translated by Gillian C. Gill. Ithaca, N.Y.: Cornell University Press, 1985.

———. *This Sex Which Is Not One.* Translated by Catherine Porter with Carolyn Burke. Ithaca, N.Y.: Cornell University Press, 1985.

Jaeger, C. Stephen. "Charismatic Body—Charismatic Text." *Exemplaria* 9, no. 1 (1997): 117–37.

Jansen, Katherine Ludwig. *The Making of the Magdalen: Preaching and Popular Devotion in the Later Middle Ages.* Princeton, N.J.: Princeton University Press, 2000.

———. "Maria Magdalena: *Apostolorum Apostola.*" In Kienzle and Walker, 67–80.

Jantzen, Grace. " 'Cry Out and Write': Mysticism and the Struggle for Authority." In *Women, the Book, and the Godly: Selected Proceedings of the St Hilda's Conference, 1993, Volume 1,* edited by Lesley Smith and Jane H. M. Taylor, 67–76. Cambridge, U.K.: D. S. Brewer, 1995.

———. *Power, Gender and Christian Mysticism.* Cambridge: Cambridge University Press, 1995.

Jardine, Alice, and Paul Smith, eds. *Men in Feminism.* New York: Methuen, 1987.

Judic, Bruno. "Grégoire le Grand, un maître de la parole." In Dessì and Lauwers, 49–107.

Kamuf, Peggy. "Writing like a Woman." In *Women and Language in Literature and Society,* edited by Sally McConnell-Ginet, Ruth Borker, and Nelly Furman, 284–99. New York: Praeger, 1980.

Kantorowicz, Ernst. *The King's Two Bodies: A Study in Medieval Political Theology.* Princeton, N.J.: Princeton University Press, 1957.

Kay, Sarah. "Women's Body of Knowledge: Epistemology and Misogyny in the *Romance of the Rose.*" In *Framing Medieval Bodies,* edited by Sarah Kay and Miri Rubin, 211–35. Manchester: Manchester University Press, 1994.

Kellogg, Alfred L. *Chaucer, Langland, Arthur: Essays in Middle English Literature.* New Brunswick, N.J.: Rutgers University Press, 1972.

Kellogg, Alfred L., and Louis A. Haselmayer. "Chaucer's Satire of the Pardoner." In Kellogg, *Chaucer, Langland, Arthur: Essays in Middle English Literature,* 212–44. New Brunswick, N.J.: Rutgers University Press, 1972.

Kemmler, Fritz. *'Exempla' in Context: A Historical and Critical Study of Robert Mannyng of Brunne's 'Handlyng Synne.'* Tübingen, Germany: Gunter Narr Verlag, 1984.

Kendrick, Laura. *Chaucerian Play: Comedy and Control in the* Canterbury Tales. Berkeley and Los Angeles: University of California Press, 1988.

Kennedy, George A. *Classical Rhetoric and Its Christian and Secular Tradition from Ancient to Modern Times.* Chapel Hill: University of North Carolina Press, 1980.

Kerby-Fulton, Kathryn. "Prophet and Reformer: 'Smoke in the Vineyard.' " In *Voice of the Living Light: Hildegard of Bingen and Her World,* ed. Barbara J. Newman, 70–90. Berkeley and Los Angeles: University of California Press, 1998.

Kerby-Fulton, Kathryn, and Dyan Elliott. "Self-Image and the Visionary Role in Two Letters from the Correspondence of Elizabeth of Schönau and Hildegard of Bingen." *Vox benedictina* 2 (1985): 204–23.

Kieckhefer, Richard. "The Specific Rationality of Medieval Magic." *American Historical Review* 99 (1994): 813–36.

Kienzle, Beverly Mayne. "Maternal Imagery in the Sermons of Hélinand of Froidmont." In De Ore Domini: *Preacher and Word in the Middle Ages,* edited by Thomas L. Amos, Eugene A. Green, and Beverly Mayne Kienzle, 93–103. Kalamazoo: Medieval Institute Publications, Western Michigan University, 1989.

————. "*Operatrix in vinea Domini:* Hildegard's Public Preaching and Polemics against the Cathars." *Heresis* 26–27 (1996): 43–56.

————. "Preaching as Touchstone of Orthodoxy and Dissidence in the Middle Ages." *Medieval Sermon Studies* 43 (1999): 19–54.

————. "The Prostitute-Preacher: Patterns of Polemic Against Medieval Waldensian Women Preachers." In Kienzle and Walker, 99–113.

————, ed. *The Sermon.* Typologie des sources du moyen âge occidental 81–83. Turnhout, Belgium: Brepols, 2000.

Kienzle, Beverly Mayne, Edith Wilks Dolnikowski, Rosemary Drage Hale, Darleen Pryds, and Anne T. Thayer, eds. *Models of Holiness in Medieval Sermons.* Louvain-la-Neuve: Fédération Internationale des Instituts d'Études Médiévales, 1996.

Kienzle, Beverly Mayne, and Pamela J. Walker, eds. *Women Preachers and Prophets through Two Millennia of Christianity.* Berkeley and Los Angeles: University of California Press, 1998.

King, Karen L. "Prophetic Power and Women's Authority: The Case of the *Gospel of Mary* (Magdalene)." In Kienzle and Walker, 21–41.

Knapp, Peggy. *Chaucer and the Social Contest.* New York: Routledge, 1990.

Kruger, Steven F. "Claiming the Pardoner: Toward a Gay Reading of Chaucer's Pardoner's Tale." In *Critical Essays on Geoffrey Chaucer,* edited by Thomas C. Stillinger, 150–72. New York: G. K. Hall & Co., 1998.

Lagorio, Valerie M. "The Medieval Continental Women Mystics: An Introduction." In *An Introduction to the Medieval Mystics of Europe,* edited by Paul E. Szarmach, 184–93. Albany: State University of New York Press, 1984.

————. "Social Responsibility and the Medieval Women Mystics on the Continent." In *Spiritualität Heute und Gestern: Internationaler Kongress vom 4. bis 7. August 1982,* vol. 2, Analecta Cartusiana 35, edited by James Hogg, 95–104. Salzburg: Institut für Anglistik und Amerikanistik, 1983.

Lambert, Malcolm. *Medieval Heresy: Popular Movements from the Gregorian Reform to the Reformation.* Oxford: Basil Blackwell, 1992.

Lauwers, Michel. "*Praedicatio—Exhortatio:* L'Église, la reforme, et les laïcs (XIᵉ–XIIIᵉ siècles)." In Dessì and Lauwers, 187–232.

Lawrence, C. H. *The Friars: The Impact of the Early Mendicant Movement on Western Society.* London: Longman, 1994.

Lawton, David. *Chaucer's Narrators.* Cambridge, U.K.: D. S. Brewer, 1985.

Leclercq, Jean. "Le magistère du prédicateur au XIIIᵉ siècle." *Archives d'histoire doctrinale et littéraire du moyen âge* 21 (1946): 105–47.

Lecoy de la Marche, A. *La chaire française au moyen âge, spécialement au XIIIᵉ siècle.* Paris: Librairie Renouard, 1886.

Lees, Clare A., ed., with Thelma S. Fenster and Jo Ann McNamara. *Medieval Masculinities: Regarding Men in the Middle Ages.* Minneapolis: University of Minnesota Press, 1994.

Le Goff, Jacques. "Trades and Professions as Represented in Medieval Confessors' Manuals." In *Time, Work & Culture in the Middle Ages.* Translated by Arthur Goldhammer. Chicago: University of Chicago Press, 1980.

Lehmann, Paul. *Die Parodie im Mittelalter.* Stuttgart: Anton Hiersemann, 1963.

Leicester, H. Marshall, Jr. "The Art of Impersonation: A General Prologue to the *Canterbury Tales.*" *PMLA* 95 (March 1980): 213–24.

———. " 'Synne Horrible': The Pardoner's Exegesis of His Tale, and Chaucer's." In *Acts of Interpretation: The Text in Its Contexts, 700–1600: Essays on Medieval and Renaissance Literature in Honor of E. Talbot Donaldson,* edited by Mary J. Carruthers and Elizabeth D. Kirk, 25–50. Norman, Okla.: Pilgrim Books, 1982.

Lewis, Charlton T. *An Elementary Latin Dictionary.* Oxford: Oxford University Press, 1891.

Leyser, C. "Masculinity in Flux: Nocturnal Emission and the Limits of Celibacy in the Early Middle Ages." In *Masculinity in Medieval Europe,* edited by D. M. Hadley (London: Longman, 1999), 103–20.

Lochrie, Karma. *Margery Kempe and Translations of the Flesh.* Philadelphia: University of Pennsylvania Press, 1991.

Longère, Jean. *La prédication médiévale.* Paris: Études Augustiniennes, 1983.

Maier, Christoph. *Preaching the Crusades: Mendicant Friars and the Cross in the Thirteenth Century.* Cambridge: Cambridge University Press, 1994.

Mann, Jill. *Chaucer and Medieval Estates Satire: The Literature of Social Classes and the* General Prologue *to the* Canterbury Tales. Cambridge: Cambridge University Press, 1973.

Martin, John Hilary. "The Injustice of Not Ordaining Women: A Problem for Medieval Theologians." *Theological Studies* 48, no. 2 (1987): 303–10.

McAlpine, Monica. "The Pardoner's Homosexuality and How It Matters." *PMLA* 95 (1980): 8–22.

McNamara, Jo Ann. "The *Herrenfrage:* The Restructuring of the Gender System, 1050–1150." In *Medieval Masculinities: Regarding Men in the Middle Ages,* edited by Clare A. Lees, with Thelma S. Fenster and Jo Ann McNamara, 3–29. Minneapolis: University of Minnesota Press, 1994.

———. "The Rhetoric of Orthodoxy: Clerical Authority and Female Innovation in the Struggle with Heresy." In *Maps of Flesh and Light: The Religious Ex-*

perience of Medieval Women Mystics, edited by Ulrike Wiethaus, 9–27. Syracuse, N.Y.: Syracuse University Press, 1993.

McSheffrey, Shannon. *Gender and Heresy: Women and Men in Lollard Communities, 1420–1530.* Philadelphia: University of Pennsylvania Press, 1995.

Merrix, Robert P. "Sermon Structure in the Pardoner's Tale." In *Geoffrey Chaucer's the Pardoner's Tale,* edited by Harold Bloom, 125–38. New York: Chelsea House, 1988.

Minnis, Alastair J. "The Author's Two Bodies? Authority and Fallibility in Late-Medieval Textual Theory." In *Of the Making of Books: Medieval Manuscripts, Their Scribes and Readers: Essays presented to M. B. Parkes,* edited by P. R. Robinson and Rivkah Zim, 259–79. Aldershot, U.K.: Scolar, 1997.

———. "Chaucer's Pardoner and the 'Office of Preacher.'" In *Intellectuals and Writers in Fourteenth-Century Europe,* edited by Piero Boitani and Anna Torti, 88–119. Cambridge: D. S. Brewer, 1986.

———. "*De impedimento sexus:* Women's Bodies and Medieval Impediments to Female Ordination." In *Medieval Theology and the Natural Body,* edited by Peter Biller and A. J. Minnis, 109–39. York Studies in Medieval Theology 1. York, U.K.: York Medieval Press, 1997.

———. *Medieval Theory of Authorship.* London: Scolar Press, 1984.

———. "Medium and Message: Henry of Ghent on Scriptural Style." In *Literature and Religion in the Later Middle Ages,* edited by Richard G. Newhauser and John A. Alford, 209–35. Binghamton, N.Y.: Medieval & Renaissance Texts & Studies, 1995.

Mohl, Ruth. *The Three Estates in Medieval and Renaissance Literature.* New York: Columbia University Press, 1933.

Moore, Arthur K. "The Pardoner's Interruption of the *Wife of Bath's Prologue.*" *Modern Language Quarterly* 10 (1949): 49–57.

Moore, R. I. *The Formation of a Persecuting Society: Power and Deviance in Western Europe, 950–1250.* Oxford: Basil Blackwell, 1990.

Morenzoni, Franco. *Des écoles aux paroisses: Thomas de Chobham et la promotion de la prédication au début du XIIIᵉ siècle.* Paris: Institut d'Études Augustiniennes, 1995.

———. "Parole du prédicateur et inspiration divine d'après les *Artes praedicandi.*" In Dessì and Lauwers, 271–90.

Morrison, Karl F. "Incentives for Studying the Liberal Arts." In *The Seven Liberal Arts in the Middle Ages,* edited by David L. Wagner, 32–57. Bloomington: Indiana University Press, 1983.

Morrison, Susan Signe. "Don't Ask, Don't Tell: The Wife of Bath and Vernacular Translations." *Exemplaria* 8, no. 1 (1996): 97–123.

Muessig, Carolyn. "Audience and Preacher: *Ad Status* Sermons and Social Classification." In *Preacher, Sermon, and Audience,* edited by Carolyn Muessig, 255–76. Leiden: Brill, 2002.

———. "Prophecy and Song: Teaching and Preaching by Medieval Women." In Kienzle and Walker, 146–58.

Murphy, James J. *Rhetoric in the Middle Ages: A History of Rhetorical Theory from*

Saint Augustine to the Renaissance. Berkeley and Los Angeles: University of California Press, 1974.

Murray, Jacqueline. "Thinking about Gender: The Diversity of Medieval Perspectives." In *Power of the Weak: Studies on Medieval Women,* edited by Jennifer Carpenter and Sally-Beth MacLean, 1–26. Urbana: University of Illinois Press, 1995.

Natali, Carlo. "Paradeigma: The Problems of Human Acting and the Use of Examples in Some Greek Authors of the 4th Century B.C." *Rhetoric Society Quarterly* 19 (1989): 141–52.

Newman, Barbara J. *From Virile Woman to WomanChrist.* Philadelphia: University of Pennsylvania Press, 1995.

————. "Hildegard and Her Hagiographers: The Remaking of Female Sainthood." In *Gendered Voices: Medieval Saints and Their Interpreters,* edited by Catherine M. Mooney, 1–22. Philadelphia: University of Pennsylvania Press, 1999.

————. " 'Sibyl of the Rhine': Hildegard's Life and Times." In *Voice of the Living Light,* ed. Newman, 1–29.

————. *Sister of Wisdom: St. Hildegard's Theology of the Feminine.* Berkeley and Los Angeles: University of California Press, 1987.

————. "Three-Part Invention: The *Vita S. Hildegardis* and Mystical Hagiography." In *Hildegard of Bingen: The Context of Her Thought and Art,* edited by Charles Burnett and Peter Dronke, 189–210. London: The Warburg Institute, 1998.

————, ed. *Voice of the Living Light: Hildegard of Bingen and Her World.* Berkeley and Los Angeles: University of California Press, 1998.

Niermeyer, J. F. *Mediae Latinitatis Lexicon Minus.* Leiden: Brill, 1976.

Nykrog, Per. *Les fabliaux.* 2d ed. Publications romanes et françaises. Geneva: Droz, 1973.

Olson, Glending. "Rhetorical Circumstances and the Canterbury Storytelling." *Studies in the Age of Chaucer, Proceedings No. 1, 1984: Reconstructing Chaucer.* Edited by Paul Strohm and Thomas Heffernan. Knoxville, Tenn.: New Chaucer Society, 1985.

Ong, Walter J. "Gospel, Existence, and Print." Review essay. *Modern Language Quarterly* 35, no. 1 (1974): 66–77.

Owen, Charles A., Jr. *Pilgrimage and Storytelling: The Dialectic of "Ernest" and "Game."* Norman: University of Oklahoma Press, 1977.

Owst, G. R. *Literature and Pulpit in Medieval England: A Neglected Chapter in the History of English Letters and of the English People.* Cambridge: Cambridge University Press, 1933.

————. *Preaching in Medieval England: An Introduction to Sermon Manuscripts of the Period c.1350–1450.* Cambridge: Cambridge University Press, 1926.

Partner, Nancy F. "Introduction." In *Studying Medieval Women: Sex, Gender, Feminism (Speculum* 68 [1993]), edited by Nancy F. Partner, 305–8. Cambridge, Mass.: Medieval Academy of America, 1993.

Paton, Bernadette. *Preaching Friars and the Civic Ethos: Siena, 1380–1480.* Westfield Publications in Medieval Studies 7. London: Centre for Medieval Studies, Queen Mary and Westfield College, University of London, 1992.

Patterson, Lee. *Chaucer and the Subject of History*. Madison: University of Wisconsin Press, 1991.

———. "Chaucerian Confession: Penitential Literature and the Pardoner." *Medievalia et Humanistica*, n.s., 7 (1976): 153–73.

———. "The 'Parson's Tale' and the Quitting of the 'Canterbury Tales.'" *Traditio* 34 (1978): 331–80.

Pearsall, Derek. *The Canterbury Tales*. London: George Allen & Unwin, 1985.

———. "Chaucer's Pardoner: The Death of a Salesman." *Chaucer Review* 17, no. 4 (1983): 358–65.

Petry, Ray C. "Emphasis on the Gospel and Christian Reform in Late Medieval Preaching." *Church History* 16, no. 2 (1947): 75–91.

Peuchmaurd, M. "Mission canonique et prédication: Le prêtre ministre de la parole dans la querelle entre mendiants et séculiers au XIIIᶜ siècle." *Recherches de théologie ancienne et médiévale* 30 (1963): 122–44, 251–76.

Pitkin, Hanna. "Representing as 'Acting For': The Analogies." In *The Concept of Representation*, 112–43. Berkeley and Los Angeles: University of California Press, 1967.

Polo de Beaulieu, Marie Anne. "Exempla: A Discussion and a Case Study; II. *Mulier* and *Femina:* The Representation of Women in the *Scala celi* of Jean Gobi." In *Medieval Women and the Sources of Medieval History*, edited by Joel T. Rosenthal, 50–65. Athens: University of Georgia Press, 1990.

Poor, Sara S. "Cloaking the Body in Text: The Question of Female Authorship in the Writings of Mechthild von Magdeburg." *Exemplaria* 12, no. 2 (2000): 417–53.

———. "Mechthild von Magdeburg, Gender, and the 'Unlearned Tongue.'" *Journal of Medieval and Early Modern Studies* 31, no. 2 (2001): 213–50.

Pryds, Darleen. "Proclaiming Sanctity through Proscribed Acts: The Case of Rose of Viterbo." In Kienzle and Walker, 159–72.

Raming, Ida. *The Exclusion of Women from the Priesthood: Divine Law or Sex Discrimination?* Translated by Norman R. Adams. Metuchen, N.J.: Scarecrow Press, 1976.

Reames, Sherry L. *The* Legenda aurea: *A Reexamination of Its Paradoxical History*. Madison: University of Wisconsin Press, 1985.

Revard, Carter. "Gilote et Johan: An Interlude in B.L. MS. Harley 2253." *Studies in Philology* 79 (1982): 122–46.

Rice, Eugene F., Jr. *Saint Jerome in the Renaissance*. Baltimore: Johns Hopkins University Press, 1985.

Roberts, Phyllis B. "Master Stephen Langton Preaches to the People and Clergy: Sermon Texts from Twelfth-Century Paris." *Traditio* 36 (1980): 237–68.

Robertson, D. W., Jr. "The Cultural Tradition of *Handlyng Synne*." *Speculum* 22 (1947): 162–85.

Robson, C. A. *Maurice of Sully and the Medieval Vernacular Homily: With the Text of Maurice's French Homilies from a Sens Cathedral Chapter MS*. Oxford: Basil Blackwell, 1952.

Rouse, Richard H., and Mary A. Rouse. *Preachers, Florilegia, and Sermons: Studies on the* Manipulus Florum *of Thomas of Ireland.* Studies and Texts 47. Toronto: Pontifical Institute of Mediaeval Studies, 1979.

Rubin, Miri. *Corpus Christi: The Eucharist in Late Medieval Culture.* Cambridge: Cambridge University Press, 1991.

Ruether, Rosemary Radford. "Misogynism and Virginal Feminism in the Fathers of the Church." In *Religion and Sexism: Images of Woman in the Jewish and Christian Traditions,* edited by Rosemary Radford Ruether. New York: Simon and Schuster, 1974.

Rusconi, Roberto. *Predicazione e vita religiosa nella società italiana da Carlo Magno alla Controriforma.* Turin: Loescher, 1981.

Sahlin, Claire L. *Birgitta of Sweden and the Voice of Prophecy.* Woodbridge, Suffolk, U.K.: Boydell Press, 2001.

———. "Gender and Prophetic Authority in Birgitta of Sweden's *Revelations.*" In *Gender and Text in the Later Middle Ages,* edited by Jane Chance, 69–95. Gainesville: University of Florida Press, 1996.

———. "The Prophetess as Preacher: Birgitta of Sweden and the Voice of Prophecy." *Medieval Sermon Studies* 40 (autumn 1997): 29–44.

———. "The Virgin Mary and Birgitta of Sweden's Prophetic Vocation." In *Maria i Sverige under tusen år: Föredrag vid symposiet i Vadstena 6–10 oktober 1994,* edited by Sven-Erik Brodd and Alf Härdelin, 227–54. Skellefteå, Sweden: Artos, 1996.

Savage, Anne, and Nicholas Watson. *Anchoritic Spirituality: Ancrene Wisse and Associated Works.* Classics of Western Spirituality. Mahwah, N.J.: Paulist Press, 1991.

Saxer, Victor. *Le culte de Marie Madeleine en occident: Des origines à la fin du moyen âge.* 2 vols. Auxerre: Publications de la Société des Fouilles Archéologiques et des Monuments Historiques de l'Yonne; Paris: Clavreuil, 1959.

Sayers, Jane. *Innocent III: Leader of Europe, 1198–1216.* London: Longman, 1994.

Scanlon, Larry. *Narrative, Authority, and Power: The Medieval Exemplum and the Chaucerian Tradition.* Cambridge: Cambridge University Press, 1994.

Schaeffer, John D. "The Dialectic of Orality and Literacy: The Case of Book 4 of Augustine's *De doctrina christiana.*" *PMLA* 111 (October 1996): 1133–45.

Schibanoff, Susan. "The New Reader and Female Textuality in Two Early Commentaries on Chaucer." *Studies in the Age of Chaucer* 10 (1988): 71–108.

Scott, Karen. "St. Catherine of Siena, 'Apostola.'" *Church History* 61 (March 1992): 34–46.

———. "'This is why I have put you among your neighbors': St. Bernard's and St. Catherine's Understanding of the Love of God and Neighbor." In *Atti del simposio internazionale Cateriniano-Bernardiniano, Siena, 17–20 aprile 1980,* edited by Domenico Maffei and Paolo Nardi, 279–94. Siena: Accademia Senese degli Intronati, 1982.

———. "Urban Spaces, Women's Networks, and the Lay Apostolate in the Siena of Catherine Benincasa." In *Creative Women in Medieval and Early-Modern*

Italy, edited by E. Ann Matter and John Coakley, 105–19. Philadelphia: University of Pennsylvania Press, 1994.

Sedgewick, G. G. "The Progress of Chaucer's Pardoner, 1880–1940." *Modern Language Quarterly* 1, no. 4 (1940): 431–58.

Shahar, Shulamith. *The Fourth Estate. A History of Women in the Middle Ages.* Translated by Chaya Galai. London: Methuen, 1983.

Sider, Robert Dick. *Ancient Rhetoric and the Art of Tertullian.* Oxford: Oxford University Press, 1971.

Smalley, Beryl. *The Study of the Bible in the Middle Ages.* Notre Dame, Ind.: University of Notre Dame Press, 1964.

Solterer, Helen. *The Master and Minerva: Disputing Women in French Medieval Culture.* Berkeley and Los Angeles: University of California Press, 1995.

Specht, Henrik. " 'Ethopoeia' or Impersonation: A Neglected Species of Medieval Characterization." *Chaucer Review* 21 (1986): 1–15.

Spencer, H. Leith. *English Preaching in the Late Middle Ages.* Oxford: Clarendon Press, 1993.

Staley, Lynn. "Julian of Norwich and the Late-Fourteenth-Century Crisis of Authority." In David Aers and Lynn Staley, *The Powers of the Holy: Religion, Politics, and Gender in Late Medieval English Culture,* 107–78. University Park: Pennsylvania State University Press, 1996.

———. *Margery Kempe's Dissenting Fictions.* University Park: Pennsylvania State University Press, 1994.

Stapleton, M. L. *Harmful Eloquence: Ovid's* Amores *from Antiquity to Shakespeare.* Ann Arbor: University of Michigan Press, 1996.

Stock, Brian. *The Implications of Literacy: Written Language and Models of Interpretation in the Eleventh and Twelfth Centuries.* Princeton, N.J.: Princeton University Press, 1983.

Stolpe, Sven, ed. *Birgitta: På Svenska, in English, auf Deutsch.* Borås, Sweden: Bokförlaget Legenda, 1973.

Straus, Barrie Ruth. "The Subversive Discourse of the Wife of Bath: Phallocentric Discourse and the Imprisonment of Criticism." In *Chaucer: Contemporary Critical Essays,* edited by Valerie Allen and Ares Axiotis, 126–44. New York: St. Martin's Press, 1996.

Swanson, Jenny. *John of Wales: A Study of the Works and Ideas of a Thirteenth-Century Friar.* Cambridge: Cambridge University Press, 1989.

Swanson, Robert N. "Angels Incarnate: Clergy and Masculinity from Gregorian Reform to Reformation." In *Masculinity in Medieval Europe,* ed. D. M. Hadley, 160–77. London: Longman, 1999.

———. "Chaucer's Parson and Other Priests." *Studies in the Age of Chaucer* 13 (1991): 41–80.

———. *Religion and Devotion in Europe, c.1215–c.1515.* Cambridge: Cambridge University Press, 1995.

Szittya, Penn. *The Antifraternal Tradition in Medieval Literature.* Princeton, N.J.: Princeton University Press, 1986.

Thomson, J. A. F. "Orthodox Religion and the Origins of Lollardy." *History,* n.s., 74, no. 240–42 (1989): 39–55.

Trout, John M. "Preaching by the Laity in the Twelfth Century." *Studies in Medieval Culture* 4, no. 1 (1973): 92–108.

Tugwell, Simon. "*De huiusmodi sermonibus texitur omnis recta predicatio:* Changing Attitudes toward the Word of God." In *De l'homélie au sermon: Histoire de la prédication médiévale,* edited by Jacqueline Hamesse and Xavier Hermand, 159–68. Louvain-la-Neuve: Université Catholique de Louvain, Publications de l'Institut d'Études Médiévales, 1993.

van Engen, John. "Late Medieval Anticlericalism: The Case of the New Devout." In *Anticlericalism in Late Medieval and Early Modern Europe,* edited by Peter A. Dykema and Heiko A. Oberman, 19–52. Leiden: Brill, 1993.

Vauchez, André. *The Laity in the Middle Ages: Religious Beliefs and Devotional Practices.* Edited by Daniel E. Bornstein. Translated by Margery J. Schneider. Notre Dame, Ind.: University of Notre Dame Press, 1993.

Vecchio, Silvana. "Dalla predicazione alla conversazione: Il *Liber de introductione loquendi* di Filippo da Ferrara OP." *Medieval Sermon Studies* 44 (2000): 68–86.

———. "Les langues de feu: Pentecôte et rhétorique sacrée dans les sermons des XIIᵉ et XIIIᵉ siècles." In Dessì and Lauwers, 255–69.

Voaden, Rosalynn. *God's Words, Women's Voices: The Discernment of Spirits in the Writing of Late-Medieval Women Visionaries.* York, U.K.: York Medieval Press, 1999.

Volk-Birke, Sabine. *Chaucer and Medieval Preaching: Rhetoric for Listeners in Sermons and Poetry.* Tübingen: Gunter Narr Verlag, 1991.

von Campenhausen, Hans. *Ecclesiastical Authority and Spiritual Power in the Church of the First Three Centuries.* Translated by J. A. Baker. Stanford, Calif.: Stanford University Press, 1969.

Walther, Hans. *Initia carminum ac versuum Medii Aevi posterioris Latinorum. Alphabetisches Verzeichnis der Versanfänge mittellateinischer Dichtungen.* Carmina Medii Aevi posterioris Latina I/1. Göttingen: Vandenhoeck & Ruprecht, 1969.

Ward, John O. "From Marginal Gloss to *Catena* Commentary: The Eleventh-Century Origins of a Rhetorical Teaching Tradition in the Medieval West." *Parergon,* n.s., 13, no. 2 (1996): 109–20.

Watson, Nicholas. "Conceptions of the Word: The Mother Tongue and the Incarnation of God." *New Medieval Literatures* 1 (1997): 85–124.

———. "Visions of Inclusion: Universal Salvation and Vernacular Theology in Pre-Reformation England." *Journal of Medieval and Early Modern Studies* 27, no. 2 (1997): 145–87.

———. " 'Yf wommen be double naturelly': Remaking 'Woman' in Julian of Norwich's Revelation of Love." *Exemplaria* 8, no. 1 (1996): 1–34.

Welter, J.-Th. *L'Exemplum dans la littérature religieuse et didactique du moyen âge.* Paris: Occitania, 1927.

Wenzel, Siegfried. "Chaucer and the Language of Contemporary Preaching." *Studies in Philology* 73, no. 2 (April 1976): 138–61.

———. "Notes on the *Parson's Tale.*" *Chaucer Review* 16 (1982): 237–56.

———. *Preachers, Poets, and the Early English Lyric.* Princeton, N.J.: Princeton University Press, 1986.

Wiethaus, Ulrike, ed. *Maps of Flesh and Light: The Religious Experience of Medieval Women Mystics.* Syracuse, N.Y.: Syracuse University Press, 1993.

Winstead, Karen. *Virgin Martyrs: Legends of Sainthood in Late Medieval England.* Ithaca, N.Y.: Cornell University Press, 1997.

Wogan-Browne, Jocelyn. *Saints' Lives and Women's Literary Culture c. 1150–1300: Virginity and Its Authorizations.* Oxford: Oxford University Press, 2001.

Wogan-Browne, Jocelyn, Nicholas Watson, Andrew Taylor, and Ruth Evans, eds. *The Idea of the Vernacular: An Anthology of Middle English Literary Theory, 1280–1520.* University Park: Pennsylvania State University Press, 1999.

Zink, Michel. *La prédication en langue romane avant 1300.* Paris: Éditions Honoré Champion, 1976.

Ziolkowski, Jan. *Alan of Lille's Grammar of Sex: The Meaning of Grammar to a Twelfth-Century Intellectual.* Cambridge, Mass.: Medieval Academy of America, 1985.

Index